The Far-Right in International and European Law

Since the Second World War, the international community has sought to prevent the repetition of destructive far-right forces by establishing institutions such as the United Nations and by adopting documents such as the Universal Declaration of Human Rights. Jurisprudence and conventions directly prohibit far-right speech and expression. Nevertheless, recently, violent far-right entities, such as Golden Dawn of Greece, have received unprecedented electoral support; xenophobic parties have done spectacularly well in elections; and countries such as Hungary and Poland are being led by right-wing populists who are bringing constitutional upheaval and violating basic elements of doctrines such as the rule of law.

In light of this current reality, this book critically assesses the international and European tools available for States to regulate the far-right. It conducts the analysis through a militant democracy lens. This doctrine has been considered in several arenas as a concept more generally; in the sphere of the European Convention on Human Rights; in relation to particular freedoms, such as that of association; and as a tool for challenging the far-right movement through the spectrum of political science. However, this doctrine has not yet been applied within a legal assessment of challenging the far-right as a single entity. After analysing the aims, objectives, scope and possibility of shortcomings in international and European law, the book looks at what state obligations arise from these laws. It then assesses how freedom of opinion and expression, freedom of association and freedom of assembly are provided for in international and European law, and explores what limitation grounds exist which are directly relevant to the regulation of the far-right.

The issue of the far-right is a pressing one on the agenda of politicians, academics, civil society and other groups in Europe and beyond. As such, this book will appeal to those with an interest in International, European or Human Rights Law and Political Science.

Natalie Alkiviadou is a lecturer in EU Law and Human Rights. She holds degrees from Warwick University (LLB) and Utrecht University (LLM), and a PhD from the Vrije Universiteit Amsterdam.

Routledge Research in International Law

Regional Developmentalism through Law
Establishing an African Economic Community
Jonathan Bashi Rudahindwa

China's One Belt One Road Initiative and Private International Law
Edited by Poomintr Sooksripaisarnkit and Sai Ramani Garimella

Transnational Terrorist Groups and International Criminal Law
Anna Marie Brennan

Confronting Cyberespionage Under International Law
Oğuz Kaan Pehlivan

Russian Discourses on International Law
Sociological and Philosophical Phenomenon
Edited by P. Sean Morris

Backstage Practices in Transnational Law
Lianne Boer and Sofia Stolk

International 'Criminal' Responsibility
Antinomies
Ottavio Quirico

The Future of International Courts
Regional, Institutional and Procedural Challenges
Edited by Avidan Kent, Nikos Skoutaris and Jamie Trinidad

The Far-Right in International and European Law
Natalie Alkiviadou

For a full list of titles in this series, visit https://www.routledge.com/Routledge-Research-in-International-Law/book-series/INTNLLAW

The Far-Right in International and European Law

Natalie Alkiviadou

Routledge
Taylor & Francis Group

LONDON AND NEW YORK

First published 2019
by Routledge
2 Park Square, Milton Park, Abingdon, Oxon OX14 4RN

and by Routledge
52 Vanderbilt Avenue, New York, NY 10017

Routledge is an imprint of the Taylor & Francis Group, an informa business

British Library Cataloguing-in-Publication Data
A catalogue record for this book is available from the British Library

Library of Congress Cataloging-in-Publication Data
Names: Alkiviadou, Natalie, author.
Title: The far-right in international and European law/Natalie Alkiviadou.
Description: Abingdon, Oxon; New York, NY: Routledge, 2019. |
Series: Routledge research in international law | Based on author's thesis
(doctoral – Vrije Universiteit Amsterdam, 2017) issued under title: Challenging
right-wing extremism in England and Wales and Greece: tools available in
international, European and national law | Includes index.
Identifiers: LCCN 2019000831 (print) | LCCN 2019001803 (ebook) |
ISBN 9780429021428 (ebk) | ISBN 9780367075873 (hbk)
Subjects: LCSH: Right-wing extremists—Legal status, laws, etc. | Political
crimes and offenses. | Right-wing extremists—Legal status, laws, etc.—
Europe. | Political crimes and offenses—Law and legislation—Europe.
Classification: LCC K3253 (ebook) | LCC K3253 .A45 2019 (print) |
DDC 342.08/53—dc23
LC record available at https://lccn.loc.gov/2019000831

ISBN: 978-0-367-07587-3 (hbk)
ISBN: 978-0-429-02142-8 (ebk)

Typeset in Galliard
by codeMantra

In memory of
  Shehzad Luqman, 1986–2013
  Pavlos Fyssas, 1979–2013

Contents

Acknowledgements

This book is based on my PhD, which I defended at the Vrije Universiteit Amsterdam in 2017. I would like sincerely to thank my supervisors, Professor Gareth Davies and Dr Uladzislau Belavusau, for supporting me through my PhD journey and beyond. I am fortunate to have encouragement, kindness and guidance.

I thank my mother, Caroline, and my father, Alkis, for their unequivocal love and support.

I thank my children, Markella and Andreas, for being a source of inspiration throughout. I hope you read this book in the future and find that it is no longer relevant to the society in which you live.

Abbreviations

BNP	British National Party
CERD	Committee on the Elimination of All Forms of Racial Discrimination
CJEU	Court of Justice of the European Union
CoE	Council of Europe
ECHR	European Convention on Human Rights
EComHR	European Commission of Human Rights
ECRI	European Commission against Racism and Intolerance
ECtHR	European Court of Human Rights
EDL	English Defence League
EU	European Union
FPÖ	Freiheitlichen Partei Österreichs
FRA	Fundamental Rights Agency
HRC	Human Rights Committee
ICCPR	International Covenant on Civil and Political Rights
ICERD	International Convention on the Elimination of All Forms of Racial Discrimination
ICESR	International Covenant on Economic, Social and Cultural Rights
ISP	Internet Service Provider
KKK	Klu Klux Klan
LGBTI	Lesbian, Gay, Bisexual, Transgender, Intersex
NGO	Non-Governmental Organisation
NSPA	National Socialist Party of America
OAS	Organisation of American States
OSCE	Organisation of Security and Cooperation in Europe
ÖVP	Österreichische Volkspartei
PiS	Prawo i Sprawiedliwość
TEU	Treaty on the European Union
TFEU	Treaty on the Functioning of the European Union
UDHR	Universal Declaration of Human Rights
U.K.	United Kingdom
UKIP	United Kingdom Independence Party
U.S.	United States (of America)
UN	United Nations
WHO	World Health Organisation

General introduction

The far-right: a contextual framework

> Books cannot be killed by fire. People die, but books never die. No man and no force can abolish memory. No man and no force can put thought in a concentration camp forever. In this war, we know, books are weapons. And it is a part of your dedication always to make them weapons for man's freedom.
> Franklin D. Roosevelt – 6 May 1942[1]

The destructive force of the far-right was tragically witnessed through the mass devastation brought about by the Second World War. The international community sought to prevent the repetition of such devastation through the establishment of institutions, including the United Nations (UN) and the Council of Europe (CoE), and the adoption of documents such as the Universal Declaration of Human Rights (UDHR) and the European Convention on Human Rights (ECHR). Jurisprudence and conventions, on an international and European level, directly prohibit manifestations of hate with, for example, Article 4 of the International Convention on the Elimination of All Forms of Discrimination (ICERD) prohibiting racist associations and racist expression. Nevertheless, violent far-right entities, such as *The Popular Association – Golden Dawn (Λαϊκός Σύνδεσμος-Χρυσή Αυγή)* of Greece, have received unprecedented electoral support. Greece is of particular interest to the European far-right content. Its far-right spectrum is dominated by *Golden Dawn* which is a political party simultaneously acting as a violent movement organising itself in hit squads. *Golden Dawn's* national parliamentary election results saw a dramatic rise from approximately 20,000 votes[2] to 440,000 votes[3] during the period 2009 to 2012, with a small drop in the 2015 elections where it received around 380,000.[4] Nevertheless, in 2015, Golden

---

1 Franklin D. Roosevelt: 'Message to American Booksellers Association' (23 April 1942).
2 Golden Dawn Election Results 2009: http://ekloges-prev.singularlogic.eu/v2009/pages/index.html [Accessed 1 November 2015].
3 Golden Dawn Election Results 2012: http://ekloges-prev.singularlogic.eu/v2012b/public/index.html#{"cls":"party","params":{"id":41}} [Accessed 1 November 2015].
4 Golden Dawn election Results 2015: http://ekloges.ypes.gr/current/v/public/#{"cls": "party","params":{"id":41}} [Accessed 1 November 2015].

Dawn moved from being the fifth to third largest party.[5] This development has been characterised as particularly alarming by the Fundamental Rights Agency (FRA). Following the murder of Pavlos Fyssas in 2013, the leadership and some members of *Golden Dawn* are currently on trial for leading or participating in a criminal organisation. In 2017, two members of *The National Populist Front ELAM (Εθνικό Λαϊκό Μέτωπο)*, which is a sister organisation of Golden Dawn, were voted into the Cypriot parliament. The 2018 Italian elections saw the far-right *Lega Nord*, a party promoting nativist and racist rhetoric and positions, coming third in line, superseding conservative *Forza Italia* and gaining 17.6%,[6] a considerable leap from the 2013 elections in which it received just 4.09%[7] of the vote. Overall, the far-right attracts more than 10% of Western European votes on a national or European level.[8] In the East, apart from some exceptions, such as Estonia and Slovenia, such parties receive an average support of approximately 20%.[9] Even though the far-right is regularly associated with countries marred by financial crisis, and whilst 'East Central Europe continues to be the most dynamic breeding ground for right-wing extremism,'[10] this movement is also developing in other frameworks, such as the liberal traditions of Scandinavia. For example, *Sverigedemokraterna (the Sweden Democrats)*, a party founded in 1988, first entered the National Assembly in 2010 with 5.70% of the vote. In 2014, the Sweden Democrats received 12.9% of the vote,[11] making the party the third largest in the country and by 2018 received 17.5%, retaining its third place and gaining thirteen more seats.[12] During the early 1990s, *The Sweden Democrats* were part of a neo-Nazi movement[13] before cleaning up their image, with their position remaining within a nativist, anti-immigrant and right-wing populist framework and their slogan being 'to keep Sweden Swedish.'[14] On a

---

5 Greece election results 2015: http://ekloges.ypes.gr/current/v/public/#{"cls":"main","params":{}} [Accessed 17 April 2015].

6 Italy Election Results 2018: http://electionresources.org/it/2018/senate.php?region= [Accessed 5 October 2018].

7 Italy Election Results 2013: http://electionresources.org/it/senate.php?election=2013 [Accessed 5 October 2018].

8 Friedrich-Ebert-Stiftung, 'Right-Wing Extremism in Europe Country Analyses, Counter-Strategies and Labor-Market Oriented Exit Strategies' (2013) 9.

9 Ibid.

10 Ibid.

11 Sweden Election Results 2014: http://electionresources.org/se/riksdag.php?election=2014 [Accessed 18 April 2015].

12 Sweden Election Results 2018: http://electionresources.org/se/riksdag.php?election=2018 [Accessed 5 October 2018].

13 The Telegraph: 'EU Elections 2014: "I Can Hear the Boots of the 1930s Marching through Europe"' (14 May 2014) www.telegraph.co.uk/news/worldnews/europe/eu/10823028/EU-elections-2014-I-can-hear-the-boots-of-the-1930s-marching-through-Europe.html [Accessed 5 October 2018].

14 New Statesman: 'How the Remorseless Rise of the Swedish Far Right Could Leave the Country Ungovernable' (4 July 2018) www.newstatesman.com/culture/observations/2018/07/how-remorseless-rise-swedish-far-right-could-leave-country-ungovernable [Accessed 5 October 2018].

European Parliament level, in 2014 the EU witnessed the victories of parties such as France's *Front National (National Front)*, the *United Kingdom Independence Party (UKIP)* and Denmark's *Dansk Folkeparti (The Danish People's Party)*, with the parties gaining 24.86%,[15] 26.77%[16] and 26.60%[17] of the vote, respectively, finding themselves at the top of the list for their countries.[18] Violent far-right parties are also part of the European Parliament with Greece's *Golden Dawn* receiving 9.39% of the vote and Hungary's *Jobbik Magyarországért Mozgalom (Jobbik)* receiving 14.67% of the vote in 2014 in third and second place respectively.[19] In relation to *Jobbik*, it must be noted that there exists a close proximity between this party and the ruling *Fidesz*.[20] In addition to the habitual electorate of such parties, a large section of society was wooed by this mandate, as is reflected by 'public attitudes on immigration, growing public hostility towards, for example, settled Muslim communities and public dissatisfaction with mainstream parties and their performance on immigration-related issues.'[21] Moreover, by contributing to the mainstreaming of their rhetoric, far-right parties 'help to create a broader climate conducive to radical right thinking.'[22]

On a non-party level, examples of the far-right include the *English Defence League (EDL)* which has been 'at the forefront of violence around major Muslim centres and mosques,'[23] with the United Kingdom (U.K.) banning their demonstrations on several occasions for purposes of public order.[24] It is estimated that there have been approximately seven hundred criminal convictions directly linked to the *EDL* and its members.[25] In 2011, German authorities discovered a link between the violent far-right group, *Nationalsozialistischer Untergrund (National Socialist Underground)*, and the killing of ten persons, nine immigrants and one policewoman, over a period of ten years as well as a bombing

---

15 European Parliament Election Results: www.europarl.europa.eu/elections2014-results/en/country-results-fr-2014.html#table02 [Accessed 18 April 2015].

16 Ibid.

17 Ibid.

18 The European United Left/Nordic Green Left which includes parties such as SYRIZA (Coalition for the Radical Left) received 6.92% of the votes during the EP 2014 elections.

19 European Parliament Election Results: www.europarl.europa.eu/elections2014-results/en/country-results-el-2014.html#table03 [Accessed 18 April 2015].

20 *Fidesz* Magyar Polgári Szövetség. This co-operation was noted by Kim Lane Scheppele in a New York Times article: 'Hungary without Two Thirds' (17 March 2015) http://krugman.blogs.nytimes.com/2015/03/17/hungary-without-two-thirds/ [Accessed 13 April 2016].

21 A Chatham House Report: Matthew Goodwin, 'Right Response: Understanding and Countering Populist Extremism in Europe' (2011) 11.

22 Institute for Strategic Dialogue: Matthew Goodwin & Vidhya Ramalingam, 'Briefing Paper - The New Radical Right: Violent and Non-Violent Movements in Europe' (2012) 3.

23 Ibid.

24 See, *inter alia*, Ibid., BBC: 'English Defence League March in London is Blocked' (27 August 2011): www.bbc.com/news/uk-england-london-14684704 [Accessed 10 May 2015]; BBC: 'Home Secretary Bans Telford EDL March' (12 August 2011) www.bbc.com/news/uk-england-shropshire-14506941 [Accessed 10 May 2015].

25 Institute for Strategic: 'Briefing Paper - The New Radical Right: Violent and Non-Violent Movements in Europe' (2012) 9.

in Cologne.[26] In 2007, members of *Jobbik* established a group named *Magyar Gárda Egyesület (The Hungarian Guard Association)*, which has organised several public demonstrations throughout the country and in villages inhabited by a large Roma population.[27] This association has been the subject of a European Court of Human Rights (ECtHR) judgement, discussed further in Chapter 4.

Further, there is the *subculture milieu*, which is an unstructured part of the far-right movement with, for example, the *Aryan Strike Force*, *Combat 18* and *Blood and Honour* being movements active on an international level. In the U.K., two members of the *Aryan Strike Force* were arrested in 2010 and imprisoned for preparing violent racist activities. Κρυπτεία *(Kriptia)* is a new subculture movement in Greece which uses violence against migrants.[28] It calls itself a 'national resistance organisation'[29] which pledges to 'fight until the last illegal migrant is gone'[30] and to do so will use 'relentless violence.'[31]

Moreover, the far-right phenomenon goes beyond the 'West' with examples from countries including, but not limited to, Brazil, Japan and Russia. In the latest Concluding Observations to Russia of the Committee on the Elimination of All Forms of Racial Discrimination, the violent racist attacks of neo-Nazi groups and Cossack patrols were underlined as a 'pressing problem in the State Party.'[32] In its latest Concluding Observations to Japan, the same Committee noted its concern about hate speech, including that of inciting violence by 'right-wing movements or groups that organise racist demonstrations and rallies against foreigners and minorities, in particular against Koreans.'[33]

The mandates of such parties, groups and movements vary according to the contextual setting. However, 'the centrality of the immigration issue for this party family in Europe is undisputed,'[34] a statement that can be extended to other entities such as non-party movements. More particularly, the very opposite 'others' scapegoated through the movement's rhetoric and activities are immigrants, with a particular emphasis being placed on Muslims.[35] This is particularly true of far-right entities which exist in countries with a high Muslim population. In fact, this

26 Spiegel Online International: 'The World from Berlin: "The Neo-nazi Killers Were among Us"' (15 November 2011) www.spiegel.de/international/germany/the-world-from-berlin-the-neo-nazi-killers-were-among-us-a-797948.html [Accessed 26 January 2015].

27 Examples of Jobbik's paramilitary rallies beyond the rally which was the subject of the ECtHR judgement include a 2012 demonstration - following anti-Roma speeches, the marchers proceeded to Roma houses and shouted such slogans as "You are going to die here!"

28 Nooz.gr: 'Ομάδα "Κρυπτεία": Θα χρησιμοποιήσουμε βία αλύπητα' (Kriptia: 'We will use violence relentlessly' (28 November 2017) www.nooz.gr/greece/1474522/omada-krypteia--tha-chrisimopoiisoyme-bia-alypita [Accessed 5 October 2018].

29 Ibid.

30 Ibid.

31 Ibid.

32 CERD Concluding Observations to Russia (2017) CERD/C/RUS/CO/23-24, para. 15.

33 CERD Concluding Observations to Japan (2014) CERD/C/JPN/CO/7-9, para. 11.

34 Institute for Strategic Dialogue: Matthew Goodwin & Vidhya Ramalingam, 'Briefing Paper - The New Radical Right: Violent and Non-Violent Movements in Europe' (2012) 12.

35 Ibid. 9.

characteristic is facilitated by the 'increasingly critical rhetoric and policy surrounding migration and Islam in Europe.'[36] Notwithstanding the accuracy of such statements for the reality of a large number of European countries, they must be considered with care given that the contextual reality of this movement in Central and Eastern Europe is different, resulting in the parties and groups of these areas focussing on 'mobilizing public hostility towards the Jews [and] the Roma'[37] with their northern and western counterparts, for example, placing more emphasis on anti-Islam rhetoric. Once again, these characteristics are not clear-cut since these features are not mutually exclusive but merely mark the bulk of the parties' activities. This is not to say that many of these parties limit themselves to the type of rhetoric mentioned earlier, with new objectives arising as times and contexts change, a suitable example being the discriminatory rhetoric adopted by these parties against EU immigrants in countries such as the U.K. Such rhetoric, for example, constituted a large part of the Brexit campaign. Beyond the EU, targets include the Koreans in Japan and ethnic minorities in Russia. Thus, the argument made in the framework of far-right political parties insofar as 'they appear similar but in some respects they also seem the same but different'[38] hits the nail on the head in relation to the movement more generally. In light of this, it is safer to argue that 'ethnic exclusionism and/or expulsionism are now the *sine qua non* of most extreme right movements.'[39]

On one level, this movement is characterised by an anti-minority rhetoric and/or practice, a characteristic which encompasses all the relevant counterparts such as anti-immigrant, anti-Muslim, anti-Roma and anti-Semitic. In addition to this, the movement is explicitly defined as such or implicitly linked with the notion of extremism. This positive correlation assumes that the rhetoric and activities such parties or groups promote or adopt are incongruous with the general framework in which they find themselves. In liberal democracies, it is the principles which make up a liberal democracy that are the driving force of politics and, by extension, other groupings. As a result, any potential for the existence of extremism should be measured against the aforementioned principles.[40] In this light, and as noted by Minkenberg, right-wing radicalism, which is his preferred term, is a 'political ideology or tendency based on ultra-nationalist[41] ideas which tends to be directed against liberal democracy – although not necessarily directly

---

36 Ibid.
37 Ibid. 12.
38 Ibid.
39 Christopher T. Husbands, 'Combating the Extreme Right with the Instruments of the Constitutional State: Lessons from Experiences in Western Europe' (2002) 4 *Journal of Conflict and Violence Research* 1, 53.
40 Ian Hare & James Weinstein, 'Extreme Speech and Liberalism' in *'Extreme Speech and Democracy'* (2009) www.oxfordscholarship.com [Accessed 20 August 2014] 2.
41 Ultra-nationalism can be defined as 'a great or excessive devotion to or advocacy of national interests and rights especially as opposed to international interests.' (Webster's Third New International Dictionary)

or explicitly so.'[42] It is of particular significance here to refer to the possibility of an implicit breach of the principles of a liberal democracy referred to by Minkenberg, which is a reality since, for example, far-right political parties, duly registered as such, are acting within the framework of a democratically elected system of government but, through this avenue, are promoting and adopting anti-democratic approaches and practices. This poses the interesting perplexity of a liberal democratic system which permits a far-right entity to exist within its spectrum, notwithstanding that the latter's aims and objectives are in direct contravention to the former's founding principles. The dichotomy between the freedoms of expression, association and assembly, which are central to a liberal democracy, on the one hand, and the right to non-discrimination as well as general principles such as preserving human dignity, on the other, will lie at the heart of the theoretical framework underpinning this book's analysis.

The aforementioned focus on the hostility expressed towards the aforementioned minority does not mean that groups within this framework do not adopt a discriminatory approach towards other vulnerable groups such as LGBTI (Lesbian, Gay, Bisexual, Transgender and Intersex).[43] However, while ethnic minorities and/or immigrants are the common denominator[44] amongst the far-right worldwide, from Japan to Greece, LGBTI are not, the differentiation varying, once again, according to context.[45] To illustrate this briefly, Wilders Freedom Party is pro-LGBTI whilst the majority of political parties in, for example, Southern, Central and Eastern Europe, are actively anti-LGBTI. The anti-LGBTI rhetoric of, for example, Jobbik and Golden Dawn is endless, but, to illustrate briefly, a couple are put forth here. In 2014, *Jobbik* displayed a sign reading 'The Parliament Does Not Want Any Deviants' during Budapest Pride and verbally attacked participants, whilst Golden Dawn argued that gay couples can only raise pets and not children.[46]

Whatever their preferred target groups, far-right parties are 'ambivalent if not hostile towards liberal representative democracy.'[47] There are different types of political parties that make up the far-right scene. The simplest examples that demonstrate a differentiation of the types of political parties are those 'that re-

---

42 Michael Minkenberg, 'The Radical Right in Europe Today: Trends and Patterns in East and West' in Friedrich-Ebert-Stiftung Forum Berlin: Nora Langenbacher & Britta Schellenberg, 'Is Europe on the Right Path? Right-Wing Extremism and Right-Wing Populism in Europe' (2011) 38.

43 Christopher T. Husbands, 'Combating the Extreme Right with the Instruments of the Constitutional State: Lessons from Experiences in Western Europe' (2002) 4 *Journal of Conflict and Violence Research* 1, 53.

44 Ibid.

45 See for example, Wilders pro-LGBT approach in comparison to Golden Dawn anti-LGBT rights.

46 News 247: 'Παραλήρημα Ηλιόπουλου της Χρυσής Αυγής κατά των ομόφυλων ζευγαριών' (Iliopoulos rant against gay couples): (3 May 2018) www.news247.gr/politiki/paralirima-iliopoyloy-tis-chrysis-aygis-kata-ton-omofylon-zeygarion.6608997.html [Accessed 5 October 2018].

47 A Chatham House Report: Matthew Goodwin, 'Right Response: Understanding and Countering Populist Extremism in Europe' (2011) 10.

main wedded to interwar fascism and those that eschew this tradition.'[48] Notwithstanding the differences between far-right political parties in terms of vision, mission and structure, they nevertheless share the common feature of presenting minority groups, such as immigrants, as posing a socio-cultural threat to the nation. The dire consequence of such parties is that they 'can weaken social cohesion, undermining the social fabric of democracy.'[49] The impact of such parties goes beyond these frameworks given that 'their ideas have become increasingly intertwined with mainstream politics.'[50] As noted by Carter, far-right entities 'reject the principle of fundamental human equality.'[51] Such parties are considered to be far-right as 'they unquestionably occupy the right-most position of the political spectrum'[52] and embrace 'exclusionary representations of the nation, combined with authoritarian political perspectives.'[53] Some parties may directly dismiss the functioning of a representative democracy but, even if they guise themselves behind a shield of alleged legitimacy and do not, *per se*, doubt or condemn the functioning of a liberal democracy, they are nevertheless quick to espouse extremist discourses and exclusionary approaches to issues such as immigration, thereby diverging from the key constituents of a democratic system.[54]

The element of violence is also a key consideration when looking at the far-right. Although, today, such parties are mainly of a non-violent nature with most seeking to 'disassociate themselves from historical or perceived ties to their … violent counterparts,'[55] there are situations where violence continues to mark their activities as is the case, for example in Greece. Violence is more related to non-party groups and the subculture milieu. Hence, far-right organisations come in different shapes and sizes, boasting a variety of means and methods adopted for purposes of achieving their objectives. Notwithstanding some variations in their mandates, the key elements which tie these entities together include their ethnically exclusionary and/or expulsionary rhetoric and activities conducted through an extremist framework, targeting a variety of groups due to their ethnicity and/or nationality and/or religion and/or sexual orientation and/or gender identity.

Whether it is a party, a non-party group, a subculture movement or a mélange of any of these, at the core of the matter is the reality that the far-right movement promotes ideas and beliefs which are against the spirit and values of a human

---

48 Ibid. 12.
49 Institute for Strategic Dialogue: Matthew Goodwin & Vidhya Ramalingam, 'Briefing Paper - The New Radical Right: Violent and Non-Violent Movements in Europe' (2012) 12.
50 Ibid. 9.
51 Elizabeth Carter, *'The Extreme Right in Western Europe: Success or Failure?'* (1st edn. Manchester University Press, Manchester 2005) 17.
52 Piero Ignazi, *'Extreme Right Parties in Western Europe'* (1st edn. Oxford University Press, New York 2003) 2.
53 Paul Hainsworth, *'The Politics of the Extreme Right: Form the Margins to the Mainstream'* (1st edn. Pinter, London 2000) 7.
54 Ibid.
55 Institute for Strategic Dialogue: Matthew Goodwin & Vidhya Ramalingam, 'Briefing Paper - The New Radical Right: Violent and Non-Violent Movements in Europe' (2012) 12.

rights culture, as these have been promulgated by the UDHR and the documents subsequent to it. In essence, far-right groups 'reject the principle of human equality and are hence hostile towards immigrants, minority groups and rising ethnic and cultural diversity.'[56] Moreover, the hate that constitutes the foundation of organised and semi-organised far-right groups underpins the rhetoric and actions of right-wing populist political leaders such as Donald Trump and Victor Orbán. Even in countries where such parties have not been very successful in the electoral process, they have 'nevertheless often contributed towards the mainstreaming of anti-immigrant and anti-Muslim ideas and discourse, which help to create a broader climate conducive to radical right thinking.'[57] In light of this, the far-right is no longer a phenomenon of the past. It is one of the present, which is depicted in, *inter alia*, collective violence carried out by neo-Nazis, such as *Golden Dawn* and *Jobbik*, in rallies, such as Unite the Right, and in the rise in hate speech and hate crime against foreigners living in the U.K. following the Brexit vote. It has also infiltrated policies, particularly when it comes to the treatment of the non-native other. In Europe, policies dealing with international protection are starkly marked by exclusionary and nativist conceptions on both a European and national level, transforming the Mediterranean Sea into a floating death-bed for those fleeing persecution. On a parallel note, Trump's 'Zero Tolerance' immigration policy has seen a serious violation of, amongst others, children's rights, separating minors from their families and placing them in cages. Trump has since signed an executive order allowing families to remain together while individual prosecution for irregular entry continues and, in the case of asylum seekers, occurs regardless of international refugee law.

The extreme-right: an ideology against human rights

The extreme-right movement promotes ideas and beliefs which are against the spirit and values of a functional human rights culture as these have been promulgated by the UDHR and the documents subsequent to it. In essence, far-right entities 'reject the principle of human equality and hence are hostile towards immigrants, minority groups and rising ethnic and cultural diversity.'[58] By endorsing and carrying out Islamophobic, Romaphobic, anti-Semitic, anti-immigrant and/or homophobic and transphobic rhetoric and activities, the movement itself becomes an issue that is to be looked at and addressed through a human rights lens in a two-fold manner. On the one hand, the movement violates human rights and fundamental freedoms, such as non-discrimination, and rejects principles such as equality and human dignity. On the other hand, the

---

56 A Chatham House Report, Matthew Goodwin, 'Right Response: Understanding and Countering Populist Extremism in Europe' (2011) 12.
57 Institute for Strategic Dialogue: 'Briefing Paper - The New Radical Right: Violent and Non-Violent Movements in Europe' (2012) 3.
58 A Chatham House Report, Matthew Goodwin, 'Right Response: Understanding and Countering Populist Extremism in Europe' (2011) 12.

movement exploits rights and freedoms emanating from this framework, such as the freedoms of expression, association and assembly, so as to pursue and achieve their discriminatory and, at times, violent goals. Particularly due to the dire effects of fascism and extremism on mid-twentieth Century Europe, through its post-Second World War initiatives, the international community recognised the consequences of far-right rhetoric and activity and sought to eliminate the possibility of the movement's resurgence. This was pursued through the direct recognition of non-discrimination as a principle of law and on the limitation of the aforementioned rights in the event of discriminatory and/or violent activities and expressions. As such, there exist several international and European laws, principles and policies designed to counter this phenomenon, with leading documents including, *inter alia*, the ICERD and the European Convention on Human Rights (ECHR). The framework has not remained static on any of these levels, with the UN Monitoring Bodies, such as the Committee on the Elimination of Racial Discrimination (CERD), issuing General Recommendations, such as No. 15, on Measures to Eradicate Incitement to or Acts of Discrimination and incorporating recommendations to States in relation to their handling of right-wing extremism within Concluding Observations. On a CoE level, the developments are manifested in, *inter alia*, Strasbourg case-law which prohibits hate speech and hateful association[59] as well as the Additional Protocol to the Convention on Cybercrime, concerning the criminalisation of acts of a racist and xenophobic nature committed through computer systems. In fact, one of the commitments made by the Heads of State of CoE countries in the Vienna Declaration[60] was

> to combat all ideologies, policies and practices constituting an incitement to racial hatred, violence and discrimination as well as any action or language likely to strengthen fears and tensions between groups from different racial, ethnic, national, religious or social backgrounds.

The authors of the Declaration were 'convinced that these manifestations of intolerance threaten democratic societies and their fundamental values.' Also, in 2014, a General Rapporteur against Racism and Intolerance was appointed on a CoE level. The role of the rapporteur is to deal with issues such as racist violence and hate speech. On an EU level, the development of initiatives to challenge the far-right have been limited in scope and applicability. The most central tool to challenge the far-right in EU Member States is the combined Article 2 and Article 7 mechanism of the Treaty on the European Union which seeks to tackle breaches of the rule of law, human rights and democracy which may arise, amongst others, from the rhetoric and/or activities of movements such as

---

59 See, *inter alia*, *Norwood v UK & Vona v Hungary*.
60 Vienna Declaration and Programme of Action - Adopted by the World Conference on Human Rights in Vienna on 25 June 1993, www.ohchr.org/EN/ProfessionalInterest/Pages/Vienna. aspx [Accessed 14 November 2014].

the far-right. However, upon investigating this tool further, as will be done in Chapter 5, one can discern that, to date, it is marred by too much reliance on political will and, thus, remains dormant for the moment. On this level, there is also the Framework Decision on Combating Certain Forms and Expressions of *Racism* and *Xenophobia* by Means of Criminal Law which can be used to tackle rhetoric and acts of the far-right. At the foundation of the relevant legal provisions of international conventions and jurisprudence, and, as a result, at the foundation of the analysis of this dissertation, lies the doctrine of militant democracy further discussed in Chapter 2.

Regardless of the existence of tools and the existence of State obligations arising from their status as States Parties to international and European documents and/or their membership of the EU, and, even though there have been several official acknowledgements that the far-right must be challenged, this movement is rising in Europe, propagating discriminatory ideology and, at times, carrying out violent activities, with the current socio-economic climate serving as an ideal setting in which the far-right can develop.

Approach, contribution and structure of the book

Against the aforementioned conceptual framework, this book conducts a critical analysis of the international and European tools available for States and obligations emanating, therefrom in the sphere of tackling the far-right and its by-products. The major case-law of the U.S., involving the far-right and its manifestations will be examined in order to compare its libertarian approach to free speech with the more restrictive counterparts of the international and European frameworks. The phenomenon of the far-right has been looked at within several academic spheres including political science and law. In relation to the former, academic discussion has considered, *inter alia*, the general trends and developments of the far-right, generally or within particular contexts[61] and the nature of the far-right as a political and/or non-political structure, with such books focussing on particular areas or regions,[62] the socio-economic and interpersonal

---

61 General analyses of the development of the far-right (although case-studies are used) include: Pippa Norris *'Radical Right: Voters and Parties in the Electoral Market'* (1st edn. Cambridge University Press, Cambridge 2005); Contextual analyses of the development of the far-right include: Sofia Vasilopoulou & Daphne Halikiopoulou: *'The Golden Dawn's "Nationalist Solution": Explaining the Rise of the Far Right in Greece'* (1st edn. Palgrave Pivot, London 2015); Kathy Marks *'Faces of Right-Wing Extremism'* (1st edn. Branded Books, Tucson 2014); Anders Widfeldt *'Extreme Right Parties in Scandinavia'* (1st edn. Routledge, Abingdon, New York 2015).

62 General Analysis: Cas Mudde, *'The Ideology of the Extreme Right'* (1st edn. Manchester University Press, Manchester 2003); Contextual Regional Analysis: Andrea Mammone, Emmanuel Godin & Brian Jenkins, *'Varieties of Right-Wing Extremism in Europe'* (1st edn. Routledge, Abingdon, New York 2013); Cas Mudde, *'Populist Radical Right Parties in Europe'* (1st edn. Cambridge University Press, Cambridge 2007); Cas Mudde, *'Racist Extremism in Central and Eastern Europe'* (1st edn. Routledge, Abingdon, New York 2005); Contextual Country Analysis: Stephen E. Atkins, *'Encyclopaedia of Right-Wing Extremism In Modern American History'*

reasons which have led citizens to opt to be part of the far-right electorate[63] and the advantages and disadvantages of proscribing far-right groups.[64] Legal research to date has considered elements of the far-right and, in particular, hate speech,[65] with no study, thus far, considering the far-right in its entirety.

Hate speech: are bans legitimate?

In relation to hate speech, the question of whether bans on hate speech should be permitted constitutes a significant one for scholars. In fact, at the core of the argumentation put forth by supporters of hate speech bans is that 'the behaviour they seek to restrict causes real harm to certain identifiable classes of victims.'[66] Williams holds that victims of hate speech experience 'spirit murder' and Eberle argues that they suffer 'hatred or self-hatred' or a sense of 'degradation or

(1st edn. ABC-CLIO, California 2011); Other country examples include studies on, *inter alia,* Switzerland: Marcel Alexander Niggli: *'Right-Wing Extremism in Switzerland: National and International Perspectives'* (1st edn. Nomos Verlagsgesellschaft, Baden 2009).

63 Marco Giugni & Ruud Koopmans, 'What Causes People to Vote for a Radical Right Party? A Rejoinder to van der Brug and Fennema' (2007) 19 *International Journal of Public Opinion Research* 4; Matthew J. Goodwin, *'Revolt on the Right: Explaining Support for the Radical Right in Britain'* (1st edn. Routledge, London 2014).

64 Meindert Fennema, 'Legal Repression of Extreme Right Parties and Racial Discrimination' in Ruud Koopmans & Paul Statham (eds.), *'Challenging International and Ethnic Relation Politics – Comparative European Perspectives'* (1st edn. Oxford University Press, Oxford 2000). This has also been done through a US-Europe comparative approach in Erik Bleich, *'The Freedom to be Racist? How the United States and Europe Struggle to Preserve Freedom and Combat Racism'* (1st edn. Oxford University Press 2011); Stefan Sottiaux, 'Anti-Democratic Associations: Content and Consequences in Article 11 Adjudication' (2004) 22 *Netherlands Quarterly of Human Rights* 4.

65 Michael Herz & Peter Molnar, *'The Content and Context of Hate Speech: Rethinking Regulation and Responses'* (1st edn. Cambridge University Press, Cambridge 2012); Uladzislau Belavusau, *'Fighting Hate Speech through EU Law'* (2012) 4 *Amsterdam Law Forum*; Ivan Hare & James Weinstein, *'Extreme Speech and Democracy'* (2nd edn. Oxford University Press, Oxford 2011); Erich Bleich, *'The Freedom to be Racist? How the USA and Europe Struggle to Preserve Freedom and Combat Racism'* (1st edn. Oxford University Press, Oxford 2011); Marloes van Noorloos, *'Hate Speech Revisited: A Comparative and Historical Perspective on Hate Speech Law in the Netherlands and England and Wales'* (1st edn. Intersentia Cambridge 2011); Nazil Ghanea, 'Minorities and Hatred: Protections and Implications' (2010) 17 *International Journal on Minority and Group Rights* 3; Eva Brems, 'State Regulation of Xenophobia Versus Individual Freedoms: the European View' (2002) 1 *Journal of Human Rights* 4; David Kretzmer & Francine Kershman Hazan, *'Freedom of Speech and Incitement against Democracy'* (1st edn. Brill, Leiden 2000); Meindert Fennema, 'Legal Repression of Extreme Right Parties and Racial Discrimination' in Ruud Koopmans & Paul Statham (eds.), *'Challenging International and Ethnic Relation Politics – Comparative European Perspectives'* (1st edn. Oxford University Press, Oxford 2000).

66 Claudia E. Haupt, 'Regulating Hate Speech - Damned If You Do and Damned If You Don't: Lessons Learned from Comparing the German and U.S. Approaches' (2005) 23 *Boston University International Law Journal* 2, 305.

worthlessness.'[67] As such, the harm is 'quite real.'[68] As well as pinpointing the actual harm in hate speech, Eberle also makes a more general conceptualisation, that 'restraint on freedom is part of the price of joining society.'[69] Kübler argues that at the crux of the problem of deciphering whether or not hate speech can legitimately be restricted lies the fact that the manner in which one chooses to define another emanates from basic elements of self-determination and personal autonomy. However, he finds that the harm which hate speech causes to its victims in the form of, for example, intimidation, and the further marginalisation of minorities and the potential links with violence render hate speech to be legitimately restrictable.[70] In Post's article 'Racist Speech, Democracy and the First Amendment,'[71] the author argues that, in order to ensure an harmonious existence between the freedom of expression and the limitation of racist speech, focus must be placed on the harm caused by such speech. Closely interrelated to this justification are the ideas/arguments put forth by Waldron in his 2014 book 'The Harm in Hate speech.'[72] Waldron justifies limiting hate speech on grounds of preserving human dignity and protecting members of minority groups, often targeted by such speech. The arguments put forth in that book can be considered as an extension of his article 'Dignity and Defamation: the Visibility of Hate'[73] in which the author contends that hate speech should be restricted for purposes of ensuring human dignity. On the other hand, some authors find no justification for the banning of hate speech. For example, in 'Viewpoint Absolutism and Hate Speech,' Heinze argues that there exist no justifications for restricting hate speech and that such measures are 'inherently discriminatory and should be abolished.'[74]

Legitimising hate speech bans through striking a balance

Some commentators have sought to tackle the question of how to strike a balance between combatting hate, on the one hand, and preserving democratic freedoms, such as that of expression, on the other. This concept has been dealt with by

---

67 Edward J. Eberle, 'Hate Speech, Offensive Speech, and Public Discourse in America' (1994) 29 *Wake Forest Law Review* 4, 1169. See also Charles R. Lawrence III, 'If He Hollers Let Him Go: Regulating Racist Speech on Campus' (1990) 39 *Duke Law Journal* 3, 452–457.

68 Ibid. 955.

69 Ibid. 959.

70 Friedrich Kubler, 'How Much Freedom for Racist Speech?: Transnational Aspects of a Conflict of Human Rights' (1998) 27 *Hofstra Law Review* 335.

71 Robert Post, 'Racist Speech, Democracy and the First Amendment' (1990–1991) 32 *William and Mary Law Review* 2, 267.

72 Jeremy Waldron, '*The Harm in Hate Speech*' (2nd edn. Harvard University Press, Cambridge MA 2014).

73 Jeremy Waldron, 'Dignity and Defamation: The Visibility of Hate' (2010) 123 *Harvard Law Review* 7, 1597.

74 Eric Henize 'Viewpoint Absolutism and Hate Speech' (2006) 69 *The Modern Law Review* 4, 543.

several authors who have approached it through a mélange of legal, normative and contextual avenues alone or in conjunction with each other. Kretzmer's article entitled 'Freedom of Speech and Racism'[75] is an earlier piece of work which is often included in literature. It looks at freedom of speech and racism and considers the boundaries of freedom of expression when dealing with racist speech, placing more emphasis on normative appraisals of free speech theories, such as Mill's truth argument, and individualist arguments and the way in which such theories, where applicable, have received judicial support. The central research question put forth is whether there is a case for limiting the right of racist groups, such as the *Ku Klux Klan*, from disseminating their ideologies. After establishing a definitional framework of the key terms of racist speech and freedom of speech, the paper appraises theoretical arguments for and against the restriction of racist speech and the question of legislating against hate speech, its intricacies and desirability in light of the difficulties, with the author concluding that the desirability for legislation ultimately depends on social factors. Although the paper commences with a direct reference to racist groups, no examination of the freedom of association or assembly is conducted. Defeis's 'Freedom of Speech and International Norms: A Response to Hate Speech'[76] examines the U.S.' approach to hate speech, underlining the difference in the approach it takes in comparison to most other countries and noting that it is very different to that incorporated in international law. It argues that the 'First Amendment absolutist approach has failed to accommodate equality and non-discrimination rights.'[77] It then looks at the international conventions relevant to this discussion and examines regional documents such as the ECHR. This article produces an overview of the international and European frameworks, referring to other regions such as Africa. The author's argument for a change in the U.S.' approach to hate speech is predominantly based on the breach of equality and non-discrimination that arises from the aforementioned absolutist approach, making this a significant contribution to the interrelation and interdependence of restricting hate speech and promoting the aforementioned values as a valid justification for legitimately legislating against hate. In Farrior's 'Molding the Matrix,'[78] the author offers an extensive assessment of the international framework governing hate speech, exploring the history of the prohibition of hate speech in this sphere by looking at the *travaux préparatoires* of the documents and assesses the theories that underlie these developments. The author also makes a comparison of the justifications put forth by international law for the limitation of hate speech with those of critical race theory, noting, for example, the importance both place on the potential injury of hate speech to its targets. Through the analysis of the legal and normative frameworks, Farrior concludes

---

75 David Kretzmer, 'Freedom of Speech and Racism' (1986) 8 *Cardozo Law Review* 1.

76 Elizabeth F. Defeis, 'Freedom of Speech and International Norms: A Response to Hate Speech' (1992) 29 *Stanford Journal of International Law* 57.

77 Ibid. 59.

78 Stephanie Farrior, 'Molding the Matrix: The Historical and Theoretical Foundations of International Law Concerning Hate Speech' (1996) 14 *Berkley Journal of International Law* 1.

that hate speech can be restricted for purposes of protecting the principles of equality and non-discrimination, finding that the abuse of rights theory is one of the most convincing justifications for limiting hate speech. McGonagle's article 'Wrestling Racial Equality from Tolerance of Hate Looks at the Restrictions to Hate Speech from the Ambit of Prompting the Right to Equality'[79] studies the notion of tolerance in a normative sphere and the socio-political reality behind the increasing anti-racist mandate of the international community, thereby, setting a well-rounded and original normative and contextual setting for the subsequent analysis. It then continues with the standard UN and CoE instruments and case-law, considers negationism, the effectiveness of hate speech laws and the contextual reality of Ireland. This formula is implemented in order to justify its central position that the 'objective of promoting equality and non-discrimination must not be allowed to subordinate or even subdue the right to freedom of expression.'[80] The author suggests the need to balance all the rights and interests at stake. Two earlier pieces of writing also focus on the issues of equality and non-discrimination within the sphere under consideration. 'Extreme Speech and Democracy'[81] includes a collection of essays on a wide variety of issues related to its title including, *inter alia*, the international and European frameworks governing hate speech and the issue of legislating against Holocaust denial. It incorporates examples from Europe and the U.S. to illustrate the points put forth whilst simultaneously including a section which outlines the problems of implementing comparative analyses between the approach taken by States and regions to hate speech. At the core of the discussions is the difficulty of balancing between the different rights and freedoms at stake, an issue which is further developed through a philosophical approach too. This book generally adopts an interdisciplinary approach rather than a purely legal one. In Brems's article on 'State Regulation of Xenophobia Versus Individual Freedoms,' the one research question is whether States can and should impose restrictive legal measures against anti-democratic rhetoric, organisations and individuals. She frames this question as a 'democratic dilemma'[82] with the central question being 'is the remedy then not as dangerous as the illness?'[83] The author responds to the question through a legal appreciation of the issues. She establishes the legal framework by providing an overview of the international and European documents that are relevant to anti-democratic rhetoric and activities, promulgated by groups and individuals, and offers a comparative analysis of the situation in the U.S. and Germany, putting forth an historical explanation as to the variation in stances. She then moves on to tackling the problem

---

79 Tarlach McGonangle, 'Wrestling (Racial) Equality from Tolerance of Hate Speech' (2001) 23 *Dublin University Law Journal* 21.

80 Ibid. 27.

81 Ivan Hare & James Weinstein, *'Extreme Speech and Democracy'* (2nd edn. Oxford University Press, Oxford 2011).

82 Eva Brems, 'State Regulation of Xenophobia versus Individual Freedoms: The European View' (2002) 1 *Journal of Human Rights* 4, 482.

83 Ibid.

question against the aforementioned normative background, setting out a two-fold justification for the legitimate restriction of anti-democratic groups and expression in the form of 'weighing different kinds of harm'[84] and 'defending democracy.'[85] In relation to the first, restricting a person or group of persons' freedom of expression or association is legitimate due to the harmful effects such speech has on individuals and groups. Although the author does not explicitly extend this position to association, it can be implicitly discerned from the composition of this section. In relation to the second justification, the author focusses particularly on Article 17 of the ECHR as the embodiment of militant democracy and notes that far-right ideology threatens the very foundation of the ECHR. Bleich's 'The Freedom to be Racist? How the USA and Europe Struggle to Preserve Freedom and Combat Racism'[86] explores national laws and policies of countries, such as the U.S., Germany, the U.K. and France, in the spheres of racist expression and association. It recognises the differences in approach taken by European countries, on the one hand, and the U.S. on the other, but concludes that, regardless of such variations, none of the countries has breached democratic principles. The contribution's overarching objective is to examine how the countries under consideration strike a balance between the different rights and values at stake. Interestingly, Bakken's article on 'Liberty and Equality through Freedom of Expression: The Human Rights Questions behind Hate Crime Law' takes an opposite stance to that of the majority of relevant literature. It looks at how enhancing the freedom of expression maximises liberty and equality, focussing on the justification put forth for the enactment of laws against hate crime and concludes that these laws 'actually diminish liberty and equality.'[87] The author further argues that such laws do, in fact, promote inequality as they allow for greater punishments due to the victims' race, religion, sex or national origin. The author seeks to justify his positions by looking at theories of free expression and some case-law, statistics and figures from the U.S. with a brief reference to relevant international law. It must be noted that the comparison between American and European approaches to hate speech is of particular interest and relevance to the issue of hate speech given the profoundly different approaches taken by the two on the issue, with an almost absolutist position on free speech being adopted by the former. Several articles have been written by authors such as Kiska,[88] Haupt,[89]

---

84 Ibid. 495.

85 Ibid.

86 Erich Bleich, *'The Freedom to be Racist? How the USA and Europe Struggle to Preserve Freedom and Combat Racism'* (1st edn. Oxford University Press, Oxford 2011).

87 Tim Bakken, 'Liberty and Equality through Freedom of Expression: The Human Rights Questions behind Hate Crime laws' (2013) 4 *International Journal of Human Rights* 2, 1.

88 Roger Kiska, 'Hate Speech: A Comparison between the European Court of Human Rights and the United States Supreme Court Jurisprudence' 25 *Regent University Law Review* 1, 107.

89 Claudia E. Haupt, 'Regulating Hate speech – Damned If You Do and Damned If You Don't: Lessons Learned From Comparing the German and U.S. Approaches' (2006) 23 *Boston University International Law Journal* 2.

Brugger[90] and Douglas-Scott[91] on freedom of expression through a comparative assessment of U.S.-European approaches to this freedom, with European meaning either an analysis of ECtHR case-law or an analysis of instruments available in single States, usually Germany.[92] All the authors mentioned provide normative overviews of international and/or European law, due to the distinctions between the approaches being compared which serve to reflect the pros and cons of each. Thus, these articles contribute to the build-up of literature on the treatment of hate speech and to the variations between positions adopted in the U.S., on the one hand, and in Europe and/or European countries on the other. This literature seeks to find ways to strike a balance between the values and rights at stake in cases of promoting hate through freedoms and/or to justify or reject such a balancing exercise. Principles ranging from the preservation of the principle of non-discrimination to Mill's truth argument, against the backdrop of international and national frameworks, have been assessed by authors in pursuing their objectives. One important observation that can be made from this is that, although the authors recognise the potential of organised groups, such as political parties, to promote hate, focus is placed on the freedom of expression with no concrete mention of association or assembly in the sphere of legitimately restricting hate.

90　Winfried Brugger, 'Ban on or Protection of Hate Speech? Some Observations based on German and American Law' (2002) 17 *Tulane European & Civil Law Forum* 1.

91　Sionaidh Douglas-Scott, 'The Hatefulness of Protected Speech: A Comparison of the American and European Approaches' (1999) 7 *William & Mary Bill of Rights Journal* 2.

92　See e.g., Bradley A. Appleman, 'Hate Speech: A Comparison of the Approaches Taken by the United States and Germany' (1996) 14 *Wisconsin International Law Journal* 422; Winfried Brugger, 'Ban On or Protection of Hate Speech? Some Observations Based on German and American Law' (2002) 17 *Tulane European and Civil Law Forum* 1; Winfried Brugger, 'Verbot oder Schutz von Haßrede? Rechtsvergleichende Beobachtungen zum deutschen und amerikanischen Recht' (2003) 27 *DAJV-NL* 33; Winfried Brugger 'Schutz oder Verbot aggressiver Rede? Argumente aus liberaler und kommunitaristischer Sicht' (2003) 42 *Der Staat* 77; Winfried Brugger, 'Verbot oder Schutz von Hassrede? Rechtsvergleichende Beobachtungen zum deutschen und amerikanischen Recht' (2003) 128 *Archiv Des Offentlichen Rechts* 372; Thomas W. Church & Milton Heuman, 'Punishing the Words that Wound: Thoughts on Hate Speech Regulation in Western Democracies; Annual Meeting of the Committee on Comparative Judicial Studies' *International Political Science Association*, Jerusalem, July 1–4, 1996; Roland Krotoszynski, Jr., 'A Comparative Perspective on the First Amendment: Free Speech, Militant Democracy, and the Primacy of Dignity as a Preferred Constitutional Value in Germany' (2004) 78 *Tulane European and Civil Law Forum* 1549; Friedrich Kubler, 'How much Freedom for Racist Speech?: Transnational Aspects of a Conflict of Human Rights'(1998) 27 *Hofstra Law Review* 2; Friedrich Kuibler, 'Rassenhetze und Meinungsfreiheit' (2000) 125 *Archiv Des Offentlichen Rechts* 125; Natasha L. Minsker, '"I Have a Dream-Never Forget": When Rhetoric Becomes Law, A Comparison of the Jurisprudence of Race in Germany and the United States' (1998) 14 *Harvard BlackLetter Law Journal* 1; Michel Rosenfeld, 'Hate Speech in Constitutional Jurisprudence: A Comparative Analysis' (2003) 24 *Cardozo Law Review* 1; Lars Weihe, 'Freedom of Speech: Gleichheit ohne Grenzen. Eine rechtsvergleichende Untersuchung zur Meinungsfreiheit in den USA und Deutschland' (1990) 24 *Deutsch-Amerikanische Juristen-Vereinigung Newsletter* 46; Mari J. Matsuda, 'Public Response to Racist Speech: Considering the Victim's Story' (1989) 87 *Michigan Law Review* 2320; Richard Delgado & David H. Yun, 'The Speech We Hate: First Amendment Totalitarianism, The ACLU, And the Principle of Dialogic Politics' (1995) 27 *Arizona State Law Journal* 1.

Freedom of expression: a legal assessment of theoretical issues

The third set of relevant literature is context specific, assessing the international, European and/or national legal frameworks in the arena of free speech and hate speech, with some pieces focussing on particular issues such as minority rights and the incitement to violence. The book 'Striking a Balance: Hate Speech, Freedom of Expression and Non-Discrimination,'[93] edited by Coliver, brings together a collection of essays which establish the international standards for dealing with hate speech and provides an overview of the legal regulation of hate speech in a large number of countries. This book incorporates an introductory section regarding the balancing of rights and is simultaneously a rich source of the laws in the ambit of free speech and non-discrimination in the countries under consideration. During the countries' assessments, the authors pinpoint how the balance is found between competing rights. McGoldrick and O'Donnell write on 'Hate Speech Laws: Consistency with National and International Human Rights Law.'[94] The article looks at the freedom of expression in national, European and international frameworks; extensively assesses the case of *Faurisson v France*; and sets out criteria for determining whether hate speech laws are in compliance with national and international human rights law based on the variety of jurisprudence examined therein. It is a significant contribution as it refers to a series of different national laws, such as Israeli and German, as well as case-law from different States such as Canada and Australia. Therefore, this article gives an insight into the legal reality of several countries in the sphere of hate speech and is one of the most extensive analyses of the *Faurisson* case, whilst the criteria it ultimately recommends are useful as indicators of the legitimacy of measures which restrict racist expression. For example, the authors note that restrictions on the freedom of expression for purposes of protecting the rights of others may 'extend to the protection of the community as a whole and thereby to the groups that make up that community.'[95] In van Noorloos's book 'Hate Speech Revisited: a Comparative and Historical Perspective on Hate Speech Law in The Netherlands and England & Wales,'[96] the author conducts a comparative study on the historical development of hate speech and extreme speech laws in the two jurisdictions, looking at how and why the law of the two developed as it did, also considering the impact of international and European law. This contribution offers an in-depth historical appreciation of the development of laws relevant to hate speech in the two jurisdictions. In Belavusau's book 'Freedom of Expression - Importing

---

93 Sandra Coliver, '*Striking a Balance: Hate Speech, Freedom of Expression and Non-Discrimination*' (1st edn. Article 19, International Centre against Censorship, University of Essex, Essex 1992).

94 Dominic McGoldrick & Thérèse O'Donnell, 'Hate Speech Laws: Consistency with National and International Human Rights Law' (1998) 18 *Legal Studies* 4.

95 Ibid. 484.

96 Marloes van Noorloos, '*Hate Speech Revisited: A Comparative and Historical Perspective on Hate Speech Law in The Netherlands and England & Wales*' (1st edn. Intersentia, Cambridge 2011).

European and US Constitutional Models in Transitional Democracies,'[97] the author looks at free speech in the Czech Republic, Hungary and Poland and looks at how these transitional democracies have incorporated free speech models of the CoE, the EU and the U.S. The analysis of the EU approach is significant and, along with article 'Fighting Hate Speech through EU Law,' by the same author, makes up some of the first literature on regulating hate speech using EU mechanisms. Ghanea places hate speech in the realm of minority rights. Her book 'Minorities and Hatred: Protections and Implications' looks at the protection of minorities through the restriction of hate speech. The book adopts the hypothesis that there exists a nexus between hate speech and the protection of minorities, which has not yet been adequately incorporated into international documents. To justify this position, the author examines the impact of Article 20 of the ICCPR on minorities and examines jurisprudence from several countries on the link between prohibiting hate and protecting minorities, also looking at international and European case-law. In Kretzmer and Hazan's 'Freedom of Speech and Incitement against Democracy,'[98] the authors focus particularly on inciting violence and, more particularly, consider the extent to which speech that incites violence can be legitimately restricted by democratic States. It looks at U.S. and German approaches and ECtHR case-law on incitement as well as theories of free speech and theoretical justifications of restricting speech, with the general framework emanating, in part, from the institutions' approaches to the far-right.

Although the majority of the aforementioned literature has referred to Strasbourg jurisprudence during the analysis of issues, the literature mentioned in the following focusses solely on aspects related to this Court in the sphere of hate, in particular, and, more specifically, the issues of violent speech, the role of Article 17 of the ECHR and the 'bad tendency test,' with particular focus placed on *Féret v Belgium* and *Le Pen v France*. Buyse's 'Dangerous Expressions: The ECHR, Violence and Free Speech' considers how the freedom of expression and the prevention of violence can be balanced, using, *inter alia*, jurisprudence, such as *Vona, Norwood* and *Féret*, to illustrate the main arguments. Given that the analysis looks at such cases, and since there exists an inextricable link between the far-right and violence, this article is of particular relevance to the topic under consideration. It indicates that ECtHR case-law shows an 'overlap between cases relating to hate speech and those relating to instances of violence-prone speech'[99] with the Court not always being clear as to the distinction between the two types of dangerous speech. It also demonstrates that the Court has not found a mechanism adequately to balance the prevention of violent speech and the freedom of expression. The same author has previously

---

97 Uladzislau Belavusau *'Freedom of Expression- Importing European and US Constitutional Models in Transitional Democracies'* (1st edn. Routledge, London 2013).

98 David Kretzmer & Francine Kershman Hazan, '*Freedom of Speech and Incitement against Democracy'* (1st edn. Brill, Leiden 2000).

99 Antoine Buyse, 'Dangerous Expressions, the ECHR, Violence and Free Speech' (2014) 63 *International and Comparative Law Quarterly* 2, 493.

made a relevant contribution to a book entitled 'Contested Contours – The Limits of Freedom of Expression from an Abuse of Rights Perspective – Articles 10 and 17 ECHR' which focusses on the limits of freedom of expression from an abuse of rights perspective, considering Article 10 and Article 17 of the ECHR, placing the study within the framework of totalitarian regimes and particularly those of the far-right. It assesses the role of Article 17 of the ECHR, the relationship between Article 17 of the ECHR and other articles, in particular Article 10 of the ECHR. The paper peruses case-law relevant to far-right expression and association where there has been a direct or indirect application or a discarding of Article 17 of the ECHR. From this analysis, it concludes that the Court applies Article 17 of the ECHR to situations of preventing totalitarian movements from abusing Convention rights as well as to those pertaining to revisionism, racism, anti-Semitism, Islamophobia and incitement to violence. This analysis interestingly shows that the Court has not been systematic when endeavouring to 'categorise freedom of expression cases as falling either within the Convention's protective scope (Article 10) or outside it (Article 17).'[100] It also argues that experience has demonstrated that the task of deciphering whether activities do, in fact, aim at destroying human rights and democracy is difficult. It concludes by arguing that an indirect application of Article 17 of the ECHR is the most suitable, as it enables a proportionality test of the impugned measures under consideration and, thus, from a human rights perspective, is the most suitable approach. In Sottiaux's article on 'Bad Tendencies in the ECtHR's Hate Speech Jurisprudence'[101] the author places his analysis on the U.S. 'bad tendency' formula as a means to justify the suppression of ideas that put the foundations of government at risk. He argues that, although this formula has disappeared from American case-law, it marks the ECtHR's hate speech jurisprudence, resulting in a lucid relation between the expression in question and the potential danger arising therefrom. He illustrates his arguments by focussing on *Féret v Belgium* and *Le Pen v France*, on a European level, and *R v Keegstra* on a Canadian level. The author acknowledges that the U.S.-European comparison has occurred time and again in this sphere and, instead, looks at a Euro-Canadian comparison. The article finds that the ECtHR's current approach to hate speech 'is in need of re-evaluation,'[102] with the Court currently citing a variety of negative social and personal consequences which may arise from hate speech 'without indicating how they will ultimately affect its proportionality analysis.' It turns to *Keegstra* in which the Court distinguished between discriminatory speech and speech

---

100 Antoine Buyse, 'Contested Contours – The Limits of Freedom of Expression from an Abuse of Rights Perspective – Articles 10 and 17 ECHR' in Eva Brems & Janneke Gerards (eds.), *'Shaping Rights in the ECHR: The Role of the European Court of Human Rights in Determining the Scope of Human Rights'* (1st edn. Cambridge, Cambridge University Press 2013) 185.

101 Stefan Sottiaux, 'Bad Tendencies in the ECtHR's Hate Speech Jurisprudence' (2011) 7 *European Constitutional Law Review* 1.

102 Ibid. 57.

which incites hate or discrimination,[103] as a method that should be looked at by the ECtHR for purposes of ensuring a more equitable approach to hate speech and Article 10 of the ECHR. Thus, the three aforementioned pieces of writing are directly related to the role and impact of the ECtHR in the framework of far-right manifestations, denoting key weaknesses of the Court in this sphere and seeking to advance recommendations for the improvement of its approach.

Freedom of (extreme) association?

The literature on extreme-right association is limited in comparison to its expression counterpart. Three directly relevant articles can be found. Of particular relevance to this study is Sottiaux's article 'Anti-Democratic Associations: Content and Consequences in Article 11 Adjudication' which seeks to evaluate the position of anti-democratic political parties under Article 11 of the ECHR and does so through an analysis of *Refah Partisi v Turkey*. Even though this case does not deal with the far-right, *per se*, it is a landmark case to any analysis of Article 11 and the dissolution of an association in particular, an issue of paramount importance in relation to the treatment of far-right groupings. The assessment is placed within the broader framework of Loewenstein's dilemma of whether a democracy can restrict the association of political parties without violating its very aims and objectives. The article's 'central claim is that the *Refah* Court adopted a standard which is both content and consequence-based' and, thus, resembles the U.S. Supreme Court's First Amendment jurisprudence. The article's discussion builds up to the important question of why the ECtHR's analysis in *Refah Partisi* required a sufficiently imminent risk test whilst such a counterpart is not evident in its Article 10 case-law on hate speech, with the author referring to *Jersild v Denmark* to illustrate this example. This question subsequently provides a justification of the Court's treatment of Article 11 and, namely, that this reflects 'the essential role the Strasbourg organs ascribe to political associations in preserving democracy and pluralism.'[104] Further, in Fennema's contribution to a book entitled 'Legal Repression of Extreme-Right Parties and Racial Discrimination,'[105] the author looks at the origins of anti-racist and anti-fascist legislation, explores the ICERD, with a particular focus on Article 4, considers the implementation of the ICERD by States Parties, with a particular focus on how far-right parties can be banned under such legislation, and refers to actual cases and figures looking at initiatives taken by the European Union for purposes of countering racism, while dedicating a separate section to the discussion on revisionism. The author makes several conclusions, two of which stand out. First that anti-fascist legislation had its foundations in militant democracy whereas

---

103 Ibid. 58.
104 Stefan Sottiaux, 'Anti-democratic Associations: Content and Consequences in Article 11 Adjudication' (2004) 22 *Netherlands Quarterly of Human Rights* 4, 598.
105 Meindert Fennema, 'Legal Repression of Extreme Right Parties and Racial Discrimination' in Ruud Koopmans & Paul Statham (eds.), '*Challenging International and Ethnic Relation Politics – Comparative European perspectives*' (1st edn. Oxford University Press, Oxford 2000).

anti-racist legislation is founded on the principle of equality which is not easily compatible with the freedom of expression, without extrapolating on the alleged links between the types of legislation and doctrines they pursue. Either way, this article is valuable to the academic understanding of far-right parties as it is one of a kind in providing such a lengthy normative overview of initiatives, legislation and case-law pertaining to, *inter alia*, banning far-right parties. Lastly, Bleich's article 'Hate Crime Policy in Western Europe – Responding to Racist Violence in Britain, Germany and France'[106] evaluates the different approaches taken by the three countries to combat hate crime and argues that, with a view to ensuring an efficient response, it is important to learn from best practices adopted in other States and efficiently responds to actors voicing concerns about particular problems. This article gives a comprehensive overview of the social reality of the integration of migrants in each State and the legal and policy measures adopted to counter racist violence, thereby, constituting a source of relevant background information on, *inter alia*, national legal approaches to racist violence.

Under the umbrella of the far-right, one can find hate speech, hate crime and hateful types of associations and assemblies. These issues and topics are entities within themselves but are, simultaneously, interdependent and interrelated with not only each other but also with the broader framework of the far-right movement. In this light, the first conclusion that can be drawn from the earlier review is that most literature has focussed on the theoretical and/or contextual and/or legal analysis of hate speech as an entity within itself rather than within the greater spectrum of the far-right. Further, available literature has placed more focus on hate speech than hateful types of association, while there has been no substantial assessment of the freedom of assembly in the framework of the far-right as it arises within Article 11 of the ECHR. Lastly, the comparative approach between country laws and regulations has been adopted with a predominant reliance on the U.S.-European model, with the latter meaning Europe as an entity or a particular European country, more often than not Germany, but only in relation to free speech *per se* rather than the far-right and its by-products more generally. Thus, the first reason for which this book is a new contribution to the general academic framework is that it focusses on the far-right in international and European law in its entirety rather than on just one element of its manifestation. Second, this book seeks to contribute to existing academic research by addressing the imbalance, described earlier, in relation to the focus on expression and ensure that all the rights which may be used by the far-right to promote their mandate and conduct their activities are dealt with in a comprehensive manner. In relation to this, the book goes beyond the common free speech-hate speech debate, assessing the issue of hate speech within the framework of non-discrimination as well. Third, the book provides a black letter assessment of the relevant articles and documents as well as a theoretical extrapolation of

---

106 Erik Bleich, 'Hate Crime Policy in Western Europe – Responding to Racist Violence in Britain, Germany and France' (2007) 51 *American Behavioral Scientist* 2.

their nature and composition as these emanate from the doctrine of militant democracy. This doctrine has been considered in several arenas as a concept, more generally,[107] in the sphere of the ECHR[108] in relation to particular freedoms, such as that of association,[109] and as a tool for challenging the far-right movement through the spectrum of political science.[110] However, this doctrine has not yet been applied within a legal assessment of challenging the far-right as a single entity, whilst the mélange of the positive law and theoretical analysis of all the relevant provisions to tackle the far-right has yet to be conducted. Moreover, in addition to the appraisal of the militant democratic approach of the international community to the far-right and its by-products, the book will also look at opposing positions, such as the libertarian approach to hate speech, and also critically consider other theories, such as Critical Race Theory which can be used when appraising relevant laws on the far-right and whose characteristics and positions can be found in, for example, ECtHR jurisprudence, as discussed further in Chapter 4.

To achieve its aim, which is to conduct a critical analysis of the legal treatment of the far-right at the aforementioned levels, the book is structured in the following way. Chapter 1 provides a definitional framework of key terms and notions that will be employed in this book. Chapter 2 establishes the theoretical framework, considering the approaches adopted, predominantly by philosophers and legal theorists, on the question of if, how and when freedoms can be restricted. Chapter 3 sets out the international legal framework on the regulation of the far-right and considers relevant UN Conventions and, particularly, the ICCPR and the ICERD as well as relevant jurisprudence, General Comments and General Recommendations of the Human Rights Committee (HRC) and the CERD as well as reports of relevant UN Special Rapporteurs. It also sets out the development, efficacy and potential loopholes that exist on this level. This chapter examines how international law, directly or indirectly, challenges the far-right and its by-products, looking at its aims, objectives, scope and possible shortcomings. Chapter 4 assesses the legislative and jurisprudential protection and limitations of free speech, assembly and association under the ECHR and the ECtHR's treatment of hateful activity and rhetoric. An overview will also be made of the Additional Protocol to the Cybercrime Convention, Concerning the Criminalisation of Acts of a Racist and Xenophobic Nature

---

107 See, *inter alia*, Paul Cliteur & Bastiaan Rijpkema, 'The Foundations of Militant Democracy' in Afshin Ellian & Gelijn Molier (eds.), *'The State of Exception and Militant Democracy in a Time of Terror'* (1st edn. Republic of Letters Publishing, Dordrecht 2012); András Sajó, *'Militant Democracy'* (1st edn. Eleven International Publishing, Utrecht 2004); Markus Thiel, *'The Militant Democracy Principle in Modern Democracies'* (1st edn. Routledge, London 2009).

108 Paul Harvey, 'Militant Democracy and the European Convention on Human Rights' (2004) 29 *European Law Review* 3; Patrick Macklem, 'Militant Democracy, Legal Pluralism and the Paradox of Self-Determination' (2006) 4 *I-CON* 3.

109 Stefan Sottiaux, 'Bad Tendencies in the ECtHR's Hate Speech Jurisprudence' (2011) 7 *European Constitutional Law Review* 1.

110 Alexander S. Kirshner: *'A Theory of Militant Democracy: The Ethics of Combatting Political Extremism'* (1st edn. Yale University Press 2014).

Committed through Computer Systems. Chapter 5 looks at the EU and the frameworks through which the far-right can and/or should be challenged by Member States and/or European institutions. Particularly, it will look at primary law, such as Article 7 of the Treaty on the European Union, and secondary law, such as the Council Framework Decision on Combatting Certain Forms and Expressions of Racism and Xenophobia by Means of Criminal Law.[111] The overarching objective is to consider the means available to the EU directly or indirectly to challenge the far-right and its by-products and the aims, scope and possible shortcomings of these instruments. Chapter 6 will conduct an analysis of the major U.S. case-law on hate speech and hate crime with the overarching aim of this chapter constituting a comparator with the international and European frameworks.

Bibliography

International and European documents

CERD Concluding Observations to Japan (2014) CERD/C/JPN/CO/7–9, para. 11.
CERD Concluding Observations to Russia (2017) CERD/C/RUS/CO/23–24, para. 15.
Council Framework Decision 2008/913/JHA of 28 November 2008 on Combatting Certain Forms and Expressions of Racism and Xenophobia by Means of Criminal Law.

Books

Belavusau U, 'Freedom of Expression – Importing European and US Constitutional Models in Transitional Democracies' (1st edn. Routledge, London 2013).
Bleich E, 'The Freedom to be Racist? How the USA and Europe Struggle to Preserve Freedom and Combat Racism' (1st edn. Oxford University Press, Oxford 2011).
Carter E, *The Extreme Right in Western Europe: Success or Failure?'* (eds. Manchester University Press, Manchester 2005).
Coliver S, *'Striking a Balance: Hate Speech, Freedom of Expression and Non-Discrimination'* (Article 19, International Centre against Censorship, University of Essex, Essex 1992).
Goodwin M, 'Revolt on the Right: Explaining Support for the Radical Right in Britain' (1st edn. Routledge, London 2014).
Hainsworth P, 'The Politics of the Extreme Right: Form the Margins to the Mainstream' (1st edn. Pinter, London 2000) 7.
Hare I & Weinsten J, *'Extreme Speech and Democracy'* (2nd edn. Oxford University Press, Oxford 2011).
Herz M & Molnar P, *'The Content and Context of Hate Speech: Rethinking Regulation and Responses'* (1st edn. Cambridge University Press, Cambridge 2012).
Ignazi P, *'Extreme Right Parties in Western Europe'* (1st edn. Oxford University Press, New York 2003) 2.
van Noorloos M, 'Hate Speech Revisited: A Comparative and Historical Perspective on Hate Speech Law in the Netherlands and England & Wales' (1st edn. Intersentia, Cambridge 2011).

---

111 Council Framework Decision 2008/913/JHA of 28 November 2008 on Combatting Certain Forms and Expressions of Racism and Xenophobia by Means of Criminal Law.

Kirshner A.S, 'A Theory of Militant Democracy: The Ethics of Combatting Political Extremism' (eds. Yale University Press, New Haven 2014).

Kretzmer D & Kershman Hazan F, *'Freedom of Speech and Incitement against Democracy'* (1st edn. Brill, Leiden 2000).

Sajó A, *'Militant Democracy'* (1st edn. Eleven International Publishing, Utrecht 2004).

Thiel M, 'The Militant Democracy Principle in Modern Democracies' (1st edn. Routledge, London 2009).

Waldron J, *'The Harm in Hate Speech'* (2nd edn. Harvard University Press, Cambridge MA 2014).

Book chapters

Buyse A, 'Contested Contours – The Limits of Freedom of Expression from an Abuse of Rights Perspective – Articles 10 and 17 ECHR' in Eva Brems & Janneke Gerards (eds.), *'Shaping Rights in the ECHR: The Role of the European Court of Human Rights in Determining the Scope of Human Rights'* (1st edn. Cambridge University Press, Cambridge 2013), 183–210.

Fennema M, 'Legal Repression of Extreme Right Parties and Racial Discrimination' in R Ruud Koopmans & Paul Statham (eds.), *'Challenging International and Ethnic Relation Politics – Comparative European Perspectives'* (1st edn. Oxford University Press, Oxford 2000), 119–144.

Cliteur P & Rijpkema B, 'The Foundations of Militant Democracy' in Afshin Ellian & Gelijn Molier (eds.), *'The State of Exception and Militant Democracy in a Time of Terror'* (Republic of Letters Publishing, Dordrecht 2012), 227–272.

Journal articles

Bakken T, 'Liberty and Equality through Freedom of Expression: The Human Rights Questions behind Hate Crime laws' (2013) 4 *International Journal of Human Rights* 2, 1–12.

Belavusau U, 'Fighting Hate Speech through EU Law' (2012) 4 *Amsterdam Law Forum*, 20–35.

Bleich E, 'Hate Crime Policy in Western Europe – Responding to Racist Violence in Britain, Germany and France' (2007) 51 *American Behavioral Scientist* 2, 149–165.

Brems E, 'State Regulation of Xenophobia versus Individual Freedoms: The European View' (2002) 1 *Journal of Human Rights* 4, 481–500.

Brugger W, 'Ban on or Protection of Hate Speech? Some Observations based on German and American Law' (2002) 17 *Tulane European & Civil Law Forum* 1, 1–21.

Buyse A, 'Dangerous Expressions, the ECHR, Violence and Free Speech' (2014) 63 *International and Comparative Law Quarterly* 2, 491–503.

Defeis E.F, 'Freedom of Speech and International Norms: A Response to Hate Speech' (1992) 29 *Stanford Journal of International Law* 57, 57–129.

Douglas-Scott S, 'The Hatefulness of Protected Speech: A Comparison of the American and European Approaches' (1999) 7 *William & Mary Bill of Rights Journal* 2, 305–346.

Eberle E.J, 'Hate Speech, Offensive Speech, and Public Discourse in America' (1994) 29 *Wake Forest Law Review* 4, 1135–1213.

Farrior S, 'Molding the Matrix: The Historical and Theoretical Foundations of International Law Concerning Hate Speech' (1996) 14 *Berkley Journal of International Law* 1, 1–98.

Ghanea N, 'Minorities and Hatred: Protections and Implications' (2010) 17 *International Journal on Minority and Group Rights* 3, 423–446.

Giugni M & Koopmans R, 'What Causes People to Vote for a Radical Right Party? A Rejoinder to van der Brug and Fennema' (2007) 19 *International Journal of Public Opinion Research* 4, 488–491.

Harvey P, 'Militant Democracy and the European Convention on Human Rights' (2004) 29 *European Law Review* 3, 407–420.

Haupt E.C, 'Regulating Hate Speech – Damned If You Do and Damned If You Don't: Lessons Learned from Comparing the German and U.S. Approaches' (2005) 23 *Boston University International Law Journal* 2, 300–335.

Henize E, 'Viewpoint Absolutism and Hate Speech' (2006) 69 *The Modern Law Review* 4, 543–582.

Husbands C.T, 'Combating the Extreme Right with the Instruments of the Constitutional State: Lessons from Experiences in Western Europe' (2002) 4 *Journal of Conflict and Violence Research* 1, 52–73.

Kiska R, 'Hate Speech: A Comparison between the European Court of Human Rights and the United States Supreme Court Jurisprudence' (2012) 25 *Regent University Law Review* 1, 107–151.

Kretzmer D, 'Freedom of Speech and Racism' (1986) 8 *Cardozo Law Review* 1, 446–513.

Kubler F, 'How Much Freedom for Racist Speech?:Transnational Aspects of a Conflict of Human Rights' (1998) 27 *Hofstra Law Review* 2, 336–376.

Lawrence C.R III, 'If He Hollers Let Him Go: Regulating Racist Speech on Campus' (1990) 39 *Duke Law Journal* 3, 431–483.

Macklem P, 'Militant Democracy, Legal Pluralism and the Paradox of Self-Determination' (2006) 4 *I-CON* 3, 488–516.

McGoldrick D & O'Donnell T, 'Hate Speech Laws: Consistency with National and International Human Rights Law' (1998) 18 *Legal Studies* 4, 453–485.

McGonangle T, 'Wrestling (Racial) Equality from Tolerance of Hate Speech' (2001) 23 *Dublin University Law Journal* 21, 21–54.

Post P, 'Racist Speech, Democracy and the First Amendment' (1990–1991) 32 *William and Mary Law Review* 2, 267–327.

Sottiaux S, 'Bad Tendencies in the ECtHR's Hate Speech Jurisprudence' (2011) 7 *European Constitutional Law Review* 1.

Sottiaux S, 'Anti-democratic Associations: Content and Consequences in Article 11 Adjudication' (2004) 22 *Netherlands Quarterly of Human Rights* 4, 40–63.

Waldron J, 'Dignity and Defamation: The Visibility of Hate' (2010) 123 *Harvard Law Review* 7, 1597–1657.

Websites

Election results

European Parliament Election Results: www.europarl.europa.eu/elections2014-results/en/country-results-fr-2014.html#table02.

European Parliament Election Results: www.europarl.europa.eu/elections2014-results/en/country-results-el-2014.html#table03.

Golden Dawn Election Results 2009: http://ekloges-prev.singularlogic.eu/v2009/pages/index.html.

Golden Dawn Election Results 2012: http://ekloges-prev.singularlogic.eu/v2012b/public/index.html#{"cls": "party","params":{"id":41}}.

Greece Election Results 2015: http://ekloges.ypes.gr/current/v/public/#{"cls":"main", "params":{}}.

Italy Election Results 2018: http://electionresources.org/it/2018/senate.php?region=.
Italy Election Results 2013: http://electionresources.org/it/senate.php?election=2013.
Sweden Election Results 2014: http://electionresources.org/se/riksdag.php?election=2014.
Sweden Election Results 2018: http://electionresources.org/se/riksdag.php?election=2018.

Newspaper articles

BBC: 'Home Secretary Bans Telford EDL March' (12 August 2011) www.bbc.com/news/uk-england-shropshire-14506941.
BBC: 'English Defence League March in London is Blocked' (27 August 2011) www.bbc.com/news/uk-england-london-14684704.
Fidesz Magyar Polgári Szövetség. This Co-operation was Noted by Kim Lane Scheppele in a New York Times Article: 'Hungary without Two Thirds' (17 March 2015) http://krugman.blogs.nytimes.com/2015/03/17/hungary-without-two-thirds/.
New Statesman: How the Remorseless Rise of the Swedish Far Right Could Leave the Country Ungovernable (4 July 2018) www.newstatesman.com/culture/observations/2018/07/how-remorseless-rise-swedish-far-right-could-leave-country-ungovernable.
News 247: 'Παραλήρημα Ηλιόπουλου της Χρυσής Αυγής κατά των ομόφυλων ζευγαριών' (Iliopoulos Rant against Gay Couples) (3 May 2018) www.news247.gr/politiki/paralirima-iliopoyloy-tis-chrysis-aygis-kata-ton-omofylon-zeygarion.6608997.html.
Nooz.gr: 'Ομάδα "Κρυπτεία": Θα χρησιμοποιήσουμε βία αλύπητα' (Kriptia: We Will Use Violence Relentlessly' (28 November 2017) www.nooz.gr/greece/1474522/omada-krypteia--tha-chrisimopoiisoyme-bia-alypita.
Spiegel Online International: 'The World from Berlin: "The Neo-Nazi Killers Were among Us"' (15 November 2011) www.spiegel.de/international/germany/the-world-from-berlin-the-neo-nazi-killers-were-among-us-a-797948.html.
The Telegraph: 'EU Elections 2014: "I Can Hear the Boots of the 1930s Marching through Europe"' (14 May 2014) www.telegraph.co.uk/news/worldnews/europe/eu/10823028/EU-elections-2014-I-can-hear-the-boots-of-the-1930s-marching-through-Europe.html.

Reports

A Chatham House Report: Matthew Goodwin, 'Right Response: Understanding and Countering Populist Extremism in Europe' (2011).
Friedrich-Ebert-Stiftung Forum Berlin: Nora Langenbacher & Britta Schellenberg, 'Is Europe on the Right Path? Right-Wing Extremism and Right-Wing Populism in Europe' (2011).
Institute for Strategic Dialogue: Matthew Goodwin & Vidhya Ramalingam, 'Briefing Paper – The New Radical Right: Violent and Non-Violent Movements in Europe' (2012).

Other

Roosevelt F, 'Message to American Booksellers Association' (23 April 1942).

1 The definitional and conceptual framework

The far-right: semantics and notions

Far-right movements are not easily defined, with no consensus as to their definition, and with the lines between different terms that exist within this realm remaining blurred.[1] In fact, the terms 'populist, neo-nationalist, far right, radical right and extreme right are often used interchangeably.'[2] According to Mudde, even though 'the term right-wing extremism is today quite current in the social and political jargon, there is no unequivocal definition.'[3] 'Fascism,' which is a 'heavily contested term,'[4] has also been used on occasion to describe such movements. This term can be traced back to Mussolini's Italy (1922–1943), where 'prototypal Italian fascism'[5] emanated from and could subsequently be found in countries such as France, Great Britain and the Netherlands.[6] European fascism is directly interrelated with the period between the end of the First World War and the end of the Second World War,[7] and, notwithstanding that some pre-First World War traces of fascism existed, it was that war and its consequences which 'truly forged fascism out of the primitive pre-war ore.'[8] Fascism has been defined as a term which includes phenomena such as 'hypernationalism, anti-parliamentarism, antiliberalism, populism...'[9] and as one which is '...a typical

1 Friedrich-Ebert-Stiftung Forum Berlin: Nora Langenbacher & Britta Schellenberg, 'Is Europe on the Right Path? Right-Wing Extremism and Right-Wing Populism in Europe' (2011) 41.
2 Institute for Strategic Dialogue: Matthew Goodwin & Vidhya Ramalingam, 'Briefing Paper - The New Radical Right: Violent and Non-Violent Movements in Europe' (2012) 13.
3 Cass Mudde, 'Right-Wing Extremism Analyzed: A Comparative Analysis of the Ideologies of Three Alleged Right-wing Extremist Parties (NPD, NDP, CP'86) (1995) 27 *European Journal of Political Research* 2, 205.
4 Daniel Trilling, '*Bloody Nasty People – The Rise of Britain's Far Right*' (1st edn. Verso, London 2012) 5.
5 European Parliament Committee of Inquiry into the Rise of Fascism and Racism in Europe, Report on the Findings of the Inquiry, 1985, Luxembourg, para. 30.
6 Ibid.
7 Martin Blinkhorn, '*Fascism and the Right in Europe 1919-1945*' (1st edn. Routledge, London 2000) 9.
8 Ibid.
9 European Parliament Committee of Inquiry into the Rise of Fascism and Racism in Europe, Report on the Findings of the Inquiry, 1985, Luxembourg, para. 29.

manifestation of 20th century totalitarianism; resistance to modernization...'[10] As such, and as noted in the Evrigenis Report, which was formulated by an expert committee on a EU level for the purposes of examining the rise of fascism and racism in Europe in the 1980s:

> there was widespread insistence that the phenomena under consideration must be placed in a historical perspective, some experts even maintaining that the term fascism should be confined to the movements active in interwar Europe under that name.[11]

Minkenberg also adopts this viewpoint by noting that the term fascism 'refers to specific historical phenomena.'[12] Interlinked with the term 'fascism' is 'Nazism' and variations such as Neo-Nazi. In relation to Nazism, some of the experts who composed the Evrigenis Report placed fascism and Nazism under one umbrella, arguing that 'nazism is part of a continuous ideological development in Europe,'[13] whereas others noted the difference between Nazism and fascism by making reference to, *inter alia*, 'the anti-Semitic aspect of nazism as distinguishing the two.'[14] Importantly, 'while fascist or neo-fascist movements or parties should indeed be considered right-wing extremist, not all right-wing extremist movements or parties may be considered fascist or neo-fascist.'[15] More generally, the terms Fascism, Nazism, Neo-Fascism and Neo-Nazism were the terms employed by political and academic commentators until the 1960s, with the term right-wing extremism coming into play in the 1970s.[16] In relation to the term right-wing extremism, it must be noted that this is favoured predominantly in Europe, whereas the term 'radical right' is more often used in the U.S.[17] Furthermore, the term alt-right has recently seen a rise in the U.S.[18]

Either way, it is beyond the scope of this book to assess the constituents of the different definitions used to describe the movement under consideration. Instead, it is sufficient to note that the definitional framework adopted for

10 Ibid.
11 Ibid.
12 Michael Minkenberg, 'The Radical Right in Europe today: Trends and Patterns in East and West' in Friedrich-Ebert-Stiftung Forum Berlin: Nora Langenbacher & Britta Schellenberg, 'Is Europe on the Right Path? Right-Wing Extremism and Right-Wing Populism in Europe' (2011) 39–40.
13 European Parliament Committee of Inquiry into the Rise of Fascism and Racism in Europe, Report on the Findings of the Inquiry, 1985, Luxembourg, Annex 1, p. 111.
14 Ibid. para. 34.
15 Elizabeth Carter, *'The Extreme Right in Western Europe: Success or Failure?'* (1st edn. Manchester University Press, Manchester 2005) 17.
16 Paul Hainsworth, *'The Extreme Right in Western Europe'* (1st edn. Routledge, London 2008) 8.
17 Ibid. 77.
18 Cas Mudde, *'The Far Right in America (Extremism and Democracy)'* (1st edn. Routledge, London 2017).

the purposes of analysis of the ways in which this movement is challenged does not adopt an exclusionary approach towards any of the aforementioned definitions when appraising academic and legal text, given that they are, in many cases, employed interchangeably therein. However, when referring to the movement under consideration, the term far-right will be employed throughout for purposes of coherence, given that it is relatively neutral and all-encompassing of the varying characteristics and terms employed amongst continents and spheres.

The far-right: its structural framework

The far-right is an ideology promoted by individuals and groups. For the purposes of this book, far-right rhetoric and/or activity as uttered and/or carried out by political parties, non-party groups and the subculture milieu are assessed, looking at the far-right within the sphere of an organised or semi-organised movement rather than at far-right individuals with no affiliation to a particular entity or movement. Minkenberg divided the organised groupings of this movement into three different forms: those of a political party, a non-party group and a subculture environment. The first status enjoyed by such groups is that of a registered political party functioning within a democratic regime, pursuing support through elections and seeking to influence policy and practice through actual or pursued representation in the executive and/or legislature. Second are the non-party groups which are not rigidly structured and are 'not geared towards elections or public offices but nonetheless aim to mobilize the public in general.'[19] Third are the 'small groups in the sense of a subculture environment'[20] which operate independently from the other entities and are more prone to violence than other groups.[21] This does not mean that there is always a rigid separation of entities in the structure. For example, *Golden Dawn* is a political party with characteristics of a violent subculture movement, and with a rigid rather than a loose structure. In fact, it is the status of *Golden Dawn* as a political party that constituted one of the central reasons the State repeatedly cited for not interfering with its rhetoric and actions. As noted, 'exclusion constrains radical right parties but cannot prevent the movement sector from developing comparatively strongly.'[22] As such, the variations in structures will be taken into account when assessing the legal framework, with the benchmark being that the tools and obligations are applicable to the different forms which the far-right takes.

---

19 Michael Minkenberg, 'The Radical Right in Europe Today: Trends and Patterns in East and West' in Friedrich-Ebert-Stiftung Forum Berlin: Nora Langenbacher & Britta Schellenberg, 'Is Europe on the Right Path? Right-Wing Extremism and Right-Wing Populism in Europe' (2011) 41.
20 Ibid.
21 Ibid.
22 Ibid. 49.

Hate speech

Hate speech constitutes a by-product of the far-right which does not enjoy a universally accepted formulation, with most States and institutions adopting their own understanding of what hate speech entails[23] without actually defining it.[24] Determining what constitutes hate speech in the absence of such a formulation becomes even more difficult when considering that hate speech may be 'concealed in statements which at a first glance may seem to be rational or normal'[25] and does not necessarily manifest itself through the expression of hatred or of emotions.[26] As noted by the CERD, hate speech utterers 'hijack the principles and mechanisms of democracy to legitimise racist and xenophobic platforms and hate speech.'[27] Although the CERD defines the process, it does not actually define the speech-act. One of the few documents, albeit non-binding, which has sought to elucidate the meaning of hate speech, is the Recommendation of the Council of Europe Committee of Ministers on hate speech.[28] It provides that this term is to be

> understood as covering all forms of expression which spread, incite, promote or justify racial hatred, xenophobia, anti-Semitism or other forms of hatred based on intolerance, including intolerant expression by aggressive nationalism and ethnocentrism, discrimination and hostility against minorities, migrants and people of immigrant origin.

Interestingly, the Recommendation incorporates the justification of hatred as well as its spreading, incitement and promotion, allowing for a broad spectrum of intentions to fall within its definition. Hate speech has also been mentioned, but not defined, by the ECtHR. For example, it has referred to

> all forms of expression which spread, incite, promote or justify hatred based on intolerance, including religious intolerance.[29] The inclusion of merely justifying hatred demonstrates the low threshold attached to unacceptable speech. In the framework of homophobic speech, the Court held that it is not necessary for the speech 'to directly recommend individuals to commit hateful acts'[30]

---

23 Council of Europe Committee of Experts for the Development of Human Rights Report (2007) Chapter IV, 123, para. 4.
24 Natalie Alkiviadou, 'Regulating Hate Speech in the EU' in Stavros Assimakopoulos, Fabienne H Baider & Sharon Millar (eds.), *'Online Hate Speech in the EU: A Discourse Analytical Perspective'* (1st edn. Springer Briefs in Linguistics 2017).
25 Anne Weber, *'Manual on Hate Speech'* (1997) Council of Europe Publishing, 5.
26 Ibid.
27 CERD 81st Session CERD/C/SR.2196.
28 Council of Europe's Committee of Ministers Recommendation 97 (20) on Hate Speech.
29 Gündüz v Turkey, Application no. 35071/97 (ECHR 4 December 2003) para. 40; Erbakan v Turkey, Application no. 59405/00 (6 July 2006) para. 56.
30 Vejdeland and Others v Sweden, Application no. 1813/07 (ECHR 9 February 2012) para. 54.

since attacks on persons can be committed by 'insulting, holding up to ridicule or slandering specific groups of the population'[31] and that 'speech used in an irresponsible manner may not be worthy of protection.'[32] Through this case, the Court drew the correlation between hate speech and the negative effects it can have on its victims, alleging that even violence-free speech amounting to mere insults has the potential to cause harm sufficient enough to limit free speech. Matching that with its established position as protecting even offensive, shocking and disturbing ideas is tricky to say the least. Moreover, the fact that the Court has not yet offered a definition of hate speech has been characterised as 'unsatisfactory from the point of judicial interpretation, doctrinal development and general predictability and foreseeability.'[33] It could also be argued that this has contributed to the rather controversial judgements which potentially goes against the very notion of free speech, as further discussed in Chapter 4. In addition, the FRA has offered two separate formulations of hate speech, the first being that it 'refers to the incitement and encouragement of hatred, discrimination or hostility towards an individual that is motivated by prejudice against that person because of a particular characteristic.'[34] In its 2009 report on homophobia, the FRA held that the term hate speech, as used in that particular section, 'includes a broader spectrum of verbal acts including disrespectful public discourse.'[35] The particularly problematic part of this definition is the broad reference to disrespectful public discourse, especially since institutions, such as the ECtHR, extend the freedom of expression to ideas that 'shock, offend or disturb.'[36] This is the formal position of the Court, even though in relation to hate speech cases, as briefly noted earlier and as will be extended further in Chapter 4, the Court has been overly rigorous in having a very low threshold of what it is willing to accept. In the framework of academic commentary, a plethora of definitions has been put forth to describe hate speech. In exploring its different formulations, Belavusau notes that hate speech is 'deeply rooted in the ideologies of racism, sexism, religious intolerance, xenophobia, and homophobia.'[37] In addition, he argues that pinpointing the grounds from which hate speech may arise is also a tricky task and poses the question of where limits are to be drawn.[38] According to Matsuda,

---

31 Ibid.

32 Ibid. para. 55

33 Tarlach McGonagle, 'The Council of Europe Against Online Hate Speech: Conundrums and Challenges' Expert Paper, Institute for Information Law, Faculty of Law, http://hub.coe.int/c/document_library/get_file?uuid=62fab806-724e-435a-b7a5-153ce2b57c18&groupId=10227 [Accessed 15 August 2014] 10.

34 Fundamental Rights Agency, 'Hate Speech and Hate Crimes against LGBT Persons' (2009) 1.

35 Fundamental Rights Agency, 'Homophobia and Discrimination on Grounds of Sexual Orientation and Gender Identity in the EU Member States: Part II - The Social Situation' (2009) 44.

36 The Observer and The Guardian v The United Kingdom, Application no 13585/88 (ECHR 26 November 1991) para. 59.

37 Uladzislau Belavusau, *'Freedom of Speech: Importing European and US Constitutional Models in Transitional Democracies'* (1st edn. Routledge, London 2013) 41.

38 Ibid.

hate speech that she perceives and conceptualises solely as racist speech contains three central elements: namely that the message is 'of racial inferiority, the message is directed against historically oppressed groups and the message is persecutory, hateful and degrading.'[39] McGonagle offers a broad interpretation of hate speech in terms of threshold but not in terms of content and target groups, arguing that 'virtually all racist and related declensions of noxious, identity-assailing expression could be brought within the wide embrace of the term.'[40] Smolla defines it as a 'generic term that has come to embrace the use of speech attacks based on race, ethnicity, religion and sexual orientation or preference.'[41]

Although some common elements can be discerned from these approaches to hate speech and the variations therein, it could be argued that 'hate speech seems to be whatever people choose it to mean.'[42] What can be discerned from the various extrapolations of hate speech is that it 'singles out minorities for abuse and harassment.'[43] What will become apparent in the conceptualisation of hate speech in international and European law is that (i) there is no agreement on thresholds of abuse, and (ii) LGBTI groups are inherently missing from any legislative conceptualisation of hate speech on a UN, EU and CoE level.

Hate crime

Hate crimes are committed by perpetrators due to their hatred towards the victim's group rather than the victim himself/herself.[44] Hate crime is differentiated from other forms of criminality, both because of the motivations of the offender and its effects on an individual, community and societal level. Through the committal of such crimes, the victim is targeted due to his or her identity, which, in turn, terrorises not only the victim but also other members of the group to which he or she belongs.[45] To this end, the OSCE recognises that a hate crime is also a message crime and a symbolic crime.[46] Previously, such crimes were

---

39 Mark Slagle, 'An Ethical Exploration of Free Expression and The Problem of Hate Speech' (2009) 24 *Journal of Mass Media Ethics* 4, 242.

40 Tarlach McGonagle, 'Wresting Racial Equality From Tolerance of Hate Speech' (2001) 23 *Dublin University Law Journal* 21, 4.

41 Claudia E. Haupt, 'Regulating Hate Speech - Damned If You Do and Damned If You Don't: Lessons Learned from Comparing the German and U.S. Approaches' (2005) 23 *Boston University International Law Journal* 2, 304.

42 Roger Kiska, 'Hate Speech: A Comparison Between The European Court of Human Rights and the United States Supreme Court Jurisprudence' (2012) 25 *Regent University Law Review* 1, 110.

43 Mark Slagle, 'An Ethical Exploration of Free Expression and the Problem of Hate Speech' 24 *Journal of Mass Media Ethics* 4, 238.

44 Troy A. Scotting, 'Hate Crimes and the Need for Stronger Federal Legislation' (2001) 34 *Akron Law Review* 4, 856–857.

45 Eugene McLaughlin & John Muncie, *'The SAGE Dictionary of Criminology'* (1st edn. Sage CA 2006) 196.

46 OSCE-ODIHR 'Hate Crime Laws: A Practical Guide' (2009) 7: www.osce.org/odihr/36426? download=true [Accessed 10 February 2015].

habitually given 'no more concern than other serious crimes,'[47] with this situation altering in the last twenty years as a result of 'mounting public and political attention to racist violence.'[48] This, in part, emanates from the realisation that this type of violence is 'particularly reprehensible'[49] since it 'can inflict damage above and beyond the physical injury caused by a garden-variety assault.'[50] As with hate speech, there is no universally accepted definition of hate crime. For the purposes of this book, hate crime is considered to be crimes directed at a person or persons on the grounds of the victim's association or perceived association with an ethnic, national and/or religious group, and/or due to his/her sexual orientation and/or gender identity. Unfortunately, the two latter groups are conspicuously absent from the international and European legal frameworks, an issue which will be extrapolated on throughout this book. The link between hate speech and hate crime must not be undermined. As noted by the OSCE, following an extensive survey of hate crimes in 2017, hate crimes habitually occur in contexts of intolerant and racist public discourse.[51] This has been seen in, *inter alia*, Greece, the post-Brexit U.K., Hungary and Poland.

Chapter conclusion

In conclusion, several terms are used to describe the far-right movement, sometimes interchangeably. Moreover, the composition and objective of a far-right grouping varies in time and place, directly correlating with contextual woes for the purposes of satisfying its voters and attracting new ones. Manifestations of this movement, such as hate speech and hate crime, are not defined in international and European legal documents, meaning that there exist no definitional benchmarks against which national initiatives, laws and policies in this ambit can be formulated.

Bibliography

Case law

Erbakan v Turkey, App. no. 59405/00 (ECHR 6 July 2006).
Gündüz v Turkey, App. no. 35071/97 (ECHR, 4 December 2003).
The Observer and The Guardian v The United Kingdom, App. no. 13585/88 (ECHR, 26 November 1991).
Vejdeland and Others v Sweden, App. no. 1813/07 (ECHR 9 February 2012).

---

47 Erik Bleich, 'Hate Crime Policy in Western Europe: Responding to Racist Violence in Britain, Germany and France' (2007) 51 *American Behavioral Scientist* 2, 149.
48 Ibid.
49 James Weinstein, 'First Amendment Challenges to Hate Crime Legislation: Where's the Speech?' (1992) 11 *Criminal Justice Ethics* 2, 5.
50 Ibid.
51 As demonstrated through several examples in OSCE, 'Hate Crimes in the OSCE Region – Incidents and Responses: Annual Report for 2007' (2007).

International and European documents

Convention on the Elimination of All Forms of Racial Discrimination 81st Session CERD/C/SR.2196.

Council of Europe Committee of Experts for the Development of Human Rights Report (2007).

Council of Europe's Committee of Ministers Recommendation 97 (20) on Hate Speech.

European Parliament Committee of Inquiry into the Rise of Fascism and Racism in Europe, Report on the Findings of the Inquiry, 1985, Luxembourg.

Fundamental Rights Agency, 'Hate Speech and Hate Crimes against LGBT Persons' (2009).

Fundamental Rights Agency, 'Homophobia and Discrimination on Grounds of Sexual Orientation and Gender Identity in the EU Member States: Part II – The Social Situation' (2009).

Books

Belavusau U, *'Freedom of Speech: Importing European and US Constitutional Models in Transitional Democracies'* (1st edn. Routledge, London 2013) 41.

Blinkhorn M, *'Fascism and the Right in Europe 1919–1945'* (1st edn. Routledge, London 2000) 9.

Carter E (ed.), *'The Extreme Right in Western Europe: Success or Failure?'* (Manchester University Press, Manchester 2005).

Hainsworth P, *'The Extreme Right in Western Europe'* (1st edn. Routledge, London 2008) 8.

McLaughlin E & Muncie J, *'The SAGE Dictionary of Criminology'* (1st edn. SAGE, Los Angeles CA 2006).

Mudde C, *'The Far Right in America (Extremism and Democracy)'* (1st edn. Routledge, London 2017).

Plato, *'The Republic'* (Πλάτων, 'Πολιτεία').

Trilling D, *'Bloody Nasty People – The Rise of Britain's Far Right'* (1st edn. Verso, London 2012).

Book chapters

Alkiviadou N, 'Regulating Hate Speech in the EU' in Stavros Assimakopoulos, Fabienne H Baider & Sharon Millar (eds.), *'Online Hate Speech in the EU: A Discourse Analytical Perspective'* (1st edn. Springer Briefs in Linguistics 2017).

Journal articles

Bleich E, 'Hate Crime Policy in Western Europe: Responding to Racist Violence in Britain, Germany and France.' (2007) 51 *American Behavioral Scientist* 2, 49–165.

Haupt C.E, 'Regulating Hate Speech – Damned If You Do and Damned If You Don't: Lessons Learned from Comparing the German and U.S. Approaches' (2005) 23 *Boston University International Law Journal* 2, 299–335.

Kiska R, 'Hate Speech: A Comparison between the European Court of Human Rights and the United States Supreme Court Jurisprudence' (2012) 25 *Regent University Law Review* 1, 107–151.

McGonagle T, 'Wresting Racial Equality from Tolerance of Hate Speech' (2001) 23 *Dublin University Law Journal* 21, 21–54.

Mudde C, 'Right-Wing Extremism Analyzed: A Comparative Analysis of the Ideologies of Three Alleged Right-Wing Extremist Parties (NPD, NDP, CP'86)' (1995) 27 *European Journal of Political Research* 2, 203–224.

Scotting T.A, 'Hate Crimes and the Need for Stronger Federal Legislation' (2001) 34 *Akron Law Review* 4, 1–37.

Slagle M, 'An Ethical Exploration of Free Expression and the Problem of Hate Speech' 24 *Journal of Mass Media Ethics* 4, 238–250.

Weinstein J, 'First Amendment Challenges to Hate Crime Legislation: Where's the Speech?' (1992) 11 *Criminal Justice Ethics* 2, 6–20.

Reports

Institute for Strategic Dialogue: Matthew Goodwin & Vidhya Ramalingam, 'Briefing Paper – The New Radical Right: Violent and Non-Violent Movements in Europe' (2012) 13.

Friedrich-Ebert-Stiftung Forum Berlin: Nora Langenbacher & Britta Schellenberg, 'Is Europe on the Right Path? Right-Wing Extremism and Right-Wing Populism in Europe' (2011) 41.

OSCE, 'Hate Crimes in the OSCE Region – Incidents and Responses: Annual Report for 2007' (2007).

Weber A, 'Manual on Hate Speech' (1997) Council of Europe Publishing.

Other

OSCE-ODIHR 'Hate Crime Laws: A Practical Guide' (2009): www.osce.org/odihr/36426?download=true.

McGonagle T, 'The Council of Europe against Online Hate Speech: Conundrums and Challenges' Expert Paper, Institute for Information Law, Faculty of Law http://hub.coe.int/c/document_library/get_file?uuid=62fab806-724e-435a-b7a5-153ce2b57c18&groupId=10227 [Accessed 15 August 2014] 10.

2 The Theoretical Framework

The legitimate restriction of rights: how, when and why?

In his 'Republic,' Plato argues that when there are no barriers to freedom, the consequences are that it loses its meaning and results in moral superficiality and anarchy.[1] Plato also underlined that the worst evil is too much freedom while regulated freedom is the best possession.[2] In Roman times, Cato[3] held that the State could only interfere in order to 'protect men from the injuries of one another.'[4] Later, Locke, a believer in the inherent liberty and freedom of the person, argued that, for purposes of ensuring a cohesive and secure society, people should give up a part of their freedom in order to ensure a common well-being.[5] He observed that 'all men may be restrained from invading others' rights and from doing hurt to one another...'[6] thereby recognising the potential for interference in the exercise of rights insofar as the rights of others are damaged and, as such, sowing the seeds for the harm principle which was further developed by Mill. Mill put forth the necessity of regulating rights and freedoms in some particular circumstances. He was careful first to separate the role of the State in personal affairs affecting only the individual, holding that the State

> must not interfere in the areas which are self-regarding, that is which concern the individual him/herself. Every human being is the sole custodian over his/her body and mind: one's freedom must not be compromised, and one should be encouraged to express his/her personal desires.[7]

1 Πλάτων, 'Πολιτεία' (Plato, 'The Republic') (Introduction and translation: Skouteropulos N.M) (1st edn. Πόλις, Athens 2014) (original version: 381 BC) 557.
2 Πλάτων, 'Επιστολαί' (Plato, 'Epistles') (1st edn. Κάκτος, Athens 1993) 354 e4 'ελευθερία υπερβάλλουσα πάγκακον, έμμετρος δε πανάγαθος').
3 Marcus Porcius Cato Uticensis (Cato the Younger) 95 BC, 46 BC.
4 John Trenchard & Thomas Gordon, 'Cato's letters' (ed. Ronald Hamowy) (Liberty Fund, Carmel 1995) (original version: 1755).
5 John Locke, 'Two Treaties of Government' (ed. Peter Laslett) (Cambridge University Press, Cambridge 1988) (original version: 1689) Book 2, 123–131.
6 Ibid.
7 John Stuart Mill, 'On Liberty' in Mary Warnock (ed.), 'Utilitarianism and On Liberty: Including Mill's Essay on Bentham and Selections from the Writings of Jeremy Bentham and John Austin' (2nd edn. Blackwell, Englewood Cliff NJ 2012) (original version: 1859) 95.

Through this statement, Mill recognised that the State must not involve itself in any conduct which affects the conductor only (self-regarding) and implicitly setting the foundations for his subsequent arguments that, when such conduct affects others, the State has the right to interfere (in certain situations). His particular reference to expression, when talking generally of the non-interference of the State, demonstrates the significance that Mill attached to this freedom. However, he developed a framework through which rights may indeed be regulated, which is what has come to be known as the harm principle. He held that 'the only purpose for which power can be rightfully exercised over any member of a civilised community, against his will, is to prevent harm to others.'[8] He underlined that

> as soon as any part of a person's conduct affects prejudicially the interests of others, society has jurisdiction over it and the question whether the general welfare will or will not be promoted by interfering with it, becomes open to discussion.[9]

Mill extrapolated on what was previously left implied, namely, the State's power to interfere in conduct which affects others. However, this power is not automatically granted but, instead, the issue of interference simply becomes open to discussion through an appraisal of a balancing test of competing rights. Further, Mill recognised that consequences of one's conduct may be hurtful to another but that does not amount to a violation of rights and, as such, cannot be prohibited.[10] Thus, classical theorists, such as Locke and Mill, found that rights and conduct can be limited within the general framework of protecting the rights and interests of others, preventing harm coming upon them through the actions of another, according to the severity of the harm, with a strict threshold being attached thereto. Several contemporary commentators have conceptualised the theme of harm with a view to rationalising the restrictions of rights. For example, Feinberg argued that for harm to occur there needs to be a negative effect on a person's interests and that the harm violates a person's rights.[11] However, he noted that an adequate balancing between competing rights and interests involved should be effectuated and that rights may be restricted even in cases where the consequence is merely an offence to others. Feinberg defined offence as something which does not result in the violation of a person's rights or interests but nevertheless has negative consequences on that person.[12] In such cases, he put forth the proportionality principle, arguing that means other than criminal law should be considered.[13] In theorising the legitimacy of hate speech bans, several scholars have adopted

---

8 Ibid. 94.
9 Ibid. 147.
10 Ibid.
11 Joel Feinberg, *'The Moral Limits of the Criminal Law: Harm to Others'* (1st edn. Oxford University Press, Oxford 1984) 47–48.
12 Ibid.
13 Ibid. 31.

the harm perspective. Tsesis describes hate speech as a 'societal virus'[14] and Greenawalt underlines the damaging consequences of such speech, noting that 'epithets and slurs that reflect stereotypes about race, ethnic group, religion and gender may reinforce prejudices and feelings of inferiority in seriously harmful ways.'[15] In discussing bans on racist speech, Post examines several arguments that have been put forth as justifications for such bans including, the 'intrinsic harm of racist speech'[16] insofar as there is an 'elemental wrongness'[17] to such expression, the infliction of harm to particular groups or individuals as well as to the marketplace of ideas.[18] However, harm is a concept to be handled with care, especially when confronted with a perceived threat in certain circumstances. As argued by Sunstein in *Fear and Liberty*, the people and the State are prone to exaggerating the potential of harm when confronted with a highly visible threat surmounting from a single action.[19] Another approach has been adopted by Smolla, who justifies hate speech bans not due to the intrinsic harm of such speech but, rather, on the correlation between the irrelevance of hate speech to societal dialogue and the ethicacy of its restriction.[20] On both a UN and a CoE level, as will become evident in the relevant chapters, it is the issue of harm to others and their rights, which has driven the non-judicial monitoring bodies and the Court respectively to restrict readily what they perceive to be hate speech. As a brief illustration, in dealing with homophobic speech, the ECtHR found that

> Restrictions on freedom of expression must therefore be permissible in instances where the aim of the speech is to degrade, insult or incite hatred against persons or a class of person on account of their sexual orientation.[21]

Militant democracy: legitimately restricting rights for purposes of protecting democracy

As Goebbels infamously observed 'it will always remain one of the best jokes of democracy that it provides its own deadly enemies with the means with which it can be destroyed.'[22] Militant democracy essentially seeks to prevent such

---

14 As cited in Mark Slagle, 'An Ethical Exploration of Free Expression and The Problem of Hate Speech' (2009) 24 *Journal of Mass Media Ethics* 4, 242.

15 Kent Greenawalt, *'Speech, Crime and the Uses of Language'* (1st edn. Oxford University Press, New York 1989) Chapter 2.

16 Robert C. Post, 'Racist Speech, Democracy and the First Amendment' (1990–1991) 32 *William and Mary Law Review* 2, 272.

17 Ibid.

18 Ibid. 273.

19 Patrick Macklem, 'Militant Democracy, Legal Pluralism, and the Paradox of Self-determination' (2005) 4 *International Journal of Constitutional Law* 3, 515.

20 Mark Slagle, 'An Ethical Exploration of Free Expression and the Problem of Hate Speech' (2009) 24 *Journal of Mass Media Ethics* 4, 242.

21 Vejdeland v Sweden, Application no. 1813/07, (ECHR 9 February 2012) para. 46.

22 As quoted in *Nationalsozialistische Diktatur* 1933–1945: Eine Bilanz 16 (K.D. Bracher et al. eds. Düsseldorf: Droste 1983).

'jokes' by pre-emptively challenging threats posed to democracy by phenomena, such as the far-right, through the restriction of civil and political rights,[23] in particular those which facilitate their rise to power, such as freedom of expression, association and assembly. The central objective of this doctrine is to authorise a democracy 'to protect its continued existence as a democracy.'[24] Militant democracy was initially developed on an academic level by Loewenstein in a 1937 two-part article which underlined the need democracy has to protect itself from anti-democratic threats. When he wrote the article, Loewenstein had just emigrated to the U.S. after recognising that 'his Jewish ancestry and liberal mind set would not ... be in his favour'[25] in the Nazi regime. Loewenstein's article was developed during a time when the Nazi party had risen to power through the use and, ultimately, the abuse of the democratic institutions of the Weimar Republic, thereby, rendering fascism a central tenet of the development of the author's ideas. When placing Loewenstein's writings in context, it must be taken into account that they were published before the onset of the Second World War, before the Holocaust and before the defeat of Nazi Germany.[26] Loewenstein's arguments were, thus, not a reaction to the atrocities of the time but almost a precognitive solution to them. In his writings, he noted that 'democracy and democratic tolerance have been used for their own destruction'[27] and sought to replace the opposing notion of democratic fundamentalism with a militant democracy since, 'until very recently, democratic fundamentalism and legalistic blindness were unwilling to realise that the mechanism of democracy is the Trojan horse by which the enemy enters the city.'[28] Loewenstein held that 'constitutions ... have to be stiffened and hardened when confronted by movements intent upon their destruction'[29] and that 'every possible effort must be made to rescue [democracy], even at risk and cost of violating fundamental principles.'[30] Militant democracy (*wehrhafte Demokratie* or *streitbare Demokratie*) was embedded as a constitutional doctrine in post-war Germany to prevent the repetition of the atrocities committed by the Nazi regime and, as a result, is particularly associated with it. The German Basic Law was the first European constitution to embrace the militant democratic approach with most post-Second World War constitutions

---

23 Svetlana Tyulkina, 'Militant Democracy: An Alien Concept to Australian Constitutional Law?' (2015) 36 *Adelaide Law Review* 2, 517.

24 Ibid.

25 Paul Cliteur & Bastiaan Rijpkema, 'The Foundations of Militant Democracy' in Afhisn Ellian & Gelijn Molier (eds.), *'The State of Exception and Militant Democracy in a Time of Terror'* (1st edn. Republic of Letters Publishing, Dordrecht 2012) 228.

26 Robert A. Kahn, 'Why do Europeans Ban Hate Speech? A Debate between Karl Loewenstein and Robert Post' (2013) 41 *Hofstra Law Review* 3, 560.

27 Karl Loewenstein, 'Militant Democracy and Fundamental Rights I' (1937) 31 *The American Political Science Review* 3, 423.

28 Ibid. 424.

29 Ibid. 432.

30 Ibid. 432.

following its lead.[31] Although its roots are found in the 1930s and it has subsequently been transcribed into several national constitutions,[32] with the prime example being the German one, the doctrine has received great attention in recent years, on a political, legal and academic level. Based on Loewenstein's initial explanatory framework of militant democracy, several scholarly definitions have been put forth, with no universal agreement on its meaning. For example, Harvey states that it is a system which is 'capable of defending the constitution against anti-democratic actors who use the democratic process in order to subvert it.'[33] Macklem defines it as 'a form of constitutional democracy authorised to protect civil and political freedom by pre-emptively restricting the exercise of such freedoms.'[34] Pfersmann recognises both the political and legal functionalities of the enforcement of this doctrine by holding that it is

> a political and legal structure aimed at preserving democracy against those who want to overturn it from within or those who openly want to destroy it from outside by utilizing democratic institutions as well as support within the population.[35]

In terms of the element of militancy and self-preservation, Pfersmann argues that 'democracies are always more or less militant'[36] with Sajó holding that the State's most natural characteristic is self-defence.[37] This is in line with Posner's position that liberal constitutions should take measures in self-defence.[38] To contextualise the doctrine, Macklem holds that 'neo-nazi movements ... may have also provoked States to assume militant stances towards threats to democratic institutions.'[39] In this light, militant democracy today is generally seen as the fight against extreme movements, with particular emphasis on political parties pursuing anti-democratic aims.[40]

---

31 Paul Harvey, 'Militant Democracy and the European Convention on Human Rights' (2004) 29 *European Law Review* 3, 408.

32 In 1938 Italy amended its constitution to prohibit the rise of the fascist party, article 16 of the French constitution of 1958 authorises militant state action more generally, empowering the president of the republic to take measures required by the circumstances when the institutions of the republic are under serious and immediate threat.

33 Paul Harvey, 'Militant Democracy and the European Convention on Human Rights' (2004) 29 *European Law Review* 3, 408.

34 Patrick Macklem, 'Militant Democracy, Legal Pluralism, and the Paradox of Self-determination' (2005) 4 *International Journal of Constitutional Law* 3, 488.

35 Otto Pfersmann, 'Shaping Militant Democracy: Legal Limits to Democratic Stability' in Andras Sajó (ed.), *'Militant Democracy'* (1st edn. Eleven International Publishing, Utrecht 2004) 47.

36 Ibid. 53.

37 András Sajó, 'Militant Democracy and Transition towards Democracy' in Andras Sajó (ed.), *'Militant Democracy'* (1st edn. Eleven International Publishing, Utrecht 2004) 213.

38 Richard A. Posner, *'Not a Suicide Pact: The Constitution in a Time of National Emergency'* (1st edn. Oxford University Press, Oxford 2006).

39 Patrick Macklem, 'Militant Democracy, Legal Pluralism, and the Paradox of Self-determination' (2006) 4 *International Journal of Constitutional Law* 3, 491.

40 András Sajó, 'From Militant Democracy to the Preventive State' (2006) 22 *Cardozo Law Review* 5, 2262.

However, the doctrine, its meaning and its operation are far from simple. The inherent intricacy of militant democracy is, as noted by *Sajó* 'its potentially expansive reach'[41] since 'a militant democracy can easily become an illiberal democracy, more concerned with its own stability than with political developments.'[42] Some, such as Macklem, note that 'the legality of militant democracy ... is far from clear'[43] with others, including Kelsen, taking a stricter approach, namely, that when a democracy attempts to safeguard itself from anti-democratic entities, it is no longer a democracy.[44] Both theoretical and practical questions arise when considering this doctrine including, for example, the potentially oxymoronic nature of a democracy restricting democratic rights in its name. Even the doctrine's father, Loewenstein, tackled this issue by holding that democracy 'stands for fundamental rights, for fair play for all opinions, for free speech, assembly, press. How could it address itself to curtailing these without the vary basis of its existence?'[45] Loewenstein justified the militancy of a functioning democracy by noting that it has a duty to rescue itself from the 'opportunistic platitudes of fascism ... even at the risk and cost of violating fundamental principles...'[46] Cliteur and Rijpkema pinpoint that Loewenstein had indirectly recognised the vulnerability of the democratic system, a characteristic which constitutes a sound backdrop against which the militancy of a democracy can be justified. This is essentially that democracy grants hostile entities access to its institutions. Such entities are entitled to rights and freedoms 'thereby allowing them to actually discredit and vilify her,'[47] making particular reference to rights such as free speech and assembly. Relevant to this were Popper's thoughts on an open society in which he spoke of the 'paradox of tolerance,'[48] warning that 'unlimited tolerance must lead to the disappearance of tolerance.'[49] In this way, Popper demonstrated that, actually, a liberal democracy was not violating its very foundations by restricting the rights of others but rather protecting its status as such given that too much tolerance would subsequently be hijacked by

---

41 András Sajó, 'Militant Democracy and Emotional Politics' (2012) 19 *Constellations* 4, 565: https://onlinelibrary.wiley.com/doi/pdf/10.1111/cons.12011 [Accessed 12 October 2018].

42 John E. Finn, *'Constitutions in Crisis: Political Violence and the Rule of Law'* (1st edn. Oxford University Press, Oxford 1991) 217.

43 Patrick Macklem, 'Militant Democracy, Legal Pluralism, and the Paradox of Self-determination' (2005) 4 *International Journal of Constitutional Law* 3, 488.

44 Paul Cliteur & Bastiaan Rijpkema, 'The Foundations of Militant Democracy' in Afshin Ellian & Gelijn Molier (eds.), *'The State of Exception and Militant Democracy in a Time of Terror'* (1st edn. Republic of Letters Publishing, Dordrecht 2012) 243.

45 Karl Loewenstein, 'Militant Democracy and Fundamental Rights I' (1937) 31 *The American Political Science Review* 3, 430.

46 Ibid. 432.

47 Paul Cliteur & Bastiaan Rijpkema, 'The Foundations of Militant Democracy' in Afshin Ellian & Gelijn Molier (eds.), *'The State of Exception and Militant Democracy in a Time of Terror'* (1st edn. Republic of Letters Publishing, Dordrecht 2012) 235.

48 As explained in Karl Popper 'The Open Society and Its Enemies' (published in two volumes: *The Spell of Plato and The High Tide of Prophecy: Hegel, Marx, and the Aftermath*) (1st edn. Routledge, London 1945) 546.

49 Ibid.

those who embraced totalitarian models of governance. However, who defines the enemies of Popper's open society, what is intolerance and who are the intolerant? The possibility of a mal-definition of these elements could open the door for a tyrannical rule of the majority. The potential for majoritarian tyranny is directly related with the scope for abuse by governments who allege undemocratic threats when, in essence, the use of the doctrine is to facilitate the enforcement of their own political agenda and limit their political competitors. Even in cases where restrictions are imposed on, for example, speech and association in the name of self-protection and are applied 'bona fide ... they are prone to excess.'[50] Interestingly, and although Chapter 4 will demonstrate that the ECtHR could be regarded as overly zealous in the restriction of rights when confronted particularly with hate speech, it has, at least, conjecturally underlined the role of minority opinions in a democracy by holding that

> democracy does not simply mean that the views of a majority must always prevail: a balance must be achieved which ensures the fair and proper treatment of minorities and avoids any abuse of a dominant position.[51]

The element of thresholds is of paramount importance when seeking to mitigate abuse. Cliteur and Rijpkema discuss the element of thresholds, posing the question of whether militant democracy should protect itself 'only against hostile but violent parties, or also against hostile but non-violent parties?'[52] Central to this question is the consideration of non-violent yet hostile parties, not simply due to the legal issues that may arise when balancing key rights, but also due to the fact that, as argued by Loewenstein, 'no government can rely only on force or violence, the cohesive strength of the dictatorial and authoritarian state is rooted in emotionalism.'[53] Although this statement was made when referring to Loewenstein's reality at the time, that being Nazi Germany, it can still be applicable in today's far-right context, particularly in relation to political parties which also adopt political emotionalism as a central weapon. As highlighted early on by Loewenstein, openly violent acts can easily be restricted with the intricacies lying in combatting subtler techniques related to the freedom of expression.[54] However, the latter part of his statement is offered without any theoretical explanation of how precisely to restrict subtler techniques and without any reference to parties which may not be openly violent but pursue discriminatory aims, to

---

50 András Sajó, 'Militant Democracy and Emotional Politics' 19 *Constellations* 4 (2012) 571.

51 Young James and Webster v The United Kingdom, Application nos. 7601/76; 7806/77 (ECHR 18 October 1982) para. 63.

52 Paul Cliteur & Bastiaan Rijpkema, 'The Foundations of Militant Democracy' in Afshin Ellian & Gelijn Molier (eds.), *'The State of Exception and Militant Democracy in a Time of Terror'* (1st edn. Republic of Letters Publishing, Dordrecht 2012) 243.

53 Karl Loewenstein, 'Militant Democracy and Fundamental Rights I' (1937) 31 *The American Political Science Review* 3, 432.

54 Ibid. 652.

say the least. It is Van den Bergh who sought to extrapolate on the not so obvious justification of curtailing the right of non-violent yet undemocratic parties to associate. To this end, he refers to the 'self-correcting nature of democracy'[55] which treats all ideas equally, except those which seek to destroy it.[56] Based on this premise, democracy may limit all groups which promote such ideas. In addition, there are questions such as when should restrictions be enforced? What is considered a threat to democracy? Does restriction avoid the alleged destruction of democracy or could it exacerbate the situation further, especially when faced with totalitarian and/or potentially or actually violent groups? The question of legitimacy has also been put forth. Accetti and Zuckerman contest the legality of militant democracy by arguing that there is an 'irreducible element of arbitrariness in whichever way the decision is taken as to what constitutes an enemy of democracy.'[57] They extrapolated on this by holding that the decision on who to allow as a legitimate participant of the democratic process

> is ultimately a decision over the boundaries of the political community itself, which cannot coherently be taken by democratic procedures and therefore cannot be subsumed under any prior norm.[58]

Rummens has sought to overcome the potential arbitrariness of the doctrine by suggesting that the decision on who is an enemy of democracy and, thus, impacted by restrictions in the democratic process should emanate from a decision of the people.[59] However, the complexities in terms of practicalities of this approach and the significant 're-politicization of the question of membership in the demos'[60] are inherent in Rummens's suggestion. At the crux of it, if popular decision is to trigger the enforcement of militant democratic techniques, popular decision should also mark a plethora of other decisions taken on a political level, reconceptualising as such the concept of the vote, trust in those elected and consequently, the democratic system more generally.

Moreover, the impact of militant democracy must also be taken into account when appraising the doctrine on a theoretical level. Loewenstein warned that one must not 'overestimate the ultimate efficiency of legislative provisions against fascist emotional technique.'[61] This can be reflected in the example of Germany in the 1990s. Minkenberg noted that, notwithstanding the restrictive

---

55 Paul Cliteur & Bastiaan Rijpkema, 'The Foundations of Militant Democracy' in Afshin Ellian & Gelijn Molier (eds.), *'The State of Exception and Militant Democracy in a Time of Terror'* (1st edn. Republic of Letters Publishing, Dordrecth 2012) 245.
56 Ibid.
57 Carlo Invernizzi Accettil & Ian Zuckerman, 'What's Wrong with Militant Democracy?' (2017) 65 *Political Studies* IS, 183.
58 Ibid.
59 Ibid. 187.
60 Ibid.
61 Karl Loewenstein, 'Militant Democracy and Fundamental Rights I' (1937) 31 *The American Political Science Review* 4, 652.

measures against far-right groups at the time, the State saw a rise in far-right violence, coherent mobilisation and a radicalisation of the movement's ideology and not an elimination of the threat.[62] Conceptualising on the boomerang effect of militant democracy, Rosenblum argued that the inclusion of assumed enemies of democracy in the democratic process could force them to 'reformulate their objectives in ways that are consistent with democratic partisanship.'[63] Although theoretically a possibility, in recent years the far-right has demonstrated a neater, tidier and more moderate image in a plethora of countries ranging from France to Sweden, instances of which are described in this book's introduction. However, the ideological ingredients necessary for the far-right definitional box to be ticked have remained. In addition, the constitutional upheaval that has come about with the election of governments in countries, such as Hungary and Poland, cannot be ignored when appraising Rosenblum's position. *Orbán* was relatively neat, tidy and consistent with democratic partisanship up until the point he gained power the second time around. Once at the top, he shattered the very foundations of Hungary's rule of law, constitution and democratic functioning. A pertinent observation in relation to the impact of restrictive strategies was made by Goldmann and Sonnen in their critique of the CERD's *Berlin-Brandenburg* decision involving the xenophobic statements made by a former Senator of Berlin, Sarazzin. Statements included that

> If 1.3 million Chinese are just as intelligent as Germans, but more industrious and in the foreseeable future better educated while we Germans take on ever more of a Turkish mentality, we'll have a bigger problem.[64]

In relation to this case, Goldmann and Sonnen argued that

> It might have been a pyrrhic victory. The decision allows Sarrazin and other populists to style themselves as victims of a system of mainstream political correctness which supposedly suppresses diverging views by means of criminal law.[65]

As such, militant democracy remains 'an issue of extensive debate'[66] with a central issue being the extent to which democracies can limit personal rights and

---

62 Michael Minkenberg, 'Repression and Reaction: Militant Democracy and the Radical Right in Germany and France' (2006) 40 *Patterns of Prejudice* 25, 43–44.

63 Nancy Rosenblum *'On the Side of the Angels: An Appreciation of Parties and Partisanship'* (1st edn. Princeton University Press, Princeton NJ 2008) 435–544.

64 BB Turkish Union in *Berlin Brandenburg* v Germany, Communication No 48/2010 (26 February 2013) CERD/C/82/D/48/2010, para. 2.1.

65 Matthias Goldmann & Mona Sonnen, 'Soft Authority against Hard Cases of Racially Discriminating Speech: Why the CERD Committee Needs a Margin of Appreciation Doctrine' (2016) 7 *Goettingen Journal of International Law* 1, 132.

66 Uladzislau Belavusau, *'Freedom of Speech: Importing European and US Constitutional Models in Transitional Democracies'* (1st edn. Routledge 2013) 13.

freedoms through preventive measures.[67] Notwithstanding the conjectural justifications for seeking to limit democracy in a general sense, problems do arise with the technicalities of doing so. There are intricacies related to the point at which such limitations commence and the extent to which they continue. Macklem argues that this doctrine and its legality will remain vague and open to abuse unless legal standards pertaining to definitions of entities and/or actions which should fall within the restrictive actions of a militant democracy are formulated and upheld.[68] The problems of defining threats and enemies and determining thresholds have led to this debate, and a realisation of these issues from different perspectives is significant for the subsequent analysis of the legitimacy and/or efficacy and/or relevance of the tools available to tackle the far-right on an international and European level. The problems are enhanced in relation to international and European tools which are centred predominantly on the restriction of rights on the grounds of protecting *other people* rather than democracy itself. Although one would expect a particularly high threshold of harm to be necessitated for such restrictions, Chapters 3 and 4 will demonstrate that both the UN and the CoE have allowed for the limitation of speech on grounds of mere insult and offence to others.[69]

Freedom of expression: to restrict or not?

More emphasis has been placed by scholars on the issue of limiting expression and, so, this section will consider some of these arguments which could be used when considering the restriction of expression. Responses to key questions in relation to association and assembly can be found when looking at the general conceptualisation of the restriction of rights dealt with earlier, whilst, at the same time, the analysis found in the framework of expression can be potentially extended to association and assembly which are directly interrelated to expression.[70] Associations and assemblies constitute central vehicles for expression since an association is an organised collective through which persons seek, *inter alia*, to express their opinions, whilst an assembly is another mechanism through which ideas and opinions are put forth. Despite a certain parallel between the theoretical appraisal of free speech and free association and assembly in terms of restrictions, the jurisprudential treatment of such rights has,

---

67 Ibid.
68 Patrick Macklem, 'Militant Democracy, Legal Pluralism, and the Paradox of Self-determination' (2006) 4 *International Journal of Constitutional Law* 3, 495.
69 See, *inter alia*, Vejdeland v Sweden, Application no. 1813/07 (ECHR 9 February 2012).
70 As noted, *inter alia*, by the Venice Commission:

> The right to freedom of association is intertwined with the right to freedom of thought, conscience, religion, opinion and expression. It is impossible to defend individual rights if citizens are unable to organize around common needs and interests and speak up for them publicly.

> See Venice Commission, "Opinion on the compatibility with human rights standards of the legislation on non-governmental organisations of the Republic of Azerbaijan" (14–15 October 2011) CDL-AD(2011)035, para. 84.

at times, varied. For example, ECtHR case-law demonstrates that the closer a right gets to the functional operation of democracy, the higher its protection, with freedom of association being considered closer to the core. Although more on this issue will be discussed in Chapter 4, for now it suffices to underline that, although links can be made between the theoretical appraisal of the limits (or not) of free speech and with association and assembly, these are not absolute.

Aristotle's Rhetoric supports free expression and particularly 'robust public discourse as a means to promote citizen awareness and vigilance.'[71] In Gorgias, Plato is contrary to public discourse as there is the potential to 'manipulate and misguide people who lack facility in critical reason.'[72] In Ancient Greece, there was the concept of parrhesia (παρρησία) which, as noted by Belavusau, is very difficult to translate with the closest meaning being 'the frankness in speaking the truth' with Foucault being one of the authors translating this into English as free speech.[73] In addition to the concept of parrhesia, there was also isigoria (ισηγορία) which 'describes the equal right of speech in a democracy.'[74] Thus, parrhesia refers to the freedom to express oneself in a democratic society whereas isigoria incorporates the significance of equal status amongst all citizens in the realm of expression. In Ancient Rome, Cato, as a Statesman, argued that free speech was 'the great bulwark of liberty'[75] which protected persons against an arbitrary State and was, thus, an 'essential element of natural liberty.'[76] In A Letter Concerning Toleration, Locke noted that there are certain rights which are inalienable and can only be restricted if the rights of others are affected and these include religious freedom and the freedom of thought,[77] demonstrating the great significance he placed on the freedom to think. Hobbes noted that, in relation to speech, there may be an issue of limitation as it is 'but an abuse of Speech to grieve him[78] with the tongue.'[79]

As demonstrated in this chapter, several commentators have noted that freedom of expression holds a particularly sacred place in society. This protected status has subsequently given rise to a lengthy discussion on the nature of free

---

71 Eric Heinze, *'Hate Speech and Democratic Citizenship'* (1st edn. Oxford University Press, Oxford 2016) 116.

72 Ibid. 117.

73 Michel Foucault, *'Fearless Speech'* edited by Joseph Pearson (Semiotext(e) 2001) as referred to in Uladzislau Belavusau, *'Freedom of Speech – Importing European and US Constitutional Models in Transitional Democracies'* (1st edn. Routledge, London 2013) 88.

74 Uladzislau Belavusau, *'Freedom of Speech – Importing European and US Constitutional Models in Transitional Democracies'* (1st edn. Routledge, London 2013) 88.

75 John Trenchard & Thomas Gordon, *'Cato's letters'* (ed. Ronald Hamowy) (Liberty Fund, Carmel 1995) (Original: 1755).

76 Ibid.

77 John Locke, *'An Essay Concerning Human Understanding'* (ed. Peter. H Nidditch) (1st edn. Clarendon, Oxford) (original version: 1689) Book 2, Chapter 27, 252.

78 Unless that persons 'be one whom we are obliged to govern; and then it is not to grieve, but to correct and amend': Thomas Hobbes, *'Leviathan'* (Introduction by Minogue K) (Dent, Darlington1976) (original version: 1651) 13.

79 Ibid.

speech, whether it should or could be legitimately curtailed or whether it should or could be absolute. Classical libertarian models of free speech have been formulated by theorists, such as Milton, who, in *Areopagitica*,[80] considered conflicting arguments and ideas to lie within a battlefield, with the truth always revealing itself in the end. The need to restrict expression was, thus, limited given that the truth would, in one way or another, become known. However, his understanding of this freedom was very much based on his own faith in God since 'the truth[81] he speaks of is divine, and its triumph is assured by God's own omnipotence.'[82] As noted by Fish, the religious foundations from which this argument emanates render it subjectively reasonable given that the truth is considered to be a divine creation. However, if one were to remove the theological character of this argument, the model would plummet.[83]

Mill, who developed one of the original libertarian models of free speech which has survived in time and place, held that 'there ought to exist the fullest liberty of professing and discussing, as a matter of ethical conviction, any doctrine, however immoral it may be considered.'[84] He put the importance of the freedom of expression down to four key points. First, he held that expression may be true and so should not be curtailed, given that those who are seeking to do so have no right to interfere as they are not infallible and so cannot be sure that something is in fact untrue.[85] Secondly, he argued that the opinion uttered may contain elements of the truth and so is necessary to 'supply the remainder of the truth.'[86] Thirdly, he noted that an opinion must be contested before being accepted as the truth, otherwise it will 'be held in the manner of a prejudice.'[87] Lastly, without freedom of expression, truth will become dogma thereby 'preventing the growth of any real and heartfelt conviction.'[88] Mill embraced a strict test regarding the question of the limitation of rights and, so, it can be deduced that the threshold he placed for prohibition of expression is high. For example, in relation to expression, for Mill, 'mere offensiveness does not

---

80 Milton J, '*Aeropagitica*' in Ernest Sirluck '*Two Complete Prose Works of John Milton*' (1st edn. Yale University Press, New Haven CT 1959) (original version: 1644) 486.

81 Apart from the capacity of the truth to always reveal itself, Milton argued against licensing and censorship by the State as this would be a 'dishonour and derogation to the author, to the book, to the privilege and dignity of learning.' He also noted the importance of receiving both 'good' and 'bad' information posing the rhetorical question of 'what wisdom can there be to choose, what continence to forbear without the knowledge of evil?'

82 Mark Slagle, 'An Ethical Exploration of Free Expression and the Problem of Hate Speech' (2009) 24 *Journal of Mass Media Ethics* 4, 240.

83 Stanley Fish, '*There's No Such Thing as Free Speech (And It's a Good Thing Too)*' (1st edn. Oxford University Press, Oxford 1994) 103.

84 John Stuart Mill, '*On Liberty*' in Mary Warnock (ed.), '*Utilitarianism and On Liberty: Including Mill's Essay on Bentham and Selections from the Writings of Jeremy Bentham and John Austin*' (2nd edn. Blackwell, Englewood Cliff NJ 2012) (original version: 1859) 99.

85 Ibid. 128.

86 Ibid.

87 Ibid.

88 Ibid.

constitute harm'[89] and, as such, he sought to establish some kind of threshold for unprotected speech which is attached to a certain degree of damage resulting from such speech. In relation to expression, he enhanced the stringency that is to be enforced when considering limitation by putting forth other terms and conditions that need to be met if it is to be restricted. He noted that, even if the manner in which speech is communicated is not temperate and is aggravated and objectionable, the law cannot restrict it.[90] Thus, on the one hand, Mill did not require the tone or the manner of speech to be particularly peaceful, polite or acceptable but, on the other hand, he deemed the setting in which speech is expressed and disseminated to be significant as it has the potential to influence the effects of such speech. More particularly, he argued that 'even opinions lose their immunity when the circumstances in which they are expressed are such as to constitute their expression a positive instigation to some mischievous act.'[91] This description partly rings the bell of terms used today in the realm of hate speech, including dissemination of hatred or violence, which constitute mischievous acts. It is clear that Mill placed a great emphasis on the importance of free expression as a centrifugal element to the development of a society which requires persons to 'be capable of being improved through free and equal discussion.'[92] However, he noted that the liberty principle attached to the ever so important freedom of expression does not apply to children, madmen and barbarians as they are not in a position to be improved by free and equal discussion.[93] Therefore, Milton and Mill envisioned a society where unrestricted debate and discussion of a variety of conflicting ideas was central to a flourishing democracy in which truth is revealed and effective responses to issues are determined as a result of the permitted debate.[94] Their thoughts constitute the conceptual foundations for the 'marketplace of ideas' principle first formulated as such in *Abrahams v United States* which dealt with anti-war activists.[95] In his dissenting opinion, Justice Holmes held that 'the best test of truth is the power of thought to get itself accepted in the competition of the market.'[96] When considering the writings of scholars such as Milton and Mill, one must always bear in mind the systematic and long-term repression that speech underwent, with the particular temporal setting constituting the backdrop of their writings. This

---

89 David O. Brink, 'Millian Principles, Freedom of Expression and Hate Speech' (2001) 7 *Legal Theory* 2, 120.
90 Ibid. 129.
91 John Stuart Mill, *'On Liberty'* in Mary Warnock (ed.), *'Utilitarianism and On Liberty: Including Mill's Essay on Bentham and Selections from the Writings of Jeremy Bentham and John Austin'* (2nd edn. Blackwell, Englewood Cliff 2012) (original version: 1859) 131.
92 Ibid. 136.
93 Ibid. 95, 147, 148 & 153.
94 Milton J, *'Aeropagitica'* in Ernest Sirluck *'Two Complete Prose Works of John Milton'* (1st edn. Yale University Press, New Haven CT 1959) (original version: 1644) 486.
95 Abraham v United States, 250 U.S. 616 (1919): The Court upheld the conviction of five anti-war protestors, who had been charged with Sedition for distributing anti-war pamphlets.
96 Ibid. at 630 (Holmes J., dissenting).

may have partly demonstrated the great emphasis they placed on the importance of free expression.

More recent commentaries adopting the libertarian approach include that of Chaffee who holds that, by allowing free expression, a society can discover the truth and so can proceed in the best possible way to serve its best interests and, also, serve the needs of the individual to express themselves on issues that are relevant to their quality of life.[97] Further, Meiklejohn argues that 'absolute freedom of speech is an inevitable corollary of self-rule'[98] since citizens living in a democracy have the right to take decisions regarding their government which, hence, has no power to restrict the vehicle through which this is attained, namely expression. This position is partly shared by Bollinger who, although underlining that hate speech does not contribute anything valuable to society, nevertheless concluded that hate speech should be permitted.[99] He bases this premise on the fact that the ability of a society to tolerate even the most unpleasant of viewpoints allows persons to develop a sense of toleration for something that they would like to prohibit.[100] Thus, libertarian positions of expression comprehend expression in almost absolute terms and underline its significance on an individual and societal level. Such an approach could, in theory, extend not only to the expression itself but also the vehicles of association and assembly.

It must be noted that the right to freedom of thought is one that has habitually been regarded as absolute, with little need appearing to discuss any forms of restrictions thereto. Mill refers to the 'absolute freedom of opinion and sentiment on all subjects, practical or speculative, scientific, moral or theological.'[101] Mill noted that, although freedom of thought and freedom of expression are interlinked, they also have certain distinctions in that expression affects other persons. Nevertheless he recognised that it is 'almost of as much importance as the liberty of thought itself.'[102] Mill's position in relation to freedom of thought, namely, that it is linked to expression, but, unlike expression, is absolute, can also be seen in international conventions. For example, Article 19 of the ICCPR holds that everyone shall have the right to hold opinions without interference. Part 2 of this article provides for

---

97 Zechariah Chafee, *'Free Speech in the United States'* (2nd edn. Atheneum, New York 1969) 33.

98 Alexander Meiklejohn, *'Free Speech and its Relationship to Self-Government'* (1st edn. Harper, New York 1948) 27.

99 Lee Bollinger, *'The Tolerant Society: Freedom of Speech and Extremist Speech in America'* (1st edn. Oxford University Press, Oxford 1986) 77–79. The principle of permitting expression, even if it 'shocks, offends or disturbs,' was incorporated by the ECtHR in the case of *Handyside v UK* (1976) discussed in Chapter 4. This idea is also incorporated and extended in the jurisprudence of the US Supreme Court which has permitted, *inter alia*, the burning of a cross in the front garden of an African American family, R.A.V. v City of Saint Paul (1992), radical speech by white supremacists (Klu Klux Klan) and Brandenburg v Ohio (1969).

100 Lee Bollinger, *'The Tolerant Society: Freedom of Speech and Extremist Speech in America'* (1st edn. Oxford University Press, Oxford 1986) 124.

101 John Stuart Mill, *'On Liberty'* in Mary Warnock (ed.), *'Utilitarianism and On Liberty: Including Mill's Essay on Bentham and Selections from the Writings of Jeremy Bentham and John Austin'* (2nd edn. Blackwell, Englewood Cliff New Jersey 2012) (original version: 1859) 96.

102 Ibid. 97.

expression as a separate right which may be restricted on the grounds provided for in part 3. These grounds cannot be used for purposes of restricting the freedom of opinion. However, interestingly and rather surprisingly, Article 10 of the ECHR provides for freedom of expression and incorporates the freedom of opinion as part of this right. As a result, on one level, this could appear to mean that the possibility for restriction also extends to the freedom of opinion, although no Strasbourg case-law has demonstrated this point and it would be rather bizarre for the Court's position to be that the freedom of opinion is qualified. This takes no account of the philosophical and legal principles discussed in this chapter that essentially legitimise restriction (if at all) insofar as the exercise of a particular right affects the rights of others and/or general issues such as public order.

Moving more specifically to the potential realms of hate speech, there are commentators who argue in favour of the non-prohibition of hate speech due to the inherent significance of freedom of expression. For example, Feinberg placed more emphasis on the individual level, arguing that 'no amount of offensiveness in an expressed opinion can counterbalance the vital social value of allowing unfettered personal expression.'[103] However, there are also arguments in favour of non-prohibition of hate speech which are put forth for reasons other than the sanctity of free speech. Dworkin's argument focussed on a permissibility of hate speech which he considered to be 'the price we pay for enforcing the laws that the haters and defamers oppose.'[104] Dworkin places his arguments in the more general framework of ensuring democracy. However, as noted by Heinze, he does not recognise the differences between democracies in, for example, post-colonial countries compared to their Anglo-Saxon counterpart.[105] Dworkin holds that the State must not forbid hate speech as this may 'spoil the only democratic justification we have for insisting that everyone obey laws.'[106] Thus, Dworkin adopts an interesting outlook on hate speech and the limitation of free speech, which does not emanate from the importance of free speech *per se*. Instead he argues against State arbitrariness and for the maintenance of the legitimacy of a political and legal process, which he believes would be undermined if a person or persons were prohibited from uttering an opinion before a decision is taken.[107] Dworkin contests that, although hate speech should be permitted for purposes of legitimising other anti-discrimination legislation and processes, as discussed earlier, arguments in the realm of limiting speech for purposes of preventing injury to others should not be permitted.[108] In other cases, where

103 Joel Feinberg, *'Offence to Others – The Moral Limits of the Criminal Law'* (1st edn. Oxford University Press, Oxford 1985) 39.

104 Jeremy Waldron, 'Dignity and Defamation: The Visibility of Hate' (2009) 123 *Harvard Law Review* 7, 1640.

105 Eric Heinze, *'Hate Speech and Democratic Citizenship'* (1st edn. Oxford University Press, Oxford 2016) 2.

106 Ronald Dworkin, Foreword in *'Extreme Speech and Democracy'* Ivan Hare & James Weinstein (eds.), (2nd edn. Oxford University Press, Oxford 2009) 8.

107 Ibid. 7.

108 Ronald Dworkin, *'Taking Rights Seriously'* (1st edn. Duckworth, London 1977) 274.

the aim of restriction is to satisfy the interests of policy, Dworkin notes that we should be 'with our thumbs on the free speech side of the scales'[109] demonstrating the high threshold that should be met for limiting free speech insofar as only injury to others can justify it. Further, Dworkin argues that, as a result of the importance of the general legitimacy of a State, even debates on controversial issues, such as racial intelligence, should be allowed. Waldron holds this position to be wrong, as it places too much emphasis on free speech and argues that this results in society 'bear[ing] the costs of what amounts to attacks on the dignity of minority groups.'[110] At this point, the central question is whether one should adopt Mill's aforementioned argument that even an immoral opinion should be permitted in the name of free speech, or whether such a controversial debate is to be considered to step into the grounds of harm. It is this question which lies at the heart of the debate on hate speech restriction.

Therefore, the libertarian model allows for rights to be restricted insofar as it is demonstrable that there is a serious and imminent risk of serious harm to others. Within this framework, freedom of expression has been repeatedly understood to hold a particularly significant position within the human rights framework. As such, to limit this right would entail a particularly high threshold of severity and imminence with theorists noting, for example, that mere offensiveness does not meet the threshold. It could be discerned that such a threshold could also be attached to the vehicles of expression, namely association and assembly. So, essentially, libertarians interpret free expression in a very strict manner and, as such, require a high severity of harm if expression is to be restricted. Some scholars have condemned this position with, for example, Fish, arguing that the dangers associated with such speech are far more serious and extensive than classical and contemporary libertarians believe.[111] Furthermore, hate speech finds support as free speech for other reasons apart from the particular importance of free expression. For example, Weinstein argues that the most suitable response to hate speech is not a ban but a lively counter-argument put forth by the State or citizens in order to enable society to realise the damage of such speech, urging the State to put time and resources into such activities. Thus, Weinstein adopts a libertarian approach as a strategy to fight speech rather than as a result of his particular emphasis on free speech.[112]

It must be noted that, as underlined by Heinze, opponents of hate speech bans come from different schools of thought and include communitarian writers who challenge such bans on the grounds that they manifest 'modernity's exaggerated

---

109　Frederick Schauer, *'Free Speech: A Philosophical Enquiry'* (1st edn. Cambridge University Press, Cambridge, 1982) 133.

110　Eric Barendt, 'Hate Speech': Lecture given at Hull (November 21 2013): www2.hull.ac.uk/fass/pdf/Eric%20Barendt-HATE%20SPEECH.pdf [Accessed 1 December 2015].

111　Mark Slagle, 'An Ethical Exploration of Free Expression and the Problem of Hate Speech' (2009) 24 *Journal of Mass Media Ethics* 4, 242.

112　Ibid. 246.

focus on individual legal entitlements'[113] and civic republican theorists who 'seek to limit the capacity of rights regimes to trump, hence to foreclose, collective deliberation.'[114] Either way, as noted by Schauer, 'free speech is a good card to hold,'[115] but 'it does not mean that free speech is the ace of trumps,'[116] the point of contention being at what point to accept that harm of particular speech may constitute sufficient grounds for limitation. Unfortunately, none of the international or European institutions have conducted sufficient theoretical, conceptual or contextual analysis of the harm in the speech in the cases before them, being quick to find restriction legitimate.

A theoretical approach to restricting hate speech legitimately: Critical Race Theory

Taking into account that at the heart of this book lies the concept of hate and discrimination against minority groups, Critical Race Theory will be assessed as a lens through which free speech can be restricted insofar as such speech constitutes hate speech. The points of departure set out in this theory, *vis-à-vis* hate speech, will be extended to the treatment of hateful association and assembly. Before proceeding with an analysis of Critical Race Theory, the Speech Act Theory will be briefly assessed for purposes of extrapolating on speech as an act.

Speech act theory

The Speech Act Theory sets out a structure for purposes of elucidating the meaning of expression and, subsequently, its hierarchy of effects. The Speech Act Theory was put forth by Austin in 'How to Do Things with Words' which essentially 'presented a new picture of analysing meaning.' The theory was further developed by Searle in 'Speech Acts.' At the core of Austin's writings, is the concept of meaning which is illustrated by reference to the concept of acts. Essentially, in speaking, the speaker 'with an associated intention performs a linguistic act to the hearer.'[117] The theory sets out three speaking-acts: a locutionary act as one of purely saying something; an illocutionary act as an act performing a function, such as a request; and a perlocutionary act which has an effect on the actions, thoughts or feelings of the receiver.[118] Austin presents a locutionary act as one with a certain meaning, illocutionary as one with a certain force and

---

113 Eric Heinze, *'Hate Speech and Democratic Citizenship'* (1st edn. Oxford University Press, Oxford 2016) 14.

114 Ibid.

115 Frederick Schauer, *'Free Speech: A Philosophical Enquiry'* (1st edn. Cambridge University Press, Cambridge 1982) 9.

116 Ibid.

117 Etsuko Oishi, 'Austin's Speech Act Theory and the Speech Situation' (2006) 1 *Esercizi Filosofici*, 1.

118 Uladzislau Belavusau, *'Freedom of Speech – Importing European and US Constitutional Models in Transitional Democracies'* (1st edn. Routledge, London 2013) 94.

perlocutionary as one which is to achieve a certain effect.[119] Thereby, the differentiation between the three is significant for the conceptualisation of the speech under consideration and its possible effects. However, as argued by Butler, a speech situation is 'not a simple sort of context, one that might be defined easily by spatial and temporal boundaries.'[120] As underlined by Belavusau, libertarian free speech supporters endorse the locutionary nature of a hateful form of expression,[121] thereby considering it purely as an act of saying something, with no ramifications, whereas others who do not adhere to a libertarian approach will 'articulate the intimidation and even subordination potential of such expression to amount to a performative act.'[122] It has been argued that 'because expression grows out of and helps form social relationships, expression might be seen as action. Thus, what actually is speech or conduct is a complicated question as a matter of epistemology.'[123] The recognition, by the Speech Act Theory of the capacity of speech to have an actual effect on its listener if the particular speech fell within the realm of a perlocutionary act 'stimulated criticism of the US Supreme Court's laissez-faire attitude towards hate speech'[124] by critical race theorists. Heinze notes that Critical Race Theorists describe hateful expression as 'a weapon delivering a blow as harsh as a physical assault,'[125] thereby, reflecting the actual consequences these theorists attach to expression which is hateful. As such, Critical Race Theory is discussed in the following.

Critical Race Theory

Critical Race Theory came about in the mid-1980s[126] after a realisation by scholars, activists and lawyers that 'new theories and strategies were needed to combat the subtler forms of racism that were gaining ground.'[127] Racist incidents on

---

119 Etsuko Oishi, 'Austin's Speech Act Theory and the Speech Situation' (2006) 1 *Esercizi Filosofici*, 1.

120 Judith Butler, *'Excitable Speech. A Politics of the Performative'* (1st edn. Routledge, London 1997) 4.

121 In his discussion Belavusau refers to the burning of the cross in the case of R.A.V. v City of St. Paul, 505 U.S. 377 (1992).

122 Uladzislau Belavusau, *'Freedom of Speech – Importing European and US Constitutional Models in Transitional Democracies'* (1st edn. Routledge, London 2013) 95.

123 Edward J. Eberle, 'Cross Burning, Hate Speech, and Free Speech in America' 36 *Arizona State Law Journal* 953, 964.

124 Uladzislau Belavusau, *'Freedom of Speech – Importing European and US Constitutional Models in Transitional Democracies'* (1st edn. Routledge, London 2013) 82.

125 Eric Heinze, *'Hate Speech and Democratic Citizenship'* (1st edn. Oxford University Press, Oxford 2016) 138.

126 However, it can be traced back to the black liberationist movement of the 1960s and the Critical Legal Studies movement of the 1970s and 1980s: Jeffrey Pyle, 'Race, Equality and the Rule of Law: Critical Race Theory's Attack on the Promises of Liberalism' (1999) 40 *Boston College Law Review* 3, 798.

127 Richard Delegado & Jean Stefanic *'Critical Race Theory: An Introduction'* (1st edn. New York University Press, New York 2006): www.odec.umd.edu/CD/RACE/CRT.PD [Accessed 2 December 2015].

university campuses in the U.S. prompted the writings of Critical Race Theorists, such as Matsuda, Lawrence, Delegado and Stefancic 'who wrote the phrase hate speech into the legal lexicon.'[128] The theory considers a variety of issues looked at through, for example, the civil rights lens but instead

> places them in a broader perspective that includes economics, history, context, group and self-interest, and even feelings and the unconscious ... [and ... questions the very foundations of the liberal order, including equality theory, legal reasoning, enlightenment rationalism, and neutral principles of constitutional law.[129]

For these theorists, racism 'lies at the very heart of American and Western culture.'[130] The overarching aim of Critical Race Theory is to 'eliminat[e] racial oppression'[131] and achieve 'fundamental social transformation.'[132] It can be used to look at a variety of issues from law to education to political science and more.[133] In relation to hate speech, critical race theorists argue that the libertarian model adopted for free speech and, thus, for hate speech did 'not acknowledge the imbalance of power that exists within American society.'[134] According to this theory, there is an inequality of arms as a result of an inherent prejudice held and manifested against the groups and, as such, these groups which live on the margins of society cannot possibly be deemed to be able to participate equally in a dialogue with haters. As noted, 'in a rigged game ... the argument that good speech ultimately drives out bad speech rests on a false premise unless those of us who fight racism are vigilant and unequivocal in that fight,' therefore demonstrating that the groups themselves who are targets of such speech cannot participate without the assistance of others who may work in the field of anti-racism but are not marginalised themselves. According to Matsuda, hate speech is defined as such if the message incorporates the idea of racial inferiority, is directed to a traditionally marginalised group and is hateful, degrading and

---

128 Eric Heinze, *'Hate Speech and Democratic Citizenship'* (1st edn. Oxford University Press, Oxford 2016) 15.

129 Richard Delegado & Jean Stefanic *'Critical Race Theory: An Introduction'* (1st edn. New York University Press, New York 2006): www.odec.umd.edu/CD/RACE/CRT.PD [Accessed 2 December 2015].

130 Angela Harris, 'Foreword, The Jurisprudence of Reconstruction' (1994) 82 *California Law Review* 4, 749.

131 Mari J. Matsuda, Charles R. Lawrence III, Richard Delegado & Kimberle Williams Crenshaw, *'Words that Wound: Critical Race Theory, Assaultive Speech, and the First Amendment* (New Perspectives on Law, Culture, and Society)' (1st edn. Westview Press, Boulder CO 1993) 6–7.

132 Ibid.

133 Richard Delegado & Jean Stefanic *'Critical Race Theory: An Introduction'* (1st edn. New York University Press, New York 2006): www.odec.umd.edu/CD/RACE/CRT.PD [Accessed 2 December 2015].

134 Mark Slagle, 'An Ethical Exploration of Free Expression and the Problem of Hate Speech' (2009) 24 *Journal of Mass Media Ethics* 4, 239.

menacing.[135] In this way, Matsuda attempts to encapsulate only speech which is truly hateful and menacing and to leave out generally controversial speech.[136] Given the emphasis placed on the unequal position that certain groups find themselves in due to the prejudice and marginalisation which they have historically experienced, Matsuda argues that, in the event that hate speech is directed towards society's dominant group, the libertarian model of free speech should be applied.[137] On one hand, this position could be justified by the fact that the majority group is not hampered by inequalities, prejudices and discrimination and there is no issue of inequality of arms and, as such, they can reasonably partake in an effective response with the hate speech in question not causing damage to this group's societal position which, either way, is diachronically in power. On the other, it could be hard to accept, given embedded principles of law such as the general non-discriminatory application of the law. Moreover, such a position could cause concerns as to 'where such precedents might lead.'[138] Lawrence finds that racism lies in the framework of both expression and conduct, arguing that racist speech uttered by white supremacists restrains the freedom of their targets.[139] Lawrence holds that the position of free speech absolutists is ignorant to the experiences of victims of hate speech since they 'fail to comprehend both the nature and extent of the injury inflicted by racist speech.'[140] Conceptualising on the libertarian position of the free marketplace of ideas, Lawrence argues that racist speech could be considered a failure of this market since the functional operation of the market is debilitated by racial power structures which place certain groups in inferior positions, thereby, prohibiting the proper functioning of such a market.[141]

The theory is, as might be expected, not without criticism with one of the arguments put forth against it being its 'single mindedly critical character,'[142] discussing, analysing and blaming without offering any solution to the issues it raises. As noted by Tushnet, in relation to Critical Race Theory 'critique is all there is.'[143] Other critics of the theory and the way in which this school perceives the effects of hate speech include Butler who has pointed out that

---

135 Mari J. Matsuda, Charles R. Lawrence III, Richard Delgado & Kimberle Williams Crenshaw, *'Words that Wound: Critical Race Theory, Assaultive Speech, and the First Amendment* (New Perspectives on Law, Culture, and Society)' (1st edn. Westview Press, Boulder CO 1993) 36.
136 Ibid. 36.
137 Ibid. 38.
138 Jeffrey Pyle, 'Race, Equality and the Rule of Law: Critical Race Theory's Attack on the Promises of Liberalism' (1999) 40 *Boston College Law Review* 3, 805.
139 Charles R. Lawrence III, 'If He Hollers Let Him Go: Regulating Racist Speech on Campus' (1990) 39 *Duke Law Journal* 3, 427.
140 Ibid. 457.
141 Ibid. 468.
142 Jeffrey Pyle, 'Race, Equality and the Rule of Law: Critical Race Theory's Attack on the Promises of Liberalism' (1999) 40 *Boston College Law Review* 3, 816.
143 Mark Tushnet, *'Red, White and Blue: A Critical Analysis of Constitutional Law'* (1st edn. University Press of Kansas, Lawrence KS 2015) 318.

the interrelationship between hate speech and the alleged resulting harm does not always exist.[144] Further, Heinze has argued that Critical Race Theorists adopt 'wholly abstract, decontextualised and formalist readings of international norms'[145] resulting, amongst others, in non-engagement of the theory with international human rights law.[146] Although this theory is based on American realities and issues, Möschel notes that some of the main challenges considered within the framework of Critical Race Theory are relevant and significant to Europe, but, to date, this theory has 'received scant attention in European legal scholarship.'[147] Möschel places his analysis within the framework of Continental Europe and explains the lack of Critical Race Theory therein, due to the lack of a conceptualisation of race. More particularly, he holds that the 'fear is that by referring to race one might be implicitly and normatively recognising the existence of different human races from the scientific viewpoint.'[148] This fear stands in the way of extrapolating on the theory under discussion due to the necessity to conceptualise on race. In the U.K., there has been some, albeit very limited reference, to this theory.[149] Furthermore, although Critical Race Theory tackles the phenomenon of race and racism, an equivalent parallel to tackle the theme of homophobia, biphobia and transphobia and their respective manifestations in the form of speech, associations and assemblies can be drawn. Although it is beyond the scope of this book to extrapolate further on this, these phenomena are marked by institutional, historical and other foundational elements which, in their entirety, constitute a lens through which homophobic, biphobic and transphobic speech can be assessed.

So, theorists in this arena are sensible to the societal reality of prejudices and inequalities and, as a result, underline that hate speech cannot contribute to the market place of ideas since an equal dialogue cannot come about from such speech. Critical Race Theory essentially holds that institutional racism and prejudices that are traditionally affiliated to particular groups distort any discussion on free speech when it comes to hateful speech. However, they appear to alienate themselves from placing analyses within the framework of international human rights law which is centrifugal to the content of their discussions whilst other criticisms include the inability of this theory to provide solutions to the problems it identifies. Importantly, despite the significant socio-political conceptualisation of the inequalities that underlie hate speech and the argument that hate speech leads to the further silencing of marginalised groups, whether this reality

---

144 Judith Butler, *'Excitable Speech. A Politics of the Performative'* (1st edn. Routledge, London 1997) 16.

145 Eric Heinze 'Truth, Myth and Critical Theory' in Reza Banakar *'Rights in Context: Law and Justice in Late Modern Society'* (1st edn. Routledge, London 2010) 98.

146 Ibid.

147 Mattias Möschel, 'Race in Mainland European Legal Analysis: Towards a European Critical Race Theory' (2011) 34 *Ethnic and Racial Studies* 10, 1649.

148 Ibid. 1651.

149 See: Mike Cole, 'Critical Race Theory comes to the UK' (2009) 9 *Ethnicities* 2.

is sufficient to result in the ban of fundamental rights, such as expression, is far from clear. Unfortunately, no normative analysis of the legitimacy of correlating hate speech restrictions with the need to tackle institutional prejudice in the framework of international human rights law exists.

Effects-based approach to hate speech restriction

As well as looking at the legitimacy of restricting hate speech in the sphere of Critical Race Theory, one can also consider this issue by considering the effects of hate speech as grounds upon which such regulation is justifiable. When looking at the effects of hate speech, it is important first to underline which particular groups may be affected by such speech. In this realm, Scanlon looks at the extent to which a particular expression affects the rights and interests of those affected by it. Scanlon argues that, in order for a State legitimately to regulate speech, it must determine whether and, if so, the extent to which the rights and interests of the groups of persons affected by the speech are violated. These groups include the participant, the audience, the bystander and the citizens who are damaged by the speech in question.[150] The position put forth by Scanlon is interesting as it recognises a variety of groups that may be affected by the speech with this broad understanding being significant in the realm of hate speech which affects not only the victim but also other listeners who may be persuaded by its content and society, more generally, whose equilibrium may be impacted by the speech.

Now, as to the actual effects of speech, Feinberg argues that speech which is to be prohibited must cause profound offence rather than mere nuisance and differentiates between the two in five ways. Profound offences have a particularly ominous tone, are unacceptable even to those who do not witness them, are unacceptable even if they take place in private,[151] are evident even if one attempts to disregard them and are morally unacceptable.[152] This commentator holds that racial insults result in profound outrage on the part of the victim because uttering such insults is morally wrong and because he or she is threatened by this behaviour.[153] It must be noted, however, that an understanding of the effects of hate speech, which encapsulates a wider range of victims and not just the targeted person or group but also others, as set out by Scanlon, is more pragmatic. Brink argues that hate speech 'evokes visceral, rather than articulate responses, it provokes violence or, more commonly silences through insult or intimidation.'[154] Lawrence extrapolates on the reaction hate speech often causes

150 Thomas Scanlon, '*The Difficulty of Tolerance*' (1st edn. Cambridge University Press, Cambridge 2003) 86, 99, 151, 92, 155.
151 Joel Feinberg, '*Offence to Others – The Moral Limits of the Criminal Law*' (1st edn. Oxford University Press, Oxford 1985) 58.
152 Ibid. 59.
153 Ibid.
154 David O. Brink, 'Millian Principles, Freedom of Expression and Hate Speech' (2001) 7 *Legal Theory* 2, 139.

by holding that it is an attack that 'produces an instinctive, defensive psychological reaction. Fear, rage, shock and flight all interfere with any reasoned response.' Many victims do not find words of response 'until well after the assault, when the cowardly assaulter has departed.'[155] These are very significant observations when taking into account arguments of classical theorists, such as Mill, who speak of the importance of dialogue and expression for a functional society. Brink and Lawrence's points succinctly denote one of the reasons why this argument is not applicable to hate speech given that the affront it causes to the 'other side' cannot possibly allow its representatives to engage in a reasoned discussion that will produce reasoned results. Further, hate speech 'may reinforce prejudices and feelings of inferiority in a seriously harmful way.'[156] Barendt took this one step further, adopting an interesting outlook on the effects that restrictions of hate speech have on free speech by arguing that hate speech 'silences the voice of members of the targeted group'[157] and, as a result, allowing for such expression essentially restricts certain groups from exercising this right.[158] His argument was inspired by a point made by West who held that, in the event that permitting persons to promote hate results in other speech (counter-speech) being disregarded, then this curtails rather than enhances free speech.[159] Such arguments conceptualise the freedom of expression within societal realities, comprehending the effects that hate speech has on the further marginalisation of its victims who essentially cannot respond in a free marketplace of ideas. In relation to the marketplace argument, scholars, such as Smolla, have argued that hate speech offers no value to the positive development of a society and its dialogue does not fall within the marketplace framework.[160] As such, that author argued that this type of speech 'states no fact, offers no opinion, proposes no transaction, attempts no persuasion.'[161] Brink holds that 'hate speech can poison the well of mutual respect and discourage participation in the deliberative community.'[162] Therefore, such an interpretation of the impact of hate speech eliminates the marketplace as a precursor for its permission. Further, Waldron puts forth his argumentation based on the premise of human dignity and respect. The former will be extrapolated on briefly before looking at Waldron's position. Dignity has been described as 'the very founding rock of fundamental rights in post-World War II constitutionalism.' Dignity is a central concept of international

155 Charles Lawrence, 'If He Hollers Let Him Go: Regulating Racist Speech on Campus' (1990) 39 *Duke Law Journal* 3, 452–453.
156 Eric Barendt, 'Hate Speech: Lecture given at Hull' (November 21 2013): www2.hull.ac.uk/fass/pdf/Eric%20Barendt-HATE%20SPEECH.pdf [Accessed 1 December 2015].
157 Ibid.
158 Ibid.
159 Ibid.
160 Rodney A. Smolla, '*Free Speech in an Open Society*' (1st edn. Alfred A. Knopf, New York 1993) 166–167.
161 Ibid.
162 David O. Brink, 'Millian Principles, Freedom of Expression and Hate Speech' (2001) 7 *Legal Theory* 2, 140.

human rights law, with international conventions such as the United Nations Charter and the EU Charter of Fundamental Rights referring to dignity.[163] In commenting on the case of *K.A. and A.D v Belgium*, which looked at sadomasochism, Fabre-Magnan argues that

> the emergence of the human dignity principle is the sign that there is something superior (transcendent) to individual wills ... No one can renounce the human dignity principle, obviously not for others but no more so for oneself...[164]

The interrelationship between the ancient principle and *dignitas* has been considered by scholars through various lenses. *Dignitas* includes 'worth, worthiness, dignity, rank, position, political office.'[165] Whitman argues that the origins of dignity are indeed to be found in the ancient norms of honour which were gradually developed into the principle of human dignity as we understand it today.[166] However, Feldman and Waldron[167] steer away from associating the concept of human dignity, as we know it, with that of the Roman principle of *dignitas* due to the contrasts between the two. Dignity, as we know it today, is applicable to all and is non-retractable whereas *dignitas* had to be awarded and could be taken away.

Waldron argues that hate speech targets the 'social sense of assurance on which members of vulnerable minorities rely'[168] and guarantees that all citizens adhere to principles of human dignity and respect. As such, he underlined that hate speech should be prohibited in that it is so damaging, not only on an individual level but also on a group level, that such speech can almost affect social harmony.[169] Other commentators, such as Tsesis, consider hate speech to promote destructive messages with a menacing effect on society on a group

---

163 Stephanie Hennette-Vauchez, 'A Human Dignitas? Remnants of the Ancient Legal Concept in Contemporary Dignity Jurisprudence' (2011) 9 *International Journal of Constitutional Law* 1, 34.

164 Muriel Fabre-Magnan, *'Le Saidsme N'est Pas un Droit de L'homme'* (2005) *Receuil Dalloz*, 2978–2980.

165 *'Collins Latin Dictionary and Grammar'* (Harper Collins, New York 1997) 66.

166 James Q. Whitman, 'On Nazi Honor and New European Dignity' in Christian Joerges & Navraj Singh Ghaleigh (eds.), *'Darker Legacies of Law in Europe: The Shadow of National Socialism and Fascism over Europe and its Legal Traditions'* (1st edn. Hart, Oxford 2003) 245–246.

167 In referring to dignitas, David Feldman held that it 'is not human dignity of the sort which could conceivably be treated, in a sane world, as a fundamental value or as capable of generating a fundamental constitutional right.' This statement was made in 'Human Dignity as a Legal Value – Part I' (1999) Public Law 682. On the same issue, Jeremy Waldron held that it 'may seem an unpromising idea for human rights discourse, for such disclosure is characteristically egalitarian' in Jeremy Waldron (ed.), 'Dignity and Rank: In Memory of Gregory Vlastos' (2007) 48 *Archives Européennes de Sociologie* 2.

168 Jeremy Waldron, *'The Harm in Hate Speech'* (1st edn. Harvard University Press, Cambridge MA 2014) 88.

169 Ibid. 166–167.

level and not merely on an individual one, linking it to the rise of dangerous movements. Moreover, he dismissed theories of free speech in the face of the violent realities that traditionally marginalised groups have experienced as a result of the systematic development of hate speech which subsequently become part of accepted dialogue, pinpointing examples such as slavery to illustrate this point.[170] Sunstein not only recognises the harm in hate speech but also incorporates a safety net by underlining that hate speech should be regulated if it can be demonstrated that the prohibitions are targeting harms rather than ideas.[171] The long-term effects of hate speech and the direct correlation within the continuing marginalisation of certain groups are noted by Greenwalt, who holds that 'epithets and more elaborate slurs that reflect stereotypes about race, ethnic group, religion, sexual preference and gender may cause continuing hostility and psychological damage.'[172]

Further, the issue of stereotypes could also be introduced within the framework of hate speech bans. Stereotypes can be described as 'social ideas and preconceptions that exist about a particular group. Stereotypes create in and out groups: us versus them.'[173] Timmer underlines the harmful effects of such stereotypes to include, amongst others, psychological distress and underachievement.[174] An anti-stereotyping approach for the ECtHR has been recommended and set out by Timmer, placing a particular focus on gender discrimination. Such an approach can be translated and placed within the sphere of hate speech bans. More particularly, hate speech could be deemed to contribute to the creation of stereotypes against particular groups and facilitate the construction of the 'other' which lies at the heart of the discrimination, hatred and violence emanating from the context under consideration. In fact, in *Vejdeland v Sweden*,[175] in which the ECtHR looked at homophobic speech, the concurring opinions of Judges Speilmann and Nussberger referred to a Committee of Ministers Resolution against Croatia which looked at, amongst others, statements of the sort found in the Swedish case. The Resolution held that 'these statements stigmatise homosexuals and are based upon negative, distorted, reprehensible and degrading stereotypes about the sexual behaviour of all homosexuals.' There has, thereby, been an incorporation of the issue of stereotypes within the ECtHR sphere and in relation to hate speech. This particular sphere, that of an anti-stereotyping approach, has not been developed *per se* in relation to hate speech bans but could be grounds upon which analysis can be made, always taking into account the detrimental

---

170 Alexander Tsesis, *'Destructive Messages: How Hate Speech Paves the Way for Harmful Social Movements'* (1st edn. New York University Press, New York 2002) 136.

171 Cass Sunstein, *'Democracy and the Problem of Free Speech'* (1st edn. The Free Press, New York 1993) 193.

172 Kent Greenwalt *'Fighting Words Individuals, Communities and Liberties of Speech'* (1st edn. Princeton University Press, Princeton NJ 1995) 59.

173 Alexandra Timmer, 'Toward an Anti-Stereotyping Approach for the European Court of Human Rights' (2011) 11 *Human Rights Law Review* 4, 715.

174 Ibid. 716.

175 Vejdeland v Sweden, Application no. 1813/07 (ECHR 9 February 2012).

effects of stereotyping on the victims as well as on society, more generally, given the divisions and classifications this approach results in.

In sum, as per Scanlon, there are a variety of groups who are affected by hate speech, not only the targeted victim. The very nature of hate speech distorts the possibility of producing and promoting a healthy and equal dialogue for the members of a society. This, in itself, removes hate speech from the marketplace of ideas as it offers nothing of value but, instead, comes with dire effects such as harm to dignity, the production and promotion of stereotypes and the general destruction of personal and group rights. To extend this argument further, this reality results in hate speech leading to the violation of free expression as it silences particularly vulnerable and targeted groups. Moreover, the great harm which commentators, such as Tsesis and Sunstein, link to hate speech and the effects it has, not only on an individual level but also on a societal one, makes regulation imperative for them. However, the questions that remain include who is to decide what constitutes hate speech and, thus, where to draw the line between allowing free expression, on the one hand, and preventing the harms of hate speech on the other.

Chapter conclusion

Several of the thinkers discussed earlier provide for the possibility of rights being curtailed in the name of preventing harm to others. It is the crossroad of harm and rights and the severity and threshold of such harm which constitutes the dichotomy that lies between libertarians and others. In this realm, scholarly disagreement does not lie in whether a particular right should be restricted in order to avoid harm to others but, rather, in deciphering whether something actually amounts to sufficient harm to justify such restriction. This issue becomes even more complicated in the realm of free speech as this is a right which many scholars consider to be of particular importance. The significant place held by expression has meant that libertarians and others are wary of finding that particular speech does, in fact, constitute harm. One could hold that this significance is extended to its vehicles, namely association and assembly, which are also subjects of consideration in this book. Some of the aforementioned thinkers are absolutists when it comes to restricting democratic rights, in particular when this restriction is occurring for the sake of democracy itself given the alleged oxymoronic nature of this exercise. Commentators who are against prohibiting hate speech have put forth arguments in the realm of the importance of free expression but also for other reasons, such as Dworkin's point, for purposes of general legitimacy or that to regard a system as legitimate necessarily entails that hate speech is permitted. Those who wish to regulate it have come up with a variety of arguments, such as the damage caused by hate speech on an individual and societal level and the inability of hate speech to contribute to a marketplace of ideas. Critical race theorists regard the issue not through a balancing exercise but, rather, through a radical reconceptualisation of society's power structures, arguing that, in fact, hate speech further silences the marginalised, ousting them completely from the marketplace of ideas (and equal opportunities). The theory of militant democracy is another framework through which rights and freedoms can legitimately be restricted for purposes of protecting democracy itself. The aim of this book is not to conduct an in-depth philosophical analysis of the theories at play but, rather, to consider the tools available in international and European law to tackle the far-right. The theoretical framework sets the scene for the subsequent institutional evaluation with, as will be demonstrated, the UN, the CoE and the EU all embracing restriction necessity in the name of protecting the rights and freedoms of others, with the CoE flirting slightly yet obscurely with the doctrine of militant democracy. On the other hand, the U.S., discussed in the final chapter, has steered well away from a militant democratic approach to speech and has embraced a libertarian approach to this freedom as is reflected in the First Amendment to its Constitution.

Bibliography

Case-law

Abraham v United States, 250 U.S. 616 (1919).
BB Turkish Union in *Berlin Brandenburg* v Germany, CERD/C/82/D/48/2010.
Vejdeland v Sweden, App. no. 1813/07 (ECHR 9 February 2012) para. 46.
Young James and Webster v The United Kingdom, App. nos. 7601/76; 7806/77 (ECHR 18 October 1982).

International and European documents

Venice Commission, "Opinion on the Compatibility with Human Rights Standards of the Legislation on Non-governmental Organisations of the Republic of Azerbaijan" (14–15 October 2011) CDL-AD(2011)035.

Books

Belavusau U, *'Freedom of Speech: Importing European and US Constitutional Models in Transitional Democracies'* (1st edn. Routledge, London 2013).
Bollinger L, *'The Tolerant Society: Freedom of Speech and Extremist Speech in America'* (1st edn. Oxford University Press, Oxford 1986).
Butler J, *'Excitable Speech. A Politics of the Performative'* (1st edn. Routledge, London 1997).
Chafee Z, *'Free Speech in the United States'* (2nd edn. Atheneum, New York 1969).
Delegado R & Stefanic J, *'Critical Race Theory: An Introduction'* (1st edn. New York University Press, New York 2006).
Dworkin R, *'Taking Rights Seriously'* (1st edn. Duckworth, London 1977).
Feinberg J, *'The Moral Limits of the Criminal Law: Harm to Others'* (1st edn. Oxford University Press, Oxford 1984).
Finn J.E, *Constitutions in Crisis: Political Violence and the Rule of Law* (1st edn. Oxford University Press, Oxford 1991).
Fish S, *'There's No Such Thing as Free Speech (And It's a Good Thing Too)* (1st edn. Oxford University Press, Oxford 1994) 103.

Greenawalt K, *Fighting Words Individuals, Communities and Liberties of Speech* (1st edn. Princeton University Press, Princeton NJ 1995).

Greenawalt K, *'Speech, Crime and the Uses of Language'* (1st edn. Oxford University Press, New York 1989).

Heinze E, *'Hate Speech and Democratic Citizenship'* (1st edn. Oxford University Press, Oxford 2016).

Hobbes T, *'Leviathan'* (Introduction by Minogue K) (Dent, Darlington 1976) (original version: 1651).

Locke J, *'An Essay Concerning Human Understanding'* (edited by Nidditch H.P) (1979 Clarendon Oxford) (original version: 1689).

Locke J, *'Two Treaties of Government'* (edited by Laslett P) (Cambridge University Press, Cambridge 1988) (original version: 1689).

Matsuda M.J, Lawrence C.R III, Delegado R & Williams Crenshaw K, *'Words that Wound: Critical Race Theory, Assaultive Speech, and the First Amendment'* (New Perspectives on Law, Culture, and Society) (1st edn. Westview Press, Boulder CO 1993).

Meiklejohn M, *'Free Speech and its Relationship to Self-Government'* (1st edn. Harper, New York 1948).

Πλάτων, *'Πολιτεία'* (Plato, *'The Republic'*) (Introduction and translation: Skouteropulos N.M) (1st edn. Πόλις, Athens 2014) (original version: 381 BC).

Πλάτων, *'Επιστολαί'* (Plato, *'Epistles'*) (1st edn. Κάκτος, Athens 1993).

Popper K, *'The Open Society and Its Enemies'* (1st edn. published in two volumes: Routledge, London 1995).

Posner R.A, *'Not a Suicide Pact: The Constitution in a Time of National Emergency'* (1st edn. Oxford University Press, Oxford 2006).

Rosenblum N *'On the Side of the Angels: An Appreciation of Parties and Partisanship'* (1st edn. Princeton University Press, Princeton NJ 2008).

Scanlon T, *'The Difficulty of Tolerance'* (1st edn. Cambridge University Press, Cambridge 2003).

Schauer F, *'Free Speech: A Philosophical Enquiry'* (1st edn. Cambridge University Press, Cambridge, 1982).

Smolla R.A, *'Free Speech in an Open Society'* (1st edn. Alfred A. Knopf, New York 1993).

Sunstein C, *'Democracy and the Problem of Free Speech'* (1st edn. The Free Press, New York 1993).

Trenchard J & Gordon T, *'Cato's letters'* (edited by Hamowy R) (Liberty Fund, Carmel 1995) (original version: 1755).

Tsesis A, *'Destructive Messages: How Hate Speech Paves the Way for Harmful Social Movements'* (1st edn. New York University Press, New York 2002).

Tushnet M, *'Red, White and Blue: A Critical Analysis of Constitutional Law'* (1st edn. University Press of Kansas, Lawrence KS 2015).

Waldron J, *'The Harm in Hate Speech'* (1st edn. Harvard University Press, Cambridge MA 2014).

Book chapters

Cliteur P & Rijpkema B, 'The Foundations of Militant Democracy' in Ellian A & Molier G (eds.), *'The State of Exception and Militant Democracy in a Time of Terror'* (1st edn. Republic of Letters Publishing, Dordrecht 2012), 227–272.

Dworkin R, Foreword in *'Extreme Speech and Democracy'* Ivan Hare & James Weinstein (eds.) (2nd edn. Oxford University Press, Oxford 2009).

Heinze E, 'Truth, Myth and Critical Theory' in Reza Banakar (ed.), *Rights in Context: Law and Justice in Late Modern Society* (1st edn. Routledge, London 2010), 97–126.

Milton J, *'Aeropagitica'* in Rufus Wilmot Griswold (ed.), *The Prose Works of John Milton* (1st edn. John W. Moore, Philadelphia, PA 1847) (original version: 1644), 166–193.

Mills J.S, 'On Liberty' in Mary Warnock (ed.), *Utilitarianism and On Liberty: Including Mill's Essay on Bentham and Selections from the Writings of Jeremy Bentham and John Austin* (2nd edn. Blackwell, Englewood Cliff NJ 2012) (original version: 1859), 88–180.

Pfersmann O, 'Shaping Militant Democracy: Legal Limits to Democratic Stability' in Andras Sajo (ed.), *Militant Democracy* (1st edn. Eleven International Publishing, Utrecht 2004), 47–68.

Sajó A, 'Militant Democracy and Transition towards Democracy' in Andras Sajo (ed.), *Militant Democracy* (1st edn. Eleven International Publishing, Utrecht 2004), 209–230.

Whitman Q.J, 'On Nazi Honor and New European Dignity' in Christian Joerges & Navraj Singh Ghaleigh (eds.), *Darker Legacies of Law in Europe: The Shadow of National Socialism and Fascism over Europe and Its Legal Traditions* (1st edn. Hart, Oxford 2003), 243–266.

Journal articles

Brink D.O, 'Millian Principles, Freedom of Expression and Hate Speech' (2001) 7 *Legal Theory* 2.

Cole M, 'Critical Race Theory comes to the UK' (2009) 9 *Ethnicities* 2, 119–157.

Eberle E.J, 'Cross Burning, Hate Speech, and Free Speech in America' (2004) 36 *Arizona State Law Journal* 953, 953–964.

Fabre-Magnan M, *'Le Saidsme N'est Pas un Droit de L'homme'* (2005) 43 *Receuil Dalloz*, 2973–2981.

Goldmann M & Sonnen M, 'Soft Authority against Hard Cases of Racially Discriminating Speech: Why the CERD Committee Needs a Margin of Appreciation Doctrine' (2016) 7 *Goettingen Journal of International Law* 1, 131–155.

Harris A, 'Foreword, the Jurisprudence of Reconstruction' (1994) 82 *California Law Review* 4, 973–976.

Harvey P, 'Militant Democracy and the European Convention on Human Rights' (2004) 29 *European Law Review* 3, 488–516.

Hennette-Vauchez S, 'A Human Dignitas? Remnants of the Ancient Legal Concept in Contemporary Dignity Jurisprudence' (2011) 9 *International Journal of Constitutional Law* 1, 32–57.

Invernizzi Accetti C & Zuckerman I, 'What's Wrong with Militant Democracy?' (2017) 65 *Political Studies* IS, 867–882.

Jeffrey Pyle, 'Race, Equality and the Rule of Law: Critical Race Theory's Attack on the Promises of Liberalism' (1999) 40 *Boston College Law Review* 3, 787–827.

Kahn A.R, 'Why do Europeans Ban Hate Speech? A Debate between Karl Loewenstein and Robert Post' (2013) 41 *Hofstra Law Review* 3, 545–585.

Loewenstein K, 'Militant Democracy and Fundamental Rights I' (1937) 31 *The American Political Science Review* 3, 417–432.

Macklem P, 'Militant Democracy, Legal Pluralism, and the Paradox of Self-determination' 4 *International Journal of Constitutional Law* 3, 488–516.

Minkenberg M, 'Repression and Reaction: Militant Democracy and the Radical Right in Germany and France' (2006) 40 *Patterns of Prejudice* 25, 25–44.

Möschel M, 'Race in Mainland European Legal Analysis: Towards a European Critical Race Theory' (2011) 34 *Ethnic and Racial Studies* 10, 1648–1664.

Oishi E, 'Austin's Speech Act Theory and the Speech Situation' (2006) 1 *Esercizi Filosofici*, 1–14.

Post R.C, 'Racist Speech, Democracy and the First Amendment' (1990–1991) 32 *William and Mary Law Review* 2, 267–328.

Pyle J, 'Race, Equality and the Rule of Law: Critical Race Theory's Attack on the Promises of Liberalism' (1999) 40 *Boston College Law Review* 3, 787–827.

Sajó A, 'From Militant Democracy to the Preventive State' (2006) 22 *Cardozo Law Review* 5.

Sajó A 'Militant Democracy and Emotional Politics' (2012) 19 *Constellations* 4, 2255–2294.

Slagle M, 'An Ethical Exploration of Free Expression and the Problem of Hate Speech' 24 *Journal of Mass Media Ethics* 4, 238–250.

Timmer A, 'Toward an Anti-Stereotyping Approach for the European Court of Human Rights' 11 *Human Rights Law Review* 4, 707–738.

Tyulkina S, 'Militant Democracy: An Alien Concept to Australian Constitutional Law?' (2015) 36 *Adelaide Law Review* 2, 517–539.

Waldron J, 'Dignity and Defamation: The Visibility of Hate' (2009) 123 *Harvard Law Review* 7, 1596–1657.

Other

Barendt E, 'Hate Speech': Lecture given at Hull (November 21 2013): www2.hull.ac.uk/fass/pdf/Eric%20Barendt-HATE%20SPEECH.pdf.

Collins Latin Dictionary and Grammar (Harper Collins New York 1997).

3 The United Nations

The principle of non-discrimination in UN instruments

The principle of non-discrimination, as developed by contemporary human rights law, can be traced back to the Charter of the United Nations which holds that the purposes of the UN are, amongst others, to 'achieve international co-operation ... in promoting and encouraging respect for human rights and for fundamental freedoms for all without distinction as to race, sex, language, or religion.'[1] Article 13(1), therein, underlines that the UN General Assembly will assist 'in the realization of human rights and fundamental freedoms for all without distinction as to race, sex, language or religion.'

Article 1 of the Universal Declaration of Human Rights (UDHR) states that

> all human beings are born free and equal in dignity and rights.' Paragraph 2 of the UDHR provides that 'everyone is entitled to all the rights and freedoms set forth in this Declaration, without distinction of any kind, such as race, colour, sex, language, religion, political or other opinion, national or social origin, property, birth or other status.

Article 7 of the UDHR constitutes the first effort to incorporate incitement to discrimination within the framework of discrimination, a theme which, as will be demonstrated, has been extensively developed and incorporated in instruments such as the International Convention on the Elimination of All Forms of Racial Discrimination (ICERD) and the International Covenant on Civil and Political Rights (ICCPR). Article 7 of the UDHR provides that '...all are entitled to equal protection against any discrimination in violation of this Declaration and against any incitement to such discrimination.' Further, the Preambles of the ICCPR and the International Covenant on Economic, Social and Cultural Rights (ICESCR) confirm that the 'recognition of the inherent dignity and of the equal and inalienable rights of all members of the human family is the foundation of freedom, justice and peace in the world.' The general non-discrimination clauses of the ICCPR and the ICESCR, namely Article 2(2) in both documents, follow the

---

1 Article 1.3 Charter of the United Nations 1945.

same approach as Article 2 of the UDHR. The ICESCR has habitually been dis-regarded in the framework of the far-right, with more emphasis being placed on the ICCPR, the UDHR and the ICERD. However, in an interesting reference, the monitoring body of the ICESCR noted that Belgium 'should adopt measures to ensure that xenophobia, racism and activities of racist organizations, groups or political parties are outlawed, with a view to complying with the principle of non-discrimination, set forth in article 2.2.'[2] The ICCPR incorporates a more special-ised non-discrimination clause in the form of Article 26, therein, which states that

> all persons are equal before the law and are entitled without any discrim-ination to the equal protection of the law. In this respect, the law shall prohibit any discrimination and guarantee to all persons equal and effec-tive protection against discrimination on any ground such as race, colour, sex, language, religion, political or other opinion, national or social origin, property, birth or other status.

Both Article 2 and Article 26 of the ICCPR provide for the principle of non-discrimination but, as noted by the HRC in its General Comment 18, 'Article 26 of the ICCPR does not merely duplicate the guarantee already pro-vided for in Article 2 of the same document but provides in itself an autono-mous right.[3] Article 26 of the ICCPR imposes certain obligations on States Parties when creating and implementing legislation, underlining that it must be in line with Article 26 of the ICCPR while Article 2 of the same provides for non-discrimination in relation to the enjoyment of rights as contained in the Covenant. Further, Article 26 of the ICCPR 'is not limited to those rights which are provided for in the Covenant'[4] as it seeks to regulate legislation on all matters within and beyond the ICCPR's boundaries. For example, in *Broeks v Netherlands*, the HRC held that when 'legislation is adopted in the exercise of a state's sovereign power, then such legislation must comply with Article 26 of the Covenant.'[5] The significance of the principle of non-discrimination is also reflected in Article 4 of the ICCPR which deals with derogations in times of emergency. Paragraph 1, therein, holds that States may take certain meas-ures which derogate from their obligations under this Covenant provided that, amongst others, they 'do not involve discrimination solely on the ground of race, colour, sex, language, religion or social origin.' However, the Covenant does not go as far as to make Article 26 non-derogable. In any case, the principle of non-discrimination has been established as a central tenet of several international documents. General Comment 18 of the HRC underlines that

---

2 Committee on Economic, Social and Cultural Rights Concluding Observations: Belgium (2000) ICESCR E/2001/22 7, para. 482.
3 HRC General Comment 18: 'Non-Discrimination' (1994) HRI/GEN/1/Rev.1 at 26, para. 7.
4 Ibid. para. 12.
5 Broeks v Netherlands, Communication no. 172/1984 (9 April 1987) CCPR/C/OP/2, para. 12.4.

non discrimination, together with equality before the law and equal protection of the law without any discrimination, constitute a basic and general
principle relating to the protection of human rights.[6]

In fact, the principles of equality and non-discrimination 'are central to the
human rights movement.'[7] In relation to these terms, it has been noted that
equality and non-discrimination encompass the same theme and principle, but
in a positive and negative manner respectively,[8] and are, thus, sometimes used
interchangeably.

Notwithstanding the significance of the principle of non-discrimination, it is
not defined in any of the aforementioned documents. The only effort to provide
some kind of definition of non-discrimination is when it relates to a particular
type, such as racial discrimination, discussed later. In order to fill this definitional gap, the HRC, by drawing from the definitions in the ICERD and the
Convention on the Elimination of All Forms of Discrimination against Women
(CEDAW), underlined that discrimination, as incorporated in the ICCPR,

> should be understood to imply any distinction, exclusion, restriction or
> preference which is based on any ground such as race, colour, sex, language,
> religion, political or other opinion, national or social origin, property, birth
> or other status, and which has the purpose or effect of nullifying or im-
> pairing the recognition, enjoyment or exercise by all persons, on an equal
> footing, of all rights and freedoms.[9]

Further, through its case-law, the HRC has underlined that

> not all differentiations in treatment can be deemed to be discriminatory
> under Article 26. A differentiation which is compatible with the provisions
> of the Covenant and is based on objective and reasonable grounds does not
> amount to prohibited discrimination within the meaning of Article 26.[10]

Even though the HRC notes that States Parties have an obligation to take
the necessary measures to end discrimination both in the public and private
spheres,[11] there is no jurisprudence that relates to the aforementioned articles

---

6 HRC General Comment 18: 'Non-Discrimination' (1994) HRI/GEN/1/Rev.1, para. 12.

7 Jerome Shestack, 'The Jurisprudence of Human Rights,' in Theodor Meron (ed.), *'Human Rights in International Law: Legal and Policy Issues'* (1st edn. Clarendon, Oxford 1984) 101.

8 Ann F. Bayefsky, 'The Principle of Equality or Non-discrimination in International Law' (1990) 11 *Human Rights Quarterly* 1–2, 5.

9 HRC General Comment 18: 'Non-Discrimination' (1994) HRI/GEN/1/Rev.1 at 26, para. 12.

10 See, *inter alia*, Zwaan-de Vries v The Netherlands, Communication no. 182/1984, (9 April 1987) CCPR/C/OP/2, para. 13, Süsser v Czech Republic, Communication no. 1488/2006 (28 April 2008) CCPR/C/92/D/1488/2006, para. 7.2.

11 HRC General Comment 28: 'Article 3 – Equality of Rights Between Men and Women' (2000) CCPR/C/21/Rev.1/Add.10, para. 4.

from that Committee or from the Committee on Economic, Social and Cultural Rights in relation to the far-right. Instead, complaints by victims of far-right movements have been dealt with by the CERD in the realm of racial discrimination. Nevertheless, non-discrimination, as originally developed by the International Bill of Rights,[12] set the scene for the subsequent development of particular types of discrimination. Combatting the far-right can be deemed to be a central objective of the aforementioned instruments given that international human rights law, as construed in the aftermath of the Second World War, sought to tackle the phenomenon that once brought about the destruction of the international community, that being radical extremism. For example, the drafters of the UDHR 'made it abundantly clear that the Declaration on which they were about to vote had been born out of the experience of the war that had just ended.'[13] As noted by the Lebanese delegate to the drafting process, 'the document was inspired by the opposition to barbarous doctrines of Nazism and Fascism.'[14] These doctrines emanated from discriminatory beliefs and practices, and so the principle of non-discrimination, as formulated by the international community, was a key to ensuring the objectives of the drafters. This mechanism was subsequently tailor-made to cater to the duties and rights arising from particular types of discrimination, such as racial discrimination, which lie at the heart of the far-right.

Racial discrimination: definition

Legal documents have been more open in providing definitions for racial discrimination rather than racism. Article 1(1) of the ICERD states that racial discrimination means

> any distinction, exclusion, restriction or preference based on race, colour, descent or national or ethnic origin which has the purpose or effect of nullifying or impairing the recognition, enjoyment or exercise, on an equal footing, of human rights and fundamental freedoms in the political, economic, social, cultural or any other field of public life.

Although the word 'race' is used in the definition of Article 1(1), the international community has acknowledged that race 'is not a biological fact, but a social construction.'[15] In addition, the use of this term in Article 1(1) must be read in light of the ICERD's Preamble, which stipulates, amongst other things, that

---

12 UDHR, ICCPR and ICESCR.

13 Johannes Morsink, *The Universal Declaration of Human Rights, Origins, Drafting and Intent* (1st edn. University of Pennsylvania Press, Philadelphia PA 1999) 36.

14 Ibid.

15 German Institute for Human Rights, Written Contribution to the Thematic Discussion of the Committee on the Elimination of Racial Discrimination on Racist Hate Speech (28 August 2012) 2.

any doctrine of superiority based on racial differentiation is scientifically false, morally condemnable, socially unjust and dangerous, and that there is no justification for racial discrimination, in theory or in practice, anywhere.

Another document which provides a definition of racial discrimination is the ECRI's General Policy Recommendation No. 7 on National Legislation to Combat Racism and Racial Discrimination, which holds that direct racial discrimination is 'any differential treatment based on a ground such as race, colour, language, religion, nationality or national or ethnic origin, which has no objective and reasonable justification' thereby adding language and religion to the previous list. As well as including the two additional grounds, it extrapolates on the conditions for justifying such treatment which the Policy Recommendation holds must be objective and reasonable and must seek to pursue a legitimate aim and be proportional. The Policy Recommendation adds nuance to racial discrimination in a theoretical sense. However, on a practical level, it could be argued that terms, such as objective and reasonable, are open-ended and could have a plethora of interpretations which are unavailable in the case of the aforementioned document.

The definition of racial discrimination, as provided for by the ICERD, entails separate yet interrelated practices, namely any distinction, exclusion, restriction or preference which may result in hindering the enjoyment of human rights and fundamental freedoms within a variety of sectors of public life. As noted by General Recommendation 32 of the CERD:

> the reference to public life does not limit the scope of the non-discrimination principle to acts of the public administration but should be read in light of provisions in the Convention mandating measures by States parties to address racial discrimination by any persons, group or organization.[16]

Thus, States have the obligation to protect persons from discrimination promoted by far-right groups and their representatives which are political or other associations operating within or outside the public domain. As such, even though racism and racial discrimination are often used interchangeably, especially in everyday speech, the fact remains that, correctly or not, a silent distinction is recognised within legal documents. This has resulted in more definitions arising in relation to racial discrimination. Based on the premise that racism constitutes a belief system and racial discrimination refers to the surmounting practices and omissions, it has been argued that 'it is easier to give a definition of unlawful conduct than it is to give a definition of unlawful beliefs.'[17]

---

16 CERD General Recommendation 32: 'The Meaning and Scope of Special Measures in the International Convention on the Elimination of Racial Discrimination' (2009) CERD/C/GC/32, para. 9.

17 Erica Howard, 'Race and Racism – Why does European Law have Difficulties with Definitions?' (2008) 24 *International Journal of Comparative Labour Law and Industrial Relations* 1, 16.

Victims of racial discrimination

In order to comprehend fully the meaning of racial discrimination, as conceptualised in the ICERD, it is necessary to consider who may be a potential victim of the discrimination covered therein. In General Recommendation 35, the CERD refers to groups of people who may fall within the ambit of Article 1, namely 'indigenous people, descent based groups, and immigrants or non-citizens, including migrant domestic workers, refugees and asylum seekers, as well as speech directed against women members of these and other vulnerable groups.'[18] The far-right which marks Europe today attacks the majority of groups referred to in this explanation, with the term 'other vulnerable groups' holding the potential of incorporating other groups which could possibly be targeted, as long as such targeting falls within the scope of racial discrimination. The CERD has insisted that, in appraising discrimination, 'the specific characteristics of ethnic, cultural and religious groups be taken into consideration.'[19] However, it must be noted that, as the CERD made clear in *Kamal Quereshi v Denmark*, discrimination must be particularly directed to the victim or groups of victims, as outlined earlier, given that generalised targeting does not fall within the ambit of the ICERD.[20]

Intention to discriminate

In relation to intention, the CERD has noted that 'the mere act of dissemination is penalised, despite lack of intention to commit an offence and irrespective of the consequences of the dissemination.'[21] As such, by removing the necessity of an intention, the CERD envisages discrimination in a broad manner. A 2001 Joint Statement between the Special Rapporteur on the Freedom of Opinion and Expression and the OSCE (Organization of Security and Cooperation in Europe) and OAS (Organization of American States) Representatives on Racism and the Media took an opposite view to the CERD and noted that 'no one should be penalised for the dissemination of hate speech unless it has been shown that they did so with the intention of inciting discrimination, hostility or violence.'[22] In relation to the necessity of intention, Thornberry argues that the

---

18 CERD General Recommendation 35: 'Combatting Racist Hate Speech' (2013) CERD/C/GC/35, para. 6, HRC General Comment 34: 'Article 19: Freedoms of Opinion and Expression' (2011) CCPR/C/GC/34, para. 6.

19 CERD Concluding Observations: Lao People's Democratic Republic (2005) CERD/C/LAO/CO/15, para. 169.

20 Kamal Quereshi v Denmark, Communication no. 33/2003 (2005) CERD/C/66/D/33/2003, para. 2.13.

21 CERD Study: 'Positive Measures Designed to Eradicate all Incitement to, or Acts of, Racial Discrimination: Implementation of ICERD,' Article 4, New York, UN, 1986, para. 83. This study was prepared for the Second World Conference on Racism in 1983 as A/CONF.119/10.

22 International Mechanisms for Promoting Freedom of Expression, Joint Statement on Racism and the Media by the UN Special Rapporteur on Freedom of Opinion and Expression, the

CERD's stance entails a 'total absence of culpability elements beyond the act of dissemination' and that this approach 'would do violence to basic principles of criminal liability in many if not most jurisdictions.'[23] This renders the CERD's interpretation of intention rather problematic subsequently limiting the adoption of this stance by States Parties.

In sum, apart from any forms of positive discrimination, as long as the propaganda of the organisation in question results in racial discrimination, regardless of whether this is concealed in seemingly legitimate terms and regardless of any intention on the part of the perpetrator, actions, omissions or utterances falling within the definitional framework of Article 1 of the ICERD are forbidden. The ECRI places explicit emphasis on the culpability of measures which are indirectly discriminative, thereby, allowing for a broad range of offences. However, the issue of intention has been dealt with differently by other bodies of the UN and other institutions, more generally, with intent being required as a prerequisite for finding racial discrimination.

Religion as a ground for discrimination

Unlike the ECRI's aforementioned recommendation, the definitional framework, as provided for by Article 1 of the ICERD, does not refer to religion as a ground for discrimination. Likewise CERD's General Recommendation 35 does not explicitly refer to religious groups as potential victims of practices referred to in Article 1. In General Recommendation 35, the Committee reaffirmed what had once been stated by the Human Rights Committee (HRC): namely, that 'criticism of religious leaders or commentary on religious doctrine or tenets of faith should not be prohibited or punished.'[24] Nevertheless, the CERD has recognised the existence of 'manifestations of hatred against ethnoreligious groups'[25] thereby preserving the 'principle of intersectionality.'[26] This principle has been defined in the framework of gender discrimination as 'multiple ... discrimination ... compound discrimination, interlinking forms of discrimination, multiple burdens of double or triple discrimination.'[27] In the CERD's General Recommendation 32 on Special Measures, the Committee

---

OSCE Representative on Freedom of the Media and the OAS Special Rapporteur on Freedom of Expression, London, 27 February 2001, 2. www.osce.org/fom/40120 [Accessed on 7 May 2014].

23 Patrick Thornberry, 'Forms of Hate Speech and the Convention on the Elimination of all Forms of Racial Discrimination' (2010) 5 *Religion and Human Rights* 2, 101.

24 CERD General Recommendation 35: 'Combatting Racist Hate Speech' (2003) CERD/C/GC/35, para. 6, HRC General Comment 34: 'Freedoms of Opinion and Expression' (2011) CCPR/C/GC/34, para. 48.

25 CERD General Recommendation 35: 'Combatting Racist Hate Speech' (2003) CERD/C/GC/35, para. 6.

26 Ibid.

27 UN Expert Group Report: Gender and Racial Discrimination (2000): www.un.org/womenwatch/daw/csw/genrac/report.htm [Accessed 9 May 2014] 1.

underlined that the existing grounds of discrimination under the Convention, as referred to earlier, are

> extended in practice by the notion of intersectionality whereby the Committee addresses situations of double or multiple discrimination—such as discrimination on grounds of gender or religion—when discrimination on such a ground appears to exist in combination with a ground or grounds listed in Article 1 of the Convention.[28]

Three Special Rapporteurs have highlighted the significance of this principle in the sphere of religion, underlining the difference between racist rhetoric and religious defamation and holding that extending the affirmations of the Preamble of the ICERD to religion would be a tricky task.[29] They noted that

> freedom of religion or belief also covers the rights to search for meaning by comparing different religions or belief systems, to exchange personal views on questions of religion or belief, and to exercise public criticism in such matters. For this reason, the criteria for defining religious hatred may differ from those defining racial hatred. The difficult question of what precisely constitutes religious hatred, at any rate, cannot be answered by simply applying definitions found in the area of racial hatred.[30]

Intersectionality was referred to in two CERD cases, namely *P.S.N. v Denmark* and *A.W.R.A.P. v Denmark*, which were declared inadmissible given that the respective claims were, according to the CERD, based on religious discrimination only and, as noted, 'Islam is not a religion practised solely by a particular group.'[31] The CERD summed up its position in relation to this issue by holding that 'religious questions are of relevance to the Committee when they are linked

---

28 CERD General Recommendation 32: 'The Meaning and Scope of Special Measures in the International Convention on the Elimination of Racial Discrimination' (2009) CERD/C/GC/32, para. 7.

29 OHCHR Expert Workshops on the prohibition of incitement to national, racial or religious hatred, Expert workshop on Europe (2011) Joint submission by Mr. Heiner Bielefeldt, Special Rapporteur on Freedom of Religion or Belief; Mr. Frank La Rue, Special Rapporteur on the Promotion and Protection of the Right to Freedom of Opinion and Expression; Mr. Githu Muigai, Special Rapporteur on Contemporary Forms of Racism, Racial Discrimination, Xenophobia and Related Intolerance, www.ohchr.org/Documents/Issues/Expression/ICCPR/Vienna/CRP-3Joint_SRSubmission_for_Vienna.pdf [Accessed 6 May 2014].

30 OHCHR Expert Workshops on the prohibition of incitement to national, racial or religious hatred, Expert workshop on Europe (2011) Joint submission by Mr. Heiner Bielefeldt, Special Rapporteur on Freedom of Religion or Belief; Mr. Frank La Rue, Special Rapporteur on the Promotion and Protection of the Right to Freedom of Opinion and Expression; Mr. Githu Muigai, Special Rapporteur on Contemporary Forms of Racism, Racial Discrimination, Xenophobia and Related Intolerance, www.ohchr.org/Documents/Issues/Expression/ICCPR/Vienna/CRP3Joint_SRSubmission_for_Vienna.pdf [Accessed 6 May 2014].

31 P.S.N v Denmark (2007) Communication no. 36/2006, CERD/C/71/D/36/2006, para. 6.3.

with issues of ethnicity and racial discrimination.'[32] Thus, in light of the principle of intersectionality, Islamophobic and/or other religiously motivated hate speech and activities, promulgated by far-right movements, can be condemned and prohibited under the ICERD only if interlinked with one of the grounds expressly stipulated in Article 1, these being race, colour, descent, or national or ethnic origin.

Freedom from racial discrimination

The freedom from racial discrimination is a significant constituent of international human rights law, expressed in several UN documents and initiatives as one of the many grounds from which discrimination can emanate. It is dealt with as an entity in itself by the ICERD. This Convention was adopted by the UN General Assembly in 1965, came into force in 1969 and is the first international treaty to deal directly and exclusively with the issue of racial discrimination, offering the most comprehensive international response to the issue yet. The ICERD and its monitoring body seek to eliminate racial discrimination in public and private spheres. The Convention includes a variety of provisions that contribute to its objective, such as the obligation for States to create comprehensive legislation to combat this phenomenon,[33] to guarantee effective protection and remedies for victims,[34] to provide for education and awareness raising to combat prejudices[35] and to punish racially discriminatory expression and association.[36] In the next section, the ICERD will be discussed in more detail because of its importance to the issue of far-right parties and groups which habitually promote racial hatred and discrimination. With a view to elucidating key meanings and notions, jurisprudence of the ICERD's monitoring body as well as General Recommendations and Concluding Observations prepared by this body will also be considered.

Before proceeding to the analysis of the ICERD, it is useful to mention several other international sources which are relevant to the prohibition of racial discrimination. The Charter of the United Nations, the UDHR and the International Covenants, discussed previously, all stipulate that no distinction to human rights contained therein must be made on the basis of several factors, including race.[37] In 1994, the Special Rapporteur on Contemporary Forms of Racism, Racial Discrimination, Xenophobia and Related Intolerance[38] was appointed to focus on these issues by transmitting appeals and communications to States, undertake fact-finding visits, publish country reports and submit annual or thematic reports

---

32 CERD Report 66th session and 67th session (2005) A/60/18, para. 246.
33 Article 2(d) ICERD.
34 Article 6, ICERD.
35 Article 7, ICERD.
36 Article 4, ICERD.
37 Article 55(c) of the United Nations Charter, Article 2 of the UDHR and Article 2 of the ICCPR and ICESCR.
38 Appointed by the Commission on Human Rights Resolution 1993/20.

to the Human Rights Council and interim reports to the UN General Assembly on the Rapporteur's work.[39] Several of the documents issued by this organ will be considered later on. Further, in 1997, the UN General Assembly adopted Resolution 52/11 which incorporated its decision to hold a World Conference against Racism, Racial Discrimination, Xenophobia and Related Intolerance.[40] The World Conference, which was held in 2001 in Durban, South Africa, was an effort to contribute to the struggle of eradicating all forms of racism. The Conference resulted in the Durban Declaration and Programme of Action. Notwithstanding the non-binding nature of this initiative, the Declaration outlined a vision for the twenty-first century where racism and racial discrimination are combatted effectively with the Programme of Action, translating the Declaration's objectives into practical recommendations. In relation to the far-right, the Durban Declaration condemned 'persistence and resurgence of neo-nazism, neo-fascism and violent nationalist ideologies based on racial or national prejudice'[41] as well as racist organisations and political platforms.[42] The Programme of Action requested that all States discourage racist activities and xenophobic tendencies that result in the rejection of migrants.[43] It also urged States to enforce measures to tackle racist crime and called upon them to promote initiatives that deter and combat radical extremist movements which promote racism. With regard to the Durban Declaration, the Commission on Human Rights created the Intergovernmental Working Group to oversee the Declaration's implementation.[44] In 2003, the UN Secretary General appointed the Group of Independent Eminent Experts,[45] again for purposes of overseeing the implementation of the Durban Declaration. In relation to this institution, the UN General Assembly emphasised the role of these experts in 'mobilizing the necessary political will required for the successful implementation of the Durban Declaration and Programme of Action,'[46] thereby reflecting that political factors as well as social and legal factors are necessary for combatting racism. Through the aforementioned initiatives, the international community has recognised the significance

---

39 Mandate of Special Rapporteur on contemporary forms of racism, racial discrimination, xenophobia and related intolerance: www.ohchr.org/EN/Issues/Racism/SRRacism/Pages/OverviewMandate.aspx [Accessed 13 January 2014].

40 General Assembly Resolution 52/111 (1997): Third Decade to Combat Racism and Racial Discrimination and the convening of a world conference on racism, racial discrimination, xenophobia and related intolerance.

41 World Conference against Racism, Racial Discrimination, Xenophobia and Related Intolerance Durban Declaration (2001) A/CONF.189/12, para. 84.

42 Ibid. para. 85.

43 Ibid. para. 24.

44 Commission on Human Rights Resolution 2002/68: Racism, Racial Discrimination, Xenophobia and Related Intolerance.

45 General Assembly Resolution 56/266 (2014): Programme of Activities for the Implementation of the International Decade for People of African Descent.

46 General Assembly Resolution 59/177 (2004): Global efforts for the total elimination of racism, racial discrimination, xenophobia and related intolerance and the comprehensive implementation of and follow-up to the Durban Declaration and Programme of Action.

of dealing with this phenomenon and has taken a variety of relevant measures and established a number of institutions and groups in order to combat racism effectively. However, the most important mechanism continues to be the ICERD, which deals solely with this issue and will, therefore, be a central consideration of this chapter. Given that the analysis of this instrument is being effectuated against the backdrop of the far-right, the focus will be placed on Article 4 of the ICERD which is central to racist expression and associations. In relation to the principle of non-discrimination, 'ideas based upon racial superiority or hatred fundamentally deny the equality of human beings,'[47] and, given that racial discrimination and incitement to racial discrimination 'reject the very foundation of human rights,'[48]Article 4 of the ICERD incorporates a broad understanding of the kind of acts that fall within its ambit, also allowing for the incitement to such racial discrimination. This article provides for the prohibition of propaganda and organisations promoting racial discrimination. Moreover, it underlines the positive duty that a State has to eradicate all such ideas and acts. Article 4 of the ICERD condemns propaganda and organisations endorsing racial superiority and promoting racial discrimination. Thus, it explicitly limits the freedom of expression and association to those disseminating ideas and carrying out activities relevant to this scope. Article 4 of the ICERD is thus the most specialised tool within the international framework that equips States with the duty to punish any ideas and acts of violence against persons of another colour or ethnic origin and prohibit any organisations which promote racial discrimination. The central issues of prohibitions of speech and/or groups as well as the issue of sanctioning will be discussed later on. In light of this, Article 4 of the ICERD will be assessed from three separate yet interrelated angles, namely non-discrimination, expression and association. In view of the interrelationship between Article 4(a) and 4(b) to the freedom of expression and association, respectively, the two articles shall be appraised in the sections that deal with these two freedoms.

Monitoring ICERD obligations: the committee on the elimination of racial discrimination

In part to monitor obligations of States Parties in relation to Convention provisions, Article 8 of the ICERD established the CERD consisting of 'eighteen experts of high moral standing and acknowledged impartiality elected by States Parties.' The CERD receives periodic reports from States Parties and makes recommendations upon them to the UN General Assembly.[49] It may receive inter-State complaints[50] which are then referred to an *ad hoc* Conciliation Commission[51]

47 German Institute for Human Rights, Written Contribution to the Thematic Discussion of the Committee on the Elimination of Racial Discrimination on Racist Hate Speech (28 August 2012) 6.
48 Ibid.
49 Article 9, ICERD.
50 Article 11, ICERD.
51 Article 12, ICERD.

with a view to reaching an amicable solution. The ICERD also contains an optional clause to permit communications from individuals or groups of individuals, within States Parties' jurisdiction, claiming to be victims of a violation by that State Party of any of the rights set forth in this Convention, in response to which the CERD makes suggestions and recommendations to the State Party.[52] The CERD may consider complaints from groups of individuals as well as individuals, as stipulated in Article 14 ICERD. It is clear from the CERD's case-law that communications by non-governmental organisations (NGOs) can also be accepted. In *Zentralrat Deutscher Sinti und Roma et al. v Germany*, the CERD clarified that such an organisation could present a complaint, since 'bearing in mind the nature of the organization's activities and the groups of individuals they represent, they do satisfy the 'victim' requirement within the meaning of Article 14(1).'[53] This demonstrates that, in relation to admissibility criteria, the Committee was ready to interpret the spirit of Article 14 of the ICERD rather than simply its letter, by allowing an application from an organisation with a legitimate interest and correlation to the content of the complaint. The CERD offers clarification and explanation of legal principles and country obligations arising from the ICERD, through its General Recommendations. An important example from the perspective of this study is General Recommendation 35 dealing with combatting racist speech. Also of importance are its Concluding Observations on particular States Parties as they raise points of concern or applaud measures or initiatives taken by countries in the more general ambit of combatting racial discrimination, often making direct statements *vis-à-vis* the regulation of the far-right. Notwithstanding its non-binding nature, the CERD's jurisprudence, which has tackled, amongst other issues, hate speech and activities, contributes to the improvement of relevant laws and policies if the State Party opts to adopt the recommendations of the Committee. The relevant documentation prepared by the CERD will be discussed throughout the analysis of Article 4 of the ICERD.

Article 4 ICERD: a general overview

Article 4 of the ICERD deals with the prohibition of ideas and groups that disseminate and promote ideas of racial superiority and hatred and carry out acts of violence against minority groups. In fact, Article 4 is the provision which has 'functioned as the principal vehicle for combatting hate speech'[54] but is also central to limiting the actions of racist associations. This article also notes that incitement to racial discrimination and incitement to acts of violence constitute a prohibited activity. Article 4 of the ICERD provides that

---

52 Article 14, ICERD.
53 Zentralrat Deutscher Sinti und Roma et al. v Germany, Communication no. 38/2006 (3 March 2008) CERD/C/72/D/38/2006, para. 7.2.
54 CERD General Recommendation 35: 'Combatting Racist Hate Speech' (2013) CERD/C/GC/35, para. 8.

States Parties condemn all propaganda and all organizations which are based on ideas or theories of superiority of one race or group of persons of one colour or ethnic origin, or which attempt to justify or promote racial hatred and discrimination in any form, and undertake to adopt immediate and positive measures designed to eradicate all incitement to, or acts of, such discrimination and, to this end, with due regard to the principles embodied in the Universal Declaration of Human Rights and the rights expressly set forth in Article 5 of this Convention, *inter alia*:

a　Shall declare an offence punishable by law all dissemination of ideas based on racial superiority or hatred, incitement to racial discrimination, as well as all acts of violence or incitement to such acts against any race or group of persons of another colour or ethnic origin, and also the provision of any assistance to racist activities, including the financing thereof;

b　Shall declare illegal and prohibit organizations, and also organized and all other propaganda activities, which promote and incite racial discrimination, and shall recognize participation in such organizations or activities as an offence punishable by law.

Article 4 of the ICERD is of a mandatory character[55] and the CERD has underlined that 'the prohibition of racial discrimination is a peremptory norm of international law from which no derogation is permitted.'[56] Article 4 has been characterised as 'the most important article in the Convention.'[57] The CERD noted in its General Recommendation 15 on 'Measures to Eradicate Incitement to or Acts of Discrimination' that, when the ICERD was adopted, Article 4 was regarded as a key tool for the fight against racial discrimination.[58] As underlined by the Committee, at the time of the ICERD's adoption,

there was a widespread fear of the revival of authoritarian ideologies … Since that time, the Committee has received evidence of organized violence based on ethnic origin and the political exploitation of ethnic difference. As a result, implementation of Article 4 is now of increased importance.[59]

As such, Article 4 has always been central to any discourse on the far-right.

55　CERD General Recommendation 15: 'Measures to Eradicate Incitement to or Acts of Discrimination' (1985) A/40/18 at 120. This principle was reiterated in a number of documents including the CERD General Recommendation 35: Combatting Racist Hate Speech (2003) CERD/C/GC/35, para. 10.

56　CERD 2002 Statement on Racial Discrimination and Measures to Combat Terrorism, A/57/18 Chapter XI C.

57　Drew Mahalic & Joan Gambee Mahalic, 'The Limitation Provisions of the International Convention on the Elimination of all Forms of Racial Discrimination' (1987) 9 *Human Rights Quarterly* 1, 89.

58　General Recommendation 15: 'Measures to Eradicate Incitement to or Acts of Discrimination' (1994) A/48/18 at 114, para. 1.

59　Ibid.

General prohibition of incitement to racial discrimination

Article 4 of the ICERD declares punishable by law the incitement to racial discrimination and incitement to acts of violence and declares illegal activities which incite racial discrimination. The CERD places great importance on prohibiting incitement, recognising the major potential it has for destruction. For example, in its Concluding Observations to Poland, it expressed concern that the State dismissed cases of incitement due to the alleged low impact on society[60] and noted that 'according to the Convention, all such cases are very harmful to society.'[61] However, for incitement to racial discrimination to exist, it is necessary that there is a reasonable possibility that the statement could give rise to this type of discrimination.[62] The CERD has noted that no conditions, such as intention or the pursuit of a particular objective such as stirring up hatred, need to exist for incitement to racial discrimination to be established, given that 'article 4(a) of the Convention declares punishable the mere act of dissemination or incitement, without any conditions.'[63] More particularly, the intention of the perpetrator does not need to be established since, as emphasised by the CERD 'what is penalized ... is the mere act of incitement, without reference to any intention on the part of the offender or the result of such incitement, if any.'[64] The CERD has only provided details on the aspect of intention without an extrapolation of what can actually constitute incitement to racial discrimination under this article. This would be useful for States when drafting, incorporating, amending and/or implementing the necessary legislation and deciding on relevant case-law.

When considering the issue of incitement, the CERD often 'recommends remedying gaps in legislation, preferring specific legislation on this issue.'[65] For example, in its concluding observations to Israel, the CERD underlined the need to 'expand the definition of racism so as to include incitement on account of ethnic origin, country of origin, and religious affiliation.'[66] Even where there exists relevant legislation, the CERD does, when necessary, provide recommendations for its improvement. In its Concluding Observations to New Zealand, the Committee underlined its concern 'at the absence of a comprehensive strategy to address incitement to racial hatred committed in cyberspace,'[67] directing the States Party in this direction. Also, in its Concluding Observations to the U.K., the Committee sought to broaden the scope of the notion of incitement to

---

60 CERD Concluding Observations: Poland (2003) CERD/C/62/CO/6, para. 159.
61 Ibid.
62 Rabat Plan of Action on the Prohibition of Advocacy of National, Racial or Religious Hatred that constitutes Incitement to Discrimination, Hostility or Violence (2002) para. 6.
63 CERD Study: 'Positive Measures Designed to Eradicate all Incitement to, or Acts of, Racial Discrimination: Implementation of ICERD,' Article 4, New York, UN, 1986, para. 235. This study was prepared for the Second World Conference on Racism in 1983 as A/CONF.119/10.
64 Ibid.
65 Ibid.
66 CERD Concluding Observations: Israel (2012) CERD/C/ISR/CO/14-16, para. 14.
67 CERD Concluding Observations: New Zealand (2013) CERD/C/NZL/CO/18-20, para. 9.

include a wide range of grounds and recommended 'the extension of the crime of incitement to racial hatred to cover offences motivated by religious hatred against immigrant communities.'[68]

State obligations arising from Article 4

Article 4 of the ICERD imposes a number of specific obligations on the States Parties which are specifically interesting for the purposes of the current study. For example, the UN General Assembly has noted that, under this article, States Parties are under the obligation to adopt immediate and positive measures 'to condemn all propaganda and all organizations that are based on ideas of racial superiority ... and to eradicate all incitement to, or acts of, such discrimination.'[69] It has also been reiterated that States Parties must criminalise the incitement to imminent violence based on religion or belief.[70] The CERD has emphasised the significant character of these obligations by stating that 'the fact that Article 4 is couched in terms of States Parties' obligations, rather than inherent rights of individuals does not imply that they are matters to be left to the internal jurisdiction of States parties, and as such immune from review.'[71] The CERD itself has stressed time and again that States Parties have an obligation to draft and implement legislation to combat racial discrimination and incitement to hatred and discrimination as a central part of Article 4. Furthermore, the CERD has underlined that in order to comply with the obligations of Article 4, States Parties must not only ensure the enactment of appropriate legislation but also its effective implementation.[72] As far back as its first General Recommendation in 1972, the Committee noted that several countries had not incorporated Article 4 into their national legislation, 'the implementation of which ... is obligatory under the Convention for all States parties.'[73] Over the years, the Committee has given further instructions regarding this article. For example, in *Gelle v Denmark*, the Committee observed that 'it does not suffice, for purposes of Article 4 of the Convention, merely to declare acts of racial discrimination punishable on paper. Rather, criminal laws and other legal provisions prohibiting racial discrimination

---

68 CERD Concluding Observations: United Kingdom (2003) CERD/C/63/CO/11, para. 540.

69 General Assembly Resolution 66/143 (2012): Inadmissibility of certain practices that contribute to fuelling contemporary forms of racism, racial discrimination, xenophobia and related intolerance.

70 Human Rights Council Resolution 16/18 (2011): Combating intolerance, negative stereotyping and stigmatization of, and discrimination, incitement to violence, and violence against persons based on religion or belief, Human Rights Council Resolution 19/25 (2012): Combating intolerance, negative stereotyping and stigmatization of, and discrimination and incitement to violence and violence against persons based on religion or belief.

71 The Jewish community of Oslo et al. v Norway Communication no. 30/2003 (15 August 2005) CERD/C/67/D/30/2003.

72 CERD General Recommendation 15: 'Measures to Eradicate Incitement to or Acts of Discrimination' A/48/18 at 114 (1994) para. 2.

73 CERD General Recommendation 1: 'States Parties' Obligations' (1972) A/8718 at 37.

must also be effectively implemented by the competent national tribunals and other State institutions. This obligation is implicit in Article 4 of the Convention.[74] However, in considering remedies and redress, Article 6 of the ICERD, which more specifically relates to effective remedies, 'does not impose upon States Parties the duty to institute a mechanism of sequential remedies, up to and including the Supreme Court level, in cases of alleged racial discrimination.'[75] Further, in *Yilmaz-Dogan v The Netherlands*, the Committee observed that the expediency principle, which it has defined as 'the freedom to prosecute or not prosecute, is governed by considerations of public policy'[76] and noted that the Convention 'cannot be interpreted as challenging the *raison d'être* of that principle.'[77] Nevertheless, the Committee noted that, in light of the guarantees laid down in the Convention, the Convention should be respected in each case of alleged racial discrimination or incitement thereto.[78]

As highlighted in *Gelle v Denmark*, Article 4 of the ICERD imposes the obligation on States Parties to carry out an effective investigation into whether or not an act of racial discrimination has taken place, omission of which results in a breach of the said article.[79] In *Jama v Denmark*,[80] the Committee stipulated that States Parties must ensure that the police and judicial authorities conduct thorough investigations into allegations of acts of racial discrimination, as referred to in Article 4 of the Convention. In *L.K. v the Netherlands*, the Committee underlined that 'when threats of racial violence are made, and especially when they are made in public and by a group, it is incumbent upon the State to investigate with due diligence and expedition,'[81] thereby highlighting that investigation needs to be speedy in order to be adequate. Thus, the ICERD imposes on States the obligation to incorporate sufficient legislation to investigate and combat racial discrimination and incitement thereto without dictating the nature of the remedies imposed.

Conclusion: prohibition of discrimination and racial discrimination

In sum, non-discrimination is a central constituent of international human rights law, as initially developed by the International Bill of Rights and later incorporated in a specialised manner, namely in the form of combatting racial

---

74 Gelle v Denmark, Communication no. 34/2004 (15 March 2006) CERD/C/68/D/34/2004, para. 7.3. This was reiterated in Jama v Denmark, Adan v Denmark and TBB-Turkish Union v Germany.

75 Ibid.

76 Yilmaz-Dogan v The Netherlands, Communication. no. 1/1984 (10 August 1988) CERD/C/36/D/1/1984, para. 9.4.

77 Ibid.

78 Ibid.

79 Gelle v Denmark, Communication no. 34/2004 (15 March 2006) CERD/C/68/D/34/2004, para. 7.6.

80 Jama v Denmark, Communication no. 41/2008 (21 August 2009) CERD/C/75/D/41/2008.

81 L.K. v The Netherlands, Communication no. 4/1991 (16 March 1993) A/48/18, para. 6.6.

discrimination in the ICERD. As such, States Parties have a duty to prevent, prohibit and punish activities that are discriminatory to others. As discussed in the following section, it is upon the premise of non-discrimination that limitations to expression, assembly and association, as incorporated in the UDHR, the ICCPR and the ICERD, have been developed. Particularly, the exercise of these freedoms must not result in discrimination to others.

Freedom of expression: overview of freedom of expression in UN instruments

Freedom of opinion and expression are key components of democracies as they are, in conjunction with each other, central vehicles that allow citizens to develop and voice their ideologies and belief systems in the formal and informal public domains. The importance of freedom of expression was underlined in Resolution 59(1) of the UN General Assembly's first session, which holds that 'freedom of information is a fundamental human right and ... the touchstone of all the freedoms to which the United Nations is consecrated.'[82] Freedom of expression is enshrined, in combination with the freedom of opinion, in the UDHR and the ICCPR. General Comment 34 of the HRC underlines that expression includes, amongst others, political discourse,[83] while General Comment 25[84] emphasises the importance of freedom of expression for the exercise of public affairs. As well as providing protection to the freedom of expression, which is to be limited only if certain conditions are fulfilled, international law directly prohibits expression in the form of dissemination of ideas based on racial superiority or hatred.

The complex interrelationship between racial hatred and the freedom of expression has been recognised and tackled by a series of international initiatives. In 2011, the Office of the United Nations High Commissioner for Human Rights organised a series of expert workshops on incitement to national, racial or religious hatred, as reflected in international human rights law. In 2011, the expert workshops resulted in a large amount of information regarding racial hatred as well as recommendations for better implementation of the relevant international human rights standards. The resulting document of this initiative was the Rabat Plan of Action,[85] which incorporates the conclusions and recommendations of the final expert workshop which took place in 2012 in Rabat, as well as an analysis of the positions held by national legislation, jurisprudence

82 General Assembly Resolution 59(I): Calling of an International Conference on Freedom of Information (1946).

83 HRC General Comment 34: 'Article 19: Freedoms of Opinion and Expression' (2011) CCPR/C/GC/34, para. 11.

84 HRC General Comment 25: 'Article 25: The Right to Participate in Public Affairs, Voting Rights and the Right of Equal Access to Public Service' (1996) CCPR/C/21/Rev.1/Add.7.

85 Rabat Plan of Action on the Prohibition of Advocacy of National, Racial or Religious Hatred that constitutes Incitement to Discrimination, Hostility or Violence (2002) para. 6.

and policies in the various UN states. It makes recommendations on each point and, therefore, constitutes a significant source when evaluating the prohibition of advocacy of national, racial or religious hatred that constitutes incitement to discrimination, hostility or violence. As will be demonstrated, the freedom of expression is provided with a high level of protection within the system of the UN while the same institution is careful when it comes to especially dangerous expression, incorporating relevant limitations and prohibitions into the legal framework, particularly in light of the link between the freedom of expression and racist speech, promulgated by far-right movements. As noted in the Rabat Plan of Action, the right to freedom of expression allows the open debate and criticism of religious matters and beliefs.[86] A similar position is taken by the HRC, which has emphasised that the freedom of expression is of paramount importance in any society and that any restrictions to its exercise must meet a strict test of justification.[87]

This section shall consider the development, composition and implementation of the said freedom in various instruments of international human rights law, taking into account the balancing exercise which is effectuated between potentially conflicting rights and principles as well as prohibitive provisions. First, Article 19 of the UDHR, which established general notions pertaining to freedom of expression, shall be considered, followed by a discussion of Article 19 of the ICCPR, which deals with freedom of expression and legitimate limitations thereto, and of Article 20(2) of the ICCPR, which is particularly relevant to extreme speech. This section will close with an analysis of Article 4(a) of the ICERD, which has been formulated to prohibit the dissemination of racist ideas through expression.

Article 19 of the Universal Declaration of Human Rights

Article 19 of the UDHR provides that

> Everyone has the right to freedom of opinion and expression; this right includes freedom to hold opinions without interference and to seek, receive and impart information and ideas through any media and regardless of frontiers.

Article 19 of the UDHR does not expressly provide for any legitimate limitation that can be imposed on the freedom of expression nor does it include an express restriction of hate speech. This article recognises that opinions are to be held 'with no interference,' while no such qualification is made for the freedom of expression, thereby indirectly paving the way for restrictions of the freedom of

---

86 Ibid. para. 10.
87 See *inter alia* Kim v The Republic of Korea, Communication no. 574/1994 (4 January 1999) CCPR/C/64/D/574/1994, Park v The Republic of Korea, Communication no. 628/1995 (3 November 1998) CCPR/C/64/D/628/1995, Kungurov v Uzbekistan, Communication no. 1478/2006 (15 September 2011) CCPR/C/102/D/1478/2006.

expression formulated in later documents. Indeed, the freedom of expression, as provided for by the UDHR, falls under the general limitations of Articles 29 and 30 of the UDHR. Article 29 of the UDHR places duties on individuals towards the community and underlines that limitations to the exercise of rights and freedoms are to be imposed insofar as 'they are determined by law solely for the purpose of securing due recognition and respect for the rights and freedoms of others and of meeting the just requirements of morality, public order and the general welfare in a democratic society.' In addition, it provides that the rights and freedoms enshrined in the Declaration 'may in no case be exercised contrary to the purposes and principles of the United Nations.' Further, Article 30 of the UDHR states that

> nothing in this Declaration may be interpreted as implying for any State, group or person any right to engage in any activity or to perform any act aimed at the destruction of any of the rights and freedoms set forth herein.

This principle was also enshrined in later provisions, such as Article 5 of the ICCPR, and, in the case of expression of extremist groups, can be used as a yardstick for restriction given the potentially destructive impact of racist speech on the rights and freedoms of target groups. Further, the UDHR was drafted 'because the world community wanted to protect itself from Nazism, racism and fascism.'[88] Taking into account the historical setting in which the UDHR was drafted as well as the importance granted to equality and non-discrimination throughout, it can safely be argued that this document does not afford racist speech protection as this type of speech is excluded as a result of the limitation clauses as well as the overall spirit of the UDHR. More particularly 'the rights of equality and non-discrimination are central in the UDHR and no rights, including speech rights, may be asserted to destroy them.'[89] As a result, from the non-destruction clause enshrined in Article 30 of the UDHR, the protection against incitement, as offered by Article 7 of the UHDR, and the limitation grounds, as set out by Article 29, therein, as well as from the historical setting of the UDHR, it can be deducted that hate speech and incitement to racial discrimination are not protected by this document. However, care must be taken when applying relevant limitations and restrictions given that, as noted by the UN High Commissioner for Human Rights, 'defining the line that separates protected from unprotected speech is ultimately a decision that is best made after a thorough assessment of the circumstances of each case.'[90] Thus, the situation

---

88 Johannes Morsink, '*The Universal Declaration of Human Rights, Origins, Drafting and Intent*' (1st edn. University of Pennsylvania Press, Philadelphia PA 1999) 66.

89 Elizabeth Defeis, 'Freedom of Speech and International Laws: A Response to Hate Speech' (1992) 29 *Stanford Journal of International Law* 57, 71.

90 Opening Remarks by Navanethem Pillay, UN High Commissioner for Human Rights, 2 October 2008, Expert Seminar on the Links between Articles 19 and 20 of the International Covenant on Civil and Political Rights; See also HRC General Comment 34, para. 35.

is not as simple as it may first appear given that certain definitions need to be clarified, always taking into account the content and context of the speech in question as only then may one determine if the speech is unprotected and can, therefore, be legitimately restricted. Moreover, what lies at the heart of this exercise is coherently striking the balance between the freedom of expression and the freedom from racial discrimination. An effort to extrapolate upon what kind of speech is unprotected was made by the Rabat Plan of Action which will be discussed further in the framework of Article 20(2) of the ICCPR.

Notwithstanding the general normative framework that the Declaration sought to establish, it by no means provides a precise balance test to be used in applying the freedom of expression. Rather, the UDHR sets the scene for the more complex assessment of the actual limitations that can be imposed on this freedom which was subsequently provided for by the ICCPR, as discussed later.

Article 19 of the International Covenant on Civil and Political Rights: a general overview

The ICCPR was adopted and opened for signature, ratification and accession in 1966 and entered into force in 1976. Article 19 of the ICCPR provides for the freedom of opinion and expression. More particularly, it states that

1 Everyone shall have the right to hold opinions without interference;
2 Everyone shall have the right to freedom of expression; this right shall include freedom to seek, receive and impart information and ideas of all kinds, regardless of frontiers, either orally, in writing or in print, in the form of art, or through any other media of his choice;
3 The exercise of the rights provided for in paragraph 2 of this article carries with it special duties and responsibilities. It may therefore be subject to certain restrictions, but these shall only be such as are provided by law and are necessary:
   a For respect of the rights or reputations of others;
   b For the protection of national security or of public order (ordre public), or of public health or morals.

The freedom of opinion is granted an absolute status under the ICCPR, with Article 19 stipulating that there exists the right to hold opinions without interference. However, no such provision is incorporated in reference to the freedom of expression which is a qualified right. General Comment 34 of the HRC underlines that the freedoms of opinion and expression, mentioned in Section 1 of this provision, are closely related, 'with freedom of expression providing the vehicle for the exchange and development of opinions.'[91]

---

91 HRC General Comment 34, 'Article 19 – Freedom of Opinion and Expression' (2011) CCPR/C/GC/34, para. 2.

Monitoring ICCPR obligations: the Human Rights Committee

Article 28 of the ICCPR establishes the HRC, which is the supervisory and enforcement body of the ICCPR. States Parties undertake to submit reports on the measures they have adopted which give effect to the rights recognised therein. The HRC can consider inter-state complaints regarding violations of the rights of the ICCPR, periodic reports of the State Parties and, under the First Protocol to the ICCPR, the Committee can consider individual complaints or communications in the event of alleged violation of the rights enshrined therein. In *J.R.T and the W.G. Party V Canada*,[92] the Committee underlined that it is only authorised to consider communications submitted by individuals and not associations. This is relevant in the ambit of racist speech as this limitation prohibits organised human rights groups or groups which promote the rights of particular ethnic groups from bringing complaints to the HRC.

Restrictions to the freedom of expression under the ICCPR

Notwithstanding the central role held by the freedom of expression in the international legal framework, 'this freedom does not enjoy such a position of primacy among rights that it trumps equality rights.'[93] Bearing this in mind, restrictions are not to be imposed lightly given that, as noted by General Comment 34, Article 19(2) of the ICCPR embraces 'even expression that may be regarded as deeply offensive.'[94] In order to clarify the meaning and applicability of limitation clauses of the ICCPR and promote their legitimate implementation, the Siracusa Principles of the United Nations Economic and Social Council were construed by a group of experts in international law in an initiative led by a number of NGOs. Notwithstanding the non-binding nature of these principles, they are nevertheless pertinent to any discussion relating to the restriction of the freedoms and rights of the ICCPR given that they constitute the only constructive expert effort to provide a uniform interpretation of limitation clauses of the aforementioned Covenant. The Principles stipulate that 'the scope of a limitation referred to in the Covenant shall not be interpreted so as to jeopardise the essence of the right concerned.'[95] The restriction must be 'provided for by law' which means that it must be formulated with adequate detail so as to enable citi-

92 J.R.T and the W.G. Party v Canada (6 April 1983) Communication no. 104/1981, CCPR/C/ OP/2 at 25, para. 8(a).
93 Stephanie Farrior, 'Molding The Matrix: The Historical and Theoretical Foundations of International Law Concerning Hate Speech' (1996) 14 *Berkley Journal of International Law* 1, 3.
94 HRC General Comment 34, 'Article 19 – Freedom of Opinion and Expression' (2011) CCPR/C/ GC/34, para. 11.
95 United Nations, Economic and Social Council, Siracusa Principles on the Limitation and Derogation Provisions in the International Covenant on Civil and Political Rights, E/CN.4/1985/4, Annex (1985).

zens to conform to it.[96] It must be made accessible to the public[97] and must not equip enforcement mechanisms with unregulated discretion to restrict freedom of expression.[98] The Rabat Plan of Action underlines that restrictions to the freedom of expression are to be clearly defined without an overly broad scope, must respond to a pressing social need, must be the least intrusive measures available and be proportional to their goal.[99] The key process when determining whether speech should be prohibited is striking a proper balance between the aforementioned conflicting rights and freedoms. In relation to the ICCPR, it has been argued that it embraces a victim-centred approach when balancing free speech 'against the listener's right to have her inherent human dignity protected from hate speech injuries.'[100] Nevertheless, in imposing restrictions on this freedom, States must 'not put in jeopardy the right itself.'[101] Moreover, Article 19(3) of the ICCPR must not be interpreted as 'license to prohibit unpopular speech.'[102] Thus, restricting expression is not a simple task, with an array of factors that must be taken into account in relation to the formulation and implementation of a restriction.

Limitation grounds of Article 19 of the ICCPR

As already noted, Article 19 of the ICCPR is not an absolute right and, as such, can be limited on certain grounds. Article 19(3) of the ICCPR incorporates a three-tier test to be applied when limiting the named freedom, a test which the HRC has consistently applied in its views in individual complaints cases. Article 19(3) states that the exercise of the right of freedom of expression may be subject to certain restrictions that are provided by law and are necessary for the respect of the rights or reputations of others or for the protection of national security or of public order or of public health or morals. 'Necessary,' thereby, means that the restriction must be based on one of the grounds justifying limitations, responds to a pressing public or social need, pursues a legitimate aim and is proportionate to that aim.[103] The potentially relevant grounds to be invoked when seeking to restrict freedom of expression, in the name of combatting racist

96 Ibid.
97 Ibid.
98 HRC Concluding Observations: Lesotho (1999) CCPR/C/79/Add.106, para. 23.
99 Rabat Plan of Action on the Prohibition of Advocacy of National, Racial or Religious Hatred that constitutes Incitement to Discrimination, Hostility or Violence (2002) para. 18.
100 Nazila Ghanea, 'Minorities and Hatred: Protections and Implications' (2010) 17 *International Journal on Minority and Group Rights* 3, 433.
101 HRC General Comment 18: 'Non-Discrimination' (1994) HRI/GEN/1/Rev.1 at 26, para. 12.
102 Faurisson v France, Communication no. 550/1993 (8 November 1996) CCPR/C/58/D/550/1993, Individual opinion of Elizabeth Evatt and David Kretzmer (concurring opinion).
103 United Nations, Economic and Social Council, Siracusa Principles on the Limitation and Derogation Provisions in the International Covenant on Civil and Political Rights, E/CN.4/1985/4, Annex (1985).

speech and propaganda promulgated by far-right movements, are the respect for the rights of others, the protection of morals and the protection of public order which will be considered hereinafter. The burden is on the State Party to demonstrate whether a restriction imposed on the freedom of expression is in accordance with the Convention.[104] The first of the relevant legitimate grounds for restriction, listed in Article 19(3) of the ICCPR, is that of the respect for the rights of others. When dealing with racist speech and propaganda, this ground is the most pertinent given the impact of such activities on the rights of those who are targeted. As reiterated in General Comment 34, the term 'rights,' as construed in Article 19(3), includes human rights, as recognised in the Covenant and more generally in international human rights law.[105] Thus, a victim's right to be free from racial discrimination as a result of hate speech falls within the ambit of this clause. The term 'others' may, for example, 'refer to individual members of a community defined by its religious faith or ethnicity.'[106] In *Ross v Canada*, the HRC noted that the term 'others' may relate to other persons or to a community as a whole.[107] The Committee reiterated its position in *Faurisson v France*,[108] in which it underlined that restrictions may be permitted on statements which are of a nature to enhance or heighten anti-Semitic feelings, in order to uphold the right of Jewish communities to be protected from religious hatred. Moreover, as noted in the Update of the Preliminary Report prepared for the UN Sub-Commission on Prevention of Discrimination and Protection of Minority, 'only the concept of the rights of others, the boundaries of which are fairly clearly defined, seems apt to justify the restrictions needed in the struggle against racism.'[109] This could be because the rights of others can be objectively defined by turning to key international instruments and principles and because the 'reference to the rights of others finds an echo in certain restrictive provisions laid down in the general interest by the international instruments.'[110] Lastly, the HRC has drawn a direct correlation between racist speech and the rights and reputation of others and, particularly, the degree to which acts of racial discrimination and racial insults damage the injured party's perception of his/her own

---

104 Syargei Belyazeka v Belarus, Communication no. 1772/2008 (23 March 2012) CCPR/C/104/D/1772/2008; Dergachev v Belarus; Communication no. 921/200 (19 July 2002) CCPR/C/74/D/921/2000; Kungurov v Uzbekistan, Communication no. 1478/2006 (15 September 2011) CCPR/C/102/D/1478/2006; Komeenko and Milinkevich v Belarus, Communication no. 1553/2007 (24 April 2009) CCPR/C/95/D/1553/2007.

105 HRC General Comment 34, 'Article 19 – Freedom of Opinion and Expression' (2011) CCPR/C/GC/34, para. 28.

106 Ibid.

107 Ross v Canada, Communication no. 736/1997 (18 October 2000) CCPR/C/70/D/736/1997, para. 11.5.

108 Faurisson v France, Communication no. 550/1993 (8 November1996) CCPR/C/58/D/550/1993, para. 9.6.

109 Coliver S, *'Striking a Balance: Hate Speech, Freedom of Expression and Non-Discrimination'* (Article 19, International Centre against Censorship, University of Essex, Essex 1992) 43.

110 Ibid.

worth and reputation.[111] The HRC, thereby, employs an effects-based approach when conceptualising hate speech and the harm in hate speech, without putting forth a nexus between hate speech and the rights and reputation of others. Moreover, its methodology does not entail any conceptual, theoretical or in-depth contextual assessment. Secondly, Article 19(3) of the ICCPR states that the exercise of the freedom of expression may be subject to certain restrictions including the protection of public morals, which is also relevant to the consequences of far-right rhetoric and activity. In *Ross v Canada*, for example, the applicant, a former teacher, had been transferred to a non-teaching post as a result of his publication of books and leaflets which were deemed discriminatory against Jews. Here,

> as regards the protection of public morals, the State Party submit[ted] that Canadian society is multicultural and that it is fundamental to the moral fabric that all Canadians are entitled to equality without discrimination on the basis of race, religion or nationality.[112]

Nevertheless, the Committee did not confer an opinion on the applicability of this provision. Instead, as mentioned earlier, it found that restriction of the applicant's expression was necessary for the protection of the rights of others. The disregard by the Committee of the State Party's argument that the public morals ground was a legitimate reason to limit the freedom of expression in this case could have resulted from the abstract nature of the term 'public morals.' As argued by Mendel in a discussion on hate speech:

> public morals are not only hard to define, and change over time, but despite a number of cases on this, both nationally and internationally, it remains very difficult to identify what is being protected.[113]

This could also be a reason why this ground is hardly ever argued to constitute a legitimate reason for limitation of the freedom of expression in cases more generally. Furthermore, in enforcing this ground there is the risk of 'outlawing something which is merely not accepted by everybody.'[114] Thus, in General Comment 22, the Committee observed that the concept of morals derives from 'many social, philosophical and religious traditions'[115] and that limitation as per Article 19(3)

---

111 CERD General Recommendation 26: 'The Right to Seek Just and Adequate Reparation or Satisfaction' (2000) A/55/18, annex V at 153, para. 1.

112 Ross v Canada, Communication no. 736/1997 (18 October 2000) CCPR/C/70/D/736/1997, para. 6.11.

113 Toby Mendel, Restricting Freedom of Expression: Standards and Principles – Background Paper for meetings hosted by the UN Special Rapporteur on Freedom of Opinion and Expression: www.law-democracy.org/wp-content/uploads/2010/07/10.03.Paper-on-Restrictions-on-FOE.pdf [Accessed 10 May 2014] 15.

114 Sandra Coliver, *'Striking a Balance: Hate Speech, Freedom of Expression and Non-Discrimination'* (Article 19, International Centre against Censorship, University of Essex, Essex 1992) 43.

115 HRC General Comment 22: 'Article 18 – The Right to Freedom of Thought, Conscience and Religion' (1994) HRI/GEN/1/Rev.1 at 35, para. 8.

of the ICCPR 'must be based on principles not deriving exclusively from a single tradition.'[116] Such limitations must be interpreted in the realm of the universality of human rights and the principle of non-discrimination. In relation to the public order ground, the Siracusa Principles defined this as 'the sum of rules which ensure the functioning of society or the set of fundamental principles on which society is founded.'[117] Coliver considers this to constitute a rather problematic ground for limitation given that its 'boundaries ... are often ill-defined and, as a result, its unclear and abstract definitional scope means that it can be enforced in 'irrelevant circumstances, thus committing in reality a perversion of legitimacy.'[118] This could be the reason why, to date, the HRC has not enforced this ground as a justification for the restriction of hate speech and it is doubtful whether it will do so given the existence of the rights of others ground which, for reasons provided in the following, may be easier to apply. As such, this is not to say that extremist rhetoric does not damage public morals or public order but, instead, that these grounds are more difficult to define justly, adopt and support, especially in relation to the protection of the rights of others where the understanding of rights and the nexus between speech and victim or victims can be clearly established. Further, Article 19(3) of the ICCPR provides that any restrictions to the freedom of expression must be proportional to the legitimate aim pursued. More particularly, the HRC held that any such restrictions must meet the strict tests of necessity and proportionality[119] and must not be too broad.[120] The principle of proportionality must be 'respected not only in the law that frames the restrictions but also by the administrative and judicial authorities in applying the law.'[121] The Committee underlined that the principle of proportionality is to be applied to restrictions of freedom of expression on three interrelated scales. More particularly, any restriction must be 'appropriate to achieve their protective function,'[122] and 'must be the least intrusive instrument amongst those which might achieve their protective function; they must be proportionate to the interests to be protected.'[123] Thus, the principle of proportionality is to be applied when considering the objective of

116 Ibid.
117 United Nations, Economic and Social Council, Siracusa Principles on the Limitation and Derogation Provisions in the International Covenant on Civil and Political Rights, E/CN.4/1985/4, Annex (1985).
118 Sandra Coliver, *'Striking a Balance: Hate Speech, Freedom of Expression and Non-Discrimination'* (1st edn. Article 19 International Centre against Censorship 1992) 43.
119 Velichking v Belarus, Communication no. 1022/2001 (20 October 2005) CCPR/C/85/D/1022/2001, reiterated in HRC General Comment 34: 'Article 19 – Freedom of Opinion and Expression' (2011) CCPR/C/GC/34, para. 22.
120 HRC General Comment 34: 'Article 19 – Freedom of Opinion and Expression' (2011) CCPR/C/GC/34, para. 34.
121 Ibid.
122 Ibid. See also Marques v Angola, Communications no. 1128/2002 (18 April 2005) CCPR/C/83/D/1128/2002 and Coleman v Australia, No. 1157/2003 (10 August 2006) CCPR/C/87/D/1157/2003.
123 HRC General Comment 34: 'Article 19 – Freedom of Opinion and Expression' (2011) CCPR/C/GC/34, para. 34. See also Marques v Angola, Communications no. 1128/2002 (18 April 2005)

the restriction, the balancing of rights at stake and potential limitations thereto. As noted by the HRC, in applying the principle of proportionality, the competent authorities must take into account the type of expression as well as what its dissemination means.[124] For example, in the case of public debate concerning figures in the public and political domains, the significance placed on the freedom of expression is particularly high.[125] Applying the principle of proportionality to cases of freedom of expression is more difficult than may first appear given that it 'entails passing a value judgement on the ideas expressed.'[126] As such, the decision of the Committee, for example, to silence essentially a teacher because of allegedly anti-Semitic text and without setting out an explanatory backdrop for its decision to do so, does not bode well for the importance which the international community grants free speech (at least conjecturally).

Conclusion: freedom of expression

Freedom of expression in the form of Article 19 is the most qualified right of the Covenant. It is the only right to incorporate a qualification within itself through the reference to the 'special duties and responsibilities' that mark the exercise of this freedom. The inclusion of this requirement is a means to limit the negative consequences that may arise from the exercise of this freedom which can constitute a 'dangerous instrument.'[127] In light of the general principles of the UDHR, the careful formulation of Article 19 of the ICCPR and its limitation grounds, the HRC jurisprudence and international initiatives, such as the Rabat Plan of Action, it can be stated that hate speech, as such, cannot be considered responsible and, thus, legitimate speech under international human rights law, primarily due to the effects it is deemed to have on the rights of the victims. Noteworthy is the fact that these conclusions have been reached without the necessary socio-legal and theoretical examination of hate speech, its meaning and the impact on the rights of others in the framework of harm.

Article 20 of the ICCPR: general obligations on States Parties

While Article 19(3) of the ICCPR provides for the general limitations to be imposed on the freedom of expression, Article 20 of the same document

---

CCPR/C/83/D/1128/2002 and Coleman v Australia, No. 1157/2003 (10 August 2006) CCPR/C/87/D/1157/2003.
124 HRC General Comment 34: 'Article 19 – Freedom of Opinion and Expression' (2011) CCPR/C/GC/34, para. 34.
125 Ibid.
126 Sandra Coliver, *'Striking a Balance: Hate Speech, Freedom of Expression and Non-Discrimination'* (Article 19, International Centre against Censorship, University of Essex, Essex 1992) 52.
127 Manfred Nowak, *'U.N. Covenant on Civil and Political Rights: CCPR commentary'* (2nd edn. N. P Engel Verlag, Kehl am Rhein 2005) 457 at para. 40.

contains a specific prohibition on two types of expression. More particularly it holds that:

1   Any propaganda for war shall be prohibited by law.
2   Any advocacy of national, racial or religious hatred that constitutes incitement to discrimination, hostility or violence shall be prohibited by law.

Whilst a brief reference will be made to the background of Article 20, the following sections will focus on Article 20(2) as this is of more direct relevance to the contemporary rhetoric of the far-right. Article 20 was introduced into the ICCPR upon an initiative of the Soviet Union.[128] The *travaux préparatoires* of the ICCPR show that there was much debate as to whether an article prohibiting advocacy of national, racial or religious hatred should be incorporated in the Covenant.[129] Concerns were expressed as to the effectiveness of legislation as a means of dealing with such hatred as well as to the potential abuse of this clause to the detriment of the freedom of expression.[130] The final text of this article was adopted by 52 to 19 votes, with 12 abstentions and with several States Parties making reservations and declarations thereto.[131] For example, certain States held that there was no need for any additional legislation to secure the provisions of Article 20 as the requirements therein can be ensured through an interpretation of other articles in the ICCPR. For example, Belgium declared that

> Article 20 as a whole shall be applied taking into account the rights to freedom of thought and religion, freedom of opinion and freedom of assembly and association proclaimed in Articles 18, 19 and 20 of the Universal Declaration of Human Rights and reaffirmed in Articles 18, 19, 21 and 22 of the Covenant.[132]

Australia interpreted 'the rights provided for by articles 19, 21 and 22 as consistent with article 20; accordingly … the right is reserved not to introduce any further legislative provision on these matters.'[133] Similar approaches were followed by Malta, New Zealand, the U.K. and Luxembourg. As with Article 4 ICERD, the U.S. imposed a reservation on free speech grounds: namely that

---

128 Drew Mahalic & Joan Gambee Mahalic, 'The Limitation Provisions of the International Convention on the Elimination of all Forms of Racial Discrimination' (1987) 9 *Human Rights Quarterly* 1, 22.
129 Ibid. 21.
130 Ibid. 28.
131 Ibid. 40.
132 Declarations and Reservations ICCPR: https://treaties.un.org/Pages/ViewDetails.aspx?src=TREATY&mtdsg_no=IV-4&chapter=4&lang=en#EndDec.
133 Ibid.

Article 20 does not authorize or require legislation or other action by the United States that would restrict the right of free speech and association protected by the Constitution and laws of the United States.

Article 20 is different from the other articles of the ICCPR in that it does not set out a particular human right but instead imposes an obligation on the States to introduce limitations on the exercise of rights that have been dealt with in other articles, particularly those of expression and association. This special characteristic makes the provision rather similar in nature to Article 4 of the ICERD, which also mainly underlines the positive duty that States Parties have to prohibit practices that fall within its scope, even if these practices, as such, can be regarded as an exercise of fundamental rights. In implementing their duties under Article 20 of the ICCPR, States Parties must bear in mind their obligations under Article 19 of the ICCPR. On this point, the HRC has underlined that 'Articles 19 and 20 are compatible with and complement each other. The acts that are addressed in Article 20 are all subject to restriction pursuant to Article 19, paragraph 3.'[134] In comparing the two articles, the HRC noted that 'it is with regard to the specific forms of expression indicated in Article 20 that States Parties are obliged to have legal prohibitions.'[135] In *Ross v Canada*, the HRC underlined that 'restrictions on expression which may fall within the scope of Article 20 must also be permissible under Article 19, paragraph 3.'[136] Nowak underlines that Article 20 is closely interrelated to Article 19 but also to Articles 18 and 21.[137] The relation between Articles 20 and 21 of the ICCPR is significant in the realm of the far-right as this movement manifests itself in groups advocating hatred. However, no explanation or analysis of this interrelationship has been provided by the HRC. General Comment 11 provides that States Parties are obliged to adopt necessary legislative measures prohibiting the actions referred to in Article 20 of the ICCPR.[138] The General Comment stipulates that, in order to ensure an efficient and effective implementation of Article 20, States Parties should create legislation that renders the advocacy described in Article 20(2) to be against public policy and provide for appropriate sanctions in the event that this law is violated.[139] In relation to the appropriate sanctions reference, 'the article, thus, does not require criminal penalties, at least not for less serious forms of

---

134 HRC General Comment 34: 'Article 19 – Freedom of Opinion and Expression' (2011) CCPR/C/GC/34, para. 50.

135 Ibid. para. 52.

136 Ross v Canada Communication no 736/1997 (18 October 2000) CCPR/C/70/D/736/1997, para. 10.6.

137 Manfred Nowak, *'U.N. Covenant on Civil and Political Rights: CCPR Commentary'* (2nd edn. Kehl am Rhein: Engel 2005) 471, para. 8.

138 HRC General Comment 11: 'Article 20 – Prohibition of Propaganda for War and Inciting National, Racial or Religious Hatred' (1994) HRI/GEN/1/Rev.1 at 12, para. 1.

139 Ibid. para. 2.

hate advocacy'[140] since the word 'appropriate' is used rather than 'criminal.' The question of sanctions will be discussed in more detail further down.

Article 20(2) of the ICCPR: definitions and notions

A 2012 Report of the Special Rapporteur on the Promotion and Protection of the Right to Freedom of Opinion and Expression sought to expand on the issue of hate speech, given the continuing challenge faced in identifying ways to reconcile the need to protect the right to freedom of opinion and expression and to combat intolerance, discrimination and incitement to hatred. Notwithstanding that Special Rapporteurs do not have any legally binding powers to compel States to take action, they are in a position to examine and report back on a country situation or a specific human rights issue. Through the aforementioned report, the Special Rapporteur aspired to underline basic principles of international human rights law with the aim of identifying elements to be used in ascertaining what type of expression amounts to advocacy of national, racial or religious hatred that constitutes incitement to discrimination, hostility or violence. Such a report can be used by the Special Rapporteur when dealing with reporting duties and can subsequently be used as a guide by States Parties.

In an effort to elucidate the terms contained in Article 20(2) ICCPR, the 2012 Report of the Special Rapporteur defined advocacy as 'explicit, intentional, public and active support and promotion of hatred towards the target group.'[141] The Special Rapporteur underlined that Article 20(2) only covers advocacy for hatred, which means that the hatred must amount to advocacy which constitutes incitement and that such incitement must lead to one of the listed consequences, namely discrimination, hostility or violence. The report defines 'hatred' as 'a state of mind characterized as intense and irrational emotions of opprobrium, enmity and detestation towards the target group.'[142] 'Incitement' is said to refer 'to statements about national, racial or religious groups that create an imminent risk of discrimination, hostility or violence against persons belonging to those groups.'[143] The notion of 'discrimination' is also given a broad meaning in the Special Rapporteur's report, it being understood as

> any distinction, exclusion or restriction made on the basis of race, colour, descent, national or ethnic origin, nationality, gender, sexual orientation, language, religion, political or other opinion, age, economic position, property, marital status, disability, or any other status that has the effect or purpose of impairing or nullifying the recognition, enjoyment or exercise, on an equal footing, of

140 Sandra Coliver, '*Striking a Balance: Hate Speech, Freedom of Expression and Non-Discrimination*' (Article 19, International Centre against Censorship, University of Essex, Essex 1992) 31.
141 Report of the Special Rapporteur on the Promotion and Protection of the Right to Freedom of Opinion and Expression (2012) A/67/357, para. 44(b).
142 Ibid. para. 44(a).
143 Ibid. para. 44(c).

all human rights and fundamental freedoms in the political, economic, social, cultural, civil or any other field of public life.

As well as terms, such as race and national or ethnic origin, which often feature in international documents within this arena, the definition offered incorporates grounds such as age, financial position, property and more. Further, 'hostility' is considered to be a 'manifestation of hatred beyond a mere state of mind,'[144] but the report recognises that this theme has received little attention in relevant case-law and needs to be considered further.[145] Lastly, 'violence' is defined as the use of physical force or power against another person, or against a group or community, which either results in, or has a high likelihood of resulting in, injury, death, psychological harm, maldevelopment or deprivation. This definition goes beyond the physical effects of violence, also recognising its psychosocial effects. It is adapted from the definition of violence given in the 2002 World Report on Violence and Health of the World Health Organization (WHO) which covers a broad range of outcomes including psychological harm, deprivation and maldevelopment.[146] As is noted in the WHO report, 'many forms of violence against women, children and the elderly, for instance, can result in physical, psychological and social problems that do not necessarily lead to injury, disability or death.'[147] By incorporating the aforementioned definition, the WHO, and subsequently the Special Rapporteur on the Freedom of Opinion and Expression, recognised the fact that violence does not necessarily need to result in injury or death but, nevertheless, may result in a burden on the different actors and individuals involved. This is of particular importance given that, defining outcomes solely in terms of injury or death 'limits the understanding of the full impact of violence on individuals, communities and society at large.'[148]

Thus, the aforementioned report offers more clarity on terms which are central to Article 20 of the ICCPR. However, problems still remain as to their exact meaning, predominantly because of a lack of clarity as to thresholds. For example, what is the threshold for the given emotions to be deemed 'intense and irrational'? What is the threshold that has to be met to ensure imminence, and what is to be considered as risk? The report offers no explanation thereto.

Article 20: the threshold test

In order for Article 20(2) of the ICCPR to be applicable, a certain threshold (albeit undefined and unexplained) must be reached. This can be discerned from the formulation of this provision given that it can only be enforced when the

---

144 Ibid. para. 44(e).
145 Ibid. para. 44(e).
146 Etienne G. Krug, Linda L. Dahlberg, James A. Mercy, Anthony B. Zwi & Rafael Lozano 'World Report on Violence and Health' (World Health Organization, Geneva, 2002) 4.
147 Ibid. 5.
148 Ibid.

hatred concerned does, in fact, amount to incitement to discrimination, hostility or violence. Further, a direct correlation between the violence and the target group needs to be ascertained. The Rabat Plan of Action states that there must be a high threshold when applying Article 20 of the ICCPR.[149] Further, as noted in the 2012 Report of the Special Rapporteur on the Promotion and Protection of the Right to Freedom of Opinion and Expression, 'the threshold of the types of expression that would fall under the provisions of Article 20(2) should be high and solid.'[150] This is also confirmed by the fact that Article 20 contains two parts, one which deals with the prohibition of war and the other which deals with the prohibition of advocacy of national, racial or religious hatred. By placing these two constituents under one roof, it can be deducted that the severity of hatred which it seeks to address in the latter part is of a particularly severe nature. In determining whether particular speech reaches the necessary threshold, the Special Rapporteur on the Promotion and Protection of the Right to Freedom of Opinion and Expression followed the seven-part test proposed by the NGO Article 19, underlining that States must take into account the 'severity, intent, content, extent, likelihood or probability of harm occurring as well as the imminence and context of the speech in question.'[151] The Rabat Plan of Action holds that to assess the severity of the hatred and, therefore, determine whether the high threshold is met, the possible issues to be considered are 'the cruelty of what is said or of the harm advocated and the frequency, amount and extent of the communications.'[152]

The reason for this high threshold is that, as a matter of principle, limitations of speech must remain an exception to the rule. In order to determine this threshold, the Rabat Plan of Action clarifies that Article 20 of the ICCPR needs to be read in conjunction with the freedom of expression as protected by Article 19 of the ICCPR.[153] The interrelationship between Article 19 and Article 20, more generally, was also considered during the drafting process of the ICCPR. In General Comment 11, the HRC has likewise addressed this issue, holding that the

> required prohibitions of Article 20 are fully compatible with the rights of freedom of expression, as contained in Article 19, the exercise of which carries with it special duties and responsibilities. General Comment 34 holds that 'Article 19 and 20 are compatible with and complement each other.[154]

149 Rabat Plan of Action on the Prohibition of Advocacy of National, Racial or Religious Hatred that constitutes Incitement to Discrimination, Hostility or Violence (2002) para. 22.
150 Ibid. para. 45.
151 Ibid. para. 79.
152 Ibid. para. 22.
153 Ibid. para. 11.
154 HRC General Comment 34: 'Article 19 – 'Freedom of Opinion and Expression' (2011) CCPR/C/GC/34, para. 50.

The HRC further held that Article 20 is subject to restrictions set out in Article 19(3).[155] Indeed, the three principles applied when restricting rights and freedoms, namely legality, proportionality and necessity, must also apply to Article 20 cases.

Article 20(2): jurisprudence of the Human Rights Committee

The HRC has dealt with three separate communications which are directly connected to Article 20(2) of the ICCPR and has adopted differing stances. In *J.R.T and the W.G. Party v Canada*, the applicant argued that his Article 19 rights had been violated given that the State Party had cut off the telephone services of tape recorded messages warning callers of international Jewry and its destructive effects. Here, as well as finding no case of a breach of Article 19 of the ICCPR, given the anti-Semitic and, thus, racially discriminatory nature of the messages which the applicant sought to disseminate, the HRC held that the messages 'clearly constitute the advocacy of racial or religious hatred which Canada has an obligation under article 20 (2) of the Covenant to prohibit.'[156] The Committee reached this conclusion, however, without offering any interpretative explanation of the general meaning of the terms and concepts contained in Article 20(2) and without clarifying the threshold for hatred. Twenty years on, the HRC was again hesitant in voicing its opinion regarding the interpretation and implementation of Article 20(2) of the ICCPR, this time in a case where the first and second authors directly alleged a breach of Article 20(2) of the Convention. More particularly, in *Vassilari, Maria et al. v Greece*, the Committee dealt with alleged discrimination against the Roma. Four local associations sent a letter to the University of Patras entitled 'Objection against the Gypsies: Residents gather signatures for their removal.' The first and second applicants filed a criminal complaint against the local associations under the Anti-Racism Law. The first and second applicants contended that the Patras Court failed to appreciate the racist nature of the impugned letter and effectively to implement the Anti-Racism Law aimed at prohibiting dissemination of racist speech. Upon examination of the case, the HRC considered that the authors had not sufficiently substantiated the facts of their case for the purpose of admissibility of their complaint under Article 20(2), making this part of the communication inadmissible.[157] As a result, the HRC could not arrive at any substantive conclusions as to the application and meaning of Article 20(2). In his dissenting individual opinion in this case, Mr Abdelfattah Amor complained that the Committee had not yet provided an opinion on the

155 Ibid.
156 J. R. T. and the W. G. Party v Canada, Communication no. 104/1981 (18 July 1981) CCPR/C/ OP/2 at 25, para. 8(b).
157 Vassilari v Greece, Communication no. 1570/2007, (29 April 2009) CCPR/C/95/D/ 1570/2007, para. 6.5.

applicability of Article 20(2) when dealing with individual communications.[158] Mr Amor went on to state that the Committee's approach to this article was 'neither logical nor legally sound'[159] which he argued had resulted in the uncertainty of Article 20's scope. In the case of *Mohamed Rabbae, A.B.S and N.A v The Netherlands*, the authors claimed to be victims of, *inter alia*, a violation of their rights under Article 20(2) as a result of statements made by Geert Wilders, Leader of the Dutch Freedom Party, and particularly that Wilders's acquittal by the domestic court was in contravention of Article 20(2). This was the first time that the HRC gave a relatively extensive analysis of Article 20(2). It held that this article secures the right of persons to be free from hatred and discrimination but holds that it is 'crafted narrowly' so as to ensure a protection of free speech. It recalled that free speech may incorporate 'deeply offensive' speech and speech which is disrespectful for a religion, except if the strict threshold of Article 20(2) is met.[160] The Committee recognised that the Netherlands had established a legislative framework to meet the obligations imposed by Article 20(2), and underlined that this allowed victims to trigger and participate in a prosecution. In this light, and given the existence, suitability and triggering of the framework of the Wilders's case, the Committee found that the State Party had taken the 'necessary and proportionate measures in order to "prohibit" statements made in violation of article 20(2)'[161]and, thus, found no violation.

As noted by the NGO Article 19, 'the wording of article 20 of the ICCPR is rarely, if ever, found enshrined in domestic legislation,'[162] while there exists a 'lack of reference to Article 20 of the ICCPR by state authorities'[163] and a potential 'ignorance of these provisions.'[164] Before 2016, the HRC had not been particularly helpful in elucidating the obligations of States Parties, as these arise from Article 20(2), which could potentially limit the effectiveness of its implementation within the national systems of States Parties. However, in the case against Wilders, it essentially found that what States Parties had to demonstrate was that they established a functional and relevant legal framework for the incorporation of Article 20(2) into national law. This obligation does not, however, come with an obligation to convict.[165]

158 Ibid. Individual Opinion of Committee Member Mr. Abdelfattah Amor (dissenting) para. 1.

159 Ibid.

160 Mohamed Rabbae, A.B.S and N.A v The Netherlands, Communication no. 2124/2011 (14 July 2016) CCPR/C/117/D/2124/2011, para. 10(4).

161 Ibid. para. 10(7).

162 Article 19 – Towards an Interpretation of Article 20 of the ICCPR: Thresholds for the Prohibition of Incitement to Hatred Work in Progress A study Prepared for the Regional Expert Meeting on Article 20, Organised by the Office of the High Commissioner for Human Rights, Vienna, February 8–9, 2010, 3 www.ohchr.org/Documents/Issues/Expression/ICCPR/Vienna/CRP7Callamard.pdf [accessed 8 May 2014].

163 Ibid.

164 Ibid.

165 Mohamed Rabbae, A.B.S and N.A v The Netherlands, Communication no. 2124/2011 (14 July 2016) CCPR/C/117/D/2124/2011, para. 10 (7).

Conclusion: Article 20(2) ICCPR

In sum, Article 20(2) of the ICCPR is undoubtedly a significant article in the realm of the far-right, imposing positive obligations on States to prohibit advocacy of national, racial or religious hatred constituting incitement to discrimination, hatred or violence. In doing so, it theoretically sets a high threshold so as to encompass activities which should fall within its ambit, bypassing those which are simply unpleasant for the State or society. Yet again, definitional issues constitute a difficulty as regards the applicability of this article, a problem which the Special Rapporteur on the Promotion and Protection of the Right to Freedom of Opinion and Expression sought to rectify through the clarification of key terms. However, given the reservations imposed by some States, the lack of jurisprudence brought to the HRC on this article, the lack of threshold clarity and the decision of the Committee to find inadmissible the one case that was brought on such grounds, the article remains under-developed, with relevant speech and activities being dealt with through the reservation clauses of the freedom of expression and the freedom of association.

Article 4(a): Regulating hate speech through the ICERD

Article 4(a) of the ICERD deals with racially discriminatory expression. Since several general elements of Article 4 were considered previously, this part will only focus on the role political parties exercise in the framework of expression as well as in the long-standing debate on the due regard clause, as incorporated in the introductory section of Article 4 and as applicable to Articles 4(a) and (b). Issues of sanctions and punishment will be assessed later on. Article 4 acknowledges the role played, or potentially played, by the freedom of expression as a tool that could be used to promote racial hatred and racial discrimination, and, therefore, obliges States to

> declare an offence punishable by law all dissemination of ideas based on racial superiority or hatred, incitement to racial discrimination, as well as all acts of violence or incitement to such acts against any race or group of persons of another colour or ethnic origin, and also the provision of any assistance to racist activities, including the financing thereof.

Article 4(a): Political parties and racist expression

The CERD has underlined the significant obligations held by politicians and political parties in relation to their expression and their obligation to refrain from Article 4(a) activities. In *Jama v Denmark*, the CERD held that States Parties must draw the attention of politicians and members of political parties to the particular duties and responsibilities incumbent upon them pursuant to

Article 4 of the Convention with regard to their speech and expression.[166] In a Concluding Observation to Denmark, the CERD held that

> political parties are encouraged to take steps to promote solidarity, tolerance, respect and equality by developing voluntary codes of conduct so that their members refrain from public statements and actions that encourage or incite racial discrimination.[167]

Moreover, the CERD broadly noted that 'persons holding or carrying out functions in the public or political spheres should not be permitted to contribute to expressions of racism and xenophobia'[168] thereby interfering with the freedom of expression of public figures.

Article 4(a): Compatibility with the freedoms of expression and association

One of the central issues, both in relation to academic commentary on Article 4(a) of the ICERD and its legal formulation, is the extent to which it is compatible with the freedom of expression. When considering this issue, one must take into consideration the 'due regard' clause as incorporated in Article 4. However, since this is applicable both to the freedom of expression and the freedom of association, it will be considered after the appraisal of Article 4 (b) and the freedom of association.

The position of the CERD in relation to the compatibility of Article 4(a) and the freedom of expression is clear. In its 2001 Concluding Observations on the U.S., the CERD stated that 'the prohibition of dissemination of all ideas based upon racial superiority or hatred is compatible with the right to freedom of opinion and expression, given that a citizen's exercise of this right carries special duties and responsibilities, among which is the obligation not to disseminate racist ideas.'[169] The Committee characterised as 'the extreme position'[170] the view that the implementation of Article 4 might impair or jeopardise freedom of opinion and expression. In indicating that a balance must be struck between the obligations under Article 4 and the freedoms of expression and association,

---

166 Jama v Denmark, Communication no. 41/2008, (21 August 2009) CERD/C/75/D/41/2008, para. 9.
167 CERD Concluding Observations: Denmark (2002) CERD/C/60/CO/5, paras. 110, 115 and 116.
168 CERD Report: Sweden (1994) A/49/18 paras. 194–208, paras. 197 and 199.
169 CERD Concluding Observations: United States of America (2001) CERD/C/59/Misc.17/Rev.3, para. 12.
170 CERD Study: 'Positive Measures Designed to Eradicate all Incitement to, or Acts of, Racial Discrimination: Implementation of ICERD Article 4,' New York, UN, 1986, para. 225. This study was prepared for the Second World Conference on Racism in 1983 as A/CONF.119/10.

it noted that those freedoms are not absolute and that 'liberty is not licence.'[171] Thus, in relation to the balancing exercise between freedom from racial discrimination, on the one hand, and freedom of expression, on the other, the CERD has underlined that a balance between the two is the most suitable way forward but, in order to tilt the scale, it has reiterated the lower status of hate speech in relation to other types of speech which are granted more protection. However, notwithstanding the conjectural nature of the CERD's position, it has not yet conducted an adequate theoretical appreciation of this position and of the actual balancing of potentially competing rights, the justification of the balancing exercise and the potential effects of restrictions. When considering the balance test between the rights and duties in question and the resulting reservations that have been imposed by States Parties to the article under consideration, an interesting point to consider is the legal status of reservations in international law. Thornberry pertinently asks whether the issue of reservations to Article 4 on the grounds of expression and/or association and assembly raises the question as to 'whether the prohibition of hate speech as expressed in ICERD is simply a rule of treaty law or represents customary international law on the basis of its intrinsic relationship to the norm of non-discrimination.'[172] Discussing this issue, Thornberry refers to the decision of the International Criminal Tribunal for Rwanda (ICTR) in *Nahimana et al.*, where the trial chamber found that 'hate speech that expresses ethnic and other forms of discrimination violates the norm of customary international law prohibiting discrimination.'[173] Finding that it falls within the framework of international customary law would undoubtedly have consequences not only to the hierarchal significance of this article but also to the legitimacy of reservations imposed. However, the CERD has made no such reference. Nevertheless, when making a parallel with the ICTR case, the genocidal context and heinous consequences of the hate speech in question must be borne in mind.

Article 4 ICERD is problematic both in theory and in practice. Mahalic and Mahalic note that, the format of Article 4, which focusses primarily on protecting persons from racial discrimination, implies that 'in case of conflict the balance between competing freedoms should be struck in favour of persons' right to freedom from racial discrimination.'[174] This also seems to be the route adopted by the CERD. For example, in its General Recommendation 15, the CERD noted that 'the prohibition of the dissemination of all ideas based upon

171 Stephanie Farrior, 'Molding The Matrix: The Historical and Theoretical Foundations of International Law Concerning Hate Speech.' (1996) 14 *Berkley Journal of International Law* 1, 50.

172 Patrick Thornberry, 'Forms of Hate Speech and the Convention on the Elimination of all Forms of Racial Discrimination' (2010) 5 *Religion and Human Rights* 2, 105.

173 Nahimana et al. v the Prosecutor (28 November 2007) Case No. ICTR-99-52-A, para. 1076.

174 Stephanie Farrior, 'Molding The Matrix: The Historical and Theoretical Foundations of International Law Concerning Hate Speech.' (1996) 14 *Berkley Journal of International Law* 1, 92.

racial superiority or hatred is compatible with the right to freedom of opinion and expression.'[175] Kean considers this General Recommendation to be a strict call for protection from racist expression and notes the disregard therein of the due regard clause and the resulting obligations.[176] The strictness and rigour attached to banning racist expression and the very nature of the ICERD as a document against racial discrimination can be considered as a tilting factor of the balancing scale, leading to unjustified and/or illegitimate and/or unsubstantiated outcomes.

Sanctioning bad expression: limitations and regulations

As well as positively providing for freedom of expression and stipulating the grounds on which this freedom can be restricted, Article 20(2) of the ICCPR and Article 4 of the ICERD request that certain types of expression are punishable by law. Article 20(2) of the ICCPR stipulates that 'any advocacy of national, racial or religious hatred that constitutes incitement to discrimination, hostility or violence shall be prohibited by law,' while Article 4(a) of the ICERD declares 'an offence punishable by law all dissemination of ideas based on racial superiority or hatred, incitement to racial discrimination...' A notable difference between these two provisions is that the ICCPR states that speech and activities falling within the framework of Article 20(2) should be prohibited by law but makes no reference to whether such activities or the perpetrators should be punished, whereas Article 4(a) of the ICERD clearly underlines that the activities described therein constitute an offence punishable by law. General Comment 11 of the HRC fills the 'sanction gap' in Article 20 by noting that, for this article to be effective, there needs to be a law stipulating that propaganda and advocacy are against public policy which provides for a sanction in the event of a violation of the provisions therein.[177] Thus, this section emanates from the premise that Article 20(2) also requires the sanctioning of activities falling within its framework. The type of sanction which is appropriate for extremist expression is an intricately complex question.[178] This is particularly true, as neither Article 20 nor Article 4 stipulate precisely how these articles should be prohibited or punished. Several initiatives and documents have tried to elucidate how hate speech should be prohibited and/or punished, with varying positions emerging when dealing with the two articles. In fact, the HRC has emphasised the need to punish acts

---

175 CERD General Recommendation 15: 'Measures to Eradicate Incitement to or Acts of Discrimination' (1994) A/48/18 at 114, para. 4.

176 David Kean, *'Caste – Based Discrimination in International Human Rights Law'* (1st edn. Ashgate, Aldershot 2007) 195.

177 HRC General Recommendation11: 'Compilation of General Comments and General Recommendations Adopted by Human Rights Treaty Bodies' (1984) HRI/GEN/1/Rev.6 at 134, para. 2.

178 Stephanie Farrior, 'Molding The Matrix: The Historical and Theoretical Foundations of International Law Concerning Hate Speech' (1996) *Berkley Journal of International Law* 1, 10.

falling within the framework of Article 20(2) but grants the States discretion in choosing the type of punishment. More particularly, in its Concluding Observations to Egypt, the Committee held that 'the State Party must take whatever action is necessary to punish such acts by ensuring respect for article 20(2).'[179]

First, in relation to Article 20(2), the Special Rapporteur noted that 'there is no requirement to criminalize such expression'[180] and, more particularly, 'only serious and extreme instances of incitement to hatred, which would cross the seven-part threshold, should be criminalized.'[181] The seven-part threshold was adopted by the Special Rapporteur in his 2012 report and has been further discussed in the previous section related to the threshold discussion on Article 20. In less serious cases, the Special Rapporteur is of the view that States should adopt civil laws, underlining that there are instances where neither criminal nor civil sanctions are justifiable. Thus, 'laws to combat hate speech must be carefully construed and applied by the judiciary not to excessively curtail legitimate types of expression.'[182] The report underlines that when hate is expressed by politicians and public authorities, additional sanctions should be imposed, including those of a disciplinary nature.[183] The Rabat Plan of Action underlined that 'criminal sanctions related to unlawful forms of expression should be seen as last resort measures'[184] and that other types of action, such as civil and administrative sanctions and remedies, pecuniary and non-pecuniary damages as well as the right of correction and the right of reply must also be taken into account.

The Rabat Plan of Action recommended that, in order to clarify the situation of punishment and as a matter of general principle, without regard to a particular article, a distinction should be made between three types of expression, namely, expression that constitutes a criminal offence, expression that is not criminally punishable but may justify other types of sanctions and expression that does not give rise to any such sanctions but is still problematic in terms of the respect for the rights of others.[185] However, no explanation is made as to which types of expression fall within each section, although it nevertheless serves as a guideline for States seeking to regulate the sanctioning process of hate speech.

In relation to Article 4(a) of the ICERD, the sanctioning of prohibited activities falling within its framework constituted an intricate issue from the time of its drafting. For example, the Colombian delegate at the Conference which adopted the 1965 ICERD stated that

---

179 HRC Concluding Observations: Egypt (2002) ICCPR A/58/40 Vol. I, para. 18.
180 Report of the Special Rapporteur on the Promotion and Protection of the Right to Freedom of Opinion and Expression (2012) A/67/357, para. 47.
181 Ibid.
182 Ibid. para. 76.
183 Ibid. para. 81.
184 Rabat Plan of Action on the Prohibition of Advocacy of National, Racial or Religious Hatred that constitutes Incitement to Discrimination, Hostility or Violence (2002) para. 22.
185 Ibid. para. 6.

punishing ideas, whatever they may be, is to aid and abet tyranny, and leads
to the abuse of power ... As far as we are concerned and as far as democracy
is concerned, ideas should be fought with ideas and reasons; theories must
be refuted by arguments and not by the scaffold, prison, exile, confiscation
or fines.[186]

The Colombian approach was not adopted but neither was a solely criminal approach to Article 4 offences. Article 4 underlines that any punishment must
be granted 'with due regard to the principles embodied in the Universal Declaration of Human Rights and the rights expressly set forth in article 5 of this
Convention.' There has been a fair amount of discourse in relation to whether
hate speech and incitement to racial discrimination should fall within the ambit
of criminal law, or whether it would be more suitable to tackle such phenomena
through the civil law framework. This discourse has primarily come about due
to the fact that the nature of the punishment is not explicitly stated in the Convention itself or by the CERD.

   In addition to the fact that there is no clear route demonstrated by the CERD
on this issue, the Committee has also given mixed signals as to the nature of
punishment. Mahalic and Mahalic argue that 'most Committee members have
interpreted the phrase offense punishable by law to mean the imposition of criminal liability.'[187] This, for example can be demonstrated by the CERD requesting
States Parties to inform it of special criminal legislation designed for purposes
of the implementation of Article 4.[188] It has also referred to the criminal nature
of sanctions in other documents, including its Concluding Observations to Belgium in which it stated that 'adjustments should be made to the Constitution
and the laws to permit more effective criminal prosecution of racist, nugatory or
discriminatory writings.'[189] Further, in relation to incitement, the CERD noted
that 'the severe punishment of persons found guilty of incitement to racial hatred
has no doubt contributed to the improvements in the State Party.'[190] When talking of racism more generally and, thus, also racist expression, the CERD noted
that 'States parties should fully comply with the requirements of Article 4 of the
Convention and criminalize all acts of racism.'[191] However, in *Yilmaz-Dogan v
The Netherlands*, the Committee took a different stance and instead gave leeway
to States Parties in relation to the necessity of criminal punishment. It noted that
Article 4 does not adopt an absolutist approach to the requirement of criminal

---

186 U.N. Doc A/PV. 1406 at 42–43 (1965).
187 Drew Mahalic & Joan Gambee Mahalic, 'The Limitation Provisions of the International Convention on the Elimination of all Forms of Racial Discrimination' (1987) *9 Human Rights
   Quarterly* 1, 92.
188 Decision 3(vii) adopted by the Committee on 4 May 1973.
189 CERD Concluding Observations: Belgium (1997) CERD/C/304/Add.26, para. 226.
190 CERD Concluding Observations: Germany (1997) CERD/C/304/Add.24, para. 157.
191 CERD General Recommendation 31: The Prevention of Racial Discrimination in the Administration and Functioning of the Criminal Justice System (2005) A/60/18 (2005) 98, para. 4.

punishment by holding that 'the freedom to prosecute criminal offences ... is governed by considerations of public policy ... in the light of the guarantees laid down in the Convention.'[192] Also, in a case against Germany, the Committee acknowledged that the fact that the author who drafted a discriminatory letter against the Roma had been suspended from his employment in the police force meant that the letter 'carried consequences for its author, as disciplinary measures were taken against him.'[193] This statement reflects that the Committee considered non-criminal measures to be sufficient for the punishment of perpetrators.

In relation to Article 20(2) of the ICCPR, any advocacy of national, racial or religious hatred that constitutes incitement to discrimination, hostility or violence shall be prohibited by law, although only incitement which is of a particularly serious nature should, according to the Special Rapporteur and the Rabat Plan of Action, merit criminal punishment. The sanctioning process in the framework of Article 4 of the ICERD places more emphasis on the criminal nature of such sanctions, while also accepting other types of punishment. Moreover, the CERD has clearly stated that 'it is not the Committee's task to decide in abstract whether or not national legislation is compatible with the Convention but to consider whether there has been a violation in the particular case.'[194] Thus, the guidelines as to the nature of prohibitions and punishments to be imposed for hate speech have been contradictory at times. This is particularly so in relation to the different approach taken *vis-à-vis* Article 20(2) and Article 4(a) which, in essence, pursue very similar objectives.

Conclusion: regulating, prohibiting and sanctioning radical rhetoric

International human rights law provides for free speech, notes that this freedom carries with it special duties and responsibilities and does not consider hate speech to fall within the framework of free speech. Although a number of countries expressed reservations when ratifying the documents discussed earlier, and particularly Article 20(2) ICCPR and Article 4 (ICERD), 'ultimately, international conventions both reflect and reinforce a broad consensus that it is acceptable to constrain free speech in order to limit racist expression.'[195] This may be ensured by limiting the freedom of expression of extremist groups through Article 19 of the ICCPR when the need arises and when limitation grounds are applicable. In addition, Article 20(2) of the ICCPR and Article 4(a) of the ICERD positively

---

192 Yilmaz-Dogan v The Netherlands, Communication no. 1/1984, CERD/C/36/D/1/1984 (10 August 1988) para. 9.4.
193 Zentralrat Deutscher Sinti und Roma et al. v Germany, CERD/C/72/D/38/2006 (3 March 2008) CERD/C/72/D/38/2006, para. 7.7.
194 Er v Denmark, Communication no. 40/2007, CERD/C/71/D/40/2007 (8 August 2007) para. 7.2.
195 Erich Bleich, *'The Freedom to be Racist, How the United States and Europe Struggle to Preserve Freedom and Combat Racism'* (1st edn. Oxford University Press, Oxford 2011) 6.

oblige States to prohibit hate speech. The key problems to the applicability and enforcement of the previous articles relate to issues of definition, the type of sanction that should be applied and to the limited analysis conducted by the respective monitoring body in terms of meanings and thresholds.

An overview of freedom of association and assembly in UN instruments

As well as the freedom of expression, freedom of assembly and freedom of association are key vehicles for the promotion of political, philosophical, social and other belief systems and ideologies. Freedom of assembly and association are interrelated and are also interconnected with the freedom of expression.[196] 'All these rights allow individuals to come together and promote their ideas and interests.'[197] General Comment 25 of the HRC states that citizens' participation in public affairs and debate is facilitated by ensuring freedom of expression, assembly and association.[198]

On a UN level, the freedoms of assembly and association are protected by the UDHR and the ICCPR. These freedoms are not absolute, and as the limitation clauses incorporated in the ICCPR provision show, and as highlighted by UN Resolution 15/21 on the rights to freedom of peaceful assembly and of association, adopted by the Human Rights Council, which mandated the Special Rapporteur on the rights to freedom of peaceful assembly and of association, these freedoms

> can be subject to certain restrictions, which are prescribed by law and which are necessary in a democratic society in the interests of national security or public safety, public order (ordre public), the protection of public health or morals or the protection of the rights and freedoms of others.[199]

Further, Article 4(b) of the ICERD recognises that the freedom of association can be abused by groups promoting racial discrimination and positively requests States to prohibit such organisations. Thus, as with the freedom of expression, the international framework protects the freedom of association and assembly from State interference. At the same time, there are some limitations which can be imposed for certain types of speech, which also incorporate a State obligation to prohibit particular types of groups which associate for the purpose of promoting and inciting racial discrimination.

The freedoms of association and assembly are key themes in any discussion of the far-right, given that such movements associate as political parties as well as

---

196 Jeremy McBride 'Freedom of Association' in Rhona Smith & Christien van den Anker (eds.), *'The Essentials of Human Rights'* (1st edn. Routledge, London 2005) 18.

197 Ibid.

198 HRC General Comment 25 'General Comments under Article 40, para. 4, of the International Covenant on Civil and Political Rights' (1996) CCPR/C/21/Rev.1/Add.7, para. 1.

199 Human Rights Council Resolution 15/21 (2010): Mandate of the UNSR.

unregistered groups and non-group movements in order to promote their mission and vision. Further, the freedom of assembly, in the form of demonstrations and rallies, is also a characteristic of such movements. Thus, the next section will first consider Article 20 of the UDHR, which deals with assembly and association together. It will then appraise the freedom of assembly, as protected by the ICCPR, following which it will provide an overview of the meaning of association under international law and consider the grounds on which association can be legitimately restricted. Also, given the direct correlation between the far-right and racial discrimination, the next section will look at the ICERD and the obligation it imposes on States to prohibit organisations from promoting racial discrimination. The overarching aims of this section are to comprehend what tools international law grants States to respond to the assembly and association of far-right groups and what types of assemblies and associations fall within the net of prohibition. Namely, for purposes of restriction, is it sufficient for these groups and/or their assemblies to promote anti-democratic values or must such promotion go hand in hand with (an actual threat of) violence?

Freedom of assembly and association under the Universal Declaration of Human Rights

Article 20 of the UDHR states that:

1   Everyone has the right to freedom of peaceful assembly and association.
2   No one may be compelled to belong to an association.

The UDHR incorporates the freedoms of assembly and association in one article, Article 20 which sets out no limitation to the right to freedom of peaceful assembly and association. The freedom of assembly and association, as provided for by this document, fall under the general limitation clauses of Articles 29 and 30, as in the case of expression. Furthermore, limitations to the freedom of assembly and association, in particular, must be considered in light of the historical setting of the UDHR with the document being 'born out of the experience of the war that had just ended'[200] as explained at the start of this chapter. Thus, in addition to Article 7, which protects persons against incitement to discrimination, it can be argued that the Declaration does not afford protection to racist associations or racist assemblies of such association, taking into account the atrocities that occurred in the name of National Socialism, which triggered the development of the international human rights framework under discussion. The argument in favour of such a position is reinforced by the existence of the principles of equality and non-discrimination as protected throughout the Declaration as well as the general limitation clauses.

---

200 Johannes Morsink, *'The Universal Declaration of Human Rights, Origins, Drafting and Intent'* (1st edn. University of Pennsylvania Press, Philadelphia PA, 1999) 36.

Just as for non-discrimination and freedom of expression, the Declaration has paved the normative path for the subsequent limitations, qualifications and restrictions, as provided for by the ICCPR, and incorporated them in the clauses pertaining to assembly and association. Furthermore, the ICERD has taken a more specific leap towards combatting racial discrimination through tackling associations which promote it.

Freedom of assembly under the ICCPR

Article 21 of the ICCPR holds that:

> The right of peaceful assembly shall be recognised. No restrictions may be placed on the exercise of this right other than those imposed in conformity with the law and which are necessary in a democratic society in the interests of national security or public safety, public order (ordre public), the protection of public health or morals or the protection of the rights and freedoms of others.

The Special Rapporteur on the Rights to Freedom of Peaceful Assembly and of Association has defined assembly as 'an intentional and temporary gathering in a private or public space for a specific purpose.'[201] He also stressed that assemblies play a central role in 'mobilizing the population and formulating grievances and aspirations, facilitating the celebration of events and, importantly, influencing States public policy.'[202] In his 2012 report, the Special Rapporteur, therefore, underlined the positive duty that States have actively to protect the right to assembly and to enable the exercising of the right to freedom of peaceful assembly. Nevertheless, he emphasised that 'international human rights law only protects assemblies that are peaceful, i.e. those that are not violent, and where participants have peaceful intentions, which should be presumed.'[203] This is notwithstanding the fact that sporadic acts of violence by others must not prevent individuals from exercising this right.[204] Thus, protection is provided to assemblies which are physically non-violent but also thematically peaceful. The Special Rapporteur noted that States must refrain from interfering with the right to peaceful assembly and that the best practice is 'laws governing freedom of assembly [that] both avoid blanket time and location prohibitions and provide for the possibility of other less intrusive restrictions.'[205] Once again, prohibition is to be considered 'a measure of last resort … when a less restrictive response would not achieve the legitimate aim(s).'[206] Here, the question is whether assemblies

---

201 'Report of the Special Rapporteur on the Rights to Freedom of Peaceful Assembly and of Association' (21 May 2012) A/HRC/20/27, para. 24.
202 Ibid.
203 Ibid.
204 Ibid. para. 49.
205 Ibid. para. 39.
206 Ibid. para. 39.

of far-right groups which promote ideologies contrary to democratic values and, thus, create an environment conducive to discrimination contravene the 'peaceful intentions' condition. Taking the general stance of the UN towards speech and activities promoting racial discrimination and hate in the framework of non-discrimination and expression, and broadly interpreting the aforementioned requirement of peaceful intentions to incorporate the general notion of peace and democracy rather than just physical peace, it can be argued that any far-right assemblies are not protected by this freedom. Even though, at this point, this conclusion is based on generalised interpretations given the lack of further explanation by relevant bodies, the argument is particularly supported when considered in conjunction with Article 4 of the ICERD within this framework, which prohibits the promotion and incitement of racial discrimination, thereby, demonstrating the UN's intolerance towards such phenomena.

Freedom of association under the ICCPR: a general overview

Article 22, ICCPR stipulates that:

1   Everyone shall have the right to freedom of association with others, including the right to form and join trade unions for the protection of his interests.
2   No restrictions may be placed on the exercise of this right other than those which are prescribed by law and which are necessary in a democratic society in the interests of national security or public safety, public order (ordre public), the protection of public health or morals or the protection of the rights and freedoms of others. This article shall not prevent the imposition of lawful restrictions on members of the armed forces and of the police in their exercise of this right.

The freedom of association is a far-reaching one, encompassing a variety of activities and processes of an association. In Communication 1274/2004, the HRC observed that 'the right to freedom of association relates not only to the right to form an association, but also guarantees the right of such an association freely to carry out its statutory activities. The protection afforded by Article 22 extends to all activities of an association [...].'[207] As noted in *Kungurov v Uzbekistan*, this 'guarantees the right of such an association freely to carry out its statutory activities'[208] and, as such, 'the denial of state registration of an association must satisfy the requirements of paragraph 2...'[209]

---

207 Korneenko et al. v Belarus, Communication no. 1274/2004 (10 November 2006) CCPR/
    C/88/D/1274/2004, para. 7.2.
208 Ibid. para. 8.2.
209 Kungurov v Uzbekistan, Communication no. 1478/2006 (15 September 2011) CCPR/
    C/102/D/1478/2006, para. 8.2.

What is an association under international law?

The UN has defined an association as 'any groups of individuals or any legal entities brought together in order to collectively act, express, promote, pursue or defend a field of common interests.'[210] This definition extends '*inter alia* to civil society organizations, clubs, cooperatives, NGOs, religious associations, political parties, trade unions, foundations or even online associations such as the Internet which have been instrumental, for instance, in facilitating active citizen participation in building democratic societies.'[211] All such entities have the right to associate and this right applies for the entire life span of the association.[212] The Special Rapporteur has underlined that the right to freedom of association equally protects associations that are not registered.[213] Further, political parties are defined as 'a free association of persons, one of the aims of which is to participate in the management of public affairs, including through the presentation of candidates to free and democratic elections.'[214] Moreover, the Special Rapporteur notes that the central differences between political parties and other associations is that the former can be part of elections and subsequently form governments.[215] Far-right groups can take the form of registered political parties and, thereby, as a result of this status, enjoy particular protection under this framework. The position of the Special Rapporteur on the rights to freedom of peaceful assembly and of association is that, notwithstanding the important role played by political parties in a society, parties which adopt an extremist ideology often strike at democracy itself and, as a result, cannot enjoy the protection habitually afforded by the freedom of association.[216] Far-right groups can also take the form of unregistered subgroups which are looser in their structure. In addition to political parties, the CERD has recognised the existence of 'non-political groups and associations which disseminate ideas based on racial superiority or hatred.'[217] Based on the previous definitions, they, too, fall within the framework of an association since they seek to promote a common interest as international law does not require that they are registered or structured in a particular manner. The fact that a particular reference to such subgroups is not made in the aforementioned definition does not exclude them from the framework as it stipulates that the definition extends, *inter alia*, to the types referred to.

210 Report of the Special Rapporteur on the Rights to Freedom of Peaceful Assembly and of Association (21 May 2012) A/HRC/20/27, para. 51.
211 Ibid. para. 52.
212 Ibid. para. 75.
213 Ibid. para. 31.
214 Ibid. para. 9.
215 Ibid. para. 9.
216 HRC General Comment 18: 'Non-Discrimination' (1994) HRI/GEN/1/Rev.1, para. 5.
217 CERD Concluding Observations: Poland (1997) CERD/C/304/Add.36, para. 476.

Limiting the freedom of association under the ICCPR

The freedom of association, as enshrined in the ICCPR, is an important but not absolute human right as it can be limited for certain reasons and in certain circumstances which remind us of those in which the freedom of assembly and the freedom of expression can be limited. Article 22(2) of the ICCPR holds that such restrictions can be imposed on this right if they are prescribed by law and are necessary in a democratic society in the interests of national security or public safety, public order (ordre public), the protection of public health or morals or the protection of rights and freedoms. The HRC has tried to clarify the interpretation of the freedom of association under the ICCPR. In *Zvozskov v Belarus*, the HRC underlined that the reference to democratic society, in the context of Article 22, indicates that the functioning of association including those 'which peacefully promote ideas not necessarily favourably viewed by the government or the majority of the population, is a cornerstone of a democratic society.'[218] In *Belyatsky et al. v Belarus*, the Committee noted that 'the mere existence of reasonable and objective justification for limiting the right to freedom of association is not sufficient. The State Party must further demonstrate that the prohibition of an association is necessary to avert a real and not only hypothetic danger to national security or democratic order.'[219] General Comment 31 of the HRC, on the nature of the general legal obligation imposed on States Parties to the Covenant, holds that 'where such restrictions are made, States must demonstrate their necessity and only take such measures as are proportionate to the legitimate aim pursued.'[220] In addition, the Special Rapporteur on the Rights to Freedom of Peaceful Assembly and Association notes that any restriction should be 'strictly proportional to the legitimate aim pursued and used only when softer measures would be insufficient.'[221] The Special Rapporteur underlined that 'the suspension and the involuntary dissolution of an association are the severest types of restrictions on freedom of association'[222] and that such practices should only be permissible where there is a 'clear and imminent danger resulting in a flagrant violation of national law, in compliance with international human rights law.'[223] In relation to limitations, he stressed that 'freedom is to be considered the rule and its restriction the exception.'[224] In *Belyatsky et al. v Belarus*, the Committee held that the State

---

218 Ibid. para. 7.2.
219 Ibid. para. 7.3.
220 HRC General Comment 31: 'Nature of the General Legal Obligation on States Parties to the Covenant' (2004) CCPR/C/21/Rev.1/Add.13, para. 6.
221 Report of the Special Rapporteur on the Rights to Freedom of Peaceful Assembly and of Association (21 May 2012) A/HRC/20/27.
222 Ibid. para. 75.
223 Ibid.
224 Report of the Special Rapporteur on the Rights to Freedom of Peaceful Assembly and of Association (7 August 2013) A/68/299, para. 18.

Party must prove that 'less intrusive measures would be insufficient to achieve the same purpose.'[225] It is, thus, clear that the dissolution of an association should be a measure of last resort, imposed only when the limitation grounds, as incorporated into this article, are applicable, always taking into consideration the principle of proportionality and ensuring that the limitations are prescribed by law and are necessary in a democratic society.

In relation to the limitation of the freedom of association of political parties in the form of their prohibition, the Special Rapporteur noted that these entities can choose and promote ideas that are unpopular with authorities and the public, more generally, as this permits pluralism.[226] However, in the event that a political party or any of its candidates

> uses violence or advocates for violence or national, racial or religious hatred constituting incitement to discrimination, hostility or violence ... or when it carries out activities or acts aimed at the destruction of the rights and freedoms enshrined in international human rights law ... it can be lawfully prohibited.[227]

The word 'can' is interestingly placed here, as this means that States may opt to prohibit them but are not under an obligation to do so. This is not consistent with the obligations arising from Article 4(b) of the ICERD, as discussed further on, which oblige States to prohibit such parties.

In conclusion, notwithstanding the imposition of negative obligations on States to refrain from interfering with the aforementioned rights, the ICCPR also grants States the tools to interfere when considered necessary in order to pursue a legitimate aim. In curtailing the freedom of association, prohibitions of groups should be considered the option of last resort unless they contravene principles of international human rights law. Once again, taking into account the establishment, spirit and objectives of the international legal framework and key principles therein, such as non-discrimination and equality, States may prohibit far-right organisations under the ICCPR, but no explicit obligation to do so is contained therein.

Limiting the freedom of association and assembly under Article 4(b) of the ICERD

Article 4 of the ICERD is particularly significant in the far-right sphere, given that this movement organises itself through a variety of forms of association. Moreover, Article 4 'reflects the growing trend towards restricting racism that

---

225 Belyatsky et al. v Belarus, Communication no. 1296/2004 (24 July 2007) CCPR/C/90/D/ 1296/2004, para. 7.3.
226 Report of the Special Rapporteur on the Rights to Freedom of Peaceful Assembly and of Association (7 August 2013) A/68/299, para. 38.
227 Ibid.

spread throughout the world in the postwar era.'[228] However, any limitations of the freedom of association under Article 4(b) of the ICERD must be compatible with the freedom of association. The CERD has been alert to potential abuses of this clause as is reflected, for example, in its Concluding Observations to Russia in which it expressed its concern 'that the definition of extremist activity in the federal law of July 2002 is too vague to protect ... associations against arbitrariness in its application.'[229] In order to uphold Article 4(b) effectively and ensure a balanced approach, it is necessary to strike a legitimate balance between the freedom of association, on the one hand, and the freedom from discrimination on the other. This is a particularly tricky task and 'when specific anti-racist measures are concerned, opinions may diverge as to their compatibility with the requirements of the limitation clause.'[230] The international legal framework obliges States to prohibit certain types of association. Article 4(b) of the ICERD requests that States Parties 'declare illegal and prohibit organizations, and also organized and all other propaganda activities, which promote and incite racial discrimination, and shall recognize participation in such organizations or activities as an offence punishable by law.' The CERD has underlined that 'all provisions of article 4 ... are of a mandatory character, including declaring illegal and prohibiting all organizations promoting and inciting racial discrimination.'[231] In implementing this provision, States Parties must pay due regard to the principles embodied in the UDHR and the rights set out in Article 5 of the ICCPR. So, Article 4(b) imposes direct prohibitions of particular organisations and, thus, directly limits the freedom of association and, also, potentially affects the freedom of assembly as it declares illegal and prohibits 'organized and all other propaganda activities,' including activities which may take the form of an assembly. The majority of Committee members maintain that Article 4(b) categorically requires States Parties to outlaw racist organisations as well as their activities and that States Parties do not have a choice between these two tasks but are obliged to undertake both.[232] This interpretation is in line with the stance taken during the drafting of Article 4(b) where an amendment to declare illegal and prohibit only the activities of a racist organisation and not the organisation itself was rejected.[233] As noted in General Recommendation 15 of the CERD, organisations promoting racial discrimination 'have to be declared illegal and prohibited'[234] and, not only

228 CERD Study: Positive Measures Designed to Eradicate all Incitement to, or Acts of, Racial Discrimination: Implementation of ICERD, Article 4, New York, UN, 1986, para. 4. This study was prepared for the Second World Conference on Racism in 1983 as A/CONF.119/10.
229 HRC Concluding Observations: Russian Federation (2003) ICCPR A/59/40 vol. I 20, para. 6.
230 Eva Brems, 'State Regulation of Xenophobia v Individual Freedoms: the European View' (2002) 1 *Journal of Human Rights* 4, 483.
231 CERD Concluding Observations: Norway (2003) CERD/C/63/CO/8, para. 475.
232 Ibid.
233 Human Rights Commission 22nd Sess. (874th mtg) at 60 (E/CN.4/SR.827 (1966).
234 CERD General Recommendation 15: 'Measures to eradicate incitement to or acts of discrimination' A/48/18 at 114 (1994) para. 6.

that, 'participation in these organizations is, of itself, to be punished.'[235] The CERD has granted leeway to States Parties to decide on the precise nature of the punishment, welcoming, for example, a variety of penalties, including financial penalties on parties promoting racial discrimination.[236] However, the CERD has referred to sanctions amounting from Article 4(b) as being of a criminal nature. For example, in its Concluding Observations to Zimbabwe, it expressed its concern that the relevant law 'does not adequately address all the elements of article 4, particularly as regards the prohibition and criminalization of all organizations and propaganda activities that promote and incite racial discrimination.'[237] In a report to Hungary, it recommended amendments to the Hungarian Criminal Code in order to incorporate the requirements of Article 4(b) of the ICERD. [238]

The CERD has found that organisations which advocate racial discrimination, whether or not they commit acts of violence do, in fact, breach the peace.[239] Further, the CERD has underlined that groups promoting racist ideologies should fall within the framework of Article 4(b) regardless of their size or scope.[240] In one of its reports on the U.K. and Northern Ireland, the CERD found that, failing to prohibit the *BNP* and other groups and organisations of a racist nature and by allowing them to pursue their activities, the country was failing to implement Article 4, which calls for a condemnation of all organisations attempting to justify or promote racial hatred and discrimination.[241] Furthermore, the CERD has noted that the obligations arising from Article 4(b) include the prohibition of organisations in their entirety and not simply the prohibition of their activities.[242] Indeed, many Committee members appear to share the view that Article 4(b) requires States Parties to prohibit *ad limina* the establishment of racist organisations.[243] For example, the CERD has recognised that 'Article 4(b) places a greater burden upon such States to be vigilant in proceeding against such organizations at the earliest moment.'[244] Thus, the provision demonstrates the need to protect States from the danger of permitting racist organisations to function undeterred, gaining financial support, recruiting

235 Ibid.
236 CERD Concluding Observations: Belgium (2002) CERD/C/60/CO/2, para. 42.
237 CERD Concluding Observations: Zimbabwe (2000) CERD/C/304/Add.92, para. 197.
238 CERD Concluding Observations: Hungary (2002) CERD/C/431/Add.1, paras. 372 and 376.
239 CERD, 24th Sess. (538th mtg.) at 112–113 para. 15, CERD/C/SR.538 (1981); 26th Sess. (585th mtg.) at 117–118 para. 12, CERD/C/SR.585 (1984).
240 CERD 20th Sess. (440th mtg) at 63, paras. 8, 66, para. 19 CERD/C/SR.440 (1979).
241 CERD Report on the UK (1993) A/48/18, paras. 409–425, para. 416.
242 CERD Concluding Observations: Canada (2002) A/57/18(SUPP) paras. 315–343, paras. 335 and 338.
243 Drew Mahalic & Joan Gambee Mahalic, 'The Limitation Provisions of the International Convention on the Elimination of all Forms of Racial Discrimination' (1987) 9 *Human Rights Quarterly* 1, 100.
244 CERD General Recommendation 15: 'Measures to Eradicate Incitement to or Acts of Discrimination' (1994) A/48/18 at 114, para. 46.

members, implementing their mandate and becoming powerful, thereby, rendering later prohibition difficult.[245]

In sum, it is legitimate and, under Article 4(b), an obligation for States to ban an association, whether it is a political party or an unregistered group, if they are promoting or inciting racial hatred, regardless of whether or not they are violent. However, regardless of the obligations set out in Article 4(b), the Special Rapporteur has argued that a prohibition of a political party must constitute a last resort, which renders the situation more complex than it already is because of conflicting demands on States. Nevertheless, it can safely be said that the suppression of racist political associations (including bans) finds both direct and indirect support in human rights treaties, conventions, and declarations drafted by the UN. Some such treaties, notably Article 4 of the ICERD, go as far as making it compulsory or strongly recommended for States to impose certain restrictions on racist organisations, with such measures being in line with duties and obligations arising from the UDHR and Article 5 of the ICERD. Thus, the central point upon which Article 19 of the ICCPR and Article 4 of the ICERD differ is that the latter obliges States to prohibit groups promoting racial hate and discrimination whereas the former simply lays out the tools for States to interfere. In order to ensure a uniform approach to the assembly and association of the far-right, these two articles must be read in conjunction with each other.

The due regard clause of Article 4 ICERD

The central point of interest when considering Article 4(a) and Article 4(b) of the ICERD is the potential conflict that may arise as a result of the obligations emanating from the freedom of expression and the freedom of association. The question of whether the prohibition of association under Article 4(b) is consistent with the 'due regard' clause has been a matter of debate within the academic, legal and political arenas, with the obvious concern being that the prohibition of racist organisations can lead to abuse and places undue limitation on the right to freedom of association. As a result, many State representatives have explained that their governments have not outlawed racist organisations due to 'the difficulty of reconciling the right to freedom of association with the requirements of Article 4(b).'[246] This argumentation is extended to the freedom of expression and the freedom of assembly, as reflected in the following reservations. During the drafting process of Article 4, several States Parties voiced their concerns regarding its impact on other human rights and particularly expression and association. In fact, it is this very characteristic of the ICERD which has led Article 4 to being 'the subject of

245 Ibid.
246 Ibid.

different interpretations and a substantial number of reservations'[247] which have generally taken the form of explicitly limiting national obligations under this article, in light of the right to freedom of opinion and expression and the right to freedom of peaceful assembly and association. Nevertheless, the 'due regard clause,' as incorporated therein, acts as a safety net to the freedoms in questions and constitutes the thematic backdrop against which the aforementioned balance is to be found. Namely, this clause seeks to ensure that any regulation arising from Article 4 does not disregard the freedoms of expression, association and assembly.

Article 4 of the ICERD states that the provisions in parts a, b and c must be implemented 'with due regard to the principles embodied in the UDHR and the rights expressly set forth in article 5 of this Convention' which include, *inter alia*, the freedoms of opinion, expression, assembly and association. In particular, the due regard clause was inserted to 'protect against overly broad limitations on the freedoms of expression and association.'[248] For example, during the drafting procedures, Belgium underlined the importance it attached to Article 4 being read with due regard to the UDHR and the rights outlined in Article 5 of the ICERD and considered 'that the obligations imposed by Article 4 must be reconciled with the right to freedom of opinion and expression and the right to freedom of peaceful assembly and association.'[249] France followed a similar path stating that it interpreted the due regard clause of Article 4 as 'releasing the States Parties from the obligation to enact anti-discrimination legislation which is incompatible with the freedoms of opinion and expression and of peaceful assembly and association.'[250] Italy held that 'the obligations deriving from the aforementioned Article 4 are not to jeopardize the right to freedom of opinion and expression and the right to freedom of peaceful assembly and association.'[251] This approach, being the balancing of potentially conflicting rights, has also been adopted by other States Parties, such as the U.S., which, upon signing the ICERD, placed a reservation on Article 4 which stipulated that

> the Constitution of the United States contains provisions for the protection of individual rights, such as the right of free speech, and nothing in the

---

247 McGoldrick D & O'Donnell T, 'Hate Speech Laws: Consistency with National and International Human Rights Law' (1998) 18 *Legal Studies* 469.

248 Drew Mahalic & Joan Gambee Mahalic, 'The Limitation Provisions of the International Convention on the Elimination of all Forms of Racial Discrimination' (1987) 9 *Human Rights Quarterly* 1, 89.

249 Multilateral Treaties Deposited with the Secretary-general: Status as at 1 April 2009 by United Nations (2009), United Nations Publications, ST/LEG/SER.E/2610.

250 Reservation made by France to the International Convention on the Elimination of Racial Discrimination. Acceded to the Convention on 28 July 1971.

251 Declaration of Italy made upon signature of the International Convention on the Elimination of Racial Discrimination and confirmed upon ratification: Signed on 13 March 1968 and ratified on 5 January 1976.

Convention shall be deemed to require or to authorize legislation or other action by the United States of America incompatible with the provisions of the Constitution of the United States of America.[252]

Moreover, a total of 12 States out of the 87 signatories and 177 Parties have imposed such reservations.[253]

In relation to the meaning of the due regard clause, Mahalic and Mahalic refer to the equality principle laid down in Article 1 of the UDHR, the non-discrimination clause in Article 7 of the UDHR, the right to an effective remedy in Article 8 of the UHDR and the requirements of an international order whereby the rights set out in the Declaration are fully realised, as provided for by Article 28 therein. In this light, they argue that 'to have due regard for the Universal Declaration is to have due regard for the very principles upon which Article 4(a) and Article 4(b) are premised.'[254] Furthermore, as well as the aforementioned provisions, the UDHR provides for the freedom of expression under Article 19 and the freedom of assembly and association under Article 20. These articles do not incorporate limitation clauses but, instead, fall under the general limitations provided for by Articles 29 and 30. Thus, in order to give adequate regard to the UDHR principles in this ambit, one must decipher whether the speech in question contravenes Article 29, and particularly the respect for the rights and freedoms of others, morality, public order and the general welfare of a democratic society, or whether it destroys any of the other rights set out in the Declaration. Only then can it be ascertained whether or not freedoms of expression or assembly, as provided for by Articles 19 and 20 of the UDHR, can be invoked as rationales to limiting obligations set out in Article 4 of the UDHR.

Through its jurisprudence and other instruments, the Committee has given insight into how the 'due regard' clause is to be interpreted and applied in this field. In *Jewish Community of Oslo et al. v Norway*, the Committee attempted to explain what is meant by this doctrine by stating that 'it related generally to all principles embodied in the Universal Declaration of Human Rights, not only freedom of speech.'[255] In this light it held that

> to give the right to freedom of speech a more limited role in the context of Article 4 does not deprive the due regard clause of significant meaning, all

---

252 Reservation of the U.S. made upon signing of the International Convention on the Elimination of Racial Discrimination. Signed on 28 September 1966 and ratified on 21 October 1994.

253 Austria, Bahamas, Belgium, France, Ireland, Italy, Japan, Monaco, Papa New Guinea, Switzerland, the U.K. and the U.S.

254 Drew Mahalic & Joan Gambee Mahalic, 'The Limitation Provisions of the International Convention on the Elimination of all Forms of Racial Discrimination' (1987) 9 *Human Rights Quarterly* 1, 90.

255 The Jewish community of Oslo et al. v Norway (15 August 2005) Communication no. 30/2003, (CERD/C/67/D/30/2003) para. 10.5.

the more so since all international instruments that guarantee freedom of expression provide for the possibility, under certain circumstances, of limiting the exercise of this right.[256]

On this premise, the Committee noted that Sjolie, who had headed the march of a group known as the *Bootboys* in commemoration of the Nazi leader Rudolf Hess, made statements which were 'of an exceptionally/manifestly offensive character and are, thus, not protected by the due regard clause.'[257] During the months that followed the commemoration, violence against persons of African descent occurred in the area and a Ghanian teenager was stabbed to death. Norway commenced criminal proceedings against Sjolie, but the Supreme Court found that Sjolie was exercising his right to free speech. The case was taken to the CERD which found Sjolie's speech to be racist speech without any adequate critique or analysis but, instead, 'restate[d] the relevant passage and immediately qualifies it as racially discriminatory.'[258] The Committee then noted that his acquittal by the Supreme Court of Norway gave rise to a violation of Article 4 and consequently Article 6 of the ICERD. In reaching this decision, the Committee held that the 'freedom of speech has been afforded a lower level of protection in cases of racist and hate speech dealt with by other international bodies.'[259] The Committee's approach in this case, thus, demonstrates that the 'due regard' clause cannot be enforced unconditionally and that, in the event of racist speech, it does not constitute grounds for protecting the freedom of expression. This is reaffirmed by the CERD's position in General Recommendation 15, where it notes that 'the obligation not to disseminate racist ideas is of particular importance.'[260] Indeed, the CERD has underlined that the due regard clause cannot be called to be interpreted as 'cancelling or justifying a departure from the mandatory obligations set forth in Articles 4(a) and 4(b).'[261] In *TBB-Turkish Union in Berlin/Brandenburg*, the CERD found that Germany had violated its obligations by not prosecuting Sarrazin, former Finance Senator of the Berlin Senate, for his xenophobic statements. Here, the CERD found that his statements did, in fact, constitute racist speech but noted that Article 4 provides for due regard to be granted to the rights found in the UDHR. However, the CERD found the statements to constitute racist speech, without any theorisation of the matter and without a balance test of the speech's harm and

---

256 Ibid. para. 10.3.
257 Ibid. para. 10.5.
258 Matthias Goldmann & Mona Sonnen, 'Soft Authority against Hard Cases of Racially Discriminating Speech: Why the CERD Committee Needs a Margin of Appreciation Doctrine' (2016) 7 *Goettingen Journal of International* Law 1 7, 135.
259 The Jewish community of Oslo et al. v Norway (15 August 2005) Communication no. 30/2003 (CERD/C/67/D/30/2003) para. 10.5.
260 CERD General Recommendation 15: 'Measures to Eradicate Incitement to or Acts of Discrimination' A/48/18 at 114 (1994) para. 4.
261 CERD 18th Sess. (339 mtg). at 152, CERD/C/SR.399 (1978) para. 2.

freedom of expression, something which the due regard clause pursues. As noted by Goldmann and Sonnen, the CERD did not give any space for the consideration of the nature and impact of this speech. For example, it might have been a 'polemic, yet legitimate contribution to an ongoing political debate about essential values and interests of society.'[262] Either way, and whatever the determined result, if the CERD was sincere about the role and substance of the due regard clause, a balance and a well-rounded examination of the speech in question would have been effectuated. In addition, notwithstanding its previous findings that criminal sanctions for speech should be the last resort, the committee rejected Germany's position that non-criminal measures are sufficient, once again, without any extrapolation on how it reached this position.

As well as considering the meaning of the due regard clause more closely in the previous case, the CERD has tried to tackle the conflict between the competing rights through a variety of documents, a conflict which lies at the heart of the due regard debate. As early as 1983, the CERD noted that concern that Article 4 would contravene the objectives enshrined in the freedoms of expression, assembly and association was 'another factor hindering the full application of Article 4.'[263] Instead, the Committee suggested that a 'balance has to be struck between article 4(a) and freedom of speech, and between article 4(b) and freedom of expression.'[264] In striking this balance, the Committee noted that States Parties have an 'obligation to respect the right to freedom of opinion and expression when implementing Article 4.'[265] Nevertheless, neither the 'due regard' clause, as established in the ICERD, nor the principles set out in the UDHR offer a clear understanding of the balance that needs to be struck between freedoms or of how that balance is to be reached. The CERD has attempted to elucidate the meaning of the due regard clause and its impact on the interpretation and application of Article 4. It has underlined the need to understand the UDHR, in its entirety, when considering the due regard clause. However, these attempts have occurred on a very superficial level with no due regard sincerely and effectively being given to fundamental freedoms, such as that of expression, when seeking to evaluate the role and relevance of Article 4 in a particular case.

In sum, although the due regard clause was incorporated as a safety net for the protection of key freedoms, it has not properly come into the Committee's assessment of cases. Mahalic and Mahalic argue that the due regard clause does not greatly limit the obligations arising from Article 4, given that, under

---

262 Matthias Goldmann & Mona Sonnen, 'Soft Authority against Hard Cases of Racially Discriminating Speech: Why the CERD Committee Needs a Margin of Appreciation Doctrine' (2016) 7 *Goettingen Journal of International* Law 17, 136.
263 Patrick Thornberry, 'Forms of Hate Speech and the Convention on the Elimination of all Forms of Racial Discrimination' (2010) 5 *Religion and Human Rights* 97, 110.
264 Ibid.
265 CERD Concluding Observations: Belarus (2004) CERD/C/65/CO/2, para. 264.

Article 29(3), no one can enjoy the freedom of expression or association in a manner that goes against protecting others from racial discrimination, whereas Article 30 does not allow the exercise of these freedoms in a manner which destructs the rights of others to be free from racial discrimination.[266] Also, in relation to having due regard to Article 5 of the ICERD, the Committee has stated that this article cannot be used as a tool for avoiding duties arising under Article 4.[267] However, it could be argued that the CERD is not giving due regard to free speech and association and their importance for a functioning society, in particular since it has reached decisions banning, *inter alia*, anti-Semitic speech without a contextualisation or conceptualisation of the speech in question and its resulting harm. This approach will not make States Parties any more comfortable with the article in question.

Another route? Article 5 of the ICCPR: the destruction of the rights of others

The HRC has also turned to Article 5 of the ICCPR when dealing with the far-right. Article 5(1) of the ICCPR provides that

> nothing in the present Covenant may be interpreted as implying for any State, group or person any right to engage in any activity or perform any act aimed at the destruction of any of the rights and freedoms recognized herein or at their limitation to a greater extent than is provided for in the present Covenant.

This article prohibits and addresses a type of action that would have the effect of destroying the rights of freedoms protected in the ICCPR. An interesting interpretation and implementation of Article 5 can be seen in *M.A. v Italy*,[268] where the HRC applied Article 5 rather than Article 20(2) when considering a communication that did not primarily deal with advocacy but rather with the reorganisation of a dissolved fascist party. More specifically, the HRC found that the act for which *M.A.* was convicted, that being the reorganisation of the dissolved fascist party, did not receive the protection of the ICCPR as a result of the provisions of Article 5. Unfortunately, it did not further state any reasons as to why it reached this decision and it did not provide any interpretative understanding of key themes and provisions related to the applicability of Article 5. The lack of substantive reasoning in relation to Article 5 is unfortunate, since a sound assessment of Article 5 would have provided for a better

---

266 Drew Mahalic & Joan Gambee Mahalic, 'The Limitation Provisions of the International Convention on the Elimination of all Forms of Racial Discrimination' (1987) 9 *Human Rights Quarterly* 1, 90–91.

267 CERD Sess. (449th mtg.) at 156 para. 2, CERD/C/SR.449 (1979); 27th Sess. (620th mtg.) at 297 para. 19, CERD/C/SR.620 (1983).

268 M.A v Italy, Communication no. 117/1981 (21 September 1981) Supp. No. 40 (A/39/40).

understanding of the balance to be struck between the freedom of allegedly hateful association and the destruction of the rights and freedoms of others. Such a correlation, if adequately established, could also be extended to far-right rhetoric in the realm of freedom of expression. Instead, the HRC ousted the case from any Covenant protection without an assessment of the relevant article on the grounds of the group's allegedly (although unsubstantiated) hateful nature.

Sexual orientation and gender identity: the weakest link?

There is no ICERD equivalent which tackles discrimination against sexual orientation and gender identity nor are these grounds incorporated in ICCPR articles. Instead, in *Toonen v Australia*, the HRC held that the term 'sex' in Articles 2 and 26 of the ICCPR should be taken to include sexual orientation.[269] No equivalent jurisprudence exists that can assist with the interpretation of a relevant article of the ICCPR in the framework of gender identity. The exclusion of the actual terms from the ICCPR text and the fact that no other relevant covenant or convention exists to protect persons from, *inter alia*, hate, due to their sexual orientation and gender identity demonstrates a hierarchy[270] of characteristics that are protected from haters on an international level. Whilst, on a UN level, measures were taken to rectify this loophole through, *inter alia*, the Office for the High Commissioner for Human Rights' first report on violence against persons due to their sexual orientation and gender identity in 2011,[271] several resolutions passed by the Human Rights Council on LGBTI rights[272] and the appointment in 2016 of an independent expert on sexual orientation and gender identity,[273] there is no primary UN law on the matter, with measures constituting soft law approaches to the theme. Unfortunately, as will be demonstrated in the relevant chapters, this hierarchy is a characteristic of available law at a CoE and EU level. Whilst authors, such as Henkin, argue that this loophole arises, at least in part, from the

---

269 Toonen v Australia, Communication no. 488/1992 (31 March 1994) CCPR/C/50/D/488/1992, para. 8.7.
270 For the concept of hierarchies in relation to hate regulation, see, *inter alia*, Natalie Alkiviadou, 'Regulating Hatred: Of Devils and Demons?' (2018) 18 *International Journal of Discrimination and the Law* 4.
271 Report of the United Nations High Commissioner for Human Rights, Discriminatory laws and practices and acts of violence against individuals based on their sexual orientation and gender identity (2011) A/HRC/19/41.
272 See, *inter alia*, Human Rights Council Resolution: Protection against violence and discrimination based on sexual orientation and gender identity (adopted 30 June 2016) A/HRC/RES/32/2 and Human Rights Council resolution - Human rights, sexual orientation and gender identity (adopted 17 June 2011) A/HRC/RES/17/19.
273 See: Independent Expert on sexual orientation and gender identity: www.ohchr.org/en/issues/sexualorientationgender/pages/index.aspx [Accessed 10 October 2018].

fact that 'the major human rights treaties and most national constitutions were adopted prior to the emergence of LGBTI rights consciousness or advocacy movements,'[274] this justification does not stop the UN from adopting a new document of primary nature.

Chapter conclusion

In conclusion, given the temporal framework of the birth of international human rights law, the UN considered the possibilities of associations and assemblies being powerful tools for far-right movements. As such, it sought to limit the scope of these freedoms to be used by haters through limitation grounds of certain articles and through positive obligations on States as these emanate from Article 4 ICERD and Article 20 ICCPR. With no theoretical, contextual or conceptual backdrop, the UN has extended bans and prohibitions, including criminal penalties, to non-violent speech and groups, while it has given limited to no guidance to States in relation to the intricate themes of, *inter alia,* thresholds and definitions. It has also been random in its choice to use Article 5 in *M.A v Italy* with no explanation on why this article was chosen over, for example, the enforcement of a limitation clause. The result of this is that the UN framework lacks theoretical legitimacy and faces practical obstacles in relation to State enforcement, a matter which is particularly emphatic in State responses to Article 4 ICERD and Article 20(2) ICCPR. Moreover, the low threshold of Article 4, in terms of the ban on racist speech (regardless of a conceptualisation of harm/the reaching of a particular threshold) begs the question of whether the UN is actually in line with the protection of free speech as an historically recognised tenet of a democracy. In addition, the hierarchy of some protected characteristics such as race and religion, over others, such as sexual orientation and gender identity, is nothing more than an anathema to the very foundations of international human rights law.

Bibliography

International documents

CERD general recommendations

CERD General Recommendation 15: 'Measures to Eradicate Incitement to or Acts of Discrimination' (1985) A/40/18.
CERD General Recommendation 26: The Right to Seek Just and Adequate Reparation or Satisfaction (2000) A/55/18.
CERD General Recommendation 31: The Prevention of Racial Discrimination in the Administration and Functioning of the Criminal Justice System (2005) A/60/18.

---

274 Louis Henkin, Sarah Cleveland, Laurence Helfer, Gerarld Neuman & Diane Orentlicher, *'Human Rights'* (2nd edn., Foundation Press, Cleveland OH 2009) 1208.

CERD General Recommendation 32: The Meaning and Scope of Special Measures in the International Convention on the Elimination of Racial Discrimination (2009) CERD/C/GC/32.

CERD General Recommendation 35: Combatting Racist Hate Speech (2003) CERD/C/GC/35.

CERD concluding observations/reports

CERD Concluding Observations: Belarus (2004) CERD/C/65/CO/2.

CERD Concluding Observations: Belgium (1997) CERD/C/304/Add.26.

CERD Concluding Observations: Belgium (2002) CERD/C/60/CO/2.

CERD Concluding Observations: Canada (2002) A/57/18(SUPP) paras. 315–343.

CERD Concluding Observations: Denmark (2002) CERD/C/60/CO/5.

CERD Concluding Observations: Hungary (2002) CERD/C/431/Add.1.

CERD Concluding Observations: Germany (1997) CERD/C/304/Add.24.

CERD Concluding Observations: Israel (2012) CERD/C/ISR/CO/14-16.

CERD Concluding Observations: Lao People's Democratic Republic (2005) CERD/C/LAO/CO/15.

CERD Concluding Observations: New Zealand (2013) CERD/C/NZL/CO/18-20.

CERD Concluding Observation: Norway (2003) CERD/C/63/CO/8.

CERD Concluding Observations: Poland (2003) CERD/C/62/CO/6.

CERD Concluding Observations: Poland (1997) CERD/C/304/Add.36.

CERD Concluding Observations: United Kingdom (2003) CERD/C/63/CO/11.

CERD Concluding Observations: United States of America (2001) CERD/C/59/Misc.17/Rev.3.

CERD Concluding Observations: Zimbabwe (2000) CERD/C/304/Add.92.

CERD Report: Sweden (1994) A/49/18 paras. 194–208.

CERD Report on the United Kingdom (1993) A/48/18 paras. 409–425.

CERD Report 66th session and 67th session (2005) A/60/18.

CERD: other

CERD Study: Positive Measures Designed to Eradicate all Incitement to, or Acts of, Racial Discrimination: Implementation of ICERD, Article 4, New York, UN, 1986, para. 225. This study was prepared for the Second World Conference on Racism in 1983 as A/CONF.119/10.

CERD 2002 Statement on Racial Discrimination and Measures to Combat Terrorism, A/57/18 Chapter XI C.

HRC concluding observations

HRC Concluding Observations: Egypt (2002) ICCPR A/58/40 Vol. I.

HRC Concluding Observations: Lesotho (1999) CCPR/C/79/Add.106.

HRC Concluding Observations: Russian Federation (2003) ICCPR A/59/40 vol. I 20.

HRC general comments

HRC General Comment 11: Article 20 – Prohibition of Propaganda for War and Inciting National, Racial or Religious Hatred (1994) HRI/GEN/1/Rev.1.

HRC General Comment 18: Non-Discrimination (1994) HRI/GEN/1/Rev.1.

HRC General Comment 22: Article 18 – The Right to Freedom of Thought, Conscience and Religion (1994) HRI/GEN/1/Rev.1.

HRC General Comment 25: 'Article 25 – The Right to Participate in Public Affairs, Voting Rights and the Right of Equal Access to Public Service' (1996) CCPR/C/21/Rev.1/Add.7.

HRC General Comment 28: 'Article 3 – Equality of Rights between Men and Women' (2000) CCPR/C/21/Rev.1/Add.10.

HRC General Comment 31: 'Nature of the General Legal Obligation on States Parties to the Covenant' (2004) CCPR/C/21/Rev.1/Add.13.

HRC General Comment 34: 'Article 19: Freedoms of Opinion and Expression' (2011) CCPR/C/GC/34.

HRC general recommendations

HRC General Recommendation 11: 'Compilation of General Comments and General Recommendations Adopted by Human Rights Treaty Bodies' (1984) HRI/GEN/1/Rev.6 at 134.

Human Rights Council

Human Rights Council Resolution 15/21 (2010): Mandate of the UNSR.

Human Rights Council Resolution 16/18 (2011): Combating intolerance, negative stereotyping and stigmatization of, and discrimination, incitement to violence, and violence against persons based on religion or belief.

Human Rights Council Resolution 19/25 (2012): Combating intolerance, negative stereotyping and stigmatization of, and discrimination and incitement to violence and violence against persons based on religion or belief.

Special Rapporteurs

Mandate of Special Rapporteur on contemporary forms of racism, racial discrimination, xenophobia and related intolerance: www.ohchr.org/EN/Issues/Racism/SRRacism/Pages/OverviewMandate.aspx.

OHCHR Expert Workshops on the prohibition of incitement to national, racial or religious hatred, Expert workshop on Europe (2011) Joint submission by Mr. Heiner Bielefeldt, Special Rapporteur on Freedom of Religion or Belief; Mr. Frank La Rue, Special Rapporteur on the Promotion and Protection of the Right to Freedom of Opinion and Expression; Mr. Githu Muigai, Special Rapporteur on Contemporary Forms of Racism, Racial Discrimination, Xenophobia and Related Intolerance.

Report of the Special Rapporteur on the Promotion and Protection of the Right to Freedom of Opinion and Expression (2012) A/67/357.

Report of the Special Rapporteur on the Rights to Freedom of Peaceful Assembly and of Association (2012) A/HRC/20/27.

Report of the Special Rapporteur on the Rights to Freedom Peaceful Assembly and of Association (2013) A/68/299.

General Assembly

General Assembly Resolution 59(I) (1946): Calling of an International Conference on Freedom of Information.

General Assembly Resolution 52/111 (1997): Third Decade to Combat Racism and Racial Discrimination and the convening of a world conference on racism, racial discrimination, xenophobia and related intolerance.

General Assembly Resolution 59/177 (2004): Global efforts for the total elimination of racism, racial discrimination, xenophobia and related intolerance and the comprehensive implementation of and follow-up to the Durban Declaration and Programme of Action.

General Assembly Resolution 66/143 (2012): Inadmissibility of certain practices that contribute to fuelling contemporary forms of racism, racial discrimination, xenophobia and related intolerance.

General Assembly Resolution 56/266 (2014): Programme of activities for the implementation of the International Decade for People of African Descent.

Other UN documents

CESC Concluding Observations: Belgium (2000) ICESCR E/2001/22 7.

Commission on Human Rights Resolution 2002/68: Racism, Racial Discrimination, Xenophobia and Related Intolerance.

Human Rights Council Resolution: Protection against violence and discrimination based on sexual orientation and gender identity (adopted 30 June 2016) A/HRC/RES/32/2.

Human Rights Council Resolution: Human rights, sexual orientation and gender identity (adopted 17 June 2011) A/HRC/RES/17/19.

International Mechanisms for Promoting Freedom of Expression, Joint Statement on Racism and the Media by the UN Special Rapporteur on Freedom of Opinion and Expression, the OSCE Representative on Freedom of the Media and the OAS Special Rapporteur on Freedom of Expression, London, 27 February 2001.

Rabat Plan of Action on the Prohibition of Advocacy of National, Racial or Religious Hatred that constitutes Incitement to Discrimination, Hostility or Violence (2002).

Report of the United Nations High Commissioner for Human Rights, Discriminatory laws and practices and acts of violence against individuals based on their sexual orientation and gender identity (2011) A/HRC/19/41.

United Nations, Economic and Social Council, Siracusa Principles on the Limitation and Derogation Provisions in the International Covenant on Civil and Political Rights, E/CN.4/1985/4, Annex (1985).

UN Expert Group Report: Gender and Racial Discrimination (2000): www.un.org/womenwatch/daw/csw/genrac/report.htm

World Conference against Racism, Racial Discrimination, Xenophobia and Related Intolerance Durban Declaration (2001) A/CONF.189/12.

Case-law

Belyatsky et al. v Belarus, Communication no. 1296/2004 (24 July 2007) CCPR/C/90/D/1296/2004.

Broeks v Netherlands, Communication no. 172/1984 (9 April 1987) CCPR/C/OP/2.

Coleman v Australia, no. 1157/2003 (10 August 2006) CCPR/C/87/D/1157/2003.

Dergachev v Belarus, Communication no. 921/200 (19 July 2002) CCPR/C/74/D/921/2000.

Erv Denmark, Communication no. 40/2007 (8 August 2007) CERD/C/71/D/40/2007.

Faurisson v France, Communication no. 550/1993 (8 November 1996) CCPR/C/58/D/550/1993.

Gelle v Denmark, Communication no. 34/2004 (15 March 2006) CERD/C/68/D/
34/2004.

Jama v Denmark, Communication no. 41/2008 (21 August 2009) CERD/C/75/
D/41/2008.

J.R.T. and the W.G. Party v Canada (1984) Communication no. 104/1981, CCPR/
C/OP/2.

Kamal Quereshi v Denmark, Communication no. 33/2003 (2005) CERD/C/66/
D/33/2003.

Kim v The Republic of Korea, Communication no. 574/1994 (4 January 1999) CCPR/C/
64/D/574/1994.

Korneenko et al. v Belarus, Communication no. 1274/2004 (10 November 2006)
CCPR/C/88/D/1274/2004.

Kungurov v Uzbekistan, Communication no. 1478/2006 (15 September 2011)
CCPR/C/102/D/1478/2006.

L.K. v The Netherlands, Communication no. 4/1991 (16 March 1993) A/48/18.

M.A. v Italy, Communication no. 117/1981 (21 September 1981) Supp. no. 40 (A/39/40).

Marques v Angola, Communications no. 1128/2002 (18 April 2005) CCPR/C/83/
D/1128/2002.

Mohamed Rabbae, A.B.S and N.A v The Netherlands, Communication no. 2124/2011
(14 July 2016) CCPR/C/117/D/2124/2011.

Nahimana et al. v the Prosecutor (28 November 2007) Case no. ICTR-99-52-A.

Park v The Republic of Korea, Communication no. 628/1995 (3 November 1998)
CCPR/C/64/D/628/1995.

P.S.N v Denmark (2007) Communication no. 36/2006, CERD/C/71/D/36/2006.

Ross v Canada, Communication no. 736/1997 (18 October 2000) CCPR/C/70/D/
736/1997.

Süsser v Czech Republic, Communication no. 1488/2006 (28 April 2008) CCPR/C/92/D/
1488/2006.

Syargei Belyazeka v Belarus, Communication no. 1772/2008 (23 March 2012) CCPR/C/
104/D/1772/2008.

The Jewish community of Oslo et al. v Norway (15 August 2005) Communication no.
30/2003 (CERD/C/67/D/30/2003).

Toonen v Australia, Communication no. 488/1992, U.N. Doc CCPR/C/50/D/488/
1992 (1994).

Vassilari v Greece, Communication no. 1570/2007 (29 April 2009) CCPR/C/95/
D/1570/2007.

Velichking v Belarus, Communication no. 1022/2001 (20 October 2005) CCPR/
C/85/D/1022/2001 (2005).

Yilmaz-Dogan v The Netherlands (10 August 1988) Communication no. 1/1984,
CERD/C/36/D/1/1984.

Zentralrat Deutscher Sinti und Roma et al. v Germany, CERD/C/72/D/38/2006
(3 March 2008), CERD/C/72/D/38/2006.

Zwaan-de Vries v The Netherlands, Communication no. 182/1984 (9 April 1987),
CCPR/C/OP/2.

Books

Bleich E, '*The Freedom to be Racist, How the United States and Europe Struggle to Preserve Freedom and Combat Racism*' (1st edn. Oxford University Press, Oxford 2011).

Coliver S, *'Striking a Balance: Hate Speech, Freedom of Expression and Non-Discrimination'* (Article 19, International Centre against Censorship, University of Essex, Essex 1992).

Henkin L, Cleveland S, Helfer L, Neuman G & Orentlicher D, *'Human Rights'* (2nd edn. Foundation Press, Cleveland OH 2009) 1208.

Kean D, *'Caste-Based Discrimination in International Human Rights Law'* (1st edn. Ashgate, Aldershot 2007).

McBride J, *'Freedom of Association'* in Rhona Smith & Christien van den Anker *'The Essentials of Human Rights'* (1st edn. Routledge, London 2005).

Morsink J, *'The Universal Declaration of Human Rights, Origins, Drafting and Intent'* (1st edn. University of Pennsylvania Press, Philadelphia PA 1999).

Nowak M, *'U.N. Covenant on Civil and Political Rights: CCPR Commentary'* (2nd edn. N. P Engel Verlag, Kehl am Rhein 2005).

Shestack J, 'The Jurisprudence of Human Rights,' in Theodor Meron (ed.), *'Human Rights in International Law: Legal and Policy Issues'* (1st edn. Clarendon, Oxford 1984).

Journal articles

Alkiviadou N, 'Regulating Hatred: Of Devils and Demons?' (2018) *International Journal of Discrimination and the Law* 4, https://doi.org/10.1177/1358229118796029, 218–236.

Bayefsky A.F, 'The Principle of Equality or Non-discrimination in International Law' (1990) 11 *Human Rights Quarterly* 1-2, 1–34.

Brems E, 'State Regulation of Xenophobia v Individual Freedoms: the European View' (2002) 1 *Journal of Human Rights* 4, 481–500.

Defeis E, 'Freedom of Speech and International Norms: A Response to Hate Speech' 29 *Stanford Journal of International Law* 57, 57–130.

Farrior S, 'Molding The Matrix: The Historical and Theoretical Foundations of International Law Concerning Hate Speech.' (1996) 14 *Berkley Journal of International Law* 1, 1–98.

Ghanea N, 'Minorities and Hatred: Protections and Implications' (2010) 17 *International Journal on Minority and Group Rights* 3, 423–446.

Goldmann M & Sonnen M, 'Soft Authority against Hard Cases of Racially Discriminating Speech: Why the CERD Committee Needs a Margin of Appreciation Doctrine' (2016) 7 *Goettingen Journal of International Law* 17, 131–155.

Howard R.E, 'Race and Racism – Why does European Law have Difficulties with Definitions?' 24 *International Journal of Comparative Labour Law and Industrial Relations* 1, 1–30.

Mahalic D & Mahalic J.G, 'The Limitation Provisions of the International Convention on the Elimination of all Forms of Racial Discrimination' (1987) 9 *Human Rights Quarterly* 1, 74–101.

McGoldrick D & O'Donnell T, 'Hate Speech Laws: Consistency with National and International Human Rights Law' (1998) 18 *Legal Studies* 4, 453–485.

Thornberry P, 'Forms of Hate Speech and the Convention on the Elimination of all Forms of Racial Discrimination' (2010) 5 *Religion and Human Rights* 2, 97–117.

Reports

Article 19 – Towards an Interpretation of Article 20 of the ICCPR: Thresholds for the Prohibition of Incitement to Hatred Work in Progress A study Prepared for the Regional Expert Meeting on Article 20, Organised by the Office of the High Commissioner for

Human Rights, Vienna, February 8–9, 2010: www.ohchr.org/Documents/Issues/Expression/ICCPR/Vienna/CRP7Callamard.pdf.

German Institute for Human Rights, Written Contribution to the Thematic Discussion of the Committee on the Elimination of Racial Discrimination on Racist Hate Speech (28 August 2012).

Greer S, 'The exceptions to Articles 8 to 11 of the European Convention on Human Rights' (1997), Council of Europe Publishing – Human rights files no. 15, available at: www.echr.coe.int/LibraryDocs/DG2/HRFILES/DG2-EN-HRFILES-15(1997).pdf.

Krug E.G, Dahlberg L.L, Mercy J.A, Zwi A.B & Lozano R, 'World Report on Violence and Health' (World Health Organization, Geneva, 2002).

Mendel T, Restricting Freedom of Expression: Standards and Principles – Background Paper for meetings hosted by the UN Special Rapporteur on Freedom of Opinion and Expression: www.law-democracy.org/wp-content/uploads/2010/07/10.03.Paper-on-Restrictions-on-FOE.pdf.

4   The Council of Europe

The Council of Europe

The CoE was born from the ashes of the Second World War with its founding members committing to a future that respected human rights and fundamental freedoms. The ECtHR and its case-law will lie at the epicentre of this chapter. However, a brief overview of two other important bodies and their role in the sphere of tackling the far-right will be made here. The European Commission against Racism and Intolerance (ECRI) is a body of the CoE made up of independent experts which monitors phenomena such as racism, intolerance and discrimination. It issues country reports and makes recommendations which are referred to and discussed in this book. The European Commission for Democracy through Law, also known as the Venice Commission, is an advisory body of the CoE providing legal advice to its Member States[1] in the sphere of democracy, human rights and the rule of law. Importantly for this book, it has prepared guidelines on the Prohibition and Dissolution of Political Parties discussed herein. The ECHR was opened for signature on 4 November 1950 and entered into force on 3 September 1953. The Contracting Parties undertake to secure the rights and freedoms contained in the ECHR. All of the COE's 47 Member States are parties to this Convention. It provides a system of individual judicial redress resulting in binding judgements. For that reason, the Convention has been described as the 'greatest monument to the Council'[2] that is 'the most comprehensive and developed system for supranational human rights protection.'[3]

The principle of non-discrimination in Council of Europe instruments

The principle of non-discrimination is protected by the ECHR and its Protocol 12. To elucidate the duties and obligations arising, therefrom, the ECtHR

---

1 61 Member States: The 47 CoE countries plus other countries (Algeria, Brazil, Chile, Costa Rica, Israel, Kazakhstan, the Republic of Korea, Kosovo, Kyrgyzstan, Morocco, Mexico, Peru, Tunisia and the USA).

2 Ivan Hare & James Weinsten, *'Extreme Speech and Democracy'* (2nd edn. Oxford University Press, Oxford 2011) 4.

3 Ibid.

has defined discrimination as 'treating differently, without an objective and reasonable justification, persons in relevantly similar situations.'[4] No objective and reasonable justification means that 'the distinction in issue does not pursue a legitimate aim or that there is not a reasonable relationship of proportionality between the means employed and the aim sought to be realized.'[5] Moreover, in order for an application to be successful under this article, the 'discriminatory intent or effect'[6] of the object or act or measure complained of must be established.

Article 14 of the Convention provides that

> the enjoyment of the rights and freedoms set forth in this Convention shall be secured without discrimination on any grounds such as sex, race, colour, language, religion, political or other opinion, national or social origin, association with a national minority, property, birth or other status.

This article can, thus, be enforced when a right or freedom, as set out by the Convention, is at stake, thereby, limiting its applicability and effect within that document. As noted in *Marcx v Belgium*:

> although Article 14 has no independent existence, it may play an important autonomous role by complementing the other normative provisions of the Convention and the Protocols: Article 14 safeguards individuals, placed in similar situations, from any discrimination in the enjoyment of the rights and freedoms set forth in those other provisions.[7]

Notwithstanding the 'accessory character'[8] of Article 14, its importance must not be underestimated since 'it is as though Article 14 formed an integral part of each of the provisions laying down rights and freedoms.'[9] However, the 'discrimination complaints often do not add very much to the other allegations,'[10] and, as a result, the Court decides not to deal with the Article 14 aspect of the case.[11]

Article 1 of Protocol 12 holds that

> The enjoyment of any right set forth by law shall be secured without discrimination on any ground such as sex, race, colour, language, religion,

---

4 Willis v The United Kingdom, Application no. 36042/97 (ECHR 11 September 2002) para. 48.

5 See, *inter alia*, Andrejeva v Latvia, Application no. 55707/00 (ECHR 18 February 2009) para. 81; Sejdić and Finci v Bosnia and Herzegovina, Application nos. 27996/06 and 34836/06 (22 December 2009) para. 42.

6 Aksu v Turkey, Application nos. 4149/04 and 41029/04 (ECHR 15 March 2012) para. 45.

7 Marcx v Belgium, Application no. 6833/74 (ECHR 13 June 1979) para. 32.

8 Janneke Gerards, 'The Discrimination Grounds of Article 14 of the European Convention on Human Rights' (2013) 13 *Human Rights Law Review* 1, 100.

9 Belgian Linguistics case no. 2, Application nos. 1474/62, 1677/62, 1691/62, 1769/63, 1994/63 and 2126/64 (ECHR 23 July 1968) para. 9.

10 Janneke Gerards, 'The Discrimination Grounds of Article 14 of the European Convention on Human Rights' (2013) 13 *Human Rights Law Review* 1, 100.

11 Ibid.

political or other opinion, national or social origin, association with a national minority, property, birth or other status.

It further holds that 'no one shall be discriminated against by any public authority on any grounds such as those mentioned in paragraph 1.' By applying the non-discrimination principle to any right provided for by law extends the applicability of this principle beyond the framework of the Convention and into the realm of rights and freedoms enshrined in the national legal system of a State Party, in the event that the latter is more extensive than the former. However, the Protocol has only been adopted by eighteen of the forty-seven States Parties, and, thus, its actual impact remains limited. Nevertheless, with regard to the interrelationship between Protocol 12 and Article 14, the Court has underlined that they should be understood in a similar way given that 'notwithstanding the difference in scope between those provisions, the meaning of this term in Article 1 of Protocol No. 12 was intended to be identical to that in Article 14.'[12]

Race as a ground for discrimination

Unlike the UN framework, and particularly the ICERD, at a CoE level there exists no Convention dedicated to combatting racial discrimination. The only measure implemented to tackle it has been the Additional Protocol to the Convention on Cybercrime, concerning the Criminalization of Acts of a Racist and Xenophobic Nature Committed through Computer Systems. However, as can be discerned from its title, it deals with computer systems only. Nevertheless, Article 14 of the ECHR and Article 1 of Protocol 12 both name race as a prohibited ground for discrimination, while the Court has extrapolated upon the theme of racial discrimination in the cases discussed later.

From the time of the European Commission of Human Rights (EComHR), the particularly serious nature of racial discrimination has been underlined. In *3 East African Asians v The United Kingdom*, the Commission noted that 'discrimination based on race could, in certain circumstances, of itself amount to degrading treatment within the meaning of Article 3.'[13] This viewpoint was also adopted by the Court in *Timishev v Russia,* in which it was held that racial discrimination is a 'particularly invidious kind of discrimination'[14] with 'perilous consequences.'[15] This position was reiterated in *Aksu v Turkey*[16] which dealt with Romaphobia. In *Sejdić and Finci v Bosnia and Herzegovina,* the Court held that, in the context where discrimination is based on race or ethnicity, the

---

12 Sejdić and Finci v Bosnia and Herzegovina, Application nos. 27996/06 and 34836/06 (ECHR 22 December 2009) para. 55.
13 3 East African Asians (British Protected Persons) v The United Kingdom, Application nos. 4715/70, 4783/71 and 4827/71 (EComHR 6 March 1978) para. 2
14 Timishev v Russia, Application nos. 55762/00 and 55974/00 (ECHR 13 March 2006) para. 56.
15 Ibid.
16 Aksu v Turkey, Application nos. 414904 and 41029/04 (ECHR 15 March 2012) para. 43.

notion of differential treatment without an objective and reasonable justification, as referred to earlier, 'must be interpreted as strictly as possible.'[17]

In relation to racial violence, the Court underlined that it is 'a particular affront to human dignity and, in view of its perilous consequences, requires from the authorities special vigilance and a 'vigorous reaction.'[18] In *Nachova v Bulgaria*, the Court also referred to the general obligation of States Parties, under Articles 2 and 14, to conduct effective investigations where there exists the possibility that the motivation for violence was of a racist nature.[19] This duty is also extended to cases where the motives are of a religious nature with States Parties having the duty to establish 'whether or not hatred or prejudice may have played a role in the events.'[20] However, in establishing whether such motivation exists for purposes of the enforcement of, *inter alia*, Article 14 of the ECHR, the Court adopts a standard of proof beyond reasonable doubt.[21] According to established ECtHR case-law, such a standard may be attained following the 'co-existence of sufficiently strong, clear and concordant inferences or of similar unrebutted presumptions of fact.'[22] The necessity for a high standard of proof was reiterated in subsequent cases, such as *Cobzaru v Romania*,[23] in which the Court also held that

> the expression of concern by various organisations about the numerous allegations of violence against Roma by Romanian law enforcement officers ... does not suffice to consider that it has been established that racist attitudes played a role in the applicant's ill-treatment.[24]

Interestingly, in *Milanović v Serbia*, the Court made no reference to establishing proof beyond a reasonable doubt but, instead, referred to the fact that proving religiously prejudicial motivation 'may be difficult in practice'[25] and, thus, the State's obligation to investigate is 'an obligation to use best endeavours and is not absolute.'[26] Therefore, aside from the route followed in *Milanović*, proving that such motivation is a difficult task, given that it must be proved beyond a reasonable doubt, and, thus, it is possible that such acts fall outside this framework due to difficulties *vis-à-vis* attaining this standard. In fact, the NGO

---

17 Sejdić and Finci v Bosnia and Herzegovina, Application nos. 27996/06 and 34836/06 (ECHR 22 December 2009) para. 44.
18 Nachova and Others v Bulgaria, Application nos. 43577/98 and 43579/98 (ECHR 6 July 2005) para. 145.
19 Ibid. para. 161.
20 Milanović v Serbia, Application no. 44614/07 (ECHR 20 June 2011) para. 96.
21 Nachova and Others v Bulgaria, Application nos. 43577/98 and 43579/98 (ECHR 6 July 2005) para. 147.
22 Ibid.
23 Cobzaru v Romania, Application no. 48254/99 (ECHR 26 July 2007) para. 93
24 Ibid. para. 95.
25 Milanović v Serbia , Application no. 44614/07 (20 June 2011) para. 96.
26 Ibid.

Interights, which was an intervener in *Nachova v Bulgaria*, criticised this standard as 'erecting insurmountable obstacles to establishing discrimination'[27] and recommended a balance of probabilities standard of proof for such cases.[28]

The only time that Article 14 of the ECHR was directly applied in the field under consideration was in the case of *Aksu v Turkey*. Here, the Court dealt with Romaphobic rhetoric which the applicant alleged had been promoted in three publications which had received government funding. These publications included references that Roma were 'engaged in illegal activities, lived as thieves, pickpockets, swindlers, robbers, usurpers, beggars, drug dealers, prostitutes and brothel keepers and were polygamist and aggressive.'[29] The case was dealt with under Article 8 of the ECHR, read in conjunction with Article 14. The reason for this shift in technique was that the applicant was not the one expressing the views, as the Court had habitually been confronted with, but, rather, a person of Roma origin who had been insulted by the expression. As noted by Belavusau, 'procedurally, this case illustrates the paradox that hate speech cases typically reach Strasbourg exclusively as claims against States by haters, alleging violation of their rights to free speech.'[30] Even though it found no violation of Article 8 in conjunction with Article 14, the Court reiterated the need for the State to implement effective measures to combat negative stereotyping against the Roma.[31]

Even though Article 14 of the ECHR will be surpassed in the event that another article of the Convention can be relied upon, and whilst Protocol 12 has not been extrapolated on by the Court's jurisprudence due to its limited ratification, the principle of non-discrimination is significant to any discussion on far-right movements given that their activities and ideologies emanate from an unjustified difference in the treatment of people belonging to particular groups. The Court has recognised that discrimination can result from racial and religious causes, and, as reflected in the case-law, States are under a particularly strict duty to investigate violence arising from such discrimination which, as dictated by the majority of ECtHR cases, must subsequently be proved beyond a reasonable doubt. Thus, the theoretical and jurisprudential scene has been set by the Court for future cases in the realm of the far-right within the framework of non-discrimination with Article 14 and Article 1 of Protocol 12 constituting available, but, to date, rarely used tools.

---

27 Nachova and Others v Bulgaria, Application nos. 43577/98 and 43579/98 (ECHR 6 July 2005) para. 140.

28 Ibid.

29 Aksu v Turkey, Application nos. 4149/04 and 41029/04 (ECHR 15 March 2012) para. 14.

30 Uladzislau Belavusau, 'Experts in Hate Speech Cases – Towards a Higher Standard of Proof in Strasbourg?' in Łukasz Gruszczyński & Wouter Werner, *'Deference in International Courts and Tribunals: Standard of Review and Margin of Appreciation'* (1st edn. Oxford University Press, Oxford 2014) 267.

31 Aksu v Turkey, Application nos. 4149/04 and 41029/04 (ECHR 15 March 2012) para. 75.

Freedom of expression: Article 10 of the ECHR

Article 10 of the ECHR protects the right to freedom of expression. It states that:

1   Everyone has the right to freedom of expression. This right shall include freedom to hold opinions and to receive and impart information and ideas without interference by public authority and regardless of frontiers. This Article shall not prevent States from requiring the licensing of broadcasting, television or cinema enterprises.

2   The exercise of these freedoms, since it carries with it duties and responsibilities, may be subject to such formalities, conditions, restrictions or penalties as are prescribed by law and are necessary in a democratic society, in the interests of national security, territorial integrity or public safety, for the prevention of disorder or crime, for the protection of health or morals, for the protection of the reputation or rights of others, for preventing the disclosure of information received in confidence, or for maintaining the authority and impartiality of the judiciary.

First and foremost, the provision stipulates that 'everyone' has the right to freedom of expression, including both natural and legal persons.[32] As with Article 19, Article 10 recognises that the freedom of expression, which includes the freedom to hold opinions and to receive and impart information and ideas, carries with it duties and responsibilities. Importantly, Article 10, unlike other articles of this Convention, incorporates a further qualification in the form of duties and responsibilities when exercising this right, demonstrating that the drafters realised and sought to conceptualise the dangers which potentially come with free expression and the due care that must be taken by the person expressing his or her opinion(s). A State may intervene in the exercise of these freedoms as long as the restriction is provided for by law and is necessary in a democratic society to pursue one of the aims provided for by Article 10(2). Paragraph 2 of this Article provides a broader range of limitation grounds than its ICCPR counterpart since, as well as respecting the rights or reputations of others, the protection of national security or public order and public health or morals, Article 10(2) stipulates that legitimate formalities, conditions, restrictions or penalties[33] can be made for purposes of territorial integrity, for the prevention of disorder or crime, for the prevention of disclosure of information received in confidence or for maintaining the authority and impartiality of the judiciary. Nevertheless, it is important to note that it limits the possibilities for restrictions by providing that they should be necessary in a democratic society and not simply necessary in order to achieve one of the listed objectives, as is the case in Article 19(3).

---

32 Andrew Lester, David Pannick & Javan Herberg, '*Human Rights Law and Practice*' (3rd edn. LexisNexis, New York 2009).

33 Article 10 refers to all these methods of interference rather than simply to 'restrictions' as in the case of the ICCPR.

The Convention does not include a particular provision on advocacy of national, racial or religious hatred that constitutes incitement to discrimination, hostility or violence, as is the case with the ICCPR. Nevertheless, this has not prevented the ECtHR from ruling against applicants, whom the Court considered to be uttering speech covered by Article 20 ICCPR aims, nor did it prevent it or the former EComHR from rendering such cases inadmissible. As well as the limitation clauses of Article 10, Article 17 has also been of importance in this respect. This provision will be discussed separately in 'Freedom of expression: reasonableness review of restrictions and limitations.'

According to long-standing case-law of the ECtHR, the rights set out in Article 10(1) are to be interpreted and applied in a broad manner, given that 'there is no room in general for an argument that Article 10 extends only to true information: opinions, speculations and criticism are all covered.'[34] In *Handyside v The United Kingdom*, the Court held that the 'freedom of expression constitutes one of the essential foundations of [a democratic society], one of the basic conditions for its progress and for the development of every man.'[35] The Court has repeatedly underlined the central position of the freedom of expression in a democratic and pluralist society. In *Observer and the Guardian v The United Kingdom*, it held that the freedom of expression is applicable not only to information or ideas that are 'favourably received or regarded as inoffensive or as a matter of indifference, but also to those that offend, shock or disturb.'[36] Nevertheless, as will be reflected further down, the Court has been vigorous in restricting speech which it considers harmful. In a combination of precepts of militant democracy and an effects-based conceptualisation of hate speech bans, as discussed in Chapter 2, the Court has accepted that a democracy should protect itself and its basic principles and must 'fight against abuses, committed in the exercise of freedom of speech, that openly target democratic values.'[37] This is in line with its self-preservation framework, echoing the objectives of militant democracy, namely that a democratic society is 'tolerant but not inert.'[38] There is a considerable amount of case-law of the ECtHR and the EComHR in relation to Article 10 of the ECHR, including cases involving hate speech promulgated by representatives of far-right movements. In order to consider and evaluate this jurisprudence, the section will now consider the kinds of speech protected by the freedom of expression and then look at hate speech and how this is and has been understood and interpreted by the aforementioned institutions.

---

34 Adrian Marshall Williams & Jonathan Cooper, 'Hate Speech, Holocaust Denial and International Human Rights Law' (1999) 7 *European Human Rights Law Review* 593, 593–613.

35 Handyside v The United Kingdom, Application no. 5493/72 (ECHR 7 December 1976) para. 49.

36 The Observer and The Guardian v The United Kingdom, Application no. 13585/88 (ECHR 26 November 1991) para. 59.

37 Jean-François Flauss, 'The European Court of Human Rights and the Freedom of Expression' (2009) 84 *Indiana Law Journal* 3, 837.

38 Ibid.

Freedom of expression: reasonableness review of restrictions and limitations

As noted by Buyse, 'few issues are as contested as the limits of freedom of expression.'[39] Although contestations of this freedom have been seen, for example, in States Parties responses to the incorporation of Article 4 ICERD, on a CoE level and particularly in the realm of the ECtHR, nothing appears to be contested. Instead, the Court has appeared systematically ready and willing to restrict what they consider to be hate speech. The Court has developed a tripartite justification test that emanates from Article 10(2), the key question being whether a particular interference is in line with the Convention. In determining whether there has been an interference with the freedom of expression, the Court implements the classical *Sunday Times* test which is in line with the requirements of Article 10(2). The Court must ascertain whether the interference is necessary in a democratic society, whether there is a 'pressing social need' for the interference, whether it was proportionate to the legitimate aim pursued and whether its reasons are relevant and sufficient in light of the aims listed in Article 10(2). Moreover, the interference must be 'prescribed by law,' which means it must have a basis in domestic law which is sufficiently accessible and foreseeable.

Limitation ground 1: prescribed by law

The ECtHR has held that the term 'law' must be interpreted in a manner that recognises and embraces the different types of law that make up the legal reality in the country concerned. In *Sunday Times*, the Court stated that the word 'law' includes written law as well as the case-law interpreting it. In the same case, the Court held that there are two requirements emanating from this provision. First, the law must be readily accessible to citizens, namely 'the citizen must be able to have an indication that is adequate in the circumstances of the legal rules applicable to a given case.'[40] Second, it must be 'formulated with sufficient precision to enable the citizen to regulate his conduct ... to foresee, to a degree that is reasonable in the circumstances, the consequences which a given action may entail.'[41] However, the Court recognised that, in attempting to ensure certainty and foreseeability, excessively rigid laws may result which are unable to adapt to altering circumstances and situations. As a result, the Court noted that 'many laws are inevitably couched in terms which, to a greater or lesser extent, are vague and whose interpretation and application are questions of practice.[42] In *Olsson v Sweden*, the Court underlined that the phrase 'prescribed by law' refers not

39 Antoine Buyse, 'Dangerous Expressions: The ECHR, Violence and Free Speech' (2014) 63 *International and Comparative Law Quarterly* 2, 492.
40 Sunday Times v The United Kingdom, Application no. 6538/74 (ECHR 26 April 1979) para. 47.
41 Ibid.
42 Ibid.

only to the law itself but also embraces the quality of the law, requiring it to be in line with the rule of law.[43] Further, the Court recognised that, in attempting to ensure the organic nature of the law in an ever-changing society, vagueness can be an ensuing issue. Also, in *Sanoma Uitgevers BV v The Netherlands*, the Court held that domestic law must 'afford a measure of legal protection against arbitrary interferences by public authorities with the rights safeguarded by the Convention.'[44] In *Féret v Belgium*, the Court found that the national courts relied on a national law which criminalised certain acts inspired by racism or xenophobia and, thus, the interference was indeed prescribed by law.[45] This part of the Court's test, that being the determination of whether interference has been prescribed by law, has not posed a problem for hate speech case-law and, thus, this part of the Court's review on reasonableness will not be further considered.

Limitation ground 2: necessary in a democratic society

Article 10(2) and 11(2) of the ECHR outlines that the interference in question must be 'necessary in a democratic society.' A country may legitimately restrict, for example, speech which is considered by the Court to be hate speech. Such a limitation should be, *inter alia*, necessary in a democratic society for the protection of the rights and freedoms of others. Therefore, the ECHR explicitly goes beyond the mandate of militant democracy, namely the pre-emptive restriction of rights in the name of democracy itself, to the pre-emptive restriction of rights in the name of a democratic society. The wording is similar but the meaning and impact vary substantially. Expression, association and assembly do not need to be threatening the democratic order to be limited under the ECHR and may occur to protect others in a democratic society. This is in antithesis with the ICCPR, which, in theory, adopts an even lower threshold, allowing limitation of speech, assembly and association insofar as these are necessary, without the requirement of a democratic society. Also relevant to this discussion are 20(2) of the ICCPR and Article 4 of the ICERD which directly prohibit certain types of (racist) expression and association, without any need for this to happen for purposes of, for example, protecting a particular ground, ensuring democracy or for the needs of a democratic society. As such, the threshold for restriction is, thus, much lower than what has been envisaged by constitutional theorists deliberating on militant democracy both in terms of the ECHR and the ICCPR. What is, then, a democratic society for the ECHR and the ECtHR? The Court does not really say. It merely puts forth elements which characterise such a society. For example, in *Handyside v The United Kingdom*, as well as recognising the central role held by the freedom of expression in a democratic society, the Court outlined the characteristics that make up such a society, namely 'pluralism, tolerance and

---

43 Olsson v Sweden, Application no. 10465/83 (ECHR 24 March 1998) para. 61(b).
44 Sanoma Uitgevers B.V. v The Netherlands, Application no. 38224/03 (ECHR 14 September 2010) para. 82.
45 Féret v Belgium, Application no. 15615/07 (ECHR 16 July 2009) para. 58.

broadmindedness without which there is no democratic society.'[46] In *United Communist Party of Turkey and Others v Turkey*, the Court held that 'democracy is the only political model contemplated by the Convention and, accordingly, the only one compatible with it.'[47] In *Ždanoka v Latvia*, the Court noted that 'democracy constitutes a fundamental element of the European public order.'[48]

As noted, the phrase 'democratic society' is

> arguably one of the most important clauses in the entire Convention since, in principle it gives the Strasbourg organs the widest possible discretion in condoning or condemning interferences with rights which states seek to justify by reference to one or more of the legitimate purposes in the second paragraphs of Articles 8 to 11.[49]

However, the substance and content of a democratic society test 'remains highly fluid and indeterminate'[50] just as is the case with the meaning of 'democracy' which, as discussed in Chapter 2 and further discussed in this chapter, is referred to in ECtHR jurisprudence although it is not found in Convention texts. Without a proper theoretical backdrop of these terms, the role, relevance and potentially the legitimacy of the Court's decisions are undermined. As pertinently argued by Gearty:

> To have no theory of judicial activism, other than that each article needs separately to be interpreted in the appropriate (but undefined) manner, would be to surrender intellectual interest in the vast area of judicial discretion that exists within the Convention.[51]

Through the limitation grounds, the Court embraces a militant approach to protecting grounds, such as the rights of others, as these are necessary in a democratic society. The resulting balancing test theoretically emanates from the premise that one must grant due consideration to 'the democratic importance of freedom of speech on the one hand and the harmful consequences of hate propaganda on the other hand.'[52] In *Klass v Germany*, the Court affirmed that

---

46 Handyside v The United Kingdom, Application no. 5493/72 (ECHR 7 December 1976) para. 49.

47 United Communist Party of Turkey and Others v Turkey, Application no. 133/1996/752/951 (ECHR 30 January 1998) para. 45.

48 Ždanoka v Latvia, Application no. 58278/00 (ECHR 16 March 2006) para. 98.

49 Steven Greer, 'The Exceptions to Articles 8 to 11 of the European Convention on Human Rights' (1997), Council of Europe Publishing - Human Rights Files no. 15: www.echr.coe. int/LibraryDocs/DG2/HRFILES/DG2-EN-HRFILES-15(1997).pdf [Accessed 1 October 2018] 14.

50 Conor A. Gearty, 'The European Court of Human Rights and the Protection of Civil Liberties: An Overview' (1993) 52 *The Cambridge Law Journal* 1, 96.

51 Ibid.

52 Stefan Sottiaux, 'Bad Tendencies in the ECtHR's Hate Speech Jurisprudence' (2011) 7 *European Constitutional Law Review* 1, 48.

'some compromise between the requirements for defending democratic society and individual rights is inherent in the system of the Convention.'[53] In *Thoma v Luxembourg*, the Court held that restrictions on rights guaranteed by the Convention must be narrowly construed and enforced in the interest of public and social life, in its entirety, as well as in the interest of individuals making up that society.[54] In *Ždanoka v Latvia*, the Court found that 'in order to guarantee the stability and effectiveness of a democratic system, the State may be required to take specific measures to protect itself.'[55] However, as noted in *United Communist Party of Turkey and Others v Turkey*, the problem which arises is how to strike a balance between defending democracy and protecting individual rights and freedoms. For the purpose of mitigating the potential risks involved, this balancing must be conducted meticulously, with due care and consideration given to all the actors and institutions involved. Regardless of a certain variation made by the Court when deciphering the margin of appreciation, a State should, in fact, be the guiding light in the balancing exercise between the different rights at stake so as to ensure that individuals and groups do not use and abuse the genuine aims and objectives of Article 10(1) for purposes contrary to the Convention. This is the precise outcome which the Court attempts to avoid in cases involving the far-right, either through the enforcement of Article 10(2) or of Article 17. In practice, however, and as will be demonstrated in this chapter, the Court is overly zealous in restricting what it considers to be bad speech in the name of a democratic society. The legitimacy of the Court's decisions is weakened by the lacking theoretical analysis of this democratic society which is the framework in which restrictions are permitted.

Further, in *Sunday Times v The United Kingdom*, the Court found that the adjective 'necessary' within the meaning of Article 10(2) 'is not synonymous with indispensable, neither has it the flexibility of such expressions as admissible, ordinary, useful, reasonable or desirable and that it implies the existence of a pressing social need.'[56] When assessing the pressing social need and the proportionality of the interference, the State must consider whether the expression contributes 'to any form of public debate capable of furthering progress in human affairs'[57] or whether the expression is simply aimed at destructing democratic principles and values. In relation to far-right rhetoric, the Commission directly interlinked the prohibition of National Socialist activities with the preservation of a democratic society. In *X v Austria*, the applicant was convicted on charges of neo-Nazi activities and sentenced to nine months' imprisonment for violating a constitutional act dealing with Nationalist Socialist activities. The EComHR examined whether the restriction was necessary in a democratic society and stated

53 Klass and Others v Germany, Application no. 5029/71 (ECHR 6 September 1978) para. 59.
54 Thoma v Luxembourg, Application no. 38432/97 (ECHR 29 March 2001) para. 48.
55 Ždanoka v Latvia, Application no. 58278/00 (ECHR 16 March 2006) para. 100.
56 Sunday Times v The United Kingdom, Application no. 6538/74 (ECHR 26 April 1979) para. 59.
57 Otto-Preminger-Institut v Austria, Application no. 13470/87 (ECHR 20 September 1994) para. 49.

that Austria recognised the dangers to social order brought about by National Socialism, holding that 'it is scarcely to be supposed that the EComHR, whose duty it is, after all, to preserve this democratic order in the European States will disagree with her.'[58]

Limitation ground 3: legitimate aim

In order to be accepted, interference to the freedom of expression must pursue a legitimate aim. In this realm, the legitimate aim of protecting the rights of others should be central to any discussion pertaining to hate speech, taking into account the need to protect the rights of those groups who may be subject to such hatred. In assessing limitations on the freedom of expression, the Court in *Otto-Preminger-Institut v Austria* considered whether the expressions are 'gratuitously offensive to others and, thus, an infringement of their rights and which, therefore, do not contribute to any form of public debate capable of furthering progress in human affairs.'[59] In *Seurot v France*, the Court dealt with the dismissal of a teacher who wrote an article for a school newsletter describing French people of North African origin as 'Muslim hordes that were impossible to assimilate.' Here, the Court found that the interference to the expression in question pursued at least one of the legitimate aims of the Convention, namely the protection of the reputation or rights of others.[60] In finding no violation of Article 10 in *Féret v Belgium*, the Court accepted a national restriction of racist and xenophobic expression as being necessary for the protection of the rights of others and for preventing disorder. The Court summarised the effects of hate speech on the rights of others: namely that

> insults, ridicule or defamation aimed at specific population groups or incitation to discrimination, as in this case, sufficed for the authorities to give priority to fighting hate speech when confronted by the irresponsible use of freedom of expression which undermined people's dignity, or even their safety.[61]

Given the devastating effect of the atrocities committed by Nazis during the Second World War, revisionist speech has been central to the development of the Commission's and the Court's approach to hate speech, with the institutions having adopted a stable position *vis-à-vis* any kinds of speech which seek to negate the occurrence of the Holocaust. They have dealt with such cases in the sphere of, *inter alia*, protecting the rights of others. For example, in *X v the Federal Republic of Germany*, the individual displayed pamphlets on his garden fence describing the Holocaust as a 'zionist swindle or lie.' His conviction included a civil

---

58 X v Austria, Application no. 1747/62 (EComHR 13 December 1963).
59 Otto-Preminger-Institut v Austria, Application no. 13470/87 (ECHR 20 September 1994) para. 49.
60 Seurot v France, Application no. 57383/00 (ECHR 18 May 2004).
61 Féret v Belgium, Application no. 15615/07 (ECHR 16 July 2009) para. 73.

prosecution for group defamation and a criminal conviction for incitement to hatred. The Commission affirmed that such interference is necessary in a democratic society and pursued a legitimate aim, namely, the protection of the rights of others. Here, the Commission underlined that a democratic society 'rests on the principles of tolerance and broadmindedness which the pamphlets in question clearly failed to observe.'[62] In *Remer v Germany*, the Commission held that a conviction for incitement to racial hatred by publishing information which denied that Jews had been gassed in Nazi Germany fell within the legitimate aims of preventing disorder and crime as well as protecting the rights of others.[63] However, just a month after *Remer*, in *Honsik v Austria*, the Commission did not make reference to the legitimate aims pursued in allowing restrictions on this type of expression, as contained in Article 10 of the ECHR, but instead simply stated that the restriction in question was necessary in a democratic society as incorporated in Article 10 given that, if permitted, this expression would contribute to the destruction of the rights and freedoms of the Convention. The approach in *Honsik* appears to be a mélange of Article 10 and Article 17 with the Court enforcing the former but essentially upholding the purpose of the latter, an issue which will be discussed more extensively further on.

Interrelated to revisionist speech and within the framework of promoting National Socialism as an ideology, through rhetoric of hate, more generally, the Court and, previously, the Commission, have repeatedly stressed its incongruence with the Convention's central objectives. For example, in *B.H., M.W., H.P. and G.K v Austria*, the Commission held that the prohibition of activities involving expression of National Socialist ideas was necessary in a democratic society in the interests of national security and territorial integrity as well as for the prevention of crime and, hence, found the interference to be within the realm of Article 10(2) of the ECHR. Moreover, it noted that 'National Socialism is a totalitarian doctrine incompatible with democracy and human rights and that its adherents undoubtedly pursue aims of the kind referred to in Article 17 of the ECHR.[64] This case, therefore, found a violation of Article 10 and concluded with a reference to Article 17.

Thus, hate speech has been legitimately restricted for the purpose of protecting the rights of others and, in certain contexts, for the purposes of protecting national security, territorial integrity and the prevention of crime and disorder, with *Honsik* being the only aforementioned case not clearly applying one of the legitimate aims as incorporated in the article under consideration.

Limitation ground 4: proportionality

The doctrine of proportionality is significant in considering restrictions to Article 10, as it is a key issue to be taken into account when looking at the

---

62 X v Federal Republic of Germany, Application no. 9235/81 (EComHR1982) para. 7.12.
63 Remer v Germany, Application no. 25096/95 (EComHR 6 September 1995).
64 B.H., M.W., H.P. and G.K. v Austria, Application no. 12774/87 (EComHR 12 October 1989).

reasonableness of an interference, as reflected in Article 10 cases later. As established in *Handyside*, 'every formality, condition, restriction or penalty imposed in this sphere must be proportionate to the legitimate aim pursued.'[65] In *Lehideux and Isorni v France*, the proportionality principle was the game breaker. Here, the Court noted that the choice of criminal proceedings rather than other means of intervention through the civil pathway was 'disproportionate and, as such, unnecessary in a democratic society.'[66] As a result, the Court found a breach of Article 10. As the Court noted in *Incal v Turkey*,[67] and reiterated in other cases, such as *Balsytė-Lideikienė v Lithuania*, the government must avoid resorting to criminal proceedings, particularly where it is possible to use other means. In the case against Lithuania, the Court nevertheless held that governments could adopt measures, even of a criminal nature, which have the potential to respond 'appropriately and without excess to such remarks.'[68] Furthermore, the nature and severity of the penalties are key factors to be taken into consideration when appraising the proportionality of an interference of Article 10.[69] Within the same mindset, in *Féret*, the Court considered the proportionality of the restriction which was of a non-criminal nature, thereby, reflecting the Contracting party's restraint when resorting to criminal proceedings, particularly where other means are available.

What kind of speech?

From the ECtHR's jurisprudence, one can discern a hierarchy of different forms of speech with political, artistic and commercial speech being the main identifiable categories[70] as well as freedom of the press[71] and whistleblowing.[72] Within this categorisation of speech, political speech is most highly valued. As stated in *Lingens v Austria*, the freedom of political debate 'is at the very core of the concept of a democratic society,'[73] with *Wingrove v The United Kingdom* noting that there is little scope under Article 10(2) to restrict political speech or issues

---

65 Handyside v UK, Application no. 5493/72 (ECHR 7 December 1976) para. 49.
66 Lehideux and Isorni v France, Application no. 24662/94 (ECHR 23 September 1998) para. 57.
67 Incal v Turkey, Application no. 22678/93 (ECHR 9 June 1998) para. 54.
68 Balsytė-Lideikienė v Lithuania, Application no. 72596/01 (ECHR 4 February 2009) para. 81.
69 Ibid. para. 83.
70 Ian Leigh, 'Damned If They Do, Damned If They Don't: The European Court of Human Rights and the Protection of Religion from Attack' (2011) 17 *Res Publica* 1, 57.
71 Delfi AS v Estonia, Application no. 64569/09 (ECHR 16 June 2015) para. 79.
72 Lucy Vickers, *'Freedom of Speech and Employment'* (1st edn. Oxford University Press, Oxford 2002) 1; Council of Europe Parliamentary Assembly Resolution 1729 (2010) 'Protection of Whistle-Blowers'; Heinisch v Germany, Application no. 28274/08 (ECHR 21 October 2011) para. 43.
73 Case-law includes, amongst others: Lingens v Austria, Application no. 9815/82 (ECHR 8 July 1986) para. 42; Özgurluk v Dayanisma Partisi (ÖDP v Turkey) Application no. 7819/04 (ECHR 10 May 2012) para. 28; Raelien Suisse v Switzerland, Application no. 16354/06 (ECHR 13 July 2012) para. 46.

of public interest.[74] In *Mouvement Raëlien Suisse v Switzerland*, the Court acknowledged that the varying value level and subsequent extent to which a State will enjoy a certain margin of appreciation in interpreting and imposing restriction on expression depends on a range of issues including the type of speech.[75]In this case, it held that 'there is little scope under Article 10(2) of the Convention for restrictions on political speech.'[76] As well as the type of speech and the importance attached thereto, the Court has also considered the significance of the form and tone used for the expression in question as well as its content,[77] giving the notion of expression a wide scope within the ECtHR's jurisprudence. Indeed, freedom within the realm of choice of language and manner of expression is evident in the official recognition of the freedom to shock, as referred to earlier. The right to hyperbolic and provocative language and speech is a central part of political speech and, in this light, polemical,[78] sarcastic[79] and satirical[80] language is permitted. Moreover, a certain degree of exaggeration is broadly understood to be accepted, particularly in discussions on political issues.[81]

Notwithstanding the importance of political speech, the Commission, and now the Court, have both emphasised the duties politicians have in contributing to the overall peace and coexistence of a democratic society. For example, in *Sener v Turkey*, the Commission emphasised the importance of the duties and responsibilities related to the exercise of the freedom of expression within the political sphere and observed that 'it is important for persons addressing the public on sensitive political issues to take care that they do not support unlawful political violence.'[82] Interlinked with this, and particularly significant to the ambit of xenophobic speech uttered by politicians and the weight that is to be attached to such political speech, are the two cases of *Féret* and *Le Pen*. In *Féret v Belgium*, the leader of a radical right political party, *National Front*, brought a claim to Strasbourg for his conviction of incitement to racism. This case dealt with anti-immigrant statements and recommendations made by Féret in leaflets distributed during an electoral campaign. Statements made, included, amongst others 'stop the Islamization of Belgium' and 'save our people from the risk posed by Islam, the conqueror.' Here, the Court emphasised that 'political speech that stirred hatred based on religious, ethnic or cultural prejudices was a threat to social peace and political stability in democratic States.'[83] It also un-

---

74 Wingrove v The United Kingdom, Application no. 17419/90 (ECHR 25 November 1996) para. 58; Surek v Turkey no. 1, Application no. 26682/95 (ECHR 8 July 1999) para. 6; Mouvement Raëlien Suisse v Switzerland, Application no. 16345/06 (ECHR 13 July 2012) para. 61.

75 Mouvement Raëlien Suisse v Switzerland, Application no. 16354/06 (ECHR 13 July 2012) para. 61.

76 Ibid.

77 Fedchenko v Russia, Application no. 33333/04 (ECHR 28 June 2010) para. 38.

78 Lopes Gomes da Silva v Portugal, Application no. 37698/97 (ECHR 28 September 2000) para. 35.

79 Katrami v Greece, Application no. 19331/05 (ECHR 6 December 2007).

80 Eon v France, Application no. 26118/10 (ECHR 14 June 2013) para. 61.

81 Dabrowski v Poland, Application no. 18235/02 (ECHR 19 December 2006) para. 35.

82 Şener v Turkey, Application no. 26680/95 (ECHR 18 July 2000) para. 79.

83 Féret v Belgium, Application no. 15615/07 (ECHR 16 July 2009) para. 73.

derlined the significance of politicians to take care when expressing themselves in public so as to avoid promoting feelings of intolerance but rather defending democracy and the values underlying it.[84] Therefore, although the Court recognised that political parties and their representatives

> must enjoy broad freedom of expression to be able to attract voters, where racist or xenophobic comments were concerned, the electoral context helped to kindle hatred and intolerance and the impact of this type of speech grew worse and more harmful.[85]

The Court did not further assess the meaning of harm of the impact of such speech, nor did it conduct a balancing exercise between the importance of political speech set out in *Wingrove and* the extension of speech to ideas that may shock, offend and disturb in *Handyside*.

In *Le Pen v France*, the Court dealt with a case brought by the president of the French far-right party, *National Front*, for the alleged breach of his Article 10 rights due to his conviction for inciting hatred against Muslims during an interview with *Le Monde* newspaper. He stated, *inter alia*, that 'when I tell people that when we have 25 million Muslims in France we French will have to watch our step, they often reply, 'But Le Pen, that is already the case now!' – and they are right.' Although no explicit reference was made by the Court to the particular duties of politicians in contributing to overall social cohesion and the overall responsibilities attached to political speech, as was the case in *Féret*, this line of reasoning was implicitly reflected in the judgement. For example, the Court noted the significance of allowing free political speech but also underlined the need to protect the rights of others and the importance of combatting racial discrimination.[86] The Court found this case to be inadmissible.

Hate speech: position of the ECtHR

The task of ensuring a smooth interrelationship between the freedom of expression and principles, such as equality and non-discrimination, is central to any discussion pertaining to hate speech uttered by far-right movements. This section will look at examples of the general position of the Commission and the Court when faced with hate speech, with the following sections examining the formulas construed and implemented by the institutions for purposes of ruling on hate speech. The Commission established the position that hate speech is not entitled to Convention protection in the cases of *Glimmerveen and Hagenbeek v The Netherlands* and *Kühnen v the Federal Republic of Germany*. *Glimmerveen and Hagenbeek* was the first case involving the far-right in which Article 17 was enforced. Here, the Commission dealt with a leaflet addressed to 'white Dutch

84 Ibid. para. 75.
85 Ibid. para. 76.
86 Le Pen v France, Application no. 187788/09 (ECHR 20 April 2010) para. 1.

people' which advocated a policy that sought to remove all non-white people from the Netherlands. The Commission held that this policy contained elements of racial discrimination and held the view that 'the expression of the political ideas of the applicants clearly constitutes an activity within the meaning of Article 17 of the Convention.'[87] The Commission's exclusionary approach to racist rhetoric continued in *Kuhnen v Federal Republic of Germany*, which 'left no doubts that racist expression cannot be rehabilitated even half a century after the Second World War for the sake of libertarian argument.'[88] In this case, the applicant held a seminal position in an organisation that was allegedly attempting to re-institute the Nazi party, prohibited in Germany. In this context, he prepared and disseminated pamphlets which included, amongst others, statements such as 'We are called 'Neo-Nazis'! So what! ... We are against: bigwigs, bolshevists, Zionists, crooks, cheats and parasites.' He was sentenced to three years and four months' imprisonment. The Commission found that the applicant's proposal, as expressed in the pamphlets, contravened one of the basic values underlying the Convention, 'namely that the fundamental freedoms enshrined in the Convention are best maintained by an effective political democracy.'[89] In this case, the Commission found that the applicant sought to use the freedom provided in Article 10 as a tool to carry out activities which oppose the spirit of the Convention. The Commission relied on the meaning of Article 17 to pinpoint the necessity ground of Article 10. Initially one may believe this to demonstrate an early day confusion by the Commission on how the non-destruction clause should essentially be used. However this Article 10–17 combination was extended to *Remer v Germany* six years later, which dealt with the dissemination of leaflets suggesting that gas chambers during the Nazi regime never existed.[90] More recently, the Court itself adopted the same approach. In *Perinçek v Switzerland*, which involved expression on the Armenian genocide, the Grand Chamber held that

> Since the decisive point under Article 17 – whether the applicant's statements sought to stir up hatred or violence, and whether by making them he attempted to rely on the Convention to engage in an activity or perform acts aimed at the destruction of the rights and freedoms laid down in it – is not immediately clear and overlaps with the question whether the interference with the applicant's right to freedom of expression was "necessary in a democratic society", the Court finds that the question whether Article 17 is to be applied must be joined to the merits of the applicant's complaint under Article 10 of the Convention.[91]

---

87 Glimmerveen and Hagenbeek v The Netherlands, Application nos. 8348/78 and 8406/78 (EComHR 11 October 1979).

88 Uladzislau Belavusau, *'Freedom of Speech: Importing European and US Constitutional Models in Transitional Democracies'* (1st edn. Routledge, London 2013) 49.

89 Kuhnen v Federal Republic of Germany, Application no. 12194/86 (EComHR 12 May 1988).

90 Remer v Germany, Application no. 25096/94 (EComHR 6 September 1995).

91 Perinçek v Switzerland, Application no. 27510/08 (ECHR 15 October 2015) para. 115.

In *Lehideux & Isorni v France*, the Court dealt with a publication in *Le Monde* that defended the memory of Marshal Pétain.[92] In this case, the Court enforced Article 17, holding that 'justification of a pro-Nazi policy could not be allowed to enjoy the protection afforded by Article 10.'[93] In *Garaudy v France*, the Court dealt with the publication of a book, 'The Founding Myths of Israeli Politics,' which included statements such as 'the myth of six million exterminated Jews that has become a dogma justifying and lending sanctity (as indicated by the very word Holocaust) to every act of violence.' In this case, the Court explained why revisionist speech is to be considered hateful and harmful speech by holding that

> denying crimes against humanity is therefore one of the most serious forms of racial defamation of Jews and of incitement to hatred of them. The denial or rewriting of this type of historical fact undermines the values on which the fight against racism and anti-Semitism are based and constitutes a serious threat to public order. Such acts are incompatible with democracy and human rights because they infringe the rights of others.[94]

The Court relied, once again on Article 17 ECHR in the framework of revisionism.

In the seminal case of *Jersild v Denmark*, the Court dealt with statements expressed on television by a group called the *Greenjackets* (*Grønjakkerne*), which included, *inter alia*, that 'a nigger is not a human being, it's an animal, that goes for all the other foreign workers as well, Turks, Yugoslavs and whatever they are called.' Here, the Court found that expression which was potentially insulting to particular individuals or groups and, hence, is not protected by Article 10 of the Convention.[95] The Court affirmed that 'Article 10 … should not be interpreted in such a way as to limit, derogate from or destroy the right to protection against racial discrimination under the UN Convention.'[96] In *Norwood v The United Kingdom*, the applicant was a Regional Organiser for the *BNP*, a far-right political party. He displayed a large poster in the window of his flat, supplied by the BNP, with a photograph of the Twin Towers in flames, the words 'Islam out of Britain – Protect the British People' and a symbol of a crescent and star in a prohibition sign. Here, the Court found that

> a general, vehement attack against a religious group, linking the group as a whole with a grave act of terrorism, is incompatible with the values proclaimed and guaranteed by the Convention, notably tolerance, social peace and non-discrimination.[97]

---

92 Marshal Pétain has a contradictory role in French history – both as a hero of the First World War and as a discredited chief of State of Vichy France: www.britannica.com/EBchecked/topic/453539/ [Accessed 14 June 2014] Philippe Petain.

93 Lehideux and Isorni v France, Application no. 24662/94 (ECHR 23 September 1998) para. 5.

94 Garaudy v France, Application no. 65831/01 (ECHR 25 June 2003).

95 Jersild v Denmark, Application no. 15890/89 (ECHR 23 September 1994) para. 35.

96 Ibid. para. 27.

97 Norwood v The United Kingdom, Application no. 23131/03 (ECHR 16 November 2004).

In light of its statement, the Court found this case to fall outside the scope of Article 10. In *Soulas v France*, the authors of a book discussing the alleged incompatibilities between European and Islamic cultures complained of an interference of their Article 10 rights due to their conviction by the national court for inciting hate propaganda. In reaching its judgement, the ECtHR found that phrases such as 'it is only if an ethnic civil war breaks out that the solution can be found' could potentially incite aggression against a particular group[98] and is, thus, unacceptable speech under Article 10, but it was not deemed serious enough to fall within the framework of Article 17.[99] In *Balsytė-Lideikienė v Lithuania*, the applicant was founder and owner of a company which published the Lithuanian Calendar 2000 and who received an administrative warning for statements contained in the calendar which were considered insulting to persons of Polish, Russian and Jewish origin. Statements included, amongst others,

> the soviet occupying power, with the help of the communist collaborators, among whom, in particular, were many Jews, for half a century ferociously carried out the genocide and colonisation of the Lithuanian nation.

The Court held that the passages contained statements 'inciting hatred against the Poles and the Jews. The Court considered that these statements were capable of giving the Lithuanian authorities cause for serious concern'[100] and gave the State a wide margin of appreciation to decipher and deal with the case,[101] and, as a result, found no violation of Article 10.

In *Vejdeland and Others v Sweden*, the Court dealt with homophobic speech expressed in leaflets disseminated by an association named *National Youth*. The applicants of this case had been convicted by the Swedish Supreme Court of agitation against a national or ethnic group for the dissemination of leaflets which contained, amongst others, statements that homosexuality has 'a morally destructive effect on the substance of society,' that 'HIV and AIDS appeared early with the homosexuals and that their promiscuous lifestyle was one of the main reasons for this modern-day plague gaining a foothold' and that 'homosexual lobby organisations are also trying to play down pedophilia.' In finding no violation of the freedom of expression, the Court held that 'although these statements did not directly recommend individuals to commit hateful acts, they are serious and prejudicial allegations,'[102] and, by applying *Féret*, noted that incitement to hatred does not necessarily entail a call for violence.[103] The Court also underlined that 'discrimination based on sexual orientation is as serious as

---

98 Soulas and Others v France, Application no. 15948/03 (ECHR 10 July 2008) para. 43.
99 Ibid. para. 48.
100 Balsytė-Lideikienė v Lithuania, Application no. 72596/01 (ECHR 4 November 2009) para. 79.
101 Ibid. para. 80.
102 Vejdeland and Others v Sweden, Application no. 1813/07 (ECHR 9 February 2012) para. 54.
103 Ibid. para. 55.

discrimination based on race, origin or colour.'[104] From the previous cases, it can be discerned that hate speech can be subjected to formalities, conditions, restrictions or penalties by the State. Therefore, although the Convention does not specifically limit and/or sanction speech that promotes racial or ethnic hatred,[105] or other types of hate speech, the Court predominantly deals with relevant cases, as they arise, under Article 10 or Article 17 as well as the Articles 8–14 exception of *Aksu*. The use of Article 17 to prohibit hate speech must not be taken lightly. Article 17 has a great impact on free speech in that it eliminates the speech in question from an Article 10 appraisal and thus the conjoined balancing process. The Commission and the Court have triggered this article merely on the basis of content, that content always being revisionist or negationist speech,[106]with one notable yet unexplained shift in *Norwood*.

Interestingly, the Court has not limited itself to relying on Article 17 in relation to revisionism and negationism in relation to the Holocaust but also anti-Semitism in the form that does not seek to dispute horrific historical tragedies. In *Ivanov v Russia*, the applicant, a newspaper editor, was convicted for a series of publications in his newspaper which called for the exclusion of Jews from social life, alleging the existence of a causal link between social, economic and political discomfort and the activities of Jews, and portraying the malignancy of the Jewish ethnic group. In deciding on this case, the Court relied on Article 17.

Further, probably in view of comprehending and evaluating hate speech in its entirety, the Court has sometimes made an albeit basic psycho-social appraisal of its effects. In *Féret v Belgium*, the Court held that personal attacks and defamation of groups of people violate the dignity and security of the target group. More particularly, it noted that the statements were 'inevitably of such a nature as to arouse, particularly among the less informed members of the public, feelings of distrust, rejection or hatred towards foreigners.'[107] However, in the dissenting opinion of Judge Sajó, joined by Judges Zagrebelsky and Tsotsoria, it was argued that the Court's majority viewed humans as 'nitwits … incapable of replying to arguments and counter-arguments, due to the irresistible drive of their irrational emotions.'[108] This, it was argued, contravened the idea of freedom of expression which incorporates the principle of informed choice. In addition, the Court considered the wider implications of hate propaganda within the sphere of social peace and political stability and further noted that 'to recommend solutions to immigration-related problems by advocating racial discrimination was likely to cause social tension and undermine trust in democratic institutions.'[109] In *Le Pen v France*, the applicant's statements were found to be of such nature

---

104 Ibid.
105 Unlike Article 20(2) of the ICCPR or Article 4(a) of the ICERD.
106 For a full analysis, see David Keane, 'Attacking Hate Speech under Article 17 of the European Convention on Human Rights' (2007) 25 *Netherlands Quarterly of Human Rights* 4, 642.
107 Féret v Belgium, Application no. 15615/07 (ECHR 16 July 2009) para. 69.
108 Féret v Belgium, Application no. 15615/07 (ECHR 16 July 2009).
109 Ibid. para. 77.

as to promote rejection of and hostility against the targeted community, in this case the Muslim community.[110]

When confronted with the possibility of limiting Article 10 in the name of hate speech or even, as discussed later on, of ousting it from Convention protection through Article 17, a variety of questions and ambiguities arise when seeking a balance between conflicting rights and freedoms. Namely, what is hate speech? At what point and under which conditions does speech constitute incitement to discrimination, hostility or violence? When does speech surpass the threshold of simply shocking, offending and disturbing? In some cases, such as that of *Balsytė-Lideikienė v Lithuania*, the Court made reference to the Recommendation of the CoE Committee of Ministers on hate speech[111] as a definitional framework for this phenomenon. However, there is no regular reference to this definition nor is there a formulation of a separate definition by the Commission or the Court and, while there are sporadic references to the effects of hate speech, as considered in this chapter, the aforementioned questions remain open. Establishing the meaning of hate speech, and distinguishing it from controversial yet acceptable speech, is central to any adequate legal analysis. It is a job rendered even more complicated for the ECtHR given the margin of appreciation and the resulting discretion enjoyed by Contracting Parties under certain circumstances. However, the Court has not set out a coherent test to be employed when seeking to determine whether a particular case is one of hate speech. As a result, this lacking definitional backdrop to hate speech is 'unsatisfactory from the point of judicial interpretation, doctrinal development and general predictability and foreseeability.'[112] In addition to a lack of coherence, this may also result in the possible misapplication of relevant principles, as was the case in *Willem v France* where the Court agreed with the conviction of the mayor of a French town who had publicly requested a boycott of Israeli products as a means of protesting the anti-Palestinian policies of Israel. Like the national judiciary, the ECtHR considered that the applicant had not been convicted for his political opinions but for inciting the commission of a discriminatory, and, therefore, punishable act.[113] It is, to say the least, debatable whether Article 10(2) or Article 17 aim at curtailing this genre of expression. Either way, and regardless of any technical difficulties, as noted by Belavusau and reflected in this chapter, 'the expression of racial hatred is not covered by the protective scope of Article 10(1).'[114]

110 Le Pen v France, Application no. 18788/09 (ECHR 20 April 2010).
111 Council of Europe's Committee of Ministers Recommendation 97(20) on Hate Speech (30 October 1997).
112 Tarlach McGonagle, 'The Council of Europe Against Online Hate Speech: Conundrums and Challenges' Expert Paper, Institute for Information Law, Faculty of Law http://hub.coe.int/c/document_library/get_file?uuid=62fab806-724e-435a-b7a5-153ce2b57c18&groupId=10227 [Accessed 15 August 2014] 10.
113 Willem v France, Application no. 10883/05 (ECHR 10 December 2009) para. 35.
114 Uladzislau Belavusau, *'Freedom of Speech: Importing European and US Constitutional Models in Transitional Democracies'* (1st edn. Routledge, London 2013) 49.

Violence as a key element to prohibiting expression

The majority of cases in which the ECtHR considered this theme, and particularly its glorification and/or incitement, were in relation to cases against Turkey dealing particularly with the Kurdish issue. Although the Turkish cases do not fall within the concept of the far-right *per se*, the rationales and discussions therein are pertinent to the discussion of far-right rhetoric and will, therefore, be referred to. Moreover, in relation to inciting violence though expression, the Court and Commission have been clear, stating that a conviction for the offence of incitement to violence through expression is a justified interference with freedom of expression as it seeks to ensure public safety and prevent disorder or crime.[115] Violence was also a central issue in *Erdoğdu and Ince v Turkey*, in which the Court stated that an interviewee 'expressed his view of the Kurdish question and related matters in moderate terms and he did not associate himself in any manner with the use of violence.'[116] As a result, the Court found that there had been a violation of Article 10 as the restriction imposed was to deter public discussion on important political issues rather than limiting hate speech. In *Sener v Turkey*, the Court found that the statements in question could be deemed to be shocking and disturbing for the public, but the author did not associate himself with the use of violence in any context and, on the contrary, promoted the need to employ peaceful methods in resolving the Kurdish issue. In considering inciting or fuelling violence, the Court underlined that it is necessary to take into consideration the contextual backdrop in which the expression occurs. Namely, in *Karatas v Turkey*, the Court underlined that, in light of the sensitivity of the security situation in south-eastern Turkey and the subsequent need for the authorities to be alert to acts capable of fuelling additional violence, the measures taken against the applicant can be said to meet the legitimate aims of protecting national security and territorial integrity and preventing disorder and crime.[117] The issue of violence was extrapolated on in concurring opinions in *Gerger*. More specifically, the joint concurring opinion of Judges Palm, Tulkens, Fischbach, Casadevall and Greve in *Gerger v Turkey* underlined that it is necessary to focus less on words employed and more on the context in which expression occurred. In particular, the questions that need to be answered include whether the language was intended to inflame or incite to violence and whether there was a real and genuine risk that it might actually do so. In Judge Bonello's concurring opinion in *Gerger*, it was underlined that violence needs to be real and actual with punishment of those promoting violence being justifiable in a democratic society 'only if the incitement were

---

115 Osmani v Former Yugoslav Republic of Macedonia, Application no. 50841/99 (ECHR 6 April 2000) and Glimmerveen and Hagenbeek v The Netherlands, Application nos. 8348/78 and 8406/78 (EComHR 11 October 1979).

116 Erdoğdu and Ince v Turkey, Application nos. 25067/94 and 25068/94 (ECHR 8 July 1999) para. 46.

117 Karatas v Turkey, Application no. 23168/94 (ECHR 9 July 1999) para. 44.

such as to create a clear and present danger.'[118] In *Gündüz v Turkey*, the Court recognised that some protection can be granted to expression which is contrary to the objectives of the Convention as long as it does not constitute incitement to violence or hatred. Here, the Court considered that simply defending Sharia was not to be regarded as hate speech if there is no reference to violence.[119] In *Dicle v Turkey*, the Court underlined the significant role that violence plays when determining whether hate speech exists and, thus, if expression should be restricted. More particularly, it held that the expression under consideration did 'not encourage violence, armed resistance or insurrection and does not constitute hate speech.'[120] In relation to the glorification of violence, in *Leroy v France*, the Court dealt with a restriction to the expression of a cartoonist who published a drawing of the attack on the twin towers of the World Trade Centre in a newspaper with a caption which parodied the advertising slogan of a famous brand: 'We have all dreamt of it … Hamas did it.' Here, the Court found no violation of Article 10 by stating that the drawing supported and glorified the violent destruction of the twin towers. The Court based its finding on the caption which accompanied it and noted that the applicant had expressed his moral support for those whom he presumed to be the perpetrators of the attacks.[121] Intertwined with inciting violence is the incitement to hatred, as referred to in *Féret v Belgium*. Here the Court underlined that

> incitation to hatred did not necessarily call for specific acts of violence or other offences. Insults, ridicule or defamation aimed at specific population groups or incitement to discrimination, as in this case, sufficed for the authorities to give priority to fighting hate speech when confronted by the irresponsible use of freedom of expression which undermined people's dignity, or even their safety.[122]

The comparison with classical hate speech jurisprudence and the mostly political cases of Turkey demonstrates a significant theme, namely, that, although violence is a necessary element in the prohibition of speech, such as that in the Turkish cases, this requirement is not extended to hate speech cases as reflected in, inter alia, *Féret* (Islamophobic speech) *and Vejdeland* (homophobic speech). This subsequently denotes the much lower threshold needed for the legitimisation of speech considered to be hate speech in comparison with other types of State controlled speech. The Court has yet to provide any contextual or conceptual explanation on why this large variation in thresholds exists, de-legitimising, once again, its treatment of hate speech cases.

---

118 Gerger v Turkey, Application no. 24919/94 (EComHR 8 July 1999).
119 Gündüz v Turkey, Application no. 35071/97 (ECHR 4 December 2003) para. 51.
120 Dicle v Turkey, Application no. 34685/97 (ECHR 10 February 2005) para. 17.
121 Leroy v France, Application no. 36109/03 (ECHR 2 October 2008) para. 43.
122 Féret v Belgium, Application no. 15615/07 (ECHR 16 July 2009) para. 73.

Freedom of expression: concluding comments

In sum, the freedom of expression is clearly a significant constituent of any analysis pertaining to far-right groups, associations, political parties and their representatives. Relevant cases, which initially dealt with anti-Semitism and neo-Nazi rhetoric, can be seen from the early days of the Commission. Notwithstanding that the context of the cases may have developed over time to include issues such as Islamophobia, anti-immigration rhetoric and Romaphobia, the position of the Commission and the Court has remained consistent: namely, that speech which is deemed by the Court and States to be hate speech is vigorously ousted from Convention protection. This occurs without a definitional analysis of hate speech which the Court follows and with a lacking theoretical approach *vis-à-vis* if, when and why hate speech should, in fact, be banned. Although Article 17 has popped up and, as will be demonstrated later on, has been equated with the doctrine of militant democracy, the backdrop of the Commission and now the Court's deliberation is not that doctrine. The Court is not interested in whether or not speech is destroying democracy but as per Articles 10 and 17 is interested in whether it is harming others. In conceptualising harm, when it comes to hate speech the Court does not require any element of violence to be incorporated in the speech. This has subsequently led to a low threshold that needs to be surpassed if hate speech bans and consequences are to be considered legitimate. Another particularly problematic feature of the jurisprudence is that the means to the end vary according to the importance attached to particular types of speech. More specifically, Article 17 has been predominantly reserved for older Commission cases, which anyhow involved Holocaust revisionism and negationism and newer cases on the same theme whereas all the rest, with the exception of Norwood, go through the balancing exercise of Article 10. While that is the best approach in the name of free speech, one would wish for a balance in the institutions' approach to all types of hate speech.

Freedom of assembly and association: freedom of expression: reasonableness review of restrictions and limitations

Article 11 of the ECHR on the freedom of assembly and association provides that:

1   Everyone has the right to freedom of peaceful assembly and to freedom of association with others, including the right to form and to join trade unions for the protection of his interests.
2   No restrictions shall be placed on the exercise of these rights other than such as are prescribed by law and are necessary in a democratic society in the interests of national security or public safety, for the prevention of disorder or crime, for the protection of health or morals or for the protection of the rights and freedoms of others. This Article shall not prevent the

imposition of lawful restrictions on the exercise of these rights by members of the armed forces, of the police or of the administration of the State.

In *Socialist Party and Others v Turkey*, the ECtHR underlined that the protection of opinions and the freedom to express them, within the meaning of Article 10 of the Convention, is one of the core objectives of the freedoms of assembly and association. It further held that this relationship 'applies all the more in relation to political parties in view of their essential role in ensuring pluralism and the proper functioning of democracy.'[123] Article 11 encompasses both the freedom of association and the freedom of assembly, unlike its international counterpart in the ICCPR, which deals with these two rights in separate articles. It is clear that Articles 10 and 11 are interrelated and interconnected, and, as a result, many of the central issues and standards discussed in the sphere of Article 10 are equally relevant in respect of Article 11.

In the following sections, the freedom of association will be looked at, starting with an analysis of what constitutes an association, followed by an evaluation of the circumstances in which this freedom can be restricted. After that, the freedom of assembly and how it has been assessed by the ECtHR in the realm of the far-right will be considered.

What constitutes an association?

As noted initially by the EComHR in *Young, James and Webster v The United Kingdom*, for an association to exist it must be voluntary and must pursue a common goal.[124] However, an association cannot be a casual gathering of persons seeking to enjoy each other's company but must, instead, be characterised by a certain degree of organisation and stability.[125] The EComHR and the ECtHR, the Report of the Venice Commission[126] and the EU's Charter of Fundamental Rights[127] all deem political parties to constitute an association within the realm of Article 11 of the Convention. The ECtHR holds that

> political parties are a form of association, and that, in view of the importance of democracy in the Convention system, there can be no doubt that political parties come within the scope of Article 11.[128]

123 Socialist Party and Others v Turkey, Application no. 21237/83 (ECHR 25 May 1998) para. 41.
124 Young, James and Webster v The United Kingdom, Application nos. 7601/76 and 7896/77, Commission's report of 14 December 1979, Series B, no. 39, p. 36, § 167. December 1979, Series B, no. 39 p. 36, para. 167.
125 McFeeley v The United Kingdom, Application no. 8317/78, Commission's Decision of 15 May 1980, Decisions and Reports (DR) 20, p. 44.
126 Guidelines on Prohibition and Dissolution of Political Parties and Analogous Measures Adopted by the Venice Commission at its 41st plenary session (Venice, 10–11 December, 1999).
127 Article 12(2) Charter of Fundamental Rights of the European Union.
128 Socialist Party and Others v Turkey, Application no. 21237/83 (ECHR 25 May 1998).

In a number of cases, the Court has reiterated the significant position held by political parties in a democracy. In *United Communist Party of Turkey and Others v Turkey*, the Court stated that 'in view of the role played by political parties, any measure taken against them affected both freedom of association and, consequently, democracy in the State concerned.'[129] Further, it underlined the particularly important role played by political parties in comparison to other associations or groups in a democracy given that 'by the proposal for an overall societal model which they put before the electorate and by their capacity to implement those proposals once they come to power, political parties differ from other organizations which intervene in the political arena.'[130] In *Dicle (on behalf of the Democratic Party (DEP) v Turkey)*, the Court stated that, to ensure a functional democracy, political bodies should be able to make public proposals, even if they are in conflict with mainstream governmental policy or prevailing public opinion.[131] Notwithstanding the important role an association plays or should play in a democracy, this does not mean that it is endowed with an indefinite and unmonitored capacity to participate and promote values and themes that are contrary to principles underlying democracy, nor does it mean that the methods used by it to achieve its aims and objectives can go against these principles. In *KPD v Germany*, the Commission recognised that there always exists the possibility that, in enforcing the rights as provided for by Article 11 (as well as Article 10) of the ECHR, a political party may, in fact, be seeking to pursue the destruction of democracy.[132] The Court also noted that a political party may work towards a change in the law of a State only under the condition that 'the means used to that end must be legal and democratic ... [and]... the change proposed must itself be compatible with fundamental democratic principles.'[133] As a result, a political party inciting violence or policies and practices which contravene democratic principles cannot seek protection under Article 11 against any resulting penalties. As is the case with Article 10, democracy entails concessions and compromises between individuals and groups making up a society in order to satisfy the needs of all the different associations whilst simultaneously preserving values, such as human rights and fundamental freedoms, which are inherently interrelated to democracy.

In *Vona v Hungary*, the Court dealt with the role of Article 11 in the realm of social organisations rather than political parties. It distinguished between political parties and social organisations and movements, stating that they may have

---

129 United Communist Party of Turkey and Others, Application no. 19392/92 (ECHR 30 January 1998) para. 31.

130 Refah Partisi (the Welfare Party) and Others v Turkey, Application nos. 41340/98, 41342/98 and 41344/98 (ECHR 13 February 2003) para. 87.

131 Dicle (on behalf of the Democratic Party DEP) v Turkey, Application no. 25141/94 (10 January 2012) para. 53.

132 Communist Party (KPD) v Germany, Application no. 250/57, Commission Decision of 20 July 1957, Yearbook 1, p. 222.

133 Refah Partisi (the Welfare Party) and Others v Turkey, Application nos. 41340/98, 41342/98 and 41344/98 (ECHR 13 February 2003) para. 98.

the ability to influence the development of politics and public discourse, but, unlike political parties, they enjoy fewer legal privileges to do so.[134] Nevertheless, given the actual political impact which social organisations and movements have when any danger to democracy and its principles is being evaluated, due regard must be given to this impact.[135] As a result, this article is central to any coherent analysis of the far-right which often takes the form of a political party as well as other types of associations.

Legitimate interferences to the freedom of association

The freedom of association is a central tenet of a functioning democracy. In relation to this freedom, the ECtHR noted that 'the way in which national legislation enshrines this freedom and its practical application by the authorities reveals the state of democracy in the country concerned.'[136] Nevertheless, this freedom is not granted an absolute status by the ECHR as it can be legitimately restricted for the purposes provided in part two of the article. The grounds which legitimately exist for restricting the freedom of association are nearly identical in both the ICCPR and the ECHR, with the latter including the prevention of disorder or crime whilst the former refers to the interests of public order. In deciphering whether dissolution is permitted, the ECtHR clearly considers the limitation clause, as provided for by Article 11(2). More particularly, the Court looks at whether the interference is prescribed by law, is necessary in a democratic society, pursues a legitimate aim and is proportional to the aim pursued. At a first glance, the approach taken by the Court in limiting Articles 10 and 11 is similar. However, when one looks at the relevant case-law, it becomes clear that this is not, in fact, the case. The threshold that needs to be surpassed for associations to be banned is higher than speech, with tests like the 'pressing social need' being developed in the realm of political parties, as discussed further down. Moreover, in *Refah Partisi*, the Court underlined that, where the prohibition of political parties is concerned 'only convincing and compelling reasons can justify restrictions on such parties' freedom of association.'[137] In *Vona*, the Court considered the particular status and obstacles faced by non-party groups, underlining that

> the incidental advocacy of anti-democratic ideas is not sufficient in itself to justify banning a political party on grounds of compelling necessity, and even less so in the case of an association which cannot make use of the special status granted to political parties.[138]

---

134 Vona v Hungary Application nos. 35943/10 (ECHR 9 July 2013) para. 69, para. 56.
135 Ibid.
136 Sidiropoulos and Others v Greece, Application no. 57/1997/841/1047 (ECHR 10 July 1998) para. 40.
137 Refah Partisi (the Welfare Party) and Others v Turkey, Application nos. 41340/98, 41342/98 and 41344/98 (ECHR 13 February 2003) para. 100.
138 Vona v Hungary, Application no. 35943/10 (ECHR 9 July 2013) para. 69.

The method adopted by the ECtHR, in relation to restrictions imposed on allegedly anti-democratic associations, has been predominantly established by several cases involving Turkey as well as *Vona v Hungary*, which dealt with a social association/movement rather than directly with a political party, notwithstanding an affiliation between the association, movement and political party, as will be explained further on. Even though the Turkish cases do not involve far-right movements, the methodology created and implemented by the Court as a means to assess the legitimacy of dissolution is relevant to this discussion. *Refah Partisi v Turkey* dealt with the dissolution of an Islamic political party and the suspension of the political rights of the other applicants who were leaders of the party at that time. *Vona v Hungary* included several types of association. The *Hungarian Guard Association (Magyar Gárda Egyesület)* had been founded by ten members of the political party *Movement for a Better Hungary (Jobbik Magyarországért Mozgalom)*, a far-right party. The applicant was chairman of the association. Uniformed members of the Movement held rallies and demonstrations throughout Hungary, including in villages with large Roma populations, and called for the defence of 'ethnic Hungarians' against so-called 'Gipsy criminality.' These demonstrations and rallies were not prohibited by the authorities. One of these demonstrations, involving about two-hundred activists, was organised in Tatárszentgyörgy, a village of some 1,800 inhabitants. The police were present and did not allow the march to pass through a street inhabited by Roma families. In 2007, in reaction to this event, the Budapest Chief Prosecutor's Office lodged a court action seeking the dissolution of the Association. The Prosecutor's Office was of the view that the Movement constituted a division of the Association, and indeed its activity represented a significant part of the Association. In 2008, the Budapest Regional Court ruled in favour of the Prosecutor's Office and disbanded the Association. The Regional Court acknowledged the symbiotic relationship between the Association and the Movement but noted that the legal effect of the judgement was, nevertheless, limited to the dissolution of the Association, since, in the Court's view, the Movement did not have any legal personality. In 2009, the Budapest Court of Appeal upheld the judgement of the Regional Court but established a closer connection between the two entities, also extending the scope of the judgement to the Movement. Given the central role *Vona* plays in the sphere of the Court's treatment of far-right association and assembly, and given the important legal principles developed in *Refah Partisi* and subsequently upheld in *Vona*, the analysis of the legitimate restriction of association will focus predominantly on these two cases.

Limitation ground 1: prescribed by law

In order to satisfy the expression 'prescribed by law,' the Court follows the same route of determination as it does with the freedom of expression. More particularly, the interference must be based on domestic law which is foreseeable and accessible. As mentioned in the framework of freedom of expression, it is impossible to ensure such precision given the organic nature of situations which the law seeks to regulate. A law which provides a certain extent of flexibility and discretion is not, *per se*, inconsistent with the requirement of precision provided that 'the scope of the discretion and the manner of its exercise are indicated with sufficient clarity, having regard to the legitimate aim in question, to give the individual adequate protection against arbitrary interference.'[139]

Limitation ground 2: legitimate aim

In *Refah Partisi*, the Court found that, in light of the importance of secularism in Turkey, the interference pursued the legitimate aim of protecting national security and public safety, prevention of disorder of crime and protection of the rights and freedoms of others.[140] Thus, the analysis of the legitimate aim occurred against the backdrop of secularism, with the Court taking into account an appraisal of the situation in the State under consideration and, specifically, the 'general interest in preserving the principle of secularism in that context in the country'[141] as well as its own previous statements of secularism being a fundamental principle in line with the rule of law, human rights and democracy.[142] Further, in this case, the Court held that the dissolution of a political party with an anti-democratic mandate is 'also consistent with Contracting Parties' positive obligations under Article 1 of the Convention to secure the rights and freedoms of persons within their jurisdiction.'[143] In *Vona*, the Court mentioned that the interference pursued a legitimate aim of ensuring public safety, preventing disorder and protecting the rights of others, regardless of the applicant's argument that no specific instance of disorder or violation of the rights of others had been demonstrated.[144] The Court then went on to reiterate that a State is entitled to take preventive action to ensure the protection of the rights of others, in this case Roma persons, in the event that their rights and democratic values are at serious risk, one such value being the 'co-existence of members of society free from racial segregation.'[145] In this realm, the Court noted that the removal of the threat to the rights of others could only be ensured by 'removing the organisational back-up of the Movement provided by the Association.'[146]

---

139 Margareta and Roger Andersson v Sweden, Application no. 12963/87 (ECHR 20 January 1992).
140 Refah Partisi (the Welfare Party) and Others v Turkey, Application nos. 41340/98, 41342/98 and 41344/98 (ECHR 13 February 2003) para. 67.
141 Ibid. para. 105.
142 Ibid. para 93.
143 Ibid. para. 103.
144 Vona v Hungary, Application no. 35943/10 (ECHR 9 July 2013) para. 52.
145 Ibid. para. 57.
146 Ibid. para. 71.

Limitation ground 3: necessary in a democratic society?

In *Refah Partisi*, the Court held that the dissolution of an association should constitute the last resort, with less intrusive measures being implemented when possible. In applying the necessity test, 'the right of association is accorded particular protection in the maintenance of pluralist opinion and democracy.'[147] As is the case with the freedom of expression and Article 10(2), the restrictions to Article 11 are necessary in a democratic society only when there exists a pressing social need to invoke the restrictions. In order to make this determination, the Court must consider three factors, namely whether a risk to democracy was sufficiently imminent, whether the acts and speeches of the leaders and members of the political party were imputable to the party as a whole and whether the acts and speeches imputable to the political party promoted a societal model incompatible with the concept of a democratic society.[148] Further, in determining the necessity of the impugned measure, the Court must appreciate the contextual and, sometimes, historical setting in which a particular dissolution occurs. For example, in *Refah Partisi*, the Court considered the general interest in preserving secularism in Turkey.[149] The issue of context was deemed significant in other Article 11 cases, such as *Herri Batasuna and Batasuna v Spain*, where the Court underlined that, in view of the Spanish experience in the field of terrorist attacks, a link with **Euskadi Ta Askatasuna** (ETA) and the applicant parties could objectively result in a threat to democracy.[150]

Limitation ground 4: proportionality

In *Refah Partisi*, the Court noted 'that the nature and severity of the interference are … factors to be taken into account when assessing its proportionality.'[151] In *Herri Batasuna and Batasuna v Spain*, the Court held that, in order to determine whether an interference was proportionate to the legitimate aim pursued, it must consider it in light of the case as a whole.[152] In *Refah Partisi*, the Court noted that, after the party's dissolution, only five of its MPs temporarily forfeited their parliamentary office and their role as leaders of a political party. The one

---

147 Mustafa Koçak & Esin Örücü, 'Dissolution of political parties in the Name of Democracy: Cases from Turkey and the European Court of Human Rights' (2003) 9 *European Public Law* 3, 419.
148 Refah Partisi (the Welfare Party) and Others v Turkey, Application nos. 41340/98, 41342/98 and 41344/98 (ECHR 13 February 2003) para. 104 (This test was also implemented in Vona v Hungary).
149 Ibid. para. 105.
150 Herri Batasuna and Batasuna v Spain, Application nos. 25803/04 and 25817/04 (ECHR 6 November 2009) para. 89.
151 Refah Partisi (the Welfare Party) and Others v Turkey, Application nos. 41340/98, 41342/98 and 41344/98 (ECHR 13 February 2003) para. 133.
152 Herri Batasuna and Batasuna v Spain, Application nos. 25803/04 and 25817/04 (ECHR 6 November 2009) para. 75.

hundred and fifty two remaining MPs continued to sit in Parliament. In *Vona,* the Court noted that no additional sanction was imposed on the Association or the Movement or their members who were in no way prevented from continuing political activities in other forms.

Violence as a key element in limiting association

As is the case with the freedom of expression, the issue of violence is central in ascertaining whether there has been a breach of Article 11. In *Refah Partisi*, the Court considered that the members of the party in question mentioned the possibility of resorting to force to overcome the obstacles that *Refah Partisi* was facing in the political arena.[153] The Court recognised that, while its leaders did not, in government documents, call for the use of force and violence as a political weapon, 'they did not take prompt practical steps to distance themselves from those members of [Refah] who had publicly referred with approval to the possibility of using force against politicians who opposed them.'[154] In *Vona v Hungary*, the Court underlined that, unless the impugned association can reasonably be regarded as a hotbed for violence or incarnating a negation of democratic principles, restrictions to the freedom of association are incompatible with the Convention.[155] The necessity for violence in Article 11, as set out in *Vona v Hungary*, which involves hate, as this is conceptualised in the present book, reflects the aforementioned threshold variation in terms of how hate speech and hateful associations are tackled. In brief, no element of violence is necessary for hate speech to be banned.

Limiting association: destruction of democracy

Limitations and restrictions may be imposed on practices, mandates and activities which are promoted and implemented by political parties and social organisations and movements through the enforcement of Article 11(2) and/or Article 17. In particular relation to political parties, the Court emphasised the need to protect them vigorously 'in view of their essential role in ensuring pluralism and the proper functioning of democracy.'[156] In fact, it has repeatedly underlined that the dissolution of a political party and restricting party members from carrying out their activities for a particular time period are measures to be resorted to only in the most serious of cases.[157] Notwithstanding the high threshold that is to be

---

153 Refah Partisi (the Welfare Party) and Others v Turkey, Application nos. 41340/98, 41342/98 and 41344/98 (ECHR 13 February 2003) para. 130.
154 Ibid. para. 131.
155 Vona v Hungary Application no. 35943/10 (ECHR 9 July 2013) para. 64.
156 Refah Partisi (the Welfare Party) and Others v Turkey, Application nos. 41340/98, 41342/98 and 41344/98 (ECHR 13 February 2003) para. 88.
157 See United Communist Party of Turkey and Others, Socialist Party and Others, cited earlier, and Freedom and Democracy Party (ÖZDEP) v Turkey.

attained in relation to the potential or actual destructiveness of an association, in the two central cases of *Refah Partisi v Turkey* and *Vona v Hungary,* the Court upheld the dissolution of the *Turkish Welfare Party* and the Hungarian far-right social movement and association respectively. With regard to the latter, the Court underlined that the dissolution of associations and movements is 'a sanction of comparable gravity'[158] to that of political parties and, therefore, such a measure must be as relevant and sufficient as in the case of dissolution of a political party. It also recognised that, in the case of an association and in light of its more limited national influence, 'justification for preventative restrictive measures may be less compelling than in the case of a political party.'[159] Moreover, it distinguished, yet again, between a political party and other types of association by noting that 'the incidental advocacy of anti-democratic ideas is not enough, *per se,* for banning a political party in the sense of compelling necessity and even less so in the case of an association.'[160] Despite these statements, the actual judgements reflect that the same route and analysis are taken for registered and unregistered movements and groups, with the guiding factor always being whether the interference in question is permitted under Article 11(2) or whether the activities of such an entity fall outside the scope of the Convention, as per Article 17.

In seeking to determine the potentially destructive impact of an association, the Court has warned of associations which may hide their true intentions in trying to avoid prohibitions or sanctions. In *Refah Partisi,* the Court considered that the 'constitution and programme of a political party cannot be taken into account as the sole criterion for determining its objectives and intentions.'[161] The political experience of the Contracting States has shown that, in the past, political parties with aims contrary to the fundamental principles of democracy have not revealed such aims in their official publications until after taking power. As a result, the Court notes that

> the content of the programme must be compared with the actions of the party's leaders and the positions they defend. Taken together, these acts and stances may be relevant in proceedings for the dissolution of a political party, provided that as a whole they disclose its aims and intentions.[162]

In relation to *Vona,* it was the totalitarian and racist nature of the association that led to its destructiveness. The Court made clear that it does not tolerate racist expression or activity and acknowledged that the Movement relied on a race-based opposition to the Roma minority.[163] Moreover, the Court noted that

---

158 Vona v Hungary, Application no. 35943/10 (ECHR 9 July 2013) para. 58.
159 Ibid.
160 Ibid. para. 69.
161 Refah Partisi (the Welfare Party) and Others v Turkey, Application nos. 41340/98, 41342/98 and 41344/98 (ECHR 13 February 2003) para. 101.
162 Ibid.
163 Vona v Hungary Application no. 35943/10 (ECHR 9 July 2013) para. 66.

'it is not at all improbable that totalitarian movements, organised in the form of political parties, might do away with democracy, after prospering under the democratic regime.'[164] In the concurring opinion of Judge Pinto De Albuquerque, it was underlined that the ECtHR had reiterated the significance of combatting racial discrimination including hate speech and racial violence. Furthermore, the opinion noted that 'the vulnerability of the group against whom discrimination and violence takes place has been a factor in the Court's analysis.'[165] It also emphasised the positive duty that States Parties have to

> criminalize speech or other forms of dissemination of racism, xenophobia or ethnic intolerance, prohibit every assembly and dissolve every group, organization, association or party that promotes them.[166]

Thus, as noted by the Court in *Refah Partisi* and then in *Vona*, political parties which aim for the destruction of democracy cannot enjoy Convention protection against penalties imposed on those grounds. However, due care must be taken not to surpass the legitimate objective, which, in this case, is the protection of democracy. Therefore, in the previous two cases, the Court has stipulated that limitations and restrictions are not to be taken lightly and that 'only convincing and compelling reasons can justify restrictions on such parties' freedom of association.'[167] This was a significant improvement from the pre-Vona case which also involved a racist association. In *W.P and Others v Poland*, which came about nearly ten years before *Vona*, the ECtHR showed a worrying approach to the restriction of associations in that there was no adequate jurisprudential and/or contextual analysis of the issues at stake. This case involved the registration of a series of associations by the applicants, including *The National and Patriotic Association of Polish Victims of Bolshevism and Zionism*. The aims of the organisation included 'taking action aimed at improving the living conditions of Polish victims of Bolshevism/Bolsheviks and Zionism/Zionists' and 'taking actions aimed at determined opposition to the psychological and physical murder of the Polish nation.' The Court commenced its (very minimal) analysis of this association by citing Article 17 ECHR and observed that its central aim was to 'prevent totalitarian groups from exploiting in their own interests the principles enunciated by the Convention.'[168] The Court found that the memorandum of this association 'can be seen as reviving anti-Semitism.'[169] The Court deduced, without any contextual or other investigation, that the applicants were seeking

---

164 Ibid. para. 99.
165 Vona v Hungary, Application no. 35943/10 (ECHR 9 July 2013) Concurring Opinion of Judge Pinto De Albuquerque.
166 Ibid.
167 Refah Partisi (the Welfare Party) and Others v Turkey, Application nos. 41340/98, 41342/98 and 41344/98 (ECHR 13 February 2003) para. 100.
168 W.P. and Others v Poland, Application no. 42264/98 (ECHR 22 September 2004) 11.
169 Ibid. 10.

to use Article 11 for activities which are against the spirit of the Convention,[170] and, as such, the Court enforced Article 17. The Court did not conceptualise the harm in this association, did not set thresholds that it had to surpass, did not conduct any sort of balancing exercise and, as usual, offered no theoretical analysis of the benefit of ousting this association from convention protection.

Dissolution of an association: establishing a sufficiently imminent risk

The intricately complex question of timing in the realm of dissolution of associations must be considered with due care to avoid unsubstantiated actions which constitute a breach of Article 11, on the one hand, whilst avoiding harmful consequences of destructive associations on the other. In *Refah Partisi v Turkey*, the Court held that a State may reasonably prevent the execution of a policy which is against the letter and spirit of the Convention. The Court also underlined that

> A State cannot be required to wait, before intervening, until a political party has seized power and begun to take concrete steps to implement a policy incompatible with the standards of the Convention and democracy, even though the danger of that policy for democracy is sufficiently established and imminent.[171]

In that case, the Court established a threshold for the dissolution of associations through the 'sufficiently imminent risk to democracy' test. In *Vona v Hungary*, the Court found that the State may also take such preventive measures to protect democracy against such non-party entities 'if sufficiently imminent prejudice to the rights of others undermines the fundamental values upon which a democratic society rests and functions.'[172] Here, the Court reiterated the provision related to the timing of intervention, stating that 'the State cannot be required to wait, before intervening, until a political movement takes action to undermine democracy or has recourse to violence.'[173]

The freedom of racist association and its effects in the workplace

In two cases brought against the U.K., namely, the *Associated Society of Locomotive Engineers & Firemen (ASLEF) v The United Kingdom* and *Redfearn v The United Kingdom*, the Court had to decipher the freedom of association rights in the sphere of a far-right party, namely the *BNP*, *vis- à-vis* membership

---

170 W.P. and Others v Poland, Application no. 42264/98 (ECHR 22 September 2004) 11.
171 Refah Partisi (the Welfare Party) and Others v Turkey, Application nos. 41340/98, 41342/98 and 41344/98 (ECHR 13 February 2003) para. 102.
172 Vona v Hungary Application no. 35943/10 (ECHR 9 July 2013) para. 57.
173 Ibid.

of a trade union and employment respectively. In *ASLEF v The United Kingdom*, the applicant, a trade union, alleged that it had been prevented by the national courts from expelling one of its members due to his membership of the *BNP*. In considering this case, the ECtHR held that the central question was whether the State had struck an equitable balance between the rights of the member and those of the trade Union.[174] It held that Article 11 of the ECHR entailed the right of trade unions to choose its members,[175] and so, this, in addition to the fact that no particular hardship was suffered by the member as a result of his expulsion from the trade union,[176] led to a violation of the trade union's Article 11 rights.[177] In *Redfearn v The United Kingdom*, the applicant had been dismissed by his employer following his identification as a candidate for the *BNP* in upcoming local elections. In considering whether the applicant's right to freedom of association, as enshrined in Article 11, had been violated, the ECtHR noted that the appropriate remedy for dismissing a person on his political beliefs would be a claim for unfair dismissal under national law,[178] a remedy which the applicant was not entitled to because he had not been employed for the one year qualifying period.[179] Thus, in light of the absence of this remedy and taking into consideration that the *BNP* was not illegal under national law,[180] the Court found that a 'legal system which allows dismissal from employment solely on account of the employee's membership of a political party carries with it the potential for abuse.'[181] In finding a violation of Article 11, the Court made no reference to the nature of the *BNP's* mandate, ideology, structure or objectives, which are directly interlinked with far-right extremism. This case could reflect the necessity for manifesting a particular expression for harm to be determined as the applicant had been dismissed solely for his political opinion rather than its manifestation and, had he pursued the latter in his workplace, the outcome of the case could potentially be different.

Freedom of association: concluding comments

In the ambit of association, the Court dealt with a wave of Turkish claims eventually culminating in the landmark case of *Refah Partisi* which developed significant points of law that are directly applicable to the sphere of the far-right. The Court also dealt with far-right associations in *Vona v Hungary* and *W.P. and others v Poland*. By assessing these cases and the albeit severe lack of proper

---

174 Associated Society of Locomotive Engineers & Firemen (ASLEF) v The United Kingdom, Application no. 11002/05 (ECHR 27 February 2007) para. 49.
175 Ibid. para. 39.
176 Ibid. para. 50.
177 Ibid. para. 53.
178 Ibid. para. 50.
179 Ibid. para. 51.
180 Ibid. para. 47.
181 Ibid. para. 55.

handling in the Polish case, it is concluded that the discourse pertaining to the interpretation of Article 11 and the prohibition of an association have resulted in an approach which is better rounded than the Court's stance on hate speech, which is fleeting in its content and vigorous in stance. This does not mean that the approach is well-rounded and as expected in terms of substance, content and theory, especially given the impact of banning an association on the functioning of a liberal democracy. The Court has also considered the exercise of Article 11 in the employment framework in which trade unions are endowed with the right to choose membership on grounds of ideologies and belief systems but imposes the obligation on States to protect its citizens from being dismissed from their employment on such grounds.

Freedom of assembly: a general overview

As well as the freedom of association, the freedom of assembly is a significant constituent of Article 11. The freedom of assembly constitutes a significant tool for far-right groups to promote their belief-systems through demonstrations, rallies and marches. The importance of assembly was noted in *Fáber v Hungary*, where the Court held that interferences to the freedom of assembly and expression 'other than in cases of incitement to violence or rejection of democratic principles ... do a disservice to democracy and often even endanger it.'[182] This section will consider two cases which are directly linked to the far-right use of assembly to promote ideas and values, namely *Fáber v Hungary* and *Vona v Hungary* while briefly mentioning the case of *Vajnai v Hungary*. The aim is to consider in what circumstances the Court permits this freedom to be restricted and on what grounds.

Legitimately limiting assembly

Fáber v Hungary involved the silent holding of an Árpád-striped flag by the applicant near a demonstration held by the *Hungarian Socialist Party* against racism and hatred. The police supervising the scene called on the applicant either to remove the banner or leave. The applicant refused to do so and was subsequently taken into custody and placed under interrogation, following which he was fined two hundred Euros for disobeying police instructions. In considering whether the aforementioned facts led to a breach of Articles 10 and 11, the ECtHR held that this case requires 'the right to freedom of assembly to be balanced against the right to freedom of expression and, allegedly, against the right of others to freedom of assembly.'[183] Further, it underlined that the freedom of assembly protects a demonstration that may annoy or offend persons and that the rights enshrined in this article must apply to all assemblies 'except those

---

182 Fáber v Hungary, Application no. 40721/08 (ECHR 24 July 2012) para. 37.
183 Ibid. para. 28.

where the organizers and participants have violent intentions or otherwise deny the foundations of a democratic society.'[184] It is imperative to note the link with Article 10 cases involving hate speech in which the ECtHR does not require an element of violence or violent intentions to exist for purposes of finding the hate speech ban to be legitimate. The Court further noted that the display of this particular flag, which was used by a totalitarian regime in Hungary, may create feelings of uneasiness, but these sentiments 'cannot alone set the limits of freedom of expression. To hold otherwise would mean that freedom of speech and opinion is subjected to the heckler's veto.'[185] In considering whether Article 17 could come into play, the Court recognised that, even though expression is not always allowed in certain times, places and contexts, given the obligation to protect the honour of those murdered and their relatives, it was satisfied that the use of this flag did not include any abusive element, such as the contempt for the victims of a totalitarian regime.[186] The Court did not offer any coherent explanation as to how it reached this conclusion, which can be arguably controversial given that the applicant was standing at the steps leading to the Danube embankment, the location where in 1944/1945, during the Arrow Cross regime, Jews were exterminated in large numbers, holding a flag which albeit not illegal could be deemed offensive and, to use the Court's own words, to reject democratic principles. The decision in itself is not controversial, and many scholars would argue that it is in line with the freedom under consideration and human rights law more generally. What is significant, however, is the vast difference between the treatment of speech which is revisionist or negationist in relation to the Holocaust, as discussed earlier, and this case which involved the same thoughts and ideas but, rather than being manifested in a publication or during an event for example, was done through silent symbolism. Another particular element of this case is that the Court underlined that, in determining the proportionality of a particular form of interference, the location and timing of the display of a symbol with multiple meanings plays a significant role. As noted by the dissenting opinion of Judge Keller, the flag that was being held was associated in public opinion with the Nazi regime in Hungary and was raised at a place where grave human rights violations were committed during the Second World War. If one takes into account that, in previous cases involving holocaust denial and related issues,[187] the Court and the Commission repeatedly found that such speech should not be afforded Convention protection, why then should this flag, which constitutes a form of expression during an assembly, be allowed? Notwithstanding that the Court recognised that, where an applicant expresses contempt for victims of totalitarian regimes this may call for an application of Article 17, it declared that 'it is satisfied that in the instant case no such

---

184 Ibid. para. 37.
185 Ibid. para. 57.
186 Ibid. para. 58.
187 See, *inter alia*, Kühnen v Germany, B.H., M.W., H.P. and G.K. v Austria, Walendy v Germany, Honsik v Austria and Witszch v Germany.

abusive element can be identified.'[188] It reached this conclusion loosely with no explanation on how it did so. In finding a violation of Article 10 read in light of Article 11, the Court took into account the non-violent nature of the applicant's conduct, the distance held from the other demonstration and the absence of the potential risk of disturbance.[189] So, in determining the risk of disturbance and consequently reaching its verdict, the previously discussed 'sufficiently imminent risk' test finds a counterpart in the realm of the freedom of assembly and, particularly the right to demonstrate, with emphasis on the scale of potential consequences rather than their timing. More particularly, in this case, the Court held that the mere existence of a risk is not sufficient to ban a demonstration. Instead, authorities must concretely assess the possible scale of potential disturbance in order to be able to choose the appropriate measures to neutralise the threat of violence.[190] Moreover, the peculiar element of this case is how the Court could have departed so much from previous cases involving, in particular, reviving the traumas of the Second World War.

Before proceeding to *Vona*, reference must be made to the case of *Vajnai v Hungary*, which, although dealing with the left rather than the far-right, contained similar facts to *Fáber* and the presentation of symbols. In *Vajnai*, the applicant only alleged a violation of Article 10. This case dealt with a form of visual expression during a demonstration, namely the wearing of a symbol associated with the past dictatorship and, more particularly, a five-pointed red star. The applicant was subsequently prosecuted for wearing a totalitarian symbol in public. When finding that the impugned measure breached Article 10, the Court held that this expression could not be denied Convention protection simply because it makes certain individuals or groups feel uneasy or because they are considered by some to be disrespectful.[191] The reasons for the differences between these cases shall be extrapolated upon further on.

In *Vona v Hungary*, discussed previously, the Court also dealt with the issue of demonstrations given that the group in question carried out rallies using a paramilitary formation which was 'reminiscent of the Hungarian Nazi (Arrow Cross) movement which was the backbone of the regime that was responsible for ... the mass extermination of Roma in Hungary.'[192] Although the Court recognised that it was not asked to consider the extent to which the demonstrations constituted a legitimate exercise of the freedom of assembly, the demonstrations, nevertheless, had to be taken into account with a view to revealing the association's actual objectives and mandate.[193] As a result, it made relevant comments and considerations in relation to the freedom of assembly. It held that, if the freedom of assembly is repeatedly enforced in the form of intimidating marches

---

188 Fáber v Hungary, Application no. 40721/08 (ECHR 24 July 2012) para. 58.
189 Ibid. para. 47.
190 Ibid. para. 40.
191 Vajnai v Hungary, Application no. 33629/05 (ECHR 8 July 2008) para. 57.
192 Ibid. para. 65.
193 Ibid. para. 69.

and rallies involving large groups, the State can take the necessary restrictive measures to 'avert the danger which such large-scale intimidation represents for the functioning of democracy.'[194] In deciding on the demonstrations, the EC-tHR, as well as the national courts, placed particular emphasis on the fact that the rallies involved, *inter alia*, the display of the Arrow Cross symbols which brought about a 'public menace by generating social tension and bringing about an atmosphere of impending violence.'[195] As a result, and even though the Court underlined that no violence occurred during the association's rallies, their military style formation and marching through villages, wearing ominous arm-bands reminiscent of the Arrow Cross and calling for racial division must have an 'intimidating effect on members of a racial minority, especially when they are in their homes as a captive audience.'[196] As summed up in the Concurring Opinion of Judge Pinto De Albuquerque, when considering the dissolution of a political party, one must also consider its 'overall style ... meaning its symbols, uniforms, formations, salutes, chants and other modes of expression.'[197]

In this light, the Court found that the activity of the association 'exceeds the outer limit of the scope of protection secured by the Convention for expression or assemblies and amounts to intimidation.'[198] Moreover, it pinpointed the interrelation between the freedom of expression and the freedom of assembly by underlining the fact that, in cases where expression is coupled with conduct and that conduct is

> associated with the expression of ideas that is intimidating or threatening or interferes with the free exercise or enjoyment by another of any Convention right or privilege on account of that person's race, these considerations cannot be disregarded even in the context of Articles 10 and 11.[199]

It is noteworthy in relation to symbols used during assemblies, in the cases of *Fáber v Hungary*[200] and *Vajnai v Hungary*[201] which dealt with prosecuting the holding of an Árpád-striped flag[202] and the wearing of a five-pointed red star[203] respec-

---

194 Ibid.
195 Ibid. para. 61.
196 Ibid. para. 66.
197 Ibid. Concurring Opinion of Judge Pinto De Albuquerque.
198 Ibid. para. 66.
199 Ibid.
200 Fáber v Hungary, Application no. 40721/08 (ECHR 24 July 2012).
201 Vajnai v Hungary, Application no. 33629/05 (ECHR 8 July 2008).
202 The roots of the flag go back more than eight-hundred years to a medieval dynasty. However, the flag was expropriated by the notorious Hungarian Arrow Cross Party, whose Nazi-installed puppet regime in late 1944 began murdering thousands of Jews. www.jpost.com/Jewish-World/Jewish-News/Nazi-linked-flag-surfaces-in-Hungary [Accessed 17 April 2015]. This is not an illegal symbol in Hungary.
203 The communist red star has been a banned symbol in Hungary since 1994. www.politics.hu/20080709/European-court-overturns-hungarian-prohibition-on-communist-star/ [Accessed 17 April 2015].

tively, that the Court found the impugned measures to have breached Article 10 and/or Article 11. The reason for these differentiations is that *Fáber* and *Vajnai* lacked the intimidating and threatening environment created by the assembly in its entirety within the framework of *Vona*, intimidations and threats which have not yet been required to constitute part of the justification for hate speech bans.

Freedom of assembly: concluding comments

In theory, assemblies which reject democratic principles should not be permitted.[204] However, the symbols used in *Fáber*, could, in fact, be argued to be representative of regimes and ideologies which reject democratic principles. Read in line with the Court's position on hate speech and the manner in which it has interpreted democracy and a democratic society in the realm of its ban justification, a certain confusion is created. The *Fáber* decision reinforces the position that the Court does not actually have a common line and understanding of the theory behind what it is doing *vis-à-vis* hate. The rigour of the Court, on the one hand, to ban speech that is merely insulting and offensive but, on the other hand, to allow a person to hold a symbol of a regime which if one denies publicly means being can be caught up in the Article 17 trap, simply makes no sense. The issue of violence plays a major role in deciphering whether an assembly should be permitted. As noted by the Court, if the freedom of assembly, guaranteed by Article 11 of the Convention, is not to lose out on its meaning and objective, national authorities must be tolerant towards peaceful gatherings, in situations where demonstrators do not engage in acts of violence.[205] However, violence took a broad meaning in *Vona*. More particularly, in denouncing the rallies in *Vona*, the Court underlined that violence as a condition for permitting impugned measures did not necessarily entail actual violence but also incorporated the intimidation felt by victims targeted by the rallies, thereby, extending the scope of this condition.[206] In fact, it was the intimidating and racially discriminating nature of the rallies in *Vona* which directly affected the 'others' which subsequently allowed for a restriction on such exercises of the right to assembly.[207]

Final remarks on Article 11

In a nutshell, associations which seek to destroy democracy[208] and assemblies which go beyond simply annoying or causing offence to persons who do not share the same belief system[209] and create a threatening and intimidating environment for its targets do not enjoy the rights and freedoms enshrined in the

---

204 Fáber v Hungary, Application no. 40721/08 (ECHR 24 July 2012) para. 37.
205 Ibid. para. 47.
206 Vona v Hungary, Application no. 35943/10 (ECHR 9 July 2013) para. 61.
207 Ibid. para. 66
208 The threshold as underlined in Refah Partisi (the Welfare Party) and Others v Turkey, Application nos. 41340/98, 41342/98 and 41344/98 (ECHR 13 February 2003) para. 98.
209 The threshold as underlined in Stankov and the United Macedonian Organization Ilinden v Bulgaria, Application nos. 29221/95 and 29225/95 (ECHR 2 October 2001) para. 86.

Convention. This is the general thematic framework regardless of cases, such as *Fáber*, which can be considered to be a hiccup (and potentially a positive one in the realm of free speech) when placed in the broader framework of dealing with expression and association relating to the Second World War hate. Although *W.P and Others v Poland* was legally, theoretically and jurisprudentially poor in terms of the level of analysis contained therein *Vona* represented an improvement in this realm. *Vona* is very much founded on principles developed in *Refah Partisi;* and constitutes a significant precedent for other groups and movements promoting such ethnically exclusionist and/or expulsionist rhetoric and activities.

Article 17 of the ECHR: non-destruction clause

Article 17 provides that

> Nothing in this Convention may be interpreted as implying for any State, group or person any right to engage in any activity or perform any act aimed at the destruction of any of the rights and freedoms set forth herein or at their limitation to a greater extent than is provided for in the Convention.

In relation to the application of the doctrine by the ECtHR, it has been noted that 'almost since its inception, the ECtHR has been required to consider the question of the rights of anti-democratic actors within the liberal democracies.'[210] 'Article 17 was originally included in the Convention in order to 'prevent the misappropriation of ECHR rights by those with totalitarian aims.'[211] On a practical level, the ECtHR has, on occasion, sought to extrapolate on limiting certain rights for the preservation of democracy and, in doing so, has put forth its own justifications for a militant model of democracy. As early back as *Klass v Germany*, the ECtHR underlined that 'some compromise between the requirements for defending democratic society and individual rights is inherent in the system of the Convention.'[212] In *United Communist Party of Turkey and Others v Turkey*, the problem which arose is how to strike an equitable balance between defending democracy whilst simultaneously protecting individual rights and freedoms. The resulting balancing test emanates from the premise that one must grant due consideration to 'the democratic importance of freedom of speech on the one hand and the harmful consequences of hate propaganda on the other hand.'[213] In *Thoma v Luxembourg*, the ECtHR held that restrictions on rights guaranteed by the Convention must be narrowly construed and enforced in the interest of public and social life in its entirety as well as in the interest of

---

210 Paul Harvey, 'Militant Democracy and the European Convention on Human Rights' (2004) 29 *European Law Review* 3, 407.

211 Law Commission: Hate Crime: The Case for Extending the Existing Offences Appendix A: Hate Crime and Freedom of Expression under the European Convention on Human Rights (2013) Consultation Paper no. 213.

212 Klass and Others v Germany, Application no. 502971 (ECHR 6 September 1978) para. 59

213 Stefan Sottiaux, 'Bad Tendencies in the ECtHR's Hate Speech Jurisprudence' (2011) 7 *European Constitutional Law Review* 1, 48.

individuals making up that society.[214] In *Ždanoka v Latvia*, it was held that 'in order to guarantee the stability and effectiveness of a democratic system, the State may be required to take specific measures to protect itself.'[215] In *Witzsch v Germany*, the Court similarly observed that 'the general purpose of Article 17 is to make it impossible for individuals to take advantage of a right with the aim of promoting ideas contrary to the text and the spirit of the Convention.'[216] As noted by the Court in *Ždanoka v Latvia*, the possibility exists that persons or groups may use the rights and freedoms emanating from the Convention in order to conduct themselves in such a manner as to destroy the rights or freedoms protected therein.[217] As a result, the Court considered that 'no one should be authorised to rely on the Convention's provisions in order to weaken or destroy the ideals and values of a democratic society.'[218] In *Lehideux and Isorni v France*, the concurring opinion of Judge Jambrek attempted to set out the conditions for the application of Article 17. More particularly, he held that, in order for this article to be enforced, the aim of the offending actions must be

> to spread violence or hatred, to resort to illegal or undemocratic methods, to encourage the use of violence, to undermine the nation's democratic and pluralist political system, or to pursue objectives that are racist or likely to destroy the rights and freedoms of others.[219]

Article 17 lies at the crossroads between regular situations and states of emergency, given that it may be excused from regular tests imposed by the Convention but is not as broad as Article 15.[220] What becomes emphatically apparent is that this article has been used rather recklessly in cases involving prejudicial but non-violent speech uttered by individuals and not groups or politicians, such as *Norwood*. In relation to the duties imposed on States by the spirit of this article, Buyse has argued that 'Article 17 enables States to act to protect freedoms and democracy but does not force them to do so.'[221] However, when discussing Article 17 in *Glimmerveen and J.Hagenbeek v the Netherlands*, the Commission held that, in allowing the applicants to promote their belief-system with no restriction, the Dutch authorities would, in fact, be encouraging discrimination, which is prohibited by the ECHR and the ICCPR, thereby at the very least implying a positive obligation emanating from the article in question. In *Glimmerveen and*

---

214 Thoma v Luxembourg, Application no. 38432/97 (ECHR 29 March 2001) para. 48.

215 Ždanoka v Latvia, Application no. 58278/00 (ECHR 16 March 2006) para. 100.

216 Witzsch v Germany, Application no. 7485/03 (ECHR 13 December 2005).

217 Ždanoka v Latvia, Application no. 58278/00 (ECHR 16 March 2006) para. 99.

218 Ibid.

219 Lehideux and Isorni v France, Application no. 24662/94 (ECHR 23 September 1998).

220 Buyse A, 'Contested Contours – The Limits of Freedom of Expression from an Abuse of Rights Perspective – Articles 10 and 17 ECHR' in Eva Brems & Janneke Gerards (eds.), *'Shaping Rights in the ECHR: The Role of the European Court of Human Rights in Determining the Scope of Human Rights'* (1st edn. Cambridge University Press, Cambridge 2013) 191.

221 Ibid. 190.

Hagenbeek v the Netherlands, the Commission ousted the speech in question from Convention protection through Article 17. The Commission noted that the policy promoted by the applicants contained elements of racial discrimination and, thus, held the view that 'the expression of the political ideas of the applicants clearly constitutes an activity within the meaning of Article 17 of the Convention.'[222] *Kühnen v Federal Republic of Germany*, the facts of which are described earlier, marks the beginning of the Commission's approach which can be characterised as a mélange of Article 10 and Article 17. More particularly, it found that the applicant sought to use the freedom provided for by Article 10 as a tool to carry out activities, namely, ones related to National Socialism, which oppose the spirit of the Convention and which would contribute to the destruction of the rights and freedoms set forth in the Convention. As such, the Commission held that the interference was necessary in a democratic society within the ambit of Article 10(2) of the ECHR, and so the application was manifestly ill-founded and, thus, inadmissible.[223] This approach continued in other cases such as *Ochensberger v Austria,* in which the applicant was accused of having edited, published and distributed articles which, having regard to the contents of these articles, constituted National Socialist activities. Here, the Commission agreed with the national court that the applicant's publications incited the reader to racial hatred, anti-Semitism and xenophobia. As a result, it found that the applicant was essentially seeking to use the freedom of information enshrined in Article 10 as a basis for activities which were contrary to the text and spirit of the Convention and which, if admitted, would contribute to the destruction of the rights and freedoms set forth in the Convention.[224] In *Nationaldemokratische Partei Deutschland, Bezirksverband München-Oberbayern v Germany,*[225] the applicant organisation was ordered by the Municipality to take the appropriate steps to ensure that, on the occasion of one of their meetings, the persecution of Jews under the Nazi regime was not denied or called into question. In its decision, the Municipality noted that the applicant organisation, in a local as well as in a supraregional party publication, had issued invitations to the aforementioned meeting, indicating that a well-known revisionist historian, David Irving, would attend it and comment on the question of whether the Germans and their European neighbours could further afford to accept contemporary history as means of extortion. As to the preventive nature of the interference at issue, the Commission noted the high probability of punishable statements given the subject of the discussion and the participation of Irving. In this case, the Commission found the interference of Article 10 to be justified given that the protection of public interest by preventing crime and disorder as well as the protection of

---

222 Glimmerveen and Hagenbeek v The Netherlands, Application nos. 8348/78 and 8406/78 (EComHR 11 October 1979).

223 Kühnen v Germany, Application no. 12194/86 (EComHR 12 May 1988).

224 Ochensberger v Austria, Application no. 21318/93 (EComHR 2 September 1995).

225 Nationaldemokratische Partei Deutschland, Bezirksverband München-Oberbayern v Germany, Application no. 25992/94 (EComHR 29 November 1995).

the reputation and rights of Jews surpassed the freedom of the applicant organisation to hold a meeting and that, therefore, the interference was necessary in a democratic society. The Commission fleetingly took into account Article 17 when looking at the provisions of the Penal Code and the Assembly Act which aimed to secure the peaceful coexistence of the population in Germany. It made no appraisal of this Article or its relevance to the present case and its facts and, in reaching its final conclusion, simply referred to Article 10.

On a UN level, the non-destruction clauses are found in Article 30 UDHR and Article 5 ICCPR which provide that nothing in the documents can be interpreted in a way to destroy the rights and freedoms set forth therein. The Human Rights Committee (HRC) has relied on Article 5 in relation to one case involving the far-right and, in particular, the reorganisation of a dissolved fascist party in Italy. However, unlike the ECtHR, the Committee did not develop any thoughts on democracy and its protection and did not further extrapolate on the substance of Article 5. Several scholars,[226] as well as the ECtHR itself, find the doctrine of militant democracy in Article 17 ECHR. However, due care must be taken before equating Article 17 to militant democracy. As early back as *De Becker v Belgium*, the Court noted that Article 17 'applies only to persons who threaten the democratic system of the contracting parties and then to an extent strictly proportionate to the seriousness and duration of such threat.'[227] In *W.P. and Others v Poland*, the ECtHR observed that 'the general purpose of Article 17 is to prevent totalitarian groups from exploiting in their own interests the principles enunciated by the Convention.' The Court does not make any relevance to the preservation of democracy as the central tenet of enforcing Article 17 but refers, rather, to the group's 'own interests.' The Court seems to have confused itself about the meaning of Article 17 and also by the extent that militant democracy can be used as the theoretical foundation for limiting rights, referring to the use of Article 17 against individuals in the Belgian case and groups in the Polish case. Moreover, although fleetingly referring to, for example, the 'democratic system' in *De Becker*, there is no definition either in that case or any other case of how the Court conceptualises democracy. In fact, in *United Communist Party of Turkey*, the Court stated that 'democracy ... appears to be the only political model contemplated by the Convention and, accordingly, the only one compatible with it.'[228] However, the Court has not yet told us how it understands democracy. Instead, jurisprudence reflects abstract references to elements needed for the functioning of a democracy such as the proper participation of political parties and the preservation of free speech. More particularly, Article 17 prevents a person or group from abusing Convention rights in a way that this would destroy the rights and freedoms set out in the Convention rather than

---

226 See, *inter alia*, Paul Harvey, 'Militant Democracy and the European Convention on Human Rights' (2004) 29 *European Law Review* 3.

227 De Becker v Belgium, Application no. 214/5 (ECHR 2 March 1962) para. 279.

228 Refah Partisi (the Welfare Party) and Others v Turkey, Application nos. 41340/98, 41342/98 and 41344/98 (ECHR 13 February 2002) para. 45.

democracy itself. Although the aforementioned case against Belgium clarifies the threshold of abuse necessary for Article 17 to be enforced by incorporating democracy destruction as a pre-requisite for its use, it does not equate Article 17 with militant democracy.

Assuming that Article 17 is, in fact, to be used in the way set out in *De Becker*, the lack of an understanding of what democracy constitutes, makes its militancy complicated. The way in which Article 17 has been used by the Court further complicates its relevance to the militant democracy framework. More particularly, Article 17 has been the habitual avenue by which the Court has ousted revisionist and negationist speech from Convention protection. For example, in *Garaudy v France*, the Court enforced Article 17 directly. It held that the promotion of a pro-Nazi policy could not be allowed to enjoy protection granted by Article 10 by stressing that there exists a 'category of clearly established historical facts – such as the Holocaust – whose negation or revision would be removed from the protection of Article 10 by Article 17.'[229] The Court found that the revisionist nature of the book in question is contrary to the objectives of the Convention, namely justice and peace, and is a serious threat to public order. It, therefore, held that the applicant's complaint as to an alleged violation of Article 10 was incompatible *ratione materiae* with the provisions of the Convention within the meaning of Article 35(3) and must be rejected pursuant to Article 35(4). This approach was adopted soon after in *Witzsch v Germany*, which also dealt with revisionist speech.[230] In the more recent case of *M'Bala M'Bala v France*, involving the performance of a comedian which the Court found to be anti-Semitic and negationist, the Court enforced Article 17 not because it involved a threat to the democratic system (*De Becker*) or the actions of a totalitarian group (*W.P. and Others*) but because the expression went against Convention values. Article 17 was also randomly used in *Norwood v The United Kingdom*. In this case the applicant hung a poster with illustrations of a crossed out crescent and the words 'Islam out of Britain - Protect the British People' on his apartment window. The Court enforced Article 17 holding that

> a general, vehement attack against a religious group, linking the group as a whole with a grave act of terrorism, is incompatible with the values proclaimed and guaranteed by the Convention, notably tolerance, social peace and non-discrimination.[231]

In this light, the Court underlined that the expression in question fell within the ambit of Article 17 and, thus, no assessment under Article 10 would take place. However, it offered no explanation as to how and when the line should be drawn between speech which is prohibited as a result of the provisions of Article 17 and

229 Garaudy v France, Application no. 64831/01 (ECHR 24 June 2003).
230 Witzsch v Germany, Application no. 7485/03 (ECHR 13 December 2005).
231 Norwood v The United Kingdom, Application no. 23131/03 (ECHR 16 November 2004).

speech which can be restricted as a result of the limitation clauses of Article 10. The decision to apply Article 17 in *Norwood* can be characterised as rather random and a manifestation of the unpredictable nature of this article. For example, why was Article 17 enforced in *Norwood* but not enforced, let us say, in *Féret?* The Court offers no explanation, thereto, and subsequently no explanation as to the applicability of these articles in such cases. In *De Becker v Belgium*, the Commission underlined that Article 17 applies only to persons who threaten the democratic system of the contracting parties and then to an extent strictly proportionate to the seriousness and duration of such a threat.[232] However, this line and threshold was not adopted for Norwood's poster. Moreover, no consideration was made of whether or not Norwood was acting in his capacity as a BNP member or on behalf of the party, nor was any assessment made of whether or not BNP constitutes a totalitarian group and the Court readily enforced this article, not in the name of preserving democracy but of preserving Convention values. Either way, no satisfactory extrapolation on the use of Article 17 is offered by the Court with discrepancies in the treatment of *Norwood* and *Féret* complicating the situation further.

Another issue arises from the examination of the use of Article 17 in hate speech cases: namely, that the Court has a

> higher standard of protection against Holocaust denial and related questioning of the historical facts of World War II, which it will attack directly under Article 17 of the European Convention on Human Rights, than other forms of racist or hate speech, which are examined under Article 10.[233]

This could be traced back to the temporal synergy between the collection action to tackle totalitarian groups and the drafting of Article 17. Notwithstanding the historical analogy and the fact that the ECtHR itself appears to have drawn a correlation between Article 17 and militant democracy, Article 17 cannot be substantially equated with militant democracy in the general approach of the Court nor can it be said that militant democracy is the constitutional model adopted by the ECtHR. Rather, Article 17 can be equated with a variation of this doctrine by the Court in the form of protecting democratic *values* in some cases (*M'Bala*) and democracy itself (*Refah Partisi*) in others. It could be argued that the paradox of democracy becomes even more paradoxical when fundamental rights are being restricted in the name of values rather than in the preservation of democracy itself. Therefore, although the Convention, through Article 17 and the limitation clauses of other articles, such as those in Articles 10 and 11, reflects the element of Strasbourg self-protection and self-defence, this does not necessarily mean that the ECHR has adopted a constitutional model

---

232 De Becker v Belgium, Application no. 214/56 (EComHR 8 January 1960) para. 279.
233 David Keane, 'Attacking Hate Speech under Article 17 of the European Convention on Human Rights' (2007) 25 *Netherlands Quarterly of Human Rights* 4, 642.

of militant democracy. Instead, restrictions in the non-destruction clauses and the most relied upon limitation grounds of rights, such as expression, association and assembly, emanate from the need to protect the rights of others (rather than the democratic system). The theoretical justification of limitation grounds and non-destruction clauses at both a UN and CoE level are, thus, closely intertwined with an effects-based approach to hate speech and hateful associations and assemblies with an emphasis on preventing harm to persons and groups. Either way, a link has been drawn between Article 17 and militant democracy in light of the general spirit of militant democracy, namely, the pre-emptive restriction of rights and freedoms in the name of the protection of democracy and the direct reference made by the Court to the theme of democracy protection in several cases.[234]

Article 17 and free association and assembly

The case which 'elevat[ed] the notion of militant democracy into a constitutional value at the European level'[235] was that of *Refah Partisi v Turkey*. It was following that judgement against a political party seeking to adopt the Sharia in Turkey and the 'pressing social need' test formulated therein that the Court offered a 'clear re-endorsement of militant democracy.'[236] In this case, the Court allowed the State to restrict the right of association of a political party which was considered to be a sufficiently imminent threat to democracy. The significant characteristic of the Court's approach in this case was the preventive nature of the restriction, that being the permissibility of the party ban before it came to power. The Court held that 'a state cannot be required to wait, before intervening, until a political party has seized power and begun to take concrete steps to implement a policy incompatible with the standards of the Convention and democracy.'[237] Macklem argues that the 'traditional democratic approach to such an agenda is to determine its constitutionality when it begins to conflict with the rights of others.'[238] The Court, however, pre-emptively protected the Turkish State from such a party in a preventive manner, notwithstanding the absence of substantial violence. Significantly, it did so without any conceptual extrapolation of democracy and the doctrine of militant democracy nor of any analysis of what constitutes a 'sufficiently imminent threat' which can give rise to the militant protection of a democracy. As Macklem argues, the meaning of this was

---

234 See, *inter alia*, Vona v Hungary and Refah Partisi v Turkey.
235 Carlo Invernizzi Accetti & Ian Zuckerman, 'What's Wrong with Militant Democracy?' (2015) 68 *Political Studies* IS, 192
236 Paul Harvey, 'Militant Democracy and the European Convention on Human Rights' (2004) *European Law Review* 3, 414.
237 Refah Partisi (the Welfare Party) and Others v Turkey, Application nos. 41340/98, 41342/98 and 41344/98 (ECHR 13 February 2002) para. 102.
238 Patrick Macklem, 'Militant Democracy, Legal Pluralism, and the Paradox of Self-determination' (2006) 4 *International Journal of Constitutional Law* 3, 514.

required to 'minimize the possibility of abusive state action.'[239] Furthermore, the mere plausibility of a threat was necessary for it to pass the threshold test of restriction, a point which has been argued to be an 'excessively lax standard of proof,'[240] given that the consequence is the prohibition of a political party. Especially considering the European watchdog for potential abuses of majority power, the Court should have ensured that proper thresholds and benchmarks were set for restriction, embracing a reflective standard of proof and should have conducted a theoretical appraisal of militant democracy, since the risks associated with it, as mentioned earlier, and given its poor definitional framework 'leav[es] fundamental freedoms exposed to the risk of abusive state action.'[241] An extrapolation of militant democracy *per se* is seen predominantly in cases related to prohibited associations rather than prohibited speech, probably due to the closer proximity of associations in the form of political parties to the core of a democracy's functioning. In *Refah Partisi v Turkey,* the Court underlined that political parties play a 'primordial role' in the 'proper functioning of a democracy.'[242] In relation to other types of association beyond political parties, in *Vona v Hungary* the Court found that

> Social movements may play an important role in the shaping of politics and policies, but - contrary to political parties - such organisations usually have less legally privileged opportunities to influence the political system.[243]

To this end and within the sphere of restrictive measures, the Court found that

> the State is entitled to take preventive measures to protect democracy vis-à-vis such non-party entities as well, if a sufficiently imminent prejudice to the rights of others undermines the fundamental values upon which a democratic society rests and functions. One of such values is the cohabitation of members of society without racial segregation, without which a democratic society is inconceivable.[244]

It, therefore, extended the concept of militancy to frameworks beyond political parties which may directly damage the functioning of the democratic process, applying self-protection to movements which negatively impact values upon which a democratic society rests. The extension of militancy beyond democracy protection requires a theoretical backdrop of justification, an exercise which the Court evaded.

239 Ibid.
240 Ibid. 515.
241 Patrick Macklem, 'Militant Democracy, Legal Pluralism, and the Paradox of Self-determination' (2006) 4 *International Journal of Constitutional Law* 3, 492.
242 Refah Partisi (the Welfare Party) and Others v Turkey, Application nos. 41340/98, 41342/98 and 41344/98 (ECHR 13 February 2003) para. 87.
243 Vona v Hungary, Application no. 35943/10 (ECHR 9 July 2013) para. 56.
244 Ibid. para. 57.

In relation to Article 17 being applied in the framework of association, the Court has deliberated on its use. In *Refah Partisi*, the Court clearly separated justifications for interferences, as emanating from Article 11(2) and Article 17, and held that any discussion as to the applicability of Article 17 would have to commence only after an appraisal of Article 11(2) in the realm of the given interference.[245] This position was also implemented in *Vona v Hungary*. In relation to the applicability of Article 17 in *Refah Partisi*, the Court noted that, since the complaints brought forth under Article 17 concerned the same facts as those examined under Article 11, no separate examination was necessary.[246] This is an almost distressing conclusion on Article 17 as it denotes that the treatment of Article 17, and the legal formula to be applied when seeking to determine its potential application, match that of Article 11 which, given the gravity of the cases that should fall within the framework of Article 17 and given the general abstraction in relation to the latter, renders an understanding of this article even more complicated. However, in *Vona v Hungary*, the Court actually took the time to consider the applicability of Article 17 to this case. It eliminated the possibility of recourse to Article 17, predominantly due to the lack of totalitarian elements of the association and movement in question and also due to the lack of violence during the demonstrations in question and the seriousness of the restriction imposed, that being the elimination of the legal existence of the association.[247] In these circumstances, the Court could not conclude that the association's activities were intended to justify or propagate totalitarian oppression serving totalitarian groups.[248]

In *Hizb ut-Tahrir and Others v Germany (Liberation Party)*, the applicant, describes itself as a 'global Islamic political party and/or religious society.' It was established in Jerusalem in 1953 and advocated the overthrow of governments throughout the Muslim world and their replacement by an Islamic State in the form of a recreated Caliphate. Even though this case does not come within the sphere of the far-right, the religious extremism interlinked to the case and the subsequent treatment by the Court provide important points of assessment. In this case, the ECtHR underlined that the first applicant attempted to abuse Article 11 of the ECHR for purposes which are 'clearly contrary to the values of the Convention, notably the commitment to the peaceful settlement of international conflicts and to the sanctity of human life.'[249] Further, it underlined that, during the meetings of the local section of the association chaired by the second applicant, statements calling for violence against Jews were made and that the

---

245 Refah Partisi (the Welfare Party) and Others v Turkey, Application nos. 41340/98, 41342/98 and 41344/98 (ECHR 13 February 2003) para. 96.
246 Ibid. para. 137.
247 Vona v Hungary, Application no. 35943/10 (ECHR 9 July 2013) para. 36.
248 Ibid. para. 37.
249 Hizb ut-Tahrir and Others v Germany, Application no. 31098/08 (ECHR 12 June 2012) para. 74.

leaflets handed out included the promotion of recourse to violence to establish the domination of Islam. Also, the Court underlined that Sharia is

> incompatible with the fundamental principles of democracy, particularly with regard to its criminal law and criminal procedure, its rules on the legal status of women and the way it intervenes in all spheres of private and public life in accordance with religious precepts.[250]

For these reasons, the Court found that the dissemination of the ideology promoted by *Hizb ut-Tahrir* constituted an activity falling within the scope of Article 17 of the Convention.

In *Kasymakhunov and Saybatalov v Russia*, the Court dealt with a complaint against Russia for the prohibition of *Hizb ut-Tahrir*. In considering the applicability of Article 17 to the said case, it reiterated its findings in *Hizb ut-Tahrir v Germany* and that the aims and objectives of this association were clearly contrary to the values of the Convention. Here, the Court dealt with an unregistered association operating on an international scale with approximately two hundred followers in Germany but with no known sub-organisation in Germany. Even though the entity was unregistered with a limited number of followers, the fact that its aim and objectives sought to destroy Convention values and principles led to the Court's ousting it from the protection of the Convention through the application of Article 17.[251]

Thus, in the framework of association, Article 17 has been applied in two connected cases which involved elements of radical Islam, violence and anti-Semitism. Most interesting to this discussion is, first, the decision in *Refah Partisi* that an analysis of Article 11 would have to precede any consideration of the applicability of Article 17, thereby contributing to the creation of a comprehensive appraisal of the issues at stake and, second, the non-applicability of Article 17 in *Vona*, an almost bizarre finding when comparing it with the lax approach adopted by the Court in *Norwood*. On this point, Buyse argued that the Court's stance 'was triggered by a desire to consider the merits of the case in-depth rather than dismissing it right away under Article 17.'[252]

Article 17: concluding comments

Three key issues can be deduced from an analysis of Article 17. First, in the realm of expression, this article has been applied more often by the Commission than the Court. Second, the Court, with the exception of *Norwood*, definitely shows a hierarchy of importance attached to the way revisionist and negationist

---

250 Kasymakhunov and Saybatalov v Russia, Application nos. 26261/05 and 26377/06 (ECHR 14 March 2013) para. 111.
251 Hizb ut-Tahrir and Others v German, Application no. 31098/08 (12 June 2012) para. 73.
252 Antoine Buyse, 'Dangerous Expressions: The ECHR, Violence and Free Speech' (2014) 2 *International and Comparative Law Quarterly* 63, 495.

speech are treated. Third, despite theoretical limitations to the Court's analysis of democracy and the doctrine of militant democracy and other issues related to thresholds in particular, the Court's analysis in *Refah Partisi*, as reproduced in *Vona*, as to the necessity of assessing limitation grounds before enforcing Article 17, is a contributing factor to ensuring a safer use of this article. In a nutshell, the application of this article has constituted a source of criticism given that 'it is not clear in which instances the provision applies.'[253] Buyse argues that 'this inconsistency is most probably due to the inherent tension between human rights protection and an abuse of rights clause'[254] but also due to the difficulties in proving such an abuse of rights.[255] In addition, Harris, O'Boyle and Warbrick suggest that all speech should be considered under Article 10 and its limitation grounds in order to prevent 'States from having abusive recourse to Article 17.'[256] This argument could potentially be extended to radical associations and assemblies. Leigh argues that this would result in 'greater consistency and predictability in decision-making in hate speech cases.'[257] But then again, would this not offer the chance to those acting upon totalitarian aims and objectives to taste at least a little bit of the democracy that they wish to use and abuse?

The margin of appreciation: its role in the interpretation and application of Article 10 and Article 11 of the ECHR

In dealing with cases involving, *inter alia*, alleged breaches of Articles 10 and 11, the Court has 'devised and applied its well-known margin of appreciation doctrine as an instrument to negotiate between conflicting interests in a multi-layered legal order.'[258] This doctrine has been developed by case-law of the ECtHR and now constitutes a central doctrine taken into consideration in ensuing jurisprudence. Article 1 of Protocol 15, which was developed in 2013, amends the Convention and incorporates the doctrine therein by holding that at the end of the preamble to the Convention, a new recital shall be added, which shall read as follows:

> Affirming that the High Contracting Parties, in accordance with the principle of subsidiarity, have the primary responsibility to secure the rights and freedoms defined in this Convention and the Protocols thereto, and that

253 Ibid.
254 Antoine Buyse, 'Contested Contours – The Limits of Freedom of Expression from an Abuse of Rights Perspective – Articles 10 and 17 ECHR' in Eva Brems & Janneke Gerards (eds.), *'Shaping Rights in the ECHR: The Role of the European Court of Human Rights in Determining the Scope of Human Rights'* (1st edn. Cambridge University Press, Cambridge 2013) 184.
255 Ibid. para. 188.
256 David Harris, Michael O'Boyle and Colin Warbrick, *'Law of the European Convention on Human Rights'* (2nd edn. Oxford University Press, Oxford 2009) 450.
257 Ian Leigh, 'Damned If They Do, Damned If They Don't: The European Court of Human Rights and the Protection of Religion from Attack' (2011) 17 *Res Publica* 1, 72.
258 Janneke Gerards, 'Pluralism, Deference and the Margin of Appreciation Doctrine' (2011) 1 *European Law Journal* 1, 81.

in doing so they enjoy a margin of appreciation, subject to the supervisory jurisdiction of the European Court of Human Rights established by this Convention.

Protocol 15 will enter into force as soon as all the States Parties to the Convention have signed and ratified it. This is still pending.

In *Handyside v The United Kingdom,* the Court stated that 'it is for the national authorities to make the initial assessment of the reality of the pressing social need implied by the notion of necessity in this context.'[259] This is because it is impossible to find a uniform conception of morals in all Contracting Parties and, anyhow, this conception varies according to the time and the place.[260] Also, as underlined in *Müller and Others v Switzerland*, State authorities are in a better position than international judges to rule on the necessity of a restriction given the contextual and moral framework of their country.[261] Furthermore, as well as allowing States Parties a margin of appreciation in determining whether there exists a pressing social need that would justify a restriction, the Court also provides them with leeway when deciphering other issues. For example, in *Rekvényi v Hungary*, the Court held that the national authorities enjoy a certain margin of appreciation in determining whether the impugned interference is proportionate to the legitimate aim in question.[262]

The margin of appreciation is granted to the legislature, the judiciary and other relevant bodies.[263] It can be argued that when a State is permitted, through the margin of appreciation, to decide on whether or not a particular type of speech or form of association or assembly is offensive and, therefore, a source of violation of other rights and freedoms, it is inevitably empowered with much subjectivity given that the personal and/or structural approaches, attitudes and convictions of members of governing bodies may influence any such decisions. Relevant to this argument is the finding that the impact of viewpoints on what constitutes a risk varies dramatically amongst experts and that disagreements between such experts emanate from a different set of values and value choice.[264] This is based on the hypothesis that

> culture is cognitively prior to facts in the sense that cultural values shape what individuals believe the consequences of such policies to be.[265]

---

259 Handyside v UK, Application no. 5493/72 (ECHR 7 December 1976) para. 48.

260 Ibid. para. 48.

261 Müller and Others v Switzerland, Application no. 10737/84 (ECHR 24 May 1988) para. 35.

262 Rekvényi v Hungary, Application no. 25390/94 (ECHR 20 May 1999) para. 42.

263 Handyside v UK, Application no. 5493/72 (ECHR 7 December 1976) para. 48

264 András Sajó, 'From Militant Democracy to the Preventive State' (2006) 22 *Cardozo Law Review* 5, 2289.
    The opposite view was recently presented by Dan Kahan and his co-authors (fear and democracy or fear of democracy).

265 Paul Brest & Linda Hamilton Krieger, *'Problem Solving, Decision Making, and Professional Judgment: A Guide for Lawyers and Policymakers'* (1st edn. Oxford University Press, Oxford 2010) 504.

The Contracting States do not enjoy an unmonitored and endless margin of appreciation given that the ECtHR has the last say in deciding whether an interference with the freedom of expression is in fact in line with Article 10.[266] The 'domestic margin of appreciation goes hand in hand with a European supervision.'[267] In *Sunday Times v The United Kingdom*, the Court underlined that, in exercising its supervisory powers, its role is to determine whether an interference 'was proportionate to the legitimate aim pursued and whether the reasons given by the national authorities to justify it are relevant and sufficient.'[268] In *Özgür Gundem v Turkey*, the Court noted that 'in exercising its supervisory judgement, the Court must look at interference in light of the case as a whole, including the content of the impugned statements and the context in which they were made.'[269]

The width of this margin very much depends on the type and subsequent significance of the right being considered. In the framework of expression, the Court

> has generally been particularly restrictive in its approach to the margin of appreciation but has been prepared to accept a wider margin in relation to issues likely to offend personal convictions in the religious or moral domain.[270]

This was manifested in *Soulas v France*, where the Court held that States should be granted a wider margin of appreciation in cases where they limit hate speech or discriminatory speech because of the risks they pose to social relationships and the treatment of immigrants.[271] In relation to this case, Lester, Pannick and Herberg criticised the Court's decision to uphold a restriction on anti-immigrant and Islamophobic speech. More particularly, they held that, by applying the margin of appreciation, the Court did not recognise the significance of protecting and promoting plurality of opinions.[272]The wide margin of appreciation is also granted to States if expressions 'incite to violence against an individual, a public official or a sector of the population.'[273] However, as noted by Buyse, the Court does not 'conclusively explain when this is the case.'[274] In relation to the freedom of association, the Court has underlined that the

---

266 Handyside v UK, Application no. 5493/72 (ECHR 7/12/76) para. 49.

267 Ibid.

268 Sunday Times v The United Kingdom, Application no. 6538/74 (ECHR 26 April 1979) para. 62.

269 Gundem v Turkey, Application no. 23144/93 (ECHR 16 March 2000) para. 57.

270 Lehideux and Isorni v France, Application no. 24602/94 (ECHR 23 September 1998) Joint Dissenting opinion of Judge Foighel, Loizou and Sir John Freeland.

271 Soulas and Others v France, Application no. 15948/03 (ECHR 10 July 2008) para. 38.

272 Andrew Lester, David Pannick & Javan Herberg, *'Human Rights Law and Practice'* (3rd edn. LexisNexis, New York 2009).

273 Ceylan v Turkey, Application no. 23556/94 (ECHR 8 July 1999) para. 34.

274 Antoine Buyse, 'Dangerous Expressions: The ECHR, Violence and Free Speech' (2014) 63 *International and Comparative Law Quarterly* 2, 494.

States enjoy only a narrow margin of appreciation.[275] In relation to assembly, in *Fáber v Hungary*, the Court held that adopting preventive measures to ensure public order during a demonstration and counter-demonstration enjoys a wide margin of appreciation.[276] This is due to the equal importance of the competing rights and because the national authorities are most suited to evaluate the security risks and the measures which should be implemented to overcome the risks.[277] Despite this qualitative statement regarding the wide nature of the State's discretion, the Court went on to find that there was, in fact, a violation of Article 11 of the ECHR. This is because the significance attached to this right is so great that it cannot be curtailed in any way 'so long as the person concerned does not himself commit any reprehensible act on such occasion.'[278] Interestingly, in this case, the Court underlined factors which should be considered by the State in the exercise of its margin of appreciation, particularly past violence at similar events and the impact of a counter-demonstration on the targeted demonstration. Considering these factors would allow the State to appraise the danger of violent confrontation between the two groups who are demonstrating.[279]

Thus, the margin's width depends on the right at stake, with a strict overall approach being taken to expression, association and assembly with exceptions being determined *vis-à-vis* expression which is deemed to constitute hate speech. To this end, and reflective of the situation of hate speech cases especially, it has been argued that

> the concept of the margin of appreciation has become as slippery and elusive as an eel. Again and again the Court appears to use the margin of appreciation as a substitute for coherent legal analysis of the issues at stake.[280]

The ECtHR and hate crimes

The ECtHR has dealt with several cases which involved racist crime as this is conceptualised in the current book. *Nachova and Others v Bulgaria* involved the killing of two Bulgarian nationals of Roma origin by the police. This case constituted the first platform through which the Court set out its approach to racist crimes. More particularly, the Chamber noted that

---

275 Refah Partisi (the Welfare Party) and Others v Turkey, Application nos. 41340/98, 41342/98 and 41344/98 (ECHR 13 February 2003) para.10; Vona v Hungary, Application no. 35943/10 (ECHR 9 July 2013) para. 69.

276 Fáber v Hungary, Application no. 40721/08 (ECHR 24 July 2012) para. 6.

277 Ibid. para. 42.

278 Fáber v Hungary, Application no. 40721/08 (ECHR 24 July 2012) para. 46.

279 Ibid. para. 44.

280 Lord Lester of Herne Hill, Q.C, 'Universality Versus Subsidiarity: A Reply' (1998) *European Human Rights Law Review* 73, 75–76.

it is particularly important that the official investigation is pursued with vigour and impartiality, having regard to the need to reassert continuously society's condemnation of racism and ethnic hatred and to maintain the confidence of minorities in the ability of the authorities to protect them from the threat of racist violence.[281]

This position was subsequently endorsed by the Grand Chamber and re-peated in subsequent cases, essentially attaching particular severity to hate crimes.[282] It underlines not only the significance of effective investigation, given the messages of condemnation that arise therefrom, but also the in-stilling of confidence in potential target groups. Furthermore, the Chamber noted that, in the event of racist crimes, in particular those resulting in death by State agent,

> State authorities have the additional duty to take all reasonable steps to un-mask any racist motive … Failing to do so and treating racially induced violence and brutality on an equal footing with cases that have no racist overtones would be to turn a blind eye to the specific nature of acts that are particularly destructive of fundamental rights…

This position was also endorsed by the Grand Chamber and is significant as it recognises the importance of establishing a racist motive insofar as the rac-ist crime is perpetrated by the State. The imposition of this duty comes with a recognition by the Court that proving racial motivation 'will often be ex-tremely difficult in practice'[283] and, as such, notes that the duty to investigate such motivation is an 'obligation to use best endeavours and not absolute.'[284] The aforementioned approach of the Court in relation to racist crime was applied in *Šečić v Croatia* which involved the beating of a Roma by a skinhead group. Importantly, in this case, the Court extended the additional duty to unmask any racist motive, as referred to in *Nachova*, to racist crimes committed by private individuals.[285]

The Court's position on racist crimes extends to religious and homophobic ha-tred which motivates the perpetrators. In *M.C and A.C v Romania*,[286] the Court found that authorities 'did not take reasonable steps with the aim of examining

281 Nachova and Others v Bulgaria, Application nos. 43577/98 and 43579/98 (ECHR 6 July 2005) para. 157.
282 Angelova and Iliev v Bulgaria, Application no. 55523/00 (ECHR 26 July 2007) para. 115; Sakir v Greece, Application no. 48475/09 (ECHR 24 March 2016) para. 64.
283 Nachova and Others v Bulgaria, Application nos. 43577/98 and 43579/98 (ECHR 6 July 2005) para. 159.
284 Ibid. para. 159.
285 Šečić v Croatia, Application no. 40116/02 (ECHR 31 May 2007) para. 67.
286 M.C and A.C v Romania, Application no. 12060/12 (ECHR 12 July 2016).

the role played by possible homophobic motives behind the attack,' and without such a 'rigorous approach' from the authorities

> prejudice-motivated crimes would inevitably be treated on an equal footing with cases involving no such overtones, and the resultant indifference would be tantamount to official acquiescence to, or even connivance with, hate crimes.[287]

In *Milanović v Serbia*,[288] the Court dealt with crimes fuelled by religious hate, placing such crimes on the same level of seriousness as racially motivated crimes. Here, the Court found that

> [J]ust like in respect of racially motivated attacks, when investigating violent incidents State authorities have the additional duty to take all reasonable steps to unmask any religious motive and to establish whether or not religious hatred or prejudice may have played a role in the events.[289]

Interestingly, in *Angelova and Iliev v Bulgaria*,[290] which involved the murder of a person of Roma origin, the Court underlined that the different treatment of hate crimes in comparison with other crimes was necessary in order to 'maintain the confidence of minorities in the ability of the authorities to protect them from the threat of racist violence.'[291]

In 2016, the Court dealt with a case against Greece, which involved the serious beating of an Afghan undocumented migrant living in the infamous area of Agios Panteleimon, which has been particularly affected by racist crime carried out by the hit squads of *Golden Dawn*. Following the incident, the applicant was hospitalised and upon his release was detained on grounds of illegal stay. A deportation order was issued and the applicant was under criminal investigation on the grounds of illegal entry into Greece. The applicant was released ten days later and served with his deportation order. It must be noted that the Court dealt with the condition of the victim's detention and the investigation of the violence perpetrated against him. Relevant to this discussion is the latter element, namely the investigation of the violence perpetrated against him. In the judgement, the Court referred to four reports on racist violence in Greece issued by the Ombudsperson, Amnesty International, Human Rights Watch and the Racist Violence Recording Network which, amongst others, underline the rise of racist violence in Greece and the inactivity of the Police to bring perpetrators to justice. By considering such reports, the Court placed the violence perpetrated against the applicant in the more general context of racist violence in Greece and the

---

287 Ibid. para. 124.
288 Milanović v Serbia, Application no. 44614/07 (ECHR 14 December 2010).
289 Ibid. para. 96.
290 Angelova and Iliev v Bulgaria, Application no. 55523/00 (ECHR 26 July 2010).
291 Ibid. para. 105.

approach adopted by the Police to such violence. In fact, the Court underlined the significance of placing this particular case within the general context of the rise of racist crime in Greece at the material time.[292] It noted that the Police took no steps to identify perpetrators with a history of racial violence and affiliation to extremist groups[293] and ignored the racist violence context which had been the subject of the aforementioned reports.[294] Moreover, the Court recognised the importance properly to investigate racist crimes effectively as set out in *Nachova*.[295] As a result, the Court found Greece to be in violation of Article 3 in relation to the ineffective investigation of the crime, thereby, recognising the positive obligation to investigate cases of ill-treatment, as is, in any case, the accepted position of the Court.[296]

The Additional Protocol to the Convention on Cybercrime, concerning the Criminalisation of Acts of a Racist and Xenophobic Nature Committed through Computer Systems

The Internet is one of the most powerful contemporary tools used by individuals and groups to express ideas and opinions and receive and impart information.[297] It 'magnifies the voice and multiplies the information within reach of everyone who has access to it.'[298] Notwithstanding the positive aspects of this development in the realm of free speech and exchange of ideas, the Internet also provides a platform for the promotion and dissemination of hate.[299] In fact, the Internet has seen a sharp rise in the number of far-right websites and activity.[300] As well as facilitating the promotion of hate, the Internet has also strengthened the far-right movement more generally by bringing hate groups together and converging the lines of previous fragmentation, thus, contributing to the creation of a 'collective identity that is so important to movement cohesiveness.'[301] This has occurred on an international level, thereby, 'facilitating a potential global racist subculture.'[302] Although hate existed long be-

---

292 Sakir v Greece, Application no. 48475/09 (ECHR 24 March 2016) para. 71.

293 Ibid. para. 65.

294 Ibid. para. 71.

295 Ibid. para. 64.

296 It also found Greece in violation of Article 3 in relation to the applicant's detention conditions.

297 The number of Internet users for 2014 was 2,925,249,355: www.internetlivestats.com/internet-users/#trend [Accessed 25 October 2015].

298 Report of the Special Rapporteur on the promotion and protection of the right to freedom of opinion and expression, David Kaye (22 May 2015) A/HRC/29/32, para. 11.

299 Fernne Brennan, 'Legislating against Internet Race Hate' (2009) 18 *Information and Communications Technology Law* 2, 123.

300 James Banks, 'Regulating Hate Speech Online' (2010) 24 *International Review of Law, Computers & Technology* 3, 233.

301 Barbara Perry & Patrick Olsson 'Cyberhate: The Globalization of Hate' (2009) 18 *Information and Communications Technology Law* 2, 185.

302 Ibid.

fore the creation of the Internet, this technological advancement has provided an effective and accessible means of communication and expression for hate groups and individuals whilst simultaneously adding a new dimension to the problem of regulating hate,[303] particularly due to the nature of the Internet as a global and pseudonymous medium. The CoE recognised the dangers attached to the Internet in relation to racist and xenophobic expression and, thus, put forth the Additional Protocol to the Cybercrime Convention, discussed in this section.

The CoE's Convention on Cybercrime is the first multilateral treaty that aims at combatting crimes committed through computer systems and has, to date, been ratified by forty-seven countries.[304] This Convention was signed and ratified not only by CoE States but also by the U.S. which, although it is not a member of this entity, has observer status. Interestingly, however, the U.S. acceded to the Convention only after the issue of online hate was removed from the table of discussion.[305] This reality demonstrates that 'fundamental disagreements remain as to the most appropriate and effective strategy for preventing dissemination of racist messages on the Internet'[306] which subsequently contribute to the weakening or even nullification of regulatory measures which may be adopted by particular States, given that Internet regulation requires co-operation for both technical and legal reasons, as discussed earlier. To fill some of the resulting gaps, the CoE subsequently developed an Additional Protocol to criminalise online racist and xenophobic acts committed through computer systems. This has been ratified by twenty-four countries.[307] However, the practical impact of the Protocol, without the participation of the U.S., is limited, given that the majority of impugned sites are hosted in the U.S., and no bilateral treaties for purposes of extradition exist with European countries. Either way, the CoE proceeded with the Additional Protocol, recognising the limitations in implementing a unilateral approach to the issue of online hate in the form of racist or xenophobic hate and, thereby, sought to ensure a common set of standards for participating States and promote co-operation amongst them in the criminalisation of relevant acts.[308] This document is seen as a

---

303 Dragos Cucereanu *'Aspects of Regulating Freedom of Expression on the Internet'* (1st edn. Intersentia, Cambridge 2008) 7.
304 List of signatures and ratifications: www.coe.int/en/web/conventions/full-list/-/conventions/treaty/189/signatures.
305 James Banks, 'Regulating Hate Speech Online' (2010) 24 *International Review of Law, Computers & Technology* 3, 236.
306 Dragos Cucereanu *'Aspects of Regulating Freedom of Expression on the Internet'* (1st edn. Intersentia, Cambridge 2008) 17.
307 List of signatures and ratifications: www.coe.int/en/web/conventions/full-list/-/conventions/treaty/189/signatures.
308 James Banks, 'Regulating Hate Speech Online' (2010) 24 *International Review of Law, Computers & Technology* 3, 236.

'supplement'[309] to the Convention to ensure that the latter's procedural and substantive provisions encompass racism and xenophobia online. Thus, a series of the Convention's articles apply *mutatis mutandis* to the Protocol under consideration including, amongst others, Article 13 on sanctions and measures and Article 22 on jurisdiction. However, even at first sight, this document comes with several significant limitations which will be discussed hereinafter. First, as demonstrated in its title, this Protocol tackles only racist and xenophobic hate, completely disregarding other forms of hate on grounds including, but not limited to, sexual orientation, gender identity and disability, whilst religion is considered a protected characteristic within the definitional framework set out by Article 2 of the Additional Protocol. Thus, there seems to be an unjustified prioritisation of online hate with the CoE almost arbitrarily seeking to regulate the effects of racism and xenophobia online, leaving victims of other types of hate without a respective legal framework.

The Additional Protocol defines what is meant by racist and xenophobic material, and underlines the measures to be taken at a national level in relation to the dissemination of such material,[310] racist and xenophobic threats, and insults professed through computer systems[311] as well as in relation to the denial, gross minimisation, approval or justification of genocide or crimes against humanity.[312] The Protocol also renders the intentional aiding and abetting of any of the aforementioned a criminal offence. It must be noted that, unlike Article 9 of the Cybercrime Convention which deals with child pornography, the Protocol does not criminalise the possession and procurement of racist and xenophobic material.[313] As noted in the Explanatory Note of the Protocol, in order to amount to offences, racist and xenophobic material, insults and revisionist rhetoric must occur on a public level, a point which has been incorporated for purposes adhering to Article 8 of the ECHR.[314] In relation to the acts that are to be deemed offences, it becomes clear that the freedom of expression is 'the sacred cow against which the legislation seeks to justify its apparent encroachment for the sake of providing a measure to prohibit cybercrimes motivated by race hate.'[315] To illustrate this, one can turn to Article 3 of the Additional Protocol on the dissemi-

---

309 Article 1, Additional Protocol to the Convention on Cybercrime, Concerning the Criminalisation of Acts of a Racist and Xenophobic Nature Committed through Computer Systems.
310 Ibid. Article 3.
311 Ibid. Article 4 and 5.
312 Ibid. Article 5.
313 Dragos Cucereanu *'Aspects of Regulating Freedom of Expression on the Internet'* (1st edn. Intersentia, Cambridge 2008) 50.
314 Explanatory Note to the Additional Protocol to the Convention on Cybercrime, Concerning the Criminalisation of Acts of a Racist and Xenophobic Nature Committed through Computer Systems, para. 29.
315 Fernne Brennan, 'Legislating against Internet Race Hate' (2009) 18 *Information and Communications Technology Law* 2, 124.

nation of racist and xenophobic material through computer systems, with Part 1, therein, providing that

> each party shall adopt such legislative and other measures as may be necessary to establish as a criminal offence under its domestic law, when committed intentionally and without right, the following conduct: distributing or otherwise making available, racist and xenophobic material to the public through a computer system.

However, Part 3 holds that a party may reserve the right not to apply the previous paragraph to those cases of discrimination for reasons of upholding free expression. Thus, the Protocol, as an initiative to combat online hate, has been 'thwarted through the compromise they have made to concerns about freedom of expression'[316] with much evidently less regard being had for other freedoms such as that of non-discrimination. It could, thus, be argued that the Protocol and its efficacy is undermined by the approach adopted by the CoE which grants an unequal and unjustifiable emphasis on expression rather than non-discrimination and equality.[317]

In relation to general limitations that may be imposed on the applicability of Article 3, Part 2, therein, holds that a State may choose not to attach criminal liability to conduct referred to in Part 1 if this does not promote violence or hatred insofar as other effective remedies are available. This is notwithstanding the fact that the Protocol itself is entitled as a document which seeks to criminalise racist and xenophobic acts committed through computer systems. Whilst criminalising racist and xenophobic threats has no opt-outs, Article 5 of the Additional Protocol on racist and xenophobic insults provides that a State has the right not to apply Part 1 of this article, in whole or in part, which sets out the legislative and other measures that may be adopted to criminalise racist and xenophobic insults. Although no direct reference to free expression is made here as the justifier of such limitation, it could implicitly be assumed that concerns regarding the freedom of expression led to the formulation of the aforementioned reservation available to those who want it. Many of the States which ratified the Protocol took the opportunity to incorporate reservations. It generally appears that Article 4 on racist and xenophobic threats is the one granted the most protection as it extends to private as well as public communications, unlike the other acts found in the Protocol, and offers Article 4 no opt-out possibility as others do.

The issue of intent is also significant when seeking to appraise the Protocol. This document renders illegal the dissemination of material, threats, insults and revisionist rhetoric offences as well as aiding and abetting the committal of such offences in the event that such acts and/or expressions are effectuated and/or uttered intentionally. This is particularly significant in the realm of the liability

316 Ibid. 123.
317 Ibid. 126.

of the Internet Service Provider (hereinafter ISP) which simply constitutes the platform through which problematic speech may arise. The Explanatory Report to the Additional Protocol holds that the precise meaning of 'intentionally' should be interpreted at a national level.[318] However, it did clearly stipulate that it is not sufficient for an ISP, which simply constitutes the host of the material, to be found guilty of any of the Protocol's offences if the required intent under domestic law does not exist.[319] Thus, on the one hand it does limit the liability of unknowing ISPs but leaves the general conceptualisation of intent unsure and contingent on national positions. However, the Protocol does not regulate or prohibit the finding of permissive intent in the event that an ISP is made aware of racist or xenophobic material or expression and does not take the necessary measures to remove it, thereby, leaving some doors open for finding potential liability in the inaction of ISPs. Such permissive intent is found, for example, in Germany's Information and Communications Service Act of 1997 which underlines the liability of ISPs in the event that they knew of hateful content, had the ability to block it but chose not to.[320] Further, in the realm of ISPs, the Protocol remained silent on the very significant question of jurisdiction in the event of a conflict of law between the hosting country and the other.[321] Although for EU countries, the Directive on Electronic Commerce[322] would govern with Article 3, therein providing that ISPs are governed by the laws of the Member State in which they are established,[323] the situation is not clear in the event that a non-EU country is involved in a particular dispute.[324]

Although the Protocol may contribute to promoting harmonisation on agreed upon principles and procedural, technical and legal co-operation amongst States, it remains problematic. This is the case not only due to its inherent limitations, as described earlier, but also due to the fact that the U.S. is not part of it. This, in addition to the absence of any form of extradition treaties between the U.S. and other countries in the sphere of online hate speech, deeply restricts the efficacy of the Protocol's aims and objectives. Moreover, it may well appear that the

---

318 Explanatory Note to the Additional Protocol to the Convention on Cybercrime, Concerning the Criminalisation of Acts of a Racist and Xenophobic Nature Committed through Computer Systems, para. 25.

319 Ibid.

320 Christopher D. Van Blarcum, 'Internet Hate Speech: The European Framework and the Merging American Haven' (2005) 62 *Washington and Lee Law Review* 2, 796.

321 Ibid. 801.

322 Directive 2000/31/EC of the European Parliament and of the Council of 8 June 2000 on Certain Legal Aspects of Information Society Services, In Particular Electronic Commerce, in the Internal Market ('Directive on electronic commerce').

323 It must be noted that the Directive provides for an exception to that choice of law when the receipt country's choice of law is necessary for the prevention, investigation, detection and prosecution of criminal offence including the 'fight against any incitement to hatred on grounds of race, sex, religion or nationality, and violations of human dignity concerning individual persons.' (footnote)

324 Christopher D. Van Blarcum, 'Internet Hate Speech: The European Framework and the Merging American Haven' (2005) 62 *Washington and Lee Law Review* 2, 801.

Protocol has sought to achieve the lowest possible common denominator, maybe for purposes of maximising ratification. Either way, the aforementioned delimitations may serve as stumbling blocks when seeking to meet the objectives of the Protocol. Furthermore, as well as limitations as a result of an over-emphasis on the freedom of expression, it could be argued that the Protocol constitutes an ineffective base through which online hate can be restricted since it adopts traditional conceptions of State boundaries and State sovereignty on issues such as the freedom of expression mentioned earlier and, more generally, treats the issue of online hate as any other issue using traditional means of communication, throwing in the concept of international co-operation without effectively and pragmatically considering the challenges of the Internet. However, 'the Internet is a very different animal from that we are used to, which requires handling in a different way,'[325] although this has not yet been taken on board.

Beyond the framework of the Additional Protocol and within that of the ECHR, the ECtHR has passed judgement on one case which is relevant to discussions on the far-right online. Given that this case involved far-right speech uttered online and the responsibilities of a news portal to remove the speech, the case is briefly discussed here. *Delfi v Estonia* was a seminal case in relation to Internet hate in that the Court ruled that Internet intermediaries, such as news portals, should remove hate speech uttered by its users rather than itself. Although an in-depth analysis of the facts of the case are beyond the scope of the book,[326] the significant element of the case was the Court's finding that

> ...where third-party user comments are in the form of hate speech and direct threats to the physical integrity of individuals, the member States may be entitled to impose liability on Internet news portals if they fail to take measures to remove clearly unlawful comments without delay, even without notice from the alleged victim or from third parties.[327]

This reflects the importance which the Court attaches to tackling what it perceives to be hate speech in the form of its regulation. Hate speech is, therefore, considered by the Court to be such a malice to society that even bystanders in the form of hosting news portals may incur liability if they do not remove it.

In sum, the ECtHR grants States the limitation clauses in Articles 10 and 11 of the ECHR as tools to restrict expression, associations and assemblies that go beyond the protective framework of the Convention, with 'guillotine'[328] Article 17 relevant, at least conceptually, for the most serious of

325 Fernne Brennan, 'Legislating Against Internet Race Hate' (2009) 18 *Information and Communications Technology Law* 2, 141.

326 For more on this see Natalie Alkiviadou, 'Hate Speech on Social Media Networks: Towards a Regulatory Framework?' (2018) 27 *Information & Communications Technology Law* 1, 19–35.

327 Delfi AS v Estonia, Application no. 64569/09 (ECHR 16 June 2015) para. 100.

328 Paola Lobba, 'Holocaust Denial before the European Court of Human Rights: Evolution of an Exceptional Regime' (2015) 26 *European Journal of International Law* 1, 239.

abuses. Five specific points can be discerned from the previous analysis. First, that speech interlinked to hate groups is not permitted by the Convention, whether or not it calls for violence or promotes violent sentiments. On the other hand, for an assembly or association to be deemed illegitimate, the element of violence is of centrifugal significance. Second, in particular relation to expression, the Court's assessment occurs against a weak theoretical backdrop of key notions and definitions, more particularly as to what hate speech is and at what point such speech does, in fact, become illegal. Third, that the Court offers no clear guidelines as to when Article 17 of the ECHR, rather than the limitation clauses, should be applied, a point best illustrated by the random application of Article 17 in *Norwood*. Fourth, that the Court appears to provide holocaust related speech with a sort of superiority in terms of protection. Lastly, although the margin of appreciation doctrine can be considered necessary as a regulator of a varying range of beliefs and ideologies which mark the Contracting Parties, its existence renders even more difficult the pursuit of any kind of cohesion and predictability in the judicial approach to the speech and conduct under consideration, with approach meaning the technical tackling of these cases and not the Court's general stance. In relation to hate crimes, the ECtHR has recognised that racist crimes are particularly destructive to fundamental rights, and, as such, States must take the necessary steps to determine racist motives and carry out investigations with particular vigour so as to demonstrate the condemnation of such crimes. In addition, the Additional Protocol to the Cybercrime Convention has been a significant development in tackling the far-right through regulation given that the Internet is a central platform which is used and abused by the far-right to disseminate hateful messages, target their victims and incite discrimination, violence and hatred against them although the Protocol is lacking in its scope as it is arbitrarily limited to racism and xenophobia. In addition, given the Internet's nature as a global, boundary-free entity, for the Protocol to be of practical use in combatting its hateful usage of the Internet, it would have to be signed by all countries. Notwithstanding the limitations of this Protocol, it fills a conspicuous gap in terms of regulating racism and xenophobia online. Unfortunately, it has not been ratified by the countries under consideration in this book.

Bibliography

International and European documents

Additional Protocol to the Convention on Cybercrime, Concerning the Criminalisation of Acts of a Racist and Xenophobic Nature Committed through Computer Systems.
Charter of Fundamental Rights of the European Union 2000.
Council of Europe's Committee of Ministers Recommendation 97(20) on Hate Speech (1997).
Council of Europe Parliamentary Assembly Resolution 1729 'Protection of Whistle-Blowers' (2010).

Directive 2000/31/EC of the European Parliament and of the Council of 8 June 2000 on Certain Legal Aspects of Information Society Services, In Particular Electronic Commerce, in the Internal Market ('Directive on electronic commerce').

Explanatory Note to the Additional Protocol to the Convention on Cybercrime, Concerning the Criminalisation of Acts of a Racist and Xenophobic Nature Committed through Computer Systems.

Guidelines on Prohibition and Dissolution of Political Parties and Analogous Measures Adopted by the Venice Commission at Its 41st Plenary Session (Venice, 10–11 December, 1999).

Report of the Special Rapporteur on the Promotion and Protection of the Right to Freedom of Opinion and Expression, David Kaye (22 May 2015) A/HRC/29/32.

Case-law

Aksu v Turkey, App. nos. 4149/04 and 41029/04 (ECHR 15 March 2012).

Andrejeva v Latvia, App. no. 55707/00 (ECHR 18 February 2009).

Angelova and Iliev v Bulgaria, App. no. 55523/00 (ECHR 26 July 2010).

Associated Society of Locomotive Engineers & Firemen (ASLEF) v The United Kingdom, App. no. 11002/05 (ECHR 27 February 2007).

Balsytė-Lideikienė v Lithuania, App. no. 72596/01 (ECHR 4 February 2009).

Belgian Linguistics case no. 2 (ECHR 23 July 1968).

B.H., M.W., H.P. and G.K v Austria, App. no. 12774/87 (EComHR 12 October 1989).

Ceylan v Trukey, App. no. 23556/94 (ECHR 8 July 1999).

Cobzaru v Romania, App. no. 48254/99 (ECHR 26 July 2007).

Communist Party (KPD) v Germany, App. no. 250/57, Commission Decision of 20 July 1957, Yearbook 1, p. 222.

Dabrowski v Poland, App. no. 18235/02 (ECHR 19 December 2006).

De Becker v Belgium, App. no. 214/56 (EComHR 8 January 1960).

Delfi AS v Estonia, App. no. 64569/09 (ECHR 16 June 2015).

Dicle v Turkey, App. no. 34685/97 (ECHR 10 February 2005).

3 East African Asians (British Protected Persons) v The United Kingdom, App. nos. 4715/70, 4783/71 and 4827/71 (EComHR 6 March 1978).

Eon v France, App. no. 26118/10 (ECHR 14 June 2013).

Erdoğdu and Ince v Turkey, App. nos. 25067/94 and 25068/94 (ECHR 8 July 1999).

Fáber v Hungary, App. no. 40721/08 (ECHR 24 July 2012).

Fedchenko v Russia, App. no. 33333/04 (ECHR 28 June 2010).

Féret v Belgium, App. no. 15615/07 (ECHR 16 July 2009).

Garaudy v France, App. no. 65831/01 (ECHR 25 June 2003).

Gerger v Turkey, App. no. 24919/94 (EComHR 8 July 1999).

Glimmerveen and Hagenbeek v The Netherlands, App. nos. 8348/78 and 8406/78 (EComHR 11 October 1979).

Gündüz v Turkey, App. no. 35071/97 (ECHR 4 December 2003).

Gundem v Turkey, App. no. 23144/93 (ECHR 16 March 2000).

Handyside v The United Kingdom, App. no. 5493/72 (ECHR 7 December 1976).

Heinisch v Germany, App. no. 28274/08 (ECHR 21 October 2011).

Herri Batasuna and Batasuna v Spain, App. nos. 25803/04 and 25817/04 (ECHR 6 November 2009).

Hizb ut-Tahrir and Others v Germany, App. no. 31098/08 (ECHR 12 June 2012).

Incal v Turkey, App. no. 22678/93 (ECHR 9 June 1998).

Jersild v Denmark, App. no. 15890/89 (ECHR, 23 September 1994).

Karatas v Turkey, App. no. 23168/94 (ECHR 9 July 1999).

Kasymakhunov and Saybatalov v Russia, App. nos. 26261/05 and 26377/06 (ECHR 14 March 2013).

Katrami v Greece, App. no. 19331/05 (ECHR 6 December 2007).

Kuhnen v Federal Republic of Germany, App. no. 12194/86 (EComHR 12 May 1988).

Klass and Others v Germany, App. no. 5029/71 (ECHR 6 September 1978).

Lehideux & Isorni v France, App. no. 24662/94 (ECHR 23 September 1998).

Le Pen v France, App. no. 187788/09 (ECHR 20 April 2010).

Leroy v France, App. no. 36109/03 (ECHR 2 October 2008).

Lingens v Austria, App. no. 9815/82 (ECHR 8 July 1986).

Lopes Gomes da Silva v Portugal, App. no. 37698/97 (ECHR 28 September 2000).

Marcx v Belgium, App. no. 6833/74 (ECHR 13 June 1979).

Margareta and Roger Andersson v Sweden, App. no. 12963/87 (ECHR 20 January 1992).

M.C and A.C v Romania, App. no. 12060/12 (ECHR 12 July 2016).

Milanović v Serbia, App. no. 44614/07 (ECHR 20 June 2011).

Mouvement Raëlien Suisse v Switzerland, App. no. 16345/06 (ECHR 13 July 2012).

Müller and Others v Switzerland, App. no. 10737/84 (ECHR 24 May 1988).

Nachova and Others v Bulgaria, App. nos. 43577/98 and 43579/98 (ECHR 6 July 2005).

Nationaldemokratische Partei Deutschland, Bezirksverband München-Oberbayern v Germany, App. no. 25992/94 (EComHR 29 November 1995).

Norwood v The United Kingdom, App. no. 23131/03 (ECHR 16 November 2004).

Ochensberger v Austria, App. no. 21318/93 (EComHR 2 September 1995).

Olsson v Sweden, App. no. 10465/83 (ECHR 24 March 1998).

Osmani v Former Yugoslav Republic of Macedonia, App. no. 50841/99 (ECHR 6 April 2000).

Otto-Preminger-Institut v Austria, App. no. 13470/87 (ECHR 20 September 1994).

Özgurluk v Dayanisma Partisi (ÖDP v Turkey), App. no. 7819/04 (ECHR 10 May 2012).

Perinçek v Switzerland, App. no. 27510/08 (ECHR 15 October 2015).

Raelien Suisse v Switzerland, App. no. 16354/06 (ECHR 13 July 2012).

Refah Partisi (the Welfare Party) and Others v Turkey, App. nos. 41340/98, 41342/98 and 41344/98 (ECHR 13 February 2003).

Rekvényi v Hungary, App. no. 25390/94 (ECHR 20 May 1999).

Remer v Germany, App. no. 25096/95 (EComHR 6 September 1995).

Sakir v Greece, App. no. 48475/09 (ECHR 24 March 2016).

Sanoma Uitgevers B.V. v The Netherlands, App. no. 38224/03 (ECHR 14 September 2010).

Šečić v Croatia, App. no. 40116/02 (ECHR 31 May 2007).

Sejdić and Finci v Bosnia and Herzegovina, App. nos. 27996/06 and 34836/06 (ECHR 22 December 2009).

Şener v Turkey, App. no. 26680/95 (ECHR 18 July 2000).

Seurot v France, App. no. 57383/00 (ECHR 18 May 2004).

Sidiropoulos and Others v Greece, App. no. 57/1997/841/1047 (ECHR 10 July 1998).

Socialist Party and Others v Turkey, App. no. 21237/83 (ECHR 25 May 1998).

Soulas and Others v France, App. no. 15948/03 (ECHR 10 July 2008).

Stankov and the United Macedonian Organization Ilinden v Bulgaria, App. nos. 29221/95 and 29225/95 (ECHR 2 October 2001).

Sunday Times v The United Kingdom, App. no. 6538/74 (ECHR 26 April 1979).

Surek v Turkey no. 1, App. no. 26682/95 (ECHR 8 July 1999).

The Observer and The Guardian v The United Kingdom, App. no. 13585/88 (ECHR 26 November 1991).

Thoma v Luxembourg, App. no. 38432/97 (ECHR 29 March 2001).

Timishev v Russia, App. nos. 55762/00 and 55974/00 (ECHR 13 March 2006).

United Communist Party of Turkey and Others, App. no. 19392/92 (ECHR 30 January 1998).

United Communist Party of Turkey and Others v Turkey, App. no. 133/1996/752/951 (ECHR 30 January 1998).

Vajnai v Hungary, App. no. 33629/05 (ECHR 8 July 2008).

Vejdeland and Others v Sweden, App. no. 1813/07 (ECHR 9 February 2012).

Vona v Hungary, App. no. 35943/10 (ECHR 9 July 2013).

Willem v France, App. no. 10883/05 (ECHR 10 December 2009).

Willis v The United Kingdom, App. no. 36042/97 (ECHR 11 September 2002).

Wingrove v The United Kingdom, App. no. 17419/90 (ECHR 25 November 1996).

Witzsch v Germany, App. no. 7485/03 (ECHR 13 December 2005).

X v Austria, App. no. 1747/62 (EComHR 13 December 1963).

X v Federal Republic of Germany, App. no. 9235/81 (EComHR 1982).

Young, James and Webster v The United Kingdom, App. nos. 7601/76 and 7896/77, Commission's report of 14 December 1979, Series B, no. 39, p. 36, § 167. December 1979, Series B, no. 39 p.36.

Żdanoka v Latvia, App. no. 58278/00 (ECHR 16 March 2006).

Books

Belavusau U, *'Freedom of Speech: Importing European and US Constitutional Models in Transitional Democracies'* (1st edn. Routledge, London 2013).

Brest P & Hamilton Krieger L, *'Problem Solving, Decision Making, and Professional Judgment: a Guide for Lawyers and Policymakers'* (1st edn. Oxford University Press, Oxford 2010).

Cucereanu D, *'Aspects of Regulating Freedom of Expression on the Internet'* (1st edn. Intersentia, Cambridge 2008).

Hare I & Weinstein J, *'Extreme Speech and Democracy'* (2nd edn. Oxford University Press, Oxford 2011).

Harris D, O'Boyle M & Warbrick C, *'Law of the European Convention on Human Rights'* (2nd edn. Oxford University Press, Oxford 2009).

Lester A, Pannick D & Herberg J, *'Human Rights Law and Practice'* (3rd edn. LexisNexis, New York 2009).

Vickers L, *'Freedom of Speech and Employment'* (1st edn. Oxford University Press, Oxford 2002).

Book chapters

Belavusau U, 'Experts in Hate Speech Cases – Towards a Higher Standard of Proof in Strasbourg?' in Łukasz Gruszczyński & Wouter Werner (eds.), *'Deference in International Courts and Tribunals: Standard of Review and Margin of Appreciation'* (1st edn. Oxford University Press, Oxford 2014), 254–271.

Buyse A, 'Contested Contours – The Limits of Freedom of Expression from an Abuse of Rights Perspective – Articles 10 and 17 ECHR' in Eva Brems & Janneke Gerards (eds.), *'Shaping Rights in the ECHR: The Role of the European Court of Human Rights in Determining the Scope of Human Rights'* (1st edn. Cambridge 2013), 183–210.

Articles

Alkiviadou N, 'Hate Speech on Social Media Networks: Towards a Regulatory Framework?' (2018) 27 *Information & Communications Technology Law* 1, 19–35.

Banks J, 'Regulating Hate Speech Online' (2010) 24 *International Review of Law, Computers & Technology* 3, 233–239.

Brennan F, 'Legislating against Internet Race Hate' (2009) 18 *Information and Communications Technology Law* 2, 123–153.

Buyse A, 'Dangerous Expressions: The ECHR, Violence and Free Speech' (2014) 63 *International and Comparative Law Quarterly* 2, 491–503.

Flauss J, 'The European Court of Human Rights and the Freedom of Expression' (2009) 84 *Indiana Law Journal* 3, 809–849.

Gearty C.A, 'The European Court of Human Rights and the Protection of Civil Liberties: An Overview' (1993) 52 *The Cambridge Law Journal* 1, 89–127.

Gerards J, 'The Discrimination Grounds of Article 14 of the European Convention on Human Rights' (2013) 13 *Human Rights Law Review* 1, 99–124.

Gerards J, 'Pluralism, Deference and the Margin of Appreciation Doctrine' (2011) 17 *European Law Journal* 1, 80–120.

Harvey P, 'Militant Democracy and the European Convention on Human Rights' (2004) 29 *European Law Review* 3, 488–516.

Invernizzi Accetti C & Zuckerman I, 'What's Wrong with Militant Democracy?' 68 *Political Studies* IS (2015), 867–882.

Keane D, 'Attacking Hate Speech under Article 17 of the European Convention on Human Rights' (2007) 25 *Netherlands Quarterly of Human Rights* 4, 641–633.

Koçak M & Örücü E, 'Dissolution of Political Parties in the Name of Democracy: Cases from Turkey and the European Court of Human Rights' (2003) 9 *European Public Law* 3, 399–423.

Leigh I, 'Damned If They Do, Damned If They Don't: The European Court of Human Rights and the Protection of Religion from Attack' (2011) 17 *Res Publica* 1, 55–73.

Lester A, 'Universality Versus Subsidiarity: A Reply' (1998) 1 *European Human Rights Law Review*, 73–81.

Lobba P, 'Holocaust Denial before the European Court of Human Rights: Evolution of an Exceptional Regime' (2015) 26 *European Journal of International Law* 1, 273–253.

Macklem P, 'Militant Democracy, Legal Pluralism, and the Paradox of Self-determination' (2006) 4 *International Journal of Constitutional Law* 3, 488–516.

Perry B & Olsson P 'Cyberhate: The Globalization of Hate' 18 *Information and Communications Technology Law* 2, 185–199.

Sajó A, 'From Militant Democracy to the Preventive State' (2006) 22 *Cardozo Law Review* 5, 2255–2294.

Sottiaux S, 'Bad Tendencies in the ECtHR's Hate Speech Jurisprudence' (2011) 7 *European Constitutional Law Review* 1, 40–63.

Van Blarcum C.D, 'Internet Hate Speech: The European Framework and the Merging American Haven' (2005) 62 *Washington and Lee Law Review* 2, 781–830.

Williams A.M & Cooper J, 'Hate Speech, Holocaust Denial and International Human Rights Law' (1999) 6 *European Human Rights Law Review*, 593–613.

Websites

Internet Users Live Statistics: http://www.internetlivestats.com/internet-users/#trend.

Other

Greer S, 'The Exceptions to Articles 8 to 11 of the European Convention on Human Rights' (1997) Council of Europe Publishing – Human Rights Files no. 15.

Law Commission: Hate Crime: The Case for Extending the Existing Offences Appendix A: Hate Crime and Freedom of Expression under the European Convention on Human Rights (2013) Consultation Paper no. 213.

McGonagle T, 'The Council of Europe against Online Hate Speech: Conundrums and Challenges' Expert Paper, Institute for Information Law, Faculty of Law.

5 The European Union

Rule of law: the doctrine and its origins

The rule of law is conceptually significant with 'appeals to the rule of law remain[ing] rhetorically powerful.'[1] However, the rule of law 'is an exceedingly elusive notion'[2] resulting in a 'considerable' diversity of opinions as to its meaning,[3] with the doctrine falling prey to abuse.[4] Several scholars have sought to put forth an all-embracing, contemporary definition of the rule of law. O'Donnell describes it as the state of affairs in which there exists an equitable implementation of a written and publicly announced law by competent authorities, always adhering to the principle of non-retrospective application, giving no consideration to personal characteristics such as status or class.[5] However, the definition of the rule of law remains complex, with temporal and geographical variations affecting its universal understanding and applicability as one single doctrine. Either way, it is undoubtedly a central tenet of a democratic society, interconnected with human rights and fundamental freedoms and, thus, a founding principle of the EU. To set the scene for the assessment of the protection and promotion of the rule of law within an EU framework, this section will provide a brief overview of the historical origins of the doctrine as well as its aims and objectives.

Rule of law origins

The rule of law can be traced back to Ancient Greece and, particularly, to the works of Plato and his student Aristotle.[6] Aristotle wrote that 'rightly constituted

1 Richard H. Fallon, Jr. 'The Rule of Law as a Concept in Constitutional Discourse' (1997) 97 *Columbia Law Review* 1, 1.
2 Brian Z. Tamanaha, *'On the Rule of Law: History, Politics, Theory'* (1st edn. Cambridge University Press, Cambridge 2004) 3.
3 Paul Craig, 'The Rule of Law,' Appendix 5 in House of Lords Select Committee on the Constitution, Relations between the executive, the judiciary and parliament, HL Paper 151 (2006–2007) 97.
4 Brian Z. Tamanaha, *'On the Rule of Law: History, Politics, Theory'* (1st edn. Cambridge University Press, Cambridge 2004) 4.
5 Guillermo A. O'Donnell, 'Why the Rule of Law Matters' (2004) 15 *Journal of Democracy* 4, 33.
6 Brian Z. Tamanaha, *'On the Rule of Law: History, Politics, Theory'* (1st edn. Cambridge University Press, Cambridge 2004) 7.

laws should be the final sovereign and personal rule, whether it be exercised by a single person or a body of persons, should be sovereign...'[7] The rule of law also developed during Roman times, with Cicero condemning a King who did not abide by the law, arguing that he was 'the foulest and most repellent creature imaginable,'[8] thus demonstrating the supremacy of law. The doctrine continued into the Middle Ages with particular influences emanating from 'the contest between kings and popes for supremacy, Germanic customary law, and the Magna Carta.'[9] Furthermore, in recent years, scholars have noted that Prussia was a region in which the rule of law was promoted and upheld predominantly as a result of the establishment of the Supreme Administrative Law Court having 'formalized a meaningful rule of law in Prussia that provided greater protection for individual rights.'[10] In modern times, the rule of law was further defined and embedded, mainly through the German, French and Anglo-Saxon frameworks,[11] which developed the doctrines of *rechtsstaat*, *état de droit* and the rule of law, respectively, and which all essentially sought to ensure a just society through regulating State Power and preventing its arbitrary exercise. However, the doctrines go about it in different ways and through a different set of objectives, as they stem from 'differences among political and legal histories and traditions.'[12] The term *rechtsstaat* was developed at the end of the eighteenth century 'to capture a new phenomenon, the modern state with its monopoly of force.'[13] In Germany, this doctrine 'precludes the possibility of the primacy of law over the State... Conversely, the English doctrine of the government of law is most clearly distinguished by grounding the rule of law on the superiority of law...'[14] The French *état de droit* was originally advanced by Duguit and Carré de Malberg,[15] became part of the French legal system after the Second World War and was fully realised in 1971 after the adoption of a constitutional review

7 Aristotle *'Politics'* (Translated with an Introduction, Notes and Appendixes by Ernest Barker) (1st edn. Oxford University Press, Oxford 1946) Book III, Chapter 11, para. 19 at 127.

8 Marcus Tullius Cicero, *'The Republic and the Laws'* (A New Translation by Rudd N.) (1st edn. Oxford University Press, Oxford 1998) Book II, paras. 48, 50.

9 Brian Z. Tamanaha, *'On the Rule of Law: History, Politics, Theory'* (1st edn. Cambridge University Press, Cambridge 2004) 15.

10 Kenneth F. Ledford, 'Formalizing the Rule of Law in Prussia: The Supreme Administrative Court 1876–1914' (2004) 37 *Central European History* 2, 204.

11 Michel Rosenfeld, 'The Rule of Law, and the Legitimacy of Constitutional Democracy' (2001) Cardozo Law School, Working Paper Series no. 36, 43 www-bcf.usc.edu/~usclrev/pdf/074503. pdf 5.

12 Martin Krygier, 'Rule of Law and Rechtsstaat' (2013) University of New South Wales Research Paper no. 2013–52, http://papers.ssrn.com/sol3/papers.cfm?abstract_id=2311874 [Accessed 15 April 2015], 1.

13 Ibid. 4.

14 Gustavo Gozzi, 'Rechtsstaat and Individual Rights in German Constitutional History' in Pietro Costa & Danilo Zolo (eds.), *'The Rule of Law: History, Theory and Criticism'* (1st edn. Springer Netherlands) 238.

15 Laurent Pech, *'Rule of Law in France'* in Randall Peerenboom *'Asian Discourses of Rule of Law'* (1st edn. Routledge, London 2004) 79.

of parliamentary laws.[16] Although essentially founded on the template created by its German counterpart, the French doctrine developed extensively and, today, 'does not mean State rule through law but rather constitutional state as legal guarantor of fundamental rights.'[17]

It is now necessary to pinpoint what the aforementioned doctrines actually entail by looking at the central figures in their development. In his 1885 'Introduction to the Study of the Law of the Constitution,' Dicey 'associated the rule of law with rights-based liberalism and judicial review of governmental action.'[18] Dicey's explanation of the rule of law was composed of three central tenets: namely

> the absolute supremacy of regular law as opposed to prerogative or arbitrary power ... second, equality before the law ... third, that constitutions are not the source but the consequence of individual rights defined and enforced by courts....[19]

Thus, Dicey's conception of the doctrine incorporated an understanding that it was the Courts rather than a constitution which could check the legality of an act.[20] While Dicey's explanation continues to be looked at as 'an indispensable point of departure, contemporary discussions are marked by multiple and at times competing understandings and categorizations.'[21] Further, the rule of law is looked at from two approaches, from a formal and a substantive one.[22] The former entails that this doctrine is necessary for the functioning of a legal order, regardless of the make-up of the law.[23] The latter entails that the legal system 'embraces a particular public morality.'[24]

The *rechtsstaat*, as a doctrine, has evolved over a period of approximately two hundred years and was first looked at by theorists such as Rotteck, Welcker and von Mohl.[25] German writers habitually place the analysis of the doctrine within

---

16 Michel Rosenfeld, 'The Rule of Law, and the Legitimacy of Constitutional Democracy' (2001) Cardozo Law School, Working Paper Series no. 36, 43 www-bcf.usc.edu/~usclrev/pdf/074503.pdf 28.

17 Ibid. 37.

18 Richard H. Fallon, Jr. 'The Rule of Law as a Concept in Constitutional Discourse' (1997) 97 *Columbia Law Review* 1, 1.

19 Kenneth F. Ledford, 'Formalizing the Rule of Law in Prussia: The Supreme Administrative Court 1876–1914' (2004) 37 *Central European History* 2, 206.

20 Brian Z. Tamanaha, *'On the Rule of Law: History, Politics, Theory'* (1st edn. Cambridge University Press, Cambridge 2004) 7.

21 Laurent Pech, 'The Rule of Law as a Constitutional Principle of the European Union' (2009) Jean Monnet Working Paper 04/09, 24.

22 See, *inter alia*, Paul Craig, 'Formal and Substantive Conceptions of the Rule of Law: An Analytical Framework' (1997) *Public Law* 467.

23 Dimitry Kochenov, 'The EU Rule of Law: Cutting Paths Through Confusion' (2009) 2 *Erasmus Law Review* 1, 6.

24 Ibid. 12.

25 Martin Krygier, 'Rule of Law (and Rechtsstaat)' in James D. Wright (ed.), *'International Encyclopedia of the Behavioral Sciences'* (2nd edn, Elsevier, Amsterdam 2015) 8.

the realm of Immanuel Kant's work since the *rechtsstaat* emanates from ideas formulated by him in works such as the Groundwork of the Metaphysics of Morals.[26] Notwithstanding this, the term was first created by Petersen in 1798 as an antithesis of the *polizeistaat* (Police State).[27]

In sum, this conceptualisation of the *rechtsstaat*, which underlined the importance of a constitution and the enforcement of a supreme constitution for the safeguard of citizens' rights, was prominent amongst theorists in the nineteenth century.

The liberal understanding of the *rechtsstaat* was split into natural law and positive law approaches with the former being based on its Kantian assessment. Von Rotteck, whose work was particularly influenced by Kant, argued that an individual could enjoy rights 'not as a citizen but as a legal entity'[28] and that these could be enjoyed 'even without the state.'[29] Unlike the natural law approach adopted by von Rotteck, Mohl looked at the doctrine from a positive law point of view. For example, in Mohl's assessment of the Württemberg constitution, 'he treated the reality of the State as a condition, which imposed itself on human behaviour.'[30] Conservative perspectives of *rechtsstaat*, including that of Stahl, 'who grounded his doctrine of *rechtsstaat* on the monarchic principle,'[31] considered that the *rechtsstaat* 'must determine with precision and with certainty the boundaries and the limits of its activity, as well as the free sphere of its citizens, according to the modalities of the law.'[32] Given the broad understanding that can be attached to the *rechtsstaat*, this doctrine was adopted by most Central and Eastern European countries following the cold war and before that by Portugal and Spain.[33] Thus, 'depending on time, place and author, [the rule of law's] requirements range from strong public institutions and legal certainty to substantive justice.'[34] Today, when considering the major European legal traditions of Britain, Germany and France, one may pinpoint differences and variations between the interpretation and understanding of the doctrine under consideration. However, authors, such as Pech, argue that these 'divergences should not be overstated'[35] with Kochenov arguing that 'the meaning of the

---

26 Ibid.

27 Laurent Pech, 'The Rule of Law as a Constitutional Principle of the European Union' (2009) Jean Monnet Working Paper 04/09, 32.

28 Pietro Costa & Danilo Zolo, *'The Rule of Law: History, Theory and Criticism'* (1st edn. Dordrecht, Springer 2007) 241.

29 Ibid.

30 Ibid. 242.

31 Ibid.

32 Ibid.

33 Laurent Pech, 'The Rule of Law as a Constitutional Principle of the European Union' (2009) *Jean Monnet Working Paper* 04/09, 35.

34 Armin von Bogdandy & Michael Ioannidis, 'Systemic Deficiency in the Rule of Law, What it is, What has Been Done, What Can be Done' (2014) 51 *Common Market Law Review* 59, 62.

35 Laurent Pech, 'The Rule of Law as a Constitutional Principle of the European Union' (2009) *Jean Monnet Working Paper* 04/09, 22.

concepts that correspond to the Rule of Law in the legal systems of EU Member States ... differs to a considerable extent.'[36] It must be noted that, for purposes of this study, the term 'rule of law' will be referred to without necessarily adopting the meaning of this doctrine in the English sense.

Rule of law: final comments on the rule of law as a doctrine

Thus, the rule of law 'is among the essential pillars upon which any high quality democracy rests.'[37] However, it has been argued that, even if the rule of law is in fact respected, this 'does not guarantee that violations of human dignity do not occur.'[38] This is predominantly because the rule of law is a virtue or law but not a moral value.[39] In a nutshell, issues of non-arbitrary and equal application of a just law mark the aforementioned definitions, although, as noted by one scholar, the actual application of the rule of law is marked by increasing limitations including, *inter alia*, flaws in the law, its application, access to justice and relations between the person and the State,[40] thereby undermining the objectives of the doctrine. However, for purposes of this chapter, the key elements of the rule of law shall be borne in mind as necessary prerequisites for a functional and equitable system of democratic powers.[41] As noted by Hayek, the rule of law 'is not only a safeguard, but a legal embodiment of freedom.'[42] In the end, it is against such a backdrop, rhetorical or not, that violations of principles, such as fundamental freedoms and human rights, can be assessed.

Rule of law: general overview of the rule of law in EU law

The European Commission has characterised the rule of law as 'the backbone of any modern constitutional democracy'[43] and 'one of the main values upon which the Union is based.'[44] It has been argued that 'quite paradoxically for the organization created in the wake of WWII, the EU's concern for democracy

---

36 Dimitry Kochenov, 'The EU Rule of Law: Cutting Paths through Confusion' (2009) 2 *Erasmus Law Review* 1, 14.

37 Guillermo A. O'Donnell, 'Why the Rule of Law Matters' (2004) 15 *Journal of Democracy* 4, 33.

38 András Sajó, *'Abuse: The Dark Side of Fundamental Rights'* (1st edn. Eleven International Publishing, Utrecht 2006) 17.

39 Ibid.

40 Guillermo A. O'Donnell, 'Why the Rule of Law Matters' (2004) 15 *Journal of Democracy* 4, 39.

41 See, *inter alia*, Dimitry Kochenov *'EU Enlargement and The Failure of Conditionality'* (1st edn. Kluwer International, Alphen aan den Rijn 2008) 110.

42 Friedrich von Hayek, *'The Road to Serfdom'* (1st edn. The University of Chicago Press, Chicago IL 1994) 90.

43 Communication from the Commission to the European Parliament and the Council: A New EU Framework to Strengthen the Rule of Law, COM (2014) 158 final/2, 2.

44 Ibid.

and the rule of law is of relatively recent origin.'[45] Before the incorporation of the doctrine into Treaties 'its normative basis in EU law was not quite clear.'[46] During that time, to elucidate its position in European law, the Court of Justice of the European Union (CJEU) recognised that the European Community was a 'Community based on the rule of law'[47] and the EC Treaty was a 'polity based on the rule of law.'[48] In time, the rule of law and interconnected doctrines including, *inter alia*, human rights, have increasingly influenced the formulation of primary and secondary sources of EU law. Article 2 of the Treaty on the European Union (TEU) provides that 'the Union is founded on the values of respect for human dignity, freedom, democracy, equality, the rule of law and respect for human rights.' As noted in that article, these values are necessary for a society where 'pluralism, non-discrimination, tolerance, justice, solidarity and equality between women and men prevail.' As underlined by the Commission 'the respect of the rule of law is intrinsically linked to respect for democracy and fundamental rights.'[49] The principles incorporated in Article 2 have been described as 'vague ... [but] not meaningless,'[50] with no treaty stating which interpretation should be incorporated in the European context and with no definition or elucidation of the doctrine being offered.[51] The importance of the rule of law and the other values have also been emphasised in Article 49 of the TEU, which notes that only European States, which respect these values, may apply for membership of the EU. The adherence to the rule of law is also part of the Preambles of the TEU and the Charter of Fundamental Rights. The New EU Framework to Strengthen the Rule of Law, which will be discussed further on, notes that 'the principle of the rule of law has progressively become a dominant organizational model of modern constitutional law.'[52] The European Commission holds that the principles upon which the rule of law is based include, amongst others, legality, legal certainty, respect for fundamental rights and equality before the law, notwithstanding that

---

45   Bojan Bugarič, 'Protecting Democracy and the Rule of Law in the European Union: The Hungarian Challenge' (2014) *LSE 'Europe in Question' discussion series (LEQS)* Paper no. 79/2014, 2.

46   Dimitry Kochenov, 'The EU Rule of Law: Cutting Paths through Confusion' (2009) 2 *Erasmus Law Review* 1, 17.

47   Case 294/83, Les Verts v Parliament (23 April 1986) ECLI:EU:C:1986:166, para. 23.

48   See, *inter alia*, Joined Cases C-402/05 P and C-415/05, Kadi & Al Barakaat International Foundation v Council of the European Union and Commission of the European Communities (3 September 2008) ECLI:EU:C:2008:461, para. 281.

49   Communication from the Commission to the European Parliament and the Council: A New EU Framework to strengthen the Rule of Law, COM (2014) 158 final/2, 4.

50   Bojan Bugarič, 'Protecting Democracy and the Rule of Law in the European Union: The Hungarian Challenge' (2014) *LSE 'Europe in Question' discussion series (LEQS)* Paper no. 79/2014, 15.

51   Anthony Arnull, 'The Rule of Law in The European Union' in Anthony Arnull & Daniel Wincott (eds.), *'Accountability and Legitimacy in the European Union'* (1st edn. Oxford University Press, Oxford 2002) 240.

52   Communication from the Commission to the European Parliament and the Council: A New EU Framework to Strengthen the Rule of Law, COM (2014) 158 final/2, 3.

the nature of the rule of law may vary according to a country's constitutional reality.[53] It is for purposes of promoting, amongst others, the dignified and equitable rule of law as a means of ensuring a functional democracy that Article 7 of the TEU, as discussed later, has been developed. This tool is of particular importance to this book's analysis given that it is not only one which can theoretically be used to combat the far-right in Europe, but is one that partly emanated from the handling or mishandling, as will be looked at later, of a perceived threat posed by a far-right political party, namely the *Freedom Party (Freiheitlichen Partei Österreichs – FPÖ)* of Austria. Europe is currently experiencing breaches (or risks thereto) of the core values enshrined in Article 2 TEU due to the socio-political, constitutional and/or financial developments in Member States, including, but not limited to, Hungary and Poland and the constitutional shocks brought about by the respective governments. Notwithstanding such developments, the political and academic communities in Europe seem to believe that the EU does not possess tools which are effective, both in theory and practice, for purposes of tackling the far-right.[54] Before proceeding to the following analysis, it must be noted that EU documents and judicial decisions refer to the term 'rule of law' and, in, for example, the French and German translations refer to the *état de droit* and *rechtsstaat,* respectively, as if the doctrine is the same in all legal traditions. This, as a starting point, may cause conceptual and definitional problems in relation to the interpretation and implementation of, for example, the treaty articles. It has been argued that, in order to rectify the current confusing situation, 'an autonomous Union concept of the Rule of Law needs to be identified.'[55]

Article 7 of the TEU: safeguarding the rule of law in EU member states?

Article 7 of the TEU holds that in the event of a 'clear risk of a serious breach by a Member State' of the values referred to in Article 2 TEU which include, *inter alia,* the rule of law, human rights and non-discrimination, the Council will hear the position of the State in question and may address recommendations to it as a means of overcoming the risk. If, however, there continues to be a 'serious and persistent breach' by a Member State of the said values, the State in question may have certain rights suspended, including voting rights in the Council, to be alleviated if the breach of values ceases to exist. The sanctioning mechanism preceded the preventive mechanism, having been incorporated by the Treaty of Amsterdam in 1997. The preventive mechanism came into effect in 2001 with the Treaty of Nice. Moreover, it must be noted that Article 7,

---

53 Ibid. 4.
54 Carlos Closa, Dimitry Kochenov & Joseph H.H. Weiler, 'Reinforcing Rule of Law Oversight in the European Union.' *EUI Working Papers* RSCAS 2014/25, 2.
55 Dimitry Kochenov, 'The EU Rule of Law: Cutting Paths through Confusion' (2009) 2 *Erasmus Law Review* 1, 18.

unlike other instruments such as the Charter of Fundamental Rights, is unique, innovative, if not bold, in that it applies not only to areas covered by EU Law,[56] rendering Article 7 a provision of 'strategic value.'[57] Thus, this article is composed of a two-part mechanism which includes preventive measures in the form of exchanges with the State and recommendations made to it within a spirit of removing the risk which can be imposed, in the event that the risk materialises into a serious and persistent breach of Article 2 values. Here, it must be noted that a central problem faced by the EU in relation to Article 2 is 'who is to decide what is democracy, the rule of law etc?'[58] and, therefore, who is to decide what constitutes a breach to these values? This is further complicated by the fact that the Member States' understanding of the principles enshrined in Article 2 differs and 'whether we ultimately really share values seems a much more subjective matter to verify.'[59] As such, it has been argued that, for this article to be understood comprehensively and for the Article 7 mechanism to be enforced effectively, it will be necessary to 'create an acquis on values, which does not exist.'[60]

Article 7 of the TEU seemingly 'fills a gap in the Union's approach to human rights protection'[61] through its preventive and sanctioning mechanisms. However the reality *vis-à-vis* its actual application is quite different, as will be assessed further on. When dealing with the risk or breach of principles as grounds for activating the article, the Commission has noted that a breach may include a piece of legislation or an administrative instrument.[62] The Parliament has criticised the Commission's account of what could fall within this framework, providing its own appraisal which includes a 'Member State's failure to act on violations of human rights'[63] in the areas of, *inter alia*, anti-Semitism, racism

---

56 Communication from the Commission to the Council and the European Parliament on Article 7 of the Treaty on the European Union – Respect for and Promotion of the Values on which the European Union is based, COM (2003) 606 Final, para. 1.4.

57 Wojciech Sadurisk, 'Adding a Bite to a Bark? A Story of Article 7, the EU Enlargement and Jörg Haider.' (2010) *Sydney Law Journal*, Legal Studies Research Paper no. 10/01, 29.

58 Dimitry Kochenov, 'On Policing Article 2 TEU Compliance – Reverse Solange and Systemic Infringements Analyzed' (2014) 33 *Polish Yearbook of International Law*, http://papers.ssrn.com/sol3/papers.cfm?abstract_id=2438271&download=yes 165 [Accessed 10 October 2015].

59 Jan-Werner Müller, 'Safeguarding Democracy inside the EU, Brussels and the Future of Liberal Order' (2013) Transatlantic Academy 2012-2013 Paper Series no. 3, 18.

60 Dimitry Kochenov, 'On Policing Article 2 TEU Compliance – Reverse Solange and Systemic Infringements Analyzed' (2014) 33 *Polish Yearbook of International Law*, http://papers.ssrn.com/sol3/papers.cfm?abstract_id=2438271&download=yes 165 [Accessed 10 October 2015].

61 Wojciech Sadurisk, 'Adding a Bite to a Bark? A Story of Article 7, the EU Enlargement and Jörg Haider.' (2010) *Sydney Law Journal*, Legal Studies Research Paper no. 10/01, 1.

62 Communication from the Commission to the Council and the European Parliament on Article 7 of the Treaty on the European Union – Respect for and promotion of the values on which the European Union is based, COM (2003) 606 Final, para. 1.4.4.

63 European Parliament, Committee on Constitutional Affairs, Rapporteur: Johannes Voggenhuber, Report on the Commission Communication on Article 7 of the Treaty on European Union, Respect for and promotion of the values on which the Union is based (COM(2003)606–C5-0594/2003 – 2003/2249(INI), point. 11)s.

and xenophobia.[64] In the field of the far-right, the incorporation of this failure to act enhances the efficacy of Article 7, extending its scope to the majority of situations where far-right movements, either as political parties or as non-party entities, constitute a threat to the rule of law, human rights and democracy with their rhetoric and activities being tolerated by the State.

There is a high threshold for the implementation of Article 7 with the nature of these mechanisms being described as 'a last resort.'[65] For a violation to fall within the threshold of seriousness, as incorporated in Article 7, it is probable that the breach in question will 'radically shake the very foundations of the EU.'[66] As such, the threshold is 'much higher than in individual cases of breaches of fundamental rights such as established ... by the Court of Justice.'[67] These statements, which were made by the Commission, give a general indication of the genres and seriousness of the violations which can involve only the most serious breaches of Article 2. The high threshold attached to this provision is also reflected by the Commission's elucidation of the key terms used in this article, namely the 'clear risk of a serious breach' and a 'serious and persistent breach.' More particularly, the risk or breach must not merely be an individual breach of fundamental rights but must 'concern a more systematic problem,'[68] a requirement which the Commission describes as the 'added value'[69] of the provision, saving its application for the most serious of breaches. In relation to the first part of the article and the risk of a serious breach, this must be 'clear excluding purely contingent risks from the scope of the prevention mechanism.'[70] As to the seriousness of the risk or actual breach, both the purpose and the result must be taken into account.[71] In brief, Article 7 is 'hard to satisfy'[72] especially if one takes into account the numbers and votes needed for making a reasoned proposal for the existence of a risk to Article 2 and, further, for the determination of such a breach.[73] This high threshold arises from the fact that, as noted by Kuijer, this article is one with 'far-reaching consequences' and a

---

64 Ibid.
65 Communication from the Commission to the European Parliament and the Council: A new EU Framework to strengthen the Rule of Law, COM (2014) 158 final/2, 6.
66 Communication from the Commission to the Council and the European Parliament on Article 7 of the Treaty on the European Union – Respect for and promotion of the values on which the European Union is based, COM (2003) 606 Final, 3.
67 Ibid. para. 1.4.
68 Ibid. para. 1.4.1.
69 Ibid.
70 Ibid. para. 1.4.2.
71 Ibid. para. 1.4.3.
72 Laurent Pech, 'The Rule of Law as a Constitutional Principle of the European Union' (2009) *Jean Monnet Working Paper* 04/09, 64.
73 The determination of a clear rise of a serious breach of Article 2 requires, according to Article 7, a reasoned proposal of such a breach must be made by one third of the Member States, by the European Parliament or by the European Commission. The determination of such a breach must be made by the Council, acting by a majority of four fifths of its members after obtaining the consent of the European Parliament.

'punitive nature.'[74] The actors involved in the process are the Member States, the Parliament, the Commission and the Council. Interestingly, as noted by Pech, the fact that the CJEU was not incorporated in any way in this procedure 'is a not so subtle indication that the Member States understand these mechanisms as political ones and whose value is essentially if not exclusively symbolic.'[75] In relation to this, it must be noted that extensive debate on the possibility of incorporating the CJEU in deciding Article 7 sanctions occurred in the 1990s and early 2000s, which led to an outright rejection of the Court's role in that realm.[76] Also, the European Parliament noted that this article 'may not be invoked in support of any right to, or policy of, permanent monitoring of the Member States of the Union.'[77] The reasoning behind this position could be that anything else would undermine the spirit of Article 7 and would inevitably be deemed unacceptable on an operational level, extending the powers of the Union too far. However, in a contradictory 2013 Resolution, the European Parliament requested that 'Member States be regularly assessed on their continued compliance with the fundamental values of the Union and the requirement of democracy and the rule of law.'[78]

Article 7: foundations for combating the far-right

Given that this book deals with the far-right, an interesting point to consider is an event which partially resulted in the inclusion of the preventive mechanism of Article 7(1) TEU and, namely the participation of the *FPÖ* in the Austrian government.[79] After gaining second place in the 1999 elections, the *FPÖ* formed a coalition with the *People's Party (Österreichische Volkspartei – ÖVP)*,[80]

---

74 Martin Kuijer 'Fundamental Rights Protection in the Legal Order of the European Union' in Adam Lazowski & Steven Blockmans (eds.),'*Research Handbook on EU Institutional Law*' 231 (1st edn. Edward Elgar, Cheltenham 2016).

75 Laurent Pech, 'The Rule of Law as a Constitutional Principle of the European Union' (2009) *Jean Monnet Working Paper* 04/09, 65.

76 Jan-Werner Müller, 'Safeguarding Democracy Inside the EU, Brussels and the Future of Liberal Order' (2013) *Transatlantic Academy 2012-2013 Paper Series* no. 3, 18.

77 European Parliament, Committee on Constitutional Affairs, Rapporteur: Johannes Voggenhuber, Report on the Commission Communication on Article 7 of the Treaty on European Union, Respect for and Promotion of the Values on which the Union is based (COM(2003) 606 – C5-0594/2003 – 2003/2249(INI), point. 11(a)).

78 See the European Parliament Resolutions setting out various recommendations to the EU institutions on how to strengthen the protection of Article 2 TEU, the Rui Tavares Report of 2013, the Louis Michel and the Kinga Göncz Reports of 2014.

79 Wojciech Sadurisk, 'Adding a Bite to a Bark? A Story of Article 7, the EU Enlargement and Jörg Haider' (2010) *Sydney Law Journal*, Legal Studies Research Paper no. 10/01, 3; Bojan Bugarič, 'Protecting Democracy and the Rule of Law in the European Union: The Hungarian Challenge' (2014) *LSE 'Europe in Question' Discussion Paper Series (LEQS)* Paper no. 79/2014, 14.

80 Anton Pelinka, 'The Haider Phenomenon in Austria – Examining the FPO in European Context' (2001) 9 *Journal of the International Institute* 1: http://quod.lib.umich.edu/j/jii/4750978.0009.102/--haider-phenomenon-in-austria-examining-the-fpo-in-european?rgn=main;view=fulltext [Accessed 1 November 2014].

with the *FPÖ* taking control of six of the ten ministries.[81] The *FPÖ* has been described as a populist, right-wing party, trivialising Nazi atrocities and promoting racially prejudicial rhetoric.[82] The correlation between the participation of the *FPÖ* in the Austrian government and the inclusion of the preventive mechanism in Article 7 is not only an academic assumption but also has, in fact, been underlined by a European Parliament report. As noted therein:

> respect for fundamental rights within the EU has become a major political issue, not only owing to the Charter of Fundamental Rights, but also because of the concern which the inclusion of a far-right party in the government of one of the Member States has given rise to. The political responses to that event included proposals from many quarters to strengthen the measures provided for in Article 7 of the Treaty on European Union.[83]

This short paragraph makes three separate yet interrelated observations, which are significant as they demonstrate the EU's stance on far-right parties within a human rights framework. First, it establishes an explicit link between the need to protect fundamental rights and, thus, the implicit fear of a violation of fundamental rights in an environment affected by far-right ideology. Second, it denotes that the far-right movement is not something to be taken lightly, with the EU having demonstrated 'concern' regarding such ideology within a system of government. Third, it adopts a militant model whereby the EU, acting as a single entity, needs to protect itself from the consequences of the participation of such a party in the government of a Member State. Even though the event under consideration 'provoked intense political turmoil in the European Union,'[84] the sanctioning mechanism of Article 7 was not put in place, and, instead, fourteen Member States, acting in their capacity as a group of States rather than the EU, imposed certain sanctions,[85] such as ceasing bilateral

---

81 Wojciech Sadurisk, 'Adding a Bite to a Bark? A Story of Article 7, the EU Enlargement and Jörg Haider.' (2010) *Sydney Law Journal*, Legal Studies Research Paper no. 10/01, 3, Bojan Bugarič, 'Protecting Democracy and The Rule of Law in the European Union: The Hungarian Challenge' (2014) *LSE 'Europe in Question' Discussion Paper Series (LEQS)* Paper no. 79/2014, 1.

82 Anton Pelinka, 'The Haider Phenomenon in Austria – Examining the FPO in European Context' (2001) 9 *Journal of the International Institute* 1: http://quod.lib.umich.edu/j/jii/4750978.0009.102/--haider-phenomenon-in-austria-examining-the-fpo-in-european?rgn=main;view=fulltext [Accessed 1 November 2014].

83 Committee on Constitutional Affairs, Rapporteur: Olivier Duhamel, Report on the Constitutionalisation of the Treaties (2000/2160 (INI)) FINAL 15-0289/2000, 12 October 2000, at 10.

84 Anton Pelinka, 'The Haider Phenomenon in Austria – Examining the FPO in European Context' (2001) 9 *Journal of the International Institute* 1: http://quod.lib.umich.edu/j/jii/4750978.0009.102/--haider-phenomenon-in-austria-examining-the-fpo-in-european?rgn=main;view=fulltext [Accessed 1 November 2014].

85 The sanctions were put in place in February 2000 and were officially removed in September 2000.

communications with the Austrian government.[86] As a result, the Austrian case demonstrated that 'Brussels has little if any leverage over a member country once it gains admission to the European club.'[87] The question which immediately comes to mind is why the sanctions were not imposed by the EU. The president of the Commission had noted that it was 'the duty of a strong supranational institution not to isolate one of its members, but instead to keep it firmly in the fold.'[88] An academic position which has been put forth as an explanation of the EU's decision not to impose sanctions is that, at the material time, the Austrian government had not actually violated EU Law.[89] However, this statement seems to ignore the sanctioning mechanism of Article 7 of the TEU which existed during the Austrian saga, imposing a duty on the EU and its institutions to sanction breaches of the rule of law. Instead of sanctions, on an EU level, a Committee was established to consider whether Austria complied with common European values, particularly in relation to the rights of minorities, immigrants and refugees and to comment on the nature of the *FPÖ*. The resulting report noted that

> the European history of the twentieth century reinforces the positive obligation on the part of European governments to combat any form of direct or indirect propaganda for xenophobic and racial discrimination and to react against any kind of ambiguous language which introduces a certain trivialization or negative normalization of the National Socialist past.[90]

Three significant conclusions can be drawn from this paragraph. First, that the atrocities committed during the mid-twentieth century should act as a catalyst for due care to be taken by governments in the field of far-right rhetoric and activity. Second, that the mandate of a far-right party is difficult to reconcile with common European values and, third, that the government has a general duty to combat far-right rhetoric which may include, *inter alia*, the trivialisation of Nazism. The duty of the government to ensure a just society was reiterated

86 Wojciech Sadurisk, 'Adding a Bite to a Bark? A Story of Article 7, the EU Enlargement and Jörg Haider.' (2010) *Sydney Law Journal*, Legal Studies Research Paper no. 10/01, 3, Bojan Bugarič, 'Protecting Democracy and the Rule of Law in the European Union: The Hungarian Challenge' (2014) LEQS Paper no. 79/2014, 13–14.

87 Erik K. Jenne & Cas Mudde, 'Hungary's Illiberal turn - Can Outsiders Help?' (2012) 23 *Journal of Democracy* 3, 147.

88 Statement of the former President of the European Commission, Mr. Romano Prodi, Agence Europe, 3.2.2000.

89 Michael Merlingen, Cas Mudde, Ulrich Sedelmeier, 'The Right and the Righteous? European Norms, Domestic Politics and the Sanctions against Austria' (2001) 39 *Journal of Common Market Studies* 1, 66.

90 Martti Ahtisaari, Jochen Frowein & Marcelino Oreja, Report on the Austrian Government's Commitment to the Common European Values, in particular concerning the rights of minorities, refugees and immigrants and the evolution of the political nature of the FPÖ (The Wise Men Report) 40 *International Legal Matters* 1, para. 70.

with the report noting that there is a 'clear, positive obligation on the part of the Austrian Government actively to defend the values enshrined in Art.6 of the Union Treaty, in particular human rights, democracy and the rule of law.'[91] The committee's report also recommended that the measures taken by the fourteen Member States should be lifted because 'if continued would become counter-productive'[92] the measures already having 'stirred up nationalist feelings in the country.'[93] Thus, the report helps our understanding of today's Article 7 in two ways. According to the report, a government has a horizontal responsibility *vis-à-vis* breaches of the values of Article 2 and that sanctioning measures may not always be the way forward, shedding, in this way, doubt on the sanctioning mechanism incorporated in Article 7(2). As argued, 'it is almost unanimous that imposing sanctions on Austria was highly questionable.'[94] Nevertheless, rather than arguing for the imposition of no sanctions for such an event, taking into account the horizontal duty of a State to protect the rule of law and interrelated notions, and, considering the fact that the leader of the party was promoting rhetoric which goes against the foundations of the EU, a more equitable argument could simply have been the imposition of 'less drastic measures'[95] rather than no measures at all. Finally, as well as significant observations made by the report, it was also one of the documents which promoted the need for 'preventative and monitoring procedures into Article 7 of the EU Treaty, so that a situation similar to the current situation in Austria could be dealt with within the EU from the very start.'[96]

The use of Article 7 in practice: the deteriorating cases of Hungary and Poland

The practical treatment of anti-democratic activities can be considered through a rule of law lens, on an EU level, through the cases of Hungary and Poland, particularly the constitutional and democratic turmoil brought about by *Fidesz*

---

91 Ibid. para. 107.
92 Ibid. para. 116.
93 Ibid.
94 Bojan Bugarič, 'Protecting Democracy and The Rule of Law in the European Union: The Hungarian Challenge' (2014) *LSE 'Europe in Question' Discussion Paper Series (LEQS)* Paper no. 79/2014, 17; Wojciech Sadurisk, 'Adding a Bite to a Bark? A Story of Article 7, the EU Enlargement and Jörg Haider' (2010) *Sydney Law Journal*, Legal Studies Research Paper no. 10/01,3; Bojan Bugarič, 'Protecting Democracy and the Rule of Law in the European Union: The Hungarian Challenge' (2014) *LSE 'Europe in Question' Discussion Paper Series (LEQS)* no. 79/2014, 6.
95 Wojciech Sadurisk, 'Adding a Bite to a Bark? A Story of Article 7, the EU Enlargement and Jörg Haider' (2010) *Sydney Law Journal*, Legal Studies Research Paper no. 10/01, 3; Bojan Bugarič, 'Protecting Democracy and The Rule of Law in the European Union: The Hungarian Challenge' (2014) *LSE 'Europe in Question' Discussion Paper Series (LEQS)* Paper no. 79/2014, 17.
96 Martti Ahtisaari, Jochen Frowein & Marcelino Oreja, Report on the Austrian Government's Commitment to the Common European Values, in particular concerning the rights of minorities, refugees and immigrants and the evolution of the political nature of the FPÖ (The Wise Men Report) 40 *International Legal Matters* 1, para. 177.

and the *Law and Justice party (Prawo i Sprawiedliwość – PiS)*, respectively. To do so, this section will provide a brief overview of some of the key constitutional changes that were made in the two countries and the reaction of the EU to these changes. In 2010, *Fidesz* won the majority of seats in the national parliament and soon after that, with its two-thirds majority, autonomously adopted a new Constitution[97] which came into force on 1 January 2012.[98] Amongst other things, the new Constitution 'sets a controversial change in fiscal policy, appeals to a religious and mono-ethnic ethos of Hungarian society [and] defines marriage as a union between a man and a woman...'[99] Moreover, it sought to 'eliminate any kind of checks and balances, and even the parliamentary rotation of governing parties.'[100] It has been described as being 'in a direct conflict with the fundamental values of the EU political constitution, such as democracy, the rule of law and respect for human rights.'[101] In fact, the Fundamental Rights Agency (FRA) of the EU characterised the constitutional developments in Hungary as a 'constitutional crisis.'[102] Other relevant changes include the Hungarian law which sets out criminal penalties for persons who assist asylum seekers, thereby, restricting the ability of non-governmental organisations (NGOs) to support this group of persons. In October 2015, Poland saw the largest majority government come to power since 1989 in the form of *PiS*. Since its rise to power, this party has undertaken several changes similar to those taken by Hungary. In Poland, these have included changes which affect the impartiality of the Constitutional Tribunal and media pluralism.

When considering the reaction of the EU to the Hungarian constitutional crisis, the first point that must be noted is that resort to Article 7 TEU was not completely disregarded in this case, with the European Parliament putting forth this idea as a possible course of action. However, the leading European *ÖVP* to whom the governing party belongs did not adhere to this view, and this avenue was dismissed.[103] The issue of Article 7 and Hungary was formally back on the table in 2018, as discussed later. In 2015, and following Orbán's statements on the reintroduction of the death penalty, the European Commission made clear

97 Bojan Bugarič, 'Protecting Democracy and The Rule of Law in The European Union: The Hungarian Challenge' (2014) *LSE 'Europe in Question' Discussion Paper Series (LEQS)* Paper no. 79/2014, 1.

98 Uladzislau Belavusau, 'On Age Discrimination and Beating Dead Dogs: Commission v Hungary.' (2013) 50 *Common Market Law Review* 1145, 1150.

99 Ibid.

100 Gábor Halmai, 'An Illiberal Constitutional System in the Middle of Europe' (2014) 5 *European Yearbook on Human Rights*, 497.

101 Bojan Bugarič, 'Protecting Democracy and the Rule of Law in the European Union: The Hungarian Challenge' (2014) *LSE 'Europe in Question' Discussion Paper Series (LEQS) Paper* no. 79/2014, 1.

102 Fundamental Rights Agency of the European Union, Fundamental Rights: Challenges and Achievements in 2012, Vienna: FRA 2012, 22–25.

103 Editorial Comments: Hungary's New Constitutional Order and "European Unity" (2012) 49 *Common Market Law Review* 3, 878.

that this would lead to the application of Article 7 TEU[104] and that the European Commission 'is ready to use immediately all the means at its disposal'[105] to ensure that Hungary complies with its obligations under EU law and respects Article 2 TEU. The European Parliament issued a resolution on the situation in Hungary in respect of the death penalty statements and the government's stance on immigration as well as its alleged interrelation with security threats. It urged the Commission to activate the first stage of the New EU Framework to Strengthen the Rule of Law, discussed below thereby initiating a monitoring process of the situation of democracy, the rule of law and fundamental rights, assessing a potential systematic and serious breach of Article 2 values and evaluating the emergence of a systemic threat to the rule of law in that Member State that could develop into a clear risk of a serious breach within the meaning of Article 7 TEU. The Parliament requested the Commission to report back on this matter to Parliament and the Council before September 2015.[106] There was no response and the European Parliament issued another Resolution in December 2015 reminding the Commission of the issue.[107] Essentially, years passed with soft approaches and discussions going back and forth between Brussels and Budapest. Instead of anything substantial, the European Parliament settled for a Report, namely, the Tavares Report, adopted in mid-2013, which has been characterised as 'by far the strongest and most consequential official condemnation of the *Fidesz* consolidation of power.'[108] With the adoption of this report,[109] the European Parliament has established a new framework of several avenues through which Article 2 TEU principles are to be protected and promoted.[110] Although this report emanated from and sought to tackle the situation in Hungary, the general recommendations made therein *vis-à-vis* the protection of Article 2 principles are applicable to the EU more generally and, thus, constitute additions to the EU basket of rule of law protection mechanisms. Even though some of the follow-up procedures described, such as the Article 2 Trialogue composed of EU institutions to receive and assess information provided by the Hungarian government, are designed and tailored particularly for

---

104 European Parliament Plenary – Commission Statement on the Situation in Hungary First Vice-President Timmermans Strasbourg, 19 May 2015: http://euparl.net/9353000/1/j9vvhsk-mycle0vf/vju1obotyvxq?ctx=vg09llk9rzrp&tab=1&start_tab0=5 [Accessed 6 November 2015].

105 Ibid.

106 European Parliament Resolution of 10 June 2015 on the Situation in Hungary (2015/2700(RSP) (10 June 2015)).

107 European Parliament Resolution of 16 December 2015 on the Situation in Hungary (2015/2935(RSP) (16 December 2015)).

108 Kim Lane Scheppele, 'In Praise of the Tavares Report' Hungarian Spectrum: Reflections on Politics, Economy and Culture' (2013) *Hungarian Spectrum*: https://hungarianspectrum.wordpress.com/2013/07/03/kim-lane-scheppele-in-praise-of-the-tavares-report/ [Accessed on 27 January 2015].

109 The report passed with 370 in favour, 248 against and 82 abstentions.

110 Gábor Halmai, 'An Illiberal Constitutional System in the Middle of Europe' (2014) 5 *European Yearbook on Human Rights*, 505.

this case, such a mechanism could constitute a precedent for future cases. As noted by one scholar, they are 'important tools in the toolkit that European institutions can now use to ensure that a member state of the European Union maintains its European constitutional commitments.'[111] It must be noted further that resort to Article 7 was reiterated therein, as explained later.

The most concrete mechanisms proposed by the report include the establishment of an 'Article 2 TEU Alarm Agenda'[112] to be kick-started the moment a threat to Article 2 violation is discerned. This Alarm Agenda 'effectively blocks all other dealings between the Commission and Hungary until Hungary addressed the issues raised in the report.'[113] Further, the report recognises the need to 'tackle the so-called Copenhagen dilemma'[114] where the strictness attached to pre-accession state of affairs *vis-à-vis* Article 2 standards does not continue post-accession. To this end, it calls for the 'establishment of a new mechanism to ensure compliance by all Member States with the common values enshrined in Article 2 TEU, and the continuity of the Copenhagen criteria; this mechanism could assume the form of a Copenhagen Commission...'[115] which will entail, amongst others, a noticeably enhanced role for the FRA.[116] The proposal for the creation of a Copenhagen Commission has been 'the most recent in a queue of incoherent responses'[117] to the breach of Article 2 by Member States. In addition to these mechanisms, the report reiterates, *inter alia*, the need for close co-operation between competent institutions[118] and the launching of debates on the relevant themes.[119] Moreover, it is noteworthy that Article 7 TEU was not dismissed by this document as it noted that the Conference of Presidents should consider the possibility of resorting to this mechanism in the event that Hungary does not adhere to Article 2.[120]

111 Kim Lane Scheppele, 'In Praise of the Tavares Report' Hungarian Spectrum: Reflections on Politics, Economy and Culture' (2013) *Hungarian Spectrum*: https://hungarianspectrum. wordpress.com/2013/07/03/kim-lane-scheppele-in-praise-of-the-tavares-report/ [Accessed on 27 January 2015].

112 Report on the Situation of Fundamental Rights: Standards and Practices in Hungary (pursuant to the European Parliament Resolution of 16 February 2012) Committee on Civil Liberties, Justice and Home Affairs, A7-0229/2013, para. 69.

113 Gábor Halmai, 'An Illiberal Constitutional System in the Middle of Europe' (2014) 5 *European Yearbook on Human Rights*, 506.

114 Committee on Civil Liberties, Justice and Home Affairs: 'Report on the Situation of Fundamental Rights: Standards and Practices in Hungary (pursuant to the European Parliament Resolution of 16 February 2012) A7-0229/2013 (2013) para. 72.

115 Ibid. para. 79.

116 Ibid.

117 Dimitry Kochenov, 'The Issues of Values' *University of Groningen Faculty of Law* Research Paper Series no. 19/2013, 9.

118 Report on the Situation of Fundamental Rights: Standards and Practices in Hungary (pursuant to the European Parliament resolution of 16 February 2012) Committee on Civil Liberties, Justice and Home Affairs, A7-0229/2013, para. 75.

119 Ibid. para. 76.

120 Ibid. para. 86.

These means and mechanisms have remained futile for Hungary which is steadfast in its destruction of the rule of law, its roots and its blossoms. In April 2018, the Civil Liberties Committee of the European Parliament issued a report calling for the Council to determine, in accordance with Article 7, whether there is a clear risk of a serious breach by Hungary of Article 2 TEU. This report raises the Parliament's concerns with violations to, *inter alia*, equal treatment, the rights of minorities, the functioning of the constitutional system and judicial independence. In September 2018, the European Parliament voted to trigger the sanctioning mechanism of Article 7 TEU.[121] However, there is still a long way to go for this mechanism to be put in place. Following the Austrian case, discussed earlier, the situation in Hungary constituted the first real instance where a Member State is so openly and directly violating principles including, *inter alia*, the rule of law.[122] This was followed by Poland shortly after. In Poland, the EU took a stricter stance, commencing the structured dialogue under the Rule of Law Framework relatively early on[123] with the Commission presenting a reasoned proposal for triggering Article 7 against Poland. The efficacy of the EU's stance towards Poland remains to be seen, with little hope arising given the experiences with Hungary and the inherent weakness of this Framework. It is noteworthy that Orbán's party belongs to the biggest European parliamentary group, a factor which may have contributed to the variation in the handling of Poland (which belongs to a much smaller group), demonstrating the politicised aspects of the handling of the rule of law on an EU level. The aforementioned obsession with soft law measures and the systematic shying away from Article 7, albeit with some developments, particularly in relation to Poland, points to a bleak future for Article 7 TEU ever being implemented, with doubts arising in any reasonable mind as to what kind of situations could actually meet the threshold of this article and instigate its implementation.

As such, Hungary and Poland can be referred to for purposes of responding to the question of what the EU institutions are able and/or willing to do when posed with a violation of the rule of law within its own territory. As underlined at the beginning of this assessment, this article seemingly contributes to the EU's protection of human rights through sanctions and preventive mechanisms. At a first glance, it could even be described as unique, innovative and even bold as it circumvents any limitations of the EU's powers on the supervision and sanctioning of violations to the rule of law and interrelated doctrines in its Member States. However, it has been argued that the likelihood of its actual application

---

121 Votes: 448 in favour, 197 against and 48 abstentions.
122 Bojan Bugarič, 'Protecting Democracy and the Rule of Law in the European Union: The Hungarian Challenge' (2014) *LSE 'Europe in Question' Discussion Paper Series (LEQS)* Paper no. 79/2014, 5.
123 European Commission Press Release on Poland: 'College Orientation Debate on recent developments in Poland and the Rule of Law Framework: Questions & Answers' (2016) http://europa.eu/rapid/press-release_MEMO-16-62_en.htm [Accessed 13 April 2015].

any time soon is limited[124] with the possibility that the central obstacle to its implementation could lie in the fact that, as noted by the Commission, the Article 7 procedure seeks to tackle issues through a 'comprehensive political approach.'[125] In practical terms, it is the political nature of this article with 'a lot of behind-the-scene leverage and not implying any active participation of the ECJ'[126] which limits its application, given the overt reliance on the Council for the determination of an Article 2 breach, and, further, making particular reference to Hungary, the Commission noted 'strong political unwillingness to use the mechanism provided for by Article 7 TEU.'[127] As Müller argues, it would be delusional not to acknowledge that politics play a role in the decision of the EU to intervene in a particular case,[128] especially one occurring within the national sphere. As a result, many scholars have been negative towards its potential application, referring to it as 'unusable,'[129] an 'empty gesture'[130] and a 'dead letter.'[131] In blunt terms, State representatives are just too worried to enforce Article 7 in the fear that one day it will happen to them.[132] Could this be why Article 7 has not yet been enforced to deal with the situation in *Fidesz's* Hungary which has been in power since 2010 and has been implementing a series of 'questionable policies inspired by the right-wing extremist Jobbik party'?[133]

---

124 Wojciech Sadurisk, 'Adding a Bite to a Bark? A Story of Article 7, the EU Enlargement and Jörg Haider.' (2010) *Sydney Law Journal*, Legal Studies Research Paper no. 10/01, 3; Bojan Bugarič, 'Protecting Democracy and the Rule of Law in the European Union: The Hungarian Challenge' (2014) *LSE 'Europe in Question' Discussion Paper Series (LEQS)* Paper no. 79/2014, 33–34.

125 Communication from the Commission to the Council and the European Parliament on Article 7 of the Treaty on the European Union – Respect for and Promotion of the Values on which the European Union is based, COM (2003) 606 Final, para. 1.4.1.

126 Carlos Closa, Dimitry Kochenov & Joseph H.H. Weiler, 'Reinforcing Rule of Law Oversight in the European Union' *European University Institute* Working Paper series, RSCAS 2014/25, 7.

127 Communication from the Commission to the Council and the European Parliament on Article 7 of the Treaty on the European Union – Respect for and Promotion of the Values on which the European Union is based, COM (2003) 606 Final, para. 1.4.1.

128 Jan-Werner Müller, 'Safeguarding Democracy Inside the EU – Brussels and The Future of Liberal Order' (2013) Transatlantic Academy, Paper Series 3, 13.

129 Ibid. 17.

130 Andrew Williams, 'The Indifferent Gesture: Article 7 TEU, The Fundamental Rights Agency and the UK's invasion of Iraq' (2006) 31 *European Law Review* 3, 3–27.

131 Steven Greer & Andrew Williams, 'Human Rights in the Council of Europe and the EU: Towards 'Individual', 'Constitutional' or 'Institutional' Justice?' (2009) 15 *European Law Journal* 4, 474.

132 Jan-Werner Müller, 'Safeguarding Democracy Inside the EU – Brussels and The Future of Liberal Order' (2013) *Transatlantic Academy*, Paper Series 3, 17.

133 Bojan Bugarič, 'Protecting Democracy and the Rule of Law in The European Union: The Hungarian Challenge' (2014) *LSE 'Europe in Question' Discussion Paper Series (LEQS)* Paper no. 79/2014; 17; Wojciech Sadurisk, 'Adding a Bite to a Bark? A Story of Article 7, the EU Enlargement and Jörg Haider' (2010) *Sydney Law Journal*, Legal Studies Research Paper no. 10/01, 3; Bojan Bugarič, 'Protecting Democracy and the Rule of Law in the European Union: The Hungarian Challenge' (2014) LSE 'Europe in Question' *Discussion Paper Series (LEQS)* Paper no. 79/2014, 20.

Either way, it cannot be disputed that this article contributes to the enhancement of the Union as a protector of principles of democracy and the rule of law with it also constituting a source of deterrence against abuse. It has been stated that the Hungarian case is exactly what Article 7 was created to tackle yet no constructive steps in this direction have yet been made. It is the reliance on political will for the upholding of values enshrined in Article 2, whatever these may actually mean, which has led to recommendations to make this article 'enforceable law'[134] rather than merely depending on politics and politicians. It has been argued that this mechanism 'provides an insufficient legal basis for a successful intervention,'[135] although it could be argued that it still serves for something. In fact, it is the only hard law the EU has for such violations. More particularly, as a result of this mechanism, Member States 'must always be ready to defend the legitimacy of their actions in light of principles they cannot individually set aside,'[136] even though they do not, in reality, risk being sanctioned. In 2012, due to the obstacles and limitations noted earlier, President Barosso noted that what is needed is 'a better developed set of instruments, not just the alternative between the soft power of political persuasion and the nuclear option of Article 7 TEU.'[137] However, this futility with the depiction of Article 7 as nuclear is no longer convincing for many and, in fact, justifications such as procedural or other hurdles 'are difficult to reconcile with the radical deterioration of constitutionalism on the ground in the backsliding states.'[138]

To complicate matters further, one must think of the day after triggering the sanctioning mechanism of Article 7. Let us take, for example, the case of Hungary in which the very foundations of the rule of law have been direly attacked by the government, as further described later, and let us assume that Article 7 is finally enforced. What would the actual impact of that be? Would this push the Hungarian government to conform to Article 2 values? Would they become so afraid of becoming a dead Member State in the EU's infrastructure that they would come to their senses? Or, would this cause them to become more reactionary to the very foundations of the EU which they so vociferously fight against? Would Orbán portray himself as the people's martyr who has received a final slap from a club of elitists? Finally, what would the effect on minorities, such

134 Dimitry Kochenov, 'How to Turn Article 2 TEU into a Down-to-Earth Provision?' (2013) *VerfBlog* 2013/12/08 www.verfassungsblog.de/how-to-turn-article-2-teu-into-a-down-to-earth-provision/#.VTnrfNKqqko [Accessed 24 April 2015].
135 Carlos Closa, Dimitry Kochenov & Joseph H.H Weiler, 'Reinforcing Rule of Law Oversight in The European Union' *European University Institute* Working Papers, RSCAS 2014/25, 7.
136 Laurent Pech, 'The Rule of Law as a Constitutional Principle of the European Union' (2009) *Jean Monnet* Working Paper 04/09, 67.
137 Communication from the Commission to the European Parliament and the Council: A New EU Framework to Strengthen the Rule of Law, COM (2014) 158 final/2, 2.
138 Petra Bárd & Dimitry Kochenov, 'Working Paper: Rule of Law Crisis in the New Member States of the EU' (2018) *Reconnect* Working Paper: https://reconnect-europe.eu/featured/working-paper-rule-of-law-crisis-in-the-new-member-states-of-the-eu/ [Accessed 1 September 2018].

as the Roma and LGBTI persons be, whose protection is deeply related to the European Union and the admirable civil society of Hungary that is subsequently heavily reliant on European funding? Although these questions are beyond the scope of this book, they definitely need to be considered both by EU institutions and by scholars who are pushing for Article 7 enforcement. In brief, this mechanism may actually backfire, may make the situation worse on the ground for the people, and, at the end of the day, Hungary is its people, not its government, and by 'punishing' the government we must avoid placing the people in a worse fate. Whatever one's position on this, a proper contextual and conceptual analysis of the possible risks, some of which are put forth earlier, needs to be effectuated.

Softer means: futile or strategic? A new EU framework to strengthen the rule of law

The New EU Framework to Strengthen the Rule of Law, created by the European Commission, seeks to ensure that the rule of law is adequately upheld in all Member States and to offer solutions for purposes of tackling situations of a 'systemic threat'[139] to the rule of law. More particularly, this framework is to be activated before the mechanisms of Article 7 are applicable,[140] therefore, contributing to the overall structure through which the rule of law and interrelated themes are respected and promoted by Member States and through which risks or violations of these principles are adequately dealt with by the EU. Further, it is applicable in cases where Member States are 'taking measures or are tolerating situations which are likely to systematically and adversely affect the integrity, stability or the proper functioning of the institutions and the safeguard mechanisms established at national level to secure the rule of law.'[141] This paragraph is important since it denotes that the State has a responsibility not only for directly causing a violation of the rule of law but also for tolerating a situation which violates the rule of law, which, as noted earlier, is relevant to situations where far-right parties not in power or non-party groups are threatening the democratic state of a country. Thus, in this Framework, the Commission has rectified the position it put forth in its 2003 Communication to the Parliament on Article 7, as discussed earlier, to include that the State may be guilty of any omission and not just its direct actions. This Framework decision implements a tripartite formula to achieve its objectives, namely assessments, recommendations and follow up.[142] In the event that the State does not adequately follow up the Commission's recommendations, the latter will consider activating the preventive or

---

139 Communication from the Commission to the European Parliament and the Council: A New EU Framework to Strengthen the Rule of Law, COM (2014) 158 final/2, 3.

140 Ibid.

141 Ibid. 6.

142 Communication from the Commission to the European Parliament and the Council: A New EU Framework to Strengthen the Rule of Law, COM (2014) 158 final/2, 6.

sanctioning mechanism of Article 7.[143] In relation to the assessment procedure, the Commission will consider all the relevant information and make an assessment as to the existence of 'clear indications of a systemic threat to the rule of law...'[144] In doing so, it can refer to sources of institutions, such as the CoE and the EU's Agency for Fundamental Rights.[145] If such a threat is determined, the Commission will enter into a confidential dialogue with the Member State concerned, relying always on the State's 'duty of sincere cooperation.'[146] If the Commission then finds that the Member State is not taking the steps necessary for redressing the threat, it will proceed to making a public recommendation to the State that the threat is resolved, within a set time frame, and that such solutions are then communicated to the Commission. This recommendation may also incorporate means and methods that can be implemented by the State for the resolution required.[147] The Commission will oversee the follow up of the State in question to the recommendation put forth and, if no satisfactory steps have been taken within the established temporal framework, only then will the Commission take into account the 'possibility of activating one of the mechanisms set out in Article 7 TEU.'[148] Thus, through this mechanism, the State is given enough chances through dialogue, recommendation and follow up to rectify the problem and, even if it does not take the necessary steps, the Framework does not necessarily result in the implementation of Article 7 but only the possibility of such an occurrence.

In sum, the Framework can be characterised as an 'early-warning tool to enable the Commission to enter into a structured dialogue with the Member State concerned.'[149] However, given the fact that there are no automatic legal sanctions in the event that a Member State opts to disregard the Commission's Recommendation, with recourse to Article 7 TEU only constituting a possibility, as noted earlier, this mechanism has been described as 'anything but revolutionary.'[150] Moreover, the non-binding nature of the Commission's recommendation and the mere possibility of kick-starting Article 7 renders the potential of effective implementation of this mechanism limited since, in a Member State where 'the ruling elite has made a conscious choice not to comply with EU values, engaging in a rule of law dialogue is unlikely to be fruitful.'[151] Notwithstanding the intrinsic shortcomings of this Framework, one may, at least conceptually, argue that it is too early to assess this Framework due to the fact that it is still nascent. If anything, it

---

143 Ibid. 7.
144 Ibid.
145 Ibid.
146 Ibid. 8.
147 Ibid.
148 Ibid.
149 Dimitry Kochenov & Laurent Pech 'From Bad to Worse? On the Commission and the Council's Rule of Law Initiatives' (2015) *VerfBlog* 2015/1/20 www.verfassungsblog.de/bad-worse-commission-councils-rule-law-initiatives/#.VTo7rdKqqko [Accessed 15 January 2015].
150 Ibid.
151 Ibid.

constitutes an addition to the basket of mechanisms that can be instigated when faced with rule of law threats within the EU. Either way, it remains to be seen whether it will, in fact, be implemented, with higher hopes being attached to this Framework than to the implementation of Article 7, as it will be Commissioners rather than the Heads of State who will be instigating and setting into force the mechanisms of this Framework, their actions bearing less political cost.

Council of the European Union – annual rule of law dialogue

The Council of the European Union criticised the European Commission's framework, discussed earlier, on the grounds that 'it would breach the principle of conferral'[152] and, thus, put forth its own mechanism for tackling rule of law issues, this being an annual dialogue among all Member States within the Council for the promotion of the rule of law. The Council noted that such a dialogue will occur 'on the principles of objectivity, non-discrimination and equal treatment of all Member States'[153] and that it would be conducted with a 'non-partisan and evidence-based approach'[154] noting that the principle of conferral and the identity of Member States will be respected. Essentially, this procedure is a chat about the rule of law and ideas of promoting it within the EU, with no legal or political consequences or sanctions and no mention of Article 7 TEU in the event that problems or threats are identified. Moreover, it applies equally to all Member States, providing no margin for focussing on a problematic State or States. As noted by the First Vice President of the Commission, in charge of issues including the rule of law, the Council's dialogue as well as the Commission's Framework are both 'grossly inadequate to tackle the problem of rule of law backsliding post EU accession.'[155] In fact, the term 'dialogue' in itself projects the spirit of this procedure which limits itself to discussion and talk with no consequences or actions arising, therefrom, and, as such, cannot sincerely be relied on as a protector of the rule of law in the Union. In addition, using the aforementioned statement made by Barosso as a benchmark, namely, that there is a need for instruments that are not as harsh as Article 7 and not as soft as mere political persuasion, one can reach two conclusions. First, that the Council's dialogue has not fulfilled the identified need as it is mere dialogue and, second, that the Commission's Framework, although limited in that it is non-binding, and recourse to Article 7 is not automatic in the event that all else fails, is a step up from the Council's mechanism. Either way, the current set of instruments

---

152 Ibid.
153 Conclusions of the Council of the European Union and the member states meeting within the Council on ensuring respect for the rule of law, General Affairs Council meeting Brussels, 16 December 2014.
154 Ibid.
155 Dimitry Kochenov & Laurent Pech 'From Bad to Worse? On the Commission and the Council's Rule of Law Initiatives' (2015) *VerfBlog* 2015/1/20 www.verfassungsblog.de/bad-worse-commission-councils-rule-law-initiatives/#.VTo7rdKqqko [Accessed 15 January 2015].

does not fulfil the needs, as set out by Barosso, and, in addition to the fact that Article 7 is essentially a no-go area for Member States, leaves the Union exposed to rule of law violations.

The Court of Justice of the European Union: its role and obligations

Before proceeding to look at the relevant jurisprudence, it must be noted that the CJEU is conspicuously left out of the Article 7 procedure, potentially denoting the Union's desire to keep such harsh measure free from judicial independence and more of an issue of politics, denoting that the intentions behind the article are to keep it as a tool to be handled on a diplomatic level. During the aforementioned Hungarian constitutional crisis, which has not yet been redressed, the European Commission commenced infringement under Article 258 of the Treaty on the Functioning of the European Union (TFEU) in relation to the independence of the Central Bank of Hungary, the independence of the judiciary, by looking particularly at the lowering of the retirement age of judges;[156] the abolishment of the Parliamentary Commissioner for Data Protection and replacement of this institution with a governmental agency;[157] and, more recently, the infamous Lex CEU (Central European University) and on the Law regarding foreign funded NGOs. All these changes were brought about following the election of *Fidesz* as ruling party and directly fall within the framework of the rule of law. In relation to the Central Bank, following effective discussion and co-operation with the Hungarian government, the Commission was satisfied that the government had taken the necessary steps to rectify the situation and, as such, did not proceed to bringing the case before the CJEU.[158] The procedure with the CEU and NGOs is ongoing. It is beyond the scope of this book to examine these measures in detail. Instead, an analysis of the retirement age of judges shall be made for purposes of ascertaining the role of the CJEU in the realm of the rule of law protection in Member States. This case involved the lowering of the retirement age of judges from seventy to sixty-two, putting forth arguments revolving around age discrimination. In a fast track process, the CJEU 'ruled quickly and forcefully against Hungary,'[159] and, although Hungary delayed the enforcement of the judgement

---

156 Case C-286/12, Commission v Hungary, Judgement of the Court of Justice (6 November 2012) ECLI:EU:C:2012:687.

157 Case C-288/12, Commission v Hungary, Judgement of the Court of Justice (8 April 2014) ECLI:EU:C:2014:237.

158 European Commission Press Release: Hungary - Infringements: European Commission satisfied with changes to Central Bank Statute but refers Hungary to the Court of Justice on the Independence of the Data Protection Authority and Measures Affecting the Judiciary (2012): http://europa.eu/rapid/press-release_IP-12-395_en.htm?locale=en [Accessed 27 January 2015].

159 Kim Lane Scheppele & Lane Scheppele K, 'Making Infringement Procedures More Effective: A Comment on Commission v Hungary, Case C-288/12 (8 April 2014) (Grand Chamber)' (2014) *Eutopia Law* http://eutopialaw.com/2014/04/29/making-infringement-procedures-more-effective-a-comment-on-commission-v-hungary-case-c-28812-8-april-2014-grand-chamber/ [Accessed 24 April 2015].

until all judges were essentially fired, they then compensated the judges who took early retirement. As a result, 'the decision did nothing to change the facts on the ground. The new government was able to remake the judiciary with its preferred new judges despite having lost the case.'[160] With regard to the case that dealt with the data protection commissioner, the European Commission argued that Hungary violated the independence of this officer, a view which the CJEU agreed with. As Scheppele argues, 'the case broke little new legal ground,'[161] but it was nevertheless significant because not only does it demonstrate Hungary's breach of fundamental values, but it also 'exposes the limitations of ordinary infringement proceedings for bringing a Member State into line.'[162]

The most interesting point for purposes of the present discussion is that the rule of law narrative was completely disregarded by the CJEU as if it never existed, even though the themes looked upon directly emanated from a dangerous disregard of Article 2 TEU principles, including the rule of law. As noted by Bugarič, 'they ultimately fail to address broader institutional issues that threaten the very foundations of the rule of law...'[163] In seeking to find a solution to the structural problems faced by recourse to Article 258 TFEU, in the wider framework of promoting the rule of law, human rights and democracy in Member States, Scheppele proposed an adjustment to Article 258 TFEU through the enforcement of a systemic infringement action through which, when bringing a case before the CJEU, the Commission can provide the Court with 'a holistic argument about how the pattern infringes not only specific points of European law but also its most fundamental values.'[164] Such a system would have allowed the Court to consider incidents, such as the lowering of the retirement age of judges in Hungary, in the realm of the constitutional overhaul of the country rather than looking at it in isolation. What must be noted is that the actions of the CJEU considered the aforementioned issues as single problems without placing them within the broader framework of Hungary's unconstitutional approach. This, in turn, allowed the government to 'argue that it has responded satisfactorily to the outstanding complaints without having to change anything essentially about its illiberal reforms.'[165]

160 Ibid.
161 Ibid.
162 Ibid.
163 Bojan Bugarič, 'Protecting Democracy and the Rule of Law in the European Union: The Hungarian Challenge' (2014) *LSE 'Europe in Question' Discussion Paper Series (LEQS)* Paper no. 79/2014, 15.
164 Kim Lane Scheppele, 'What Can the European Commission Do When Member States Violate Basic Principles of the European Union? The Case for Systemic Infringement Actions' (2013) *Hungarian Spectrum*: https://hungarianspectrum.wordpress.com/2013/11/27/kim-lane-scheppele-what-can-the-european-commission-do-when-member-states-violate-basic-principles-of-the-european-union-the-case-for-systemic-infringement-actions/ [Accessed 24 April 2015].
165 Erik K. Jenne & Cas Mudde, 'Hungary's Illiberal Turn - Can Outsiders Help?' (2012) 23 *Journal of Democracy* 3, 150.

In relation to Poland, in 2017 the Commission referred this country, Hungary and the Czech Republic for their refusal to conform to their legal obligations *vis-à-vis* relocation quotas of asylum seekers from Greece and Italy.[166] This is ongoing. In July 2018, the European Commission launched an infringement procedure regarding the Polish law on the Supreme Court relating to the lowering of the retirement age of judges. The outcome of both procedures remains to be seen although the 'pyrrhic'[167] precedent set by the aforementioned parallel case in relation to Hungary does not set the bench high for a constructive outcome. Further, a recent request for a preliminary ruling by Ireland is of particular interest. The question posed by the referring Court was whether Ireland may refuse to extradite a Polish citizen to Poland within the framework of the European Arrest Warrant due to the deficiency in the rule of law in Poland.

The Court found that in determining whether or not to extradite,

> the executing judicial authority must, as a first step, assess, on the basis of material that is objective, reliable, specific and properly updated, whether there is a real risk, connected with a lack of independence of the courts of the issuing Member State on account of deficiencies of that kind, of such a right being breached in the issuing Member State.[168]

As a second step, the Court held that the executing judicial authority must assess whether the requested person will, in fact, run the risk of a breach.[169]

In assessing the previous two frameworks, the CJEU referred to the proposal made by the Commission to the Council on the basis of Article 7(1) TEU as being of direct relevance to such assessments. This case is paramount to the rule of law discourse in the EU since the CJEU, unlike the Advocate General, took the lead in articulating this value into an element of primordial significance. The Court's assessment emanated from the recognition of Article 2 TEU values:

> In order to answer the questions referred, it should be recalled that EU law is based on the fundamental premise that each Member State shares with all the other Member States, and recognises that they share with it, a set of common values on which the European Union is founded, as stated in

---

166 'Relocation: Commission refers the Czech Republic, Hungary and Poland to the Court of Justice': http://europa.eu/rapid/press-release_IP-17-5002_en.htm [Accessed 15 September 2018].

167 Petra Bárd & Dimitry Kochenov, 'Working Paper: Rule of Law Crisis in the New Member States of the EU' (2018) *Reconnect* Working Paper: https://reconnect-europe.eu/featured/working-paper-rule-of-law-crisis-in-the-new-member-states-of-the-eu/ [Accessed 1 September 2018] 16.

168 Case C-216/18 PPU, Minister for Justice and Equality v LM, Judgement of the Court of Justice (25 July 2018) ECLI:EU:C:2018:586, para. 61.

169 Ibid. para. 73.

Article 2 TEU. That premise implies and justifies the existence of mutual trust between the Member States that those values will be recognised, and therefore that the EU law that implements them will be respected...

At a time when the EU has shown a very weak embracement of the rule of law, in practice and function, this decision gives hope for the paving of a proper protection of the rule of law and other Article 2 values. The knock on effect (if any) of this decision, if any, on the Union's treatment of Poland and Hungary and future defaulting Member States remains to be seen. Either way, this was a breath of fresh air in comparison with the CJEU's previous relevant case-law resulting from infringement proceedings against Hungary, in which the rule of law narrative, as the infrastructural backdrop against which violations were occurring, was absent. It now remains to be seen whether the CJEU will assess the referral of Hungary to the Commission for its non-compliance of its asylum and return legislation with EU Law, within a rule of law narrative or whether it will retreat to its pre-*Minister for Justice and Equality v LM* position.

Rule of law: concluding comments

In sum, the rule of law constitutes a theoretically effective and efficient framework through which the far-right, an accepted threat to this doctrine, may be combatted on an EU level. Once again, the preventive and sanctioning measures incorporated in the aforementioned mechanisms emanate from the EU's need to protect itself and, possibly, the country in question, from destructive forces. However, despite the growing number of available mechanisms, the fact remains that 'outside the accession framework, the EU does not enjoy a solid set of resources and procedural standards'[170] when it comes to the rule of law and, thus, practical reliance on this doctrine remains rather illusory in practice. As efficiently summed up by Kochenov and Bárd:

> The European Union and the Member States seem to be doing as little as they can against rule of law backsliding in some of the EU's constituent parts. Each of the EU institutions came up with their own plan on what to do, inventing more and more new soft law of questionable quality.[171]

Hungary and Poland are a testing ground for the efficacy and efficiency of the mechanisms available for the protection and promotion of the rule of law, within the EU, regarding the framework of State activity which is founded, in whole or

---

170 Uladzislau Belavusau, 'On Age Discrimination and Beating Dead Dogs: Commission v Hungary' (2013) 50 *Common Market Law Review* 1145, 1150.

171 Petra Bárd & Dimitry Kochenov, 'Working Paper: Rule of Law Crisis in the New Member States of the EU' (2018) *Reconnect* Working Paper: https://reconnect-europe.eu/featured/working-paper-rule-of-law-crisis-in-the-new-member-states-of-the-eu/ [Accessed 1 September 2018] 5.

in part, on far-right ideas. To date, the EU Member States and the institutions have not really done much. The effects of this are the continuum in the constitutional deterioration of the countries. For example, as aptly put in a 2014 article, some 'cosmetic changes'[172] were made by Hungary, taking minimal action on the concerns expressed by entities such as the European Parliament.[173] This indicator demonstrates that 'not by any standards do the results of the test qualify a success.'[174] It appears that the Tavares Report, although rich in innovation, ideas and good will, did not result in the amelioration of the rule of law situation in Hungary. In addition, the CJEU, when looking at by-products of this new constitutional reality, did not place its analysis within a rule of law setting in relation to Hungarian cases, but rectified this in the preliminary ruling requested by Ireland. Although a stricter stance may be discerned in relation to the EU's approach to Poland, the motivations are worrisome in themselves, and the belated proposal of the Commission *vis-à-vis* Article 7 is only a small step in the article's labyrinth. Unless the EU reconceptualises its duties towards the values set out in Article 2, the situation will continue to deteriorate in both countries, and a devastating precedent of actions will be deeply instilled. Therefore, we are very far from calling the EU an institution which seriously and systematically confronts threats from anti-democratic phenomena, such as the far-right, notwithstanding the plethora of hard and soft tools it possesses to confront them effectively and efficiently.

Charter of fundamental rights of the European Union

The interrelationship between the EU and human rights is not a simple one to assess. It has been argued that 'under the orthodox account of the EU Law, the Union lacks any general competence in the field of human rights.'[175] Nevertheless, this interrelationship is ever-developing with the Union being marked by a 'more strongly embedded paradigm of fundamental rights in the Union law.'[176] For example, Article 7 TEU now grants the EU a supervisory role in relation to the protection of Article 2 principles, such as human rights, and, since the Treaty of Nice, allows the EU to prevent breaches to the rule of law and related notions. Other initiatives have included the incorporation of Article 6 of the TEU which, *inter alia*, renders the Charter of Fundamental Rights of the EU a source of European Law and stipulates that the Union is to ratify the European Convention on Human Rights (ECHR). It has been argued that this push towards

---

172 Gábor Halmai, 'An Illiberal Constitutional System in the Middle of Europe' (2014) 5 *European Yearbook on Human Rights*, 510.

173 Ibid.

174 Ibid. 498.

175 Wojciech Sadurski, 'Adding a Bite to a Bark? A Story of Article 7, the EU Enlargement, and Jörg Haider' (2010) *Sydney Law Journal*, Legal Studies Research Paper no. 10/01, 29.

176 Uladzislau Belavusau, 'Historical Revisionism in Comparative Perspective: Law, Politics, and Surrogate Mourning' *EUI Working Papers*, Law (2013) 2013/12, 15.

endowing the EU with a role in the field of human rights has partly emanated from concerns over whether the newer Eastern Member States would continue to uphold their obligations in the ambit of democracy and human rights once their membership has been approved.[177] The Charter of Fundamental Rights of the EU was ratified in 2000 on the premise that 'the peoples of Europe, in creating an ever closer union among them, are resolved to share a peaceful future based on common values.'[178] Notwithstanding the significant step forward taken by this charter, its actual impact is restricted due to its non-binding nature and its applicability only in the event that the institutions and States implement EU Law.[179] The articles relevant to a discourse on the far-right are those pertaining to the freedom of expression, the freedom of association and assembly, the prohibition of discrimination, the general limitation clause, the non-destruction clause and the prohibition of abuse of rights. Article 11 of the Charter states that 'everyone has the right to freedom of expression. This right shall include freedom to hold opinions and to receive and impart information and ideas without interference by public authority and regardless of frontiers.' Article 12 of the Charter states that 'everyone has the right to freedom of peaceful assembly and to freedom of association at all levels...' Notwithstanding that any limitations to these rights are absent from these articles, the Charter incorporates a general limitation clause in the form of Article 52 which notes that limitation shall be 'provided for by law and respect the essence of those rights and freedoms. Subject to the principle of proportionality, limitations may be made only if they are necessary and genuinely meet objectives of general interest, recognised by the Union or the need to protect the rights and freedoms of others.' This article also states that

> in so far as this Charter contains rights which correspond to rights guaranteed by the Convention for the Protection of Human Rights and Fundamental Freedoms, the meaning and scope of those rights shall be the same as those laid down by the said Convention. This provision shall not prevent Union law providing more extensive protection.

Therefore, as in the case of the ECHR, militant democracy is also found in the Charter which permits limitations to expression, association and assembly insofar as such limitations are prescribed by law and are necessary in a democratic society, concepts which are provided for by the ECHR and which have been duly interpreted and defined by the ECtHR. However, Article 52 refers only to the meaning of these rights as covered by the Convention and not as

---

177 Michael Merlingen, Cas Mudde & Ulrich Sedelmeier, 'The Right and the Righteous? European Norms, Domestic Politics and the Sanctions against Austria' (2001) 39 *Journal of Common Market Studies* 1, 63–64.

178 Preamble, Charter of Fundamental Rights of the European Union 2000.

179 Stijn Smismans, 'The European Union's Fundamental Rights Myth' (2010) 48 *Journal of Common Market Studies* 1, 50.

interpreted by the Court. The distance kept by the EU from the CoE was further enhanced at the end of 2014 by the CJEU. In considering the EU's accession to the ECHR, the Court noted that, if this were to occur, the EU would, *inter alia*, be bound by ECtHR judgements.[180] After setting out a series of legal obstacles to acceding to the Convention, the CJEU found that to do so would be incompatible with EU law.[181] Moreover, due to the lack of relevant case-law in relation to the application of the Charter's provisions, it is not possible to ascertain, merely from this document, what kind of limitation of expression is, in fact, proportional. Even though, on an EU level, *Feryn*[182] 'marks the long-awaited birth of what can be symbolically entitled a European law of freedom of expression,'[183] this case dealt with hate speech within the employment setting and not hate speech promulgated by the far-right, and, therefore, the contextual difference does not permit us to extend principles and points developed therein to the framework of far-right rhetoric.

In addition, the Charter incorporates Article 53, which notes that the provisions therein shall not be interpreted as 'restricting or adversely affecting human rights and fundamental freedoms' as recognised by the EU, international law, international agreements, such as the ECHR, and by the Constitutions of Member States. In referring to international law, the Charter, thereby, incorporates provisions, such as those contained in the ICERD, which positively stipulate the banning of racist parties and groups. In addition, Article 54 holds that

> nothing in this Charter shall be interpreted as implying any right to engage in any activity or to perform any act aimed at the destruction of any of the rights and freedoms recognised in this Charter or at their limitation to a greater extent than is provided for herein.

Article 21 provides that

> any discrimination based on any ground such as sex, race, colour, ethnic or social origin, genetic features, language, religion or belief, political or any other opinion, membership of a national minority, property, birth, disability, age or sexual orientation shall be prohibited.

Thus, expression or association of far-right groups which results in such discrimination could be prohibited as a result of Article 21 but also in light of Article 54,

---

180 Court of Justice of the European Union Press Release No. 180/14 Luxembourg, 18 December 2014, Opinion 2/13 http://curia.europa.eu/jcms/upload/docs/application/pdf/2014-12/cp140180en.pdf [Accessed 2 December 2015].

181 Ibid.

182 Case C-54/07, Centrum voor gelijkheid van kansen en voor racismebestrijding v Firma Feryn NV (10 July 2008) ECLI:EU:C:2008:397.

183 Uladzislau Belavusau, 'Fighting Hate Speech through EU Law' (2012) 4 *Amsterdam Law Forum* 1, 22.

which prohibits the destruction of the rights and freedoms of this Charter, including the freedom from non-discrimination. Article 21 is of particular relevance to hate speech and hate crime expressed and conducted by far-right groups, given that, notwithstanding a general reference to the adoption of international law, there is no particular article dealing with racial discrimination and its prohibition within this Charter. However, given the lack of CJEU jurisprudence on central themes, such as far-right rhetoric and activity, and given that it was decided that the EU would not accede to the ECHR and is, thus, not bound to follow the interpretations set out by the ECtHR, the way in which the issue of, for example, expression is interpreted and understood in the realm of far-right rhetoric is not lucid.

In sum, the Charter provides a brief overview of rights that could be quoted by far-right groups as a justification for extremist speech or activity and provides the possibility to limit such extremism in a general manner through Articles 52, 53 and 54, with Article 21 being the only positive obligation directly imposed on Member States to prohibit racial discrimination, albeit through a broad discrimination clause. The rather generalised articles and the absence of relevant CJEU case-law mean that there does not yet exist a well-rounded insight into key meanings and notions. Instead, what is demonstrated through the aforementioned articles is the objective of the Charter simply to lay down key rights and obligations without entering into too much detail on central terms and themes, nevertheless reflecting the general spirit of the EU against actions that are contrary to human rights, whatever such spirit may entail.

1996 joint action adopted by the council concerning means to combat racism and xenophobia

The 1996 Joint Action[184] was the first comprehensive initiative taken by the EU to combat racism and xenophobia within EU Member States by promoting a harmonised criminal law amongst Member States as a means to this end. Prior to this initiative, no steps had been taken to tackle racism through EU mechanisms apart from two reports prepared by Commissions of Inquiry, as discussed later. However, during the 1990's, the EU was faced with increasing pressure from the European Parliament and civil society to incorporate measures against such discrimination.[185] Joint Actions were the legal means available between 1993 and 1999 and were later replaced by the Framework Decisions following reforms brought about by the Treaty of Amsterdam. As noted by Bell, while Joint Actions were, in theory, legally binding, 'the absence of any jurisdiction

---

184 Joint action/96/443/JHA of 15 July 1996 adopted by the Council on the basis of Article K.3 of the Treaty on European Union, Concerning Action to Combat Racism and Xenophobia.

185 Erik Bleick & Mary Clare Feldmann, 'The Rise of Race? Europeanization and Antiracist Policymaking in the EU' Paper presented at the conference 'The Impact of Europeanization on Politics and Policy in Europe: Trends and Trajectories' University of Toronto, 7–9 May 2004.

for the CJEU over Joint Actions meant that the main lever for compliance was political will,'[186] and, therefore, their actual application and legal enforceability were limited. The 1996 Joint Action had the objective of adopting rules to combat racism and xenophobia and ensure harmonisation of criminal law on this issue amongst States in order to prevent perpetrators 'from exploiting the fact that racist and xenophobic activities are classified differently in different States by moving from one country to another in order to escape criminal proceedings or avoid serving sentences...' For the purposes of this Joint Action, a plethora of activities constitute a criminal offence, with the most relevant to the far-right being the participation in the activities of groups, organisations or associations which involve discrimination; violence; or racial, ethnic or religious hatred, with other activities including the public incitement to discrimination, violence or hatred in respect of a group of persons or a member of such a group defined by reference to colour, race, religion or national or ethnic origin; the public condoning, for racist or xenophobic purposes, of crimes against humanity and human rights violations; the public dissemination of material containing expressions of racism and xenophobia; as well as public denial of certain international crimes. Such actions fall within the sphere of activities conducted and ideas professed by far-right groups. Interestingly, the Joint Action criminalises what is habitually referred to as revisionism only when it 'includes behaviour which is contemptuous of, or degrading to, a group of persons defined by reference to colour, race, religion or national or ethnic origin' whilst publicly condoning crimes against humanity and human rights violations is only criminalised when it is carried out for 'a racist or xenophobic purpose,' thereby, demonstrating the weight placed by the Joint Action on intent in that group of offences. Moreover, when reading the list of punishable activities, a similarity can be discerned between the offences listed therein and Article 4 of the ICERD. The Joint Action sought to ensure co-operation between Member States for the aforementioned offences through a variety of means, such as the seizure and confiscation of material intended for public dissemination, acknowledgement that the offences are not of a political nature in order to prevent refusal for mutual co-operation, provision of information to another Member State to initiate legal proceedings and the establishment of contact points in the Member States responsible for the collection and exchange of information for purposes of investigation and proceedings. Interestingly, the Joint Action assumed a legal and cultural cohesion between Member States not only in relation to criminal law but also in relation to the restriction of the freedom of expression and freedom of association, which are directly related to the offences listed therein. This weakness could be considered an obstacle to the proper interpretation and implementation of its provisions, a weakness which was partially rectified in the subsequent Framework Decision, as discussed later.

---

186 Mark Bell, *'Racism and Equality in the European Union'* (1st edn. Oxford Scholarship Online 2009) 157.

It has been noted that 'there is very little evidence on how the Joint Action has been applied in practice.'[187] However, two years after its entry into force, the Council noted that only Austria and Luxembourg made amendments to their legal systems in order to conform with the provisions therein.[188] Thus, the overall contribution that the Joint Action has made to the fight against racism and xenophobia remains questionable. However, it did constitute the foundation upon which the next tool, namely a Framework Decision, was developed.

Council framework decision 2009/913/JHA of 28 November 2008 on combatting certain forms and expressions of racism and xenophobia by means of criminal law

The incorporation of the fight against racism in today's Article 67.3 of the TFEU demonstrated the increasing dedication of the EU to contributing thereto. This article foresees collaboration between Member States in criminal matters pertaining to racism and xenophobia by holding that

> the Union shall endeavour to ensure a high level of security through measures to prevent and combat crime, racism and xenophobia, and through measures for co-ordination and co-operation between police and judicial authorities and other competent authorities, as well as through the mutual recognition of judgments in criminal matters and, if necessary, through the approximation of criminal laws.

In light of the provisions therein and building on the 1996 Joint Action, the Commission put forth a Framework Decision on combatting racism and xenophobia through criminal law which was adopted in 2008, after seven years of negotiations.[189] The negotiations were lengthy and complex, predominantly due to the 'disparity of the Member States legal systems and traditions as regards the protection of the right to freedom of expression.'[190] In fact, the conflicting appraisals adopted by States in the realm of restricting freedom of expression and also freedom of association are a recurring theme in the drafting of such documents, as can be reflected, for example, in the reservations imposed on Article 4 of the ICERD, discussed in the international framework. As such, the Framework Decision underlines that it respects the freedom of expression and

---

187 Ibid. 158.
188 Council of the European Union, 'Note de Comité K.4 AU Coreper' Ref 7808/1/98/ REV 1, 29 April 1998.
189 Report from the Commission to the European Parliament and the Council on the Implementation of Council Framework Decision 2008/913/JHA on Combating Certain Forms and Expressions of Racism and Xenophobia by Means of Criminal Law COM (2014) 27, 1.
190 Ibid.

the freedom of association and assembly, as provided for by the ECHR and the Charter of Fundamental Rights of the EU and, thus, adheres to the limitation clauses attached thereto and through which any conditions, limitations, restrictions to or penalties for the offences listed can be introduced. In this ambit, Article 7 of the Framework Decision holds that it shall 'not have the effect of requiring Member States to take measures in contradiction to fundamental principles relating to freedom of association and freedom of expression.' Further, in relation to criminal law, the Framework Decision recognised that full harmonisation of criminal law is not possible given that the Member States' cultural and legal traditions differ. Notwithstanding the purpose of this provision stemming from a potential to provide a realistic outlook on the objectives of this document, 'such wording leaves a certain, albeit very unclear, margin for the States to assess a pure racist ... scope of the concrete hate speech utterances.'[191]

Article 1 of the Framework Decision outlines that Member States must punish incidences of publicly inciting to violence or hatred against a particular group through public dissemination or distribution of material, publicly condoning, denying or grossly trivialising international crimes, as defined in the Statute of the International Criminal Court or the Charter of the International Military Tribunal, directed against a group, when the conduct is carried out in such a manner likely to incite to violence or hatred against such a group. However, as noted, without a CJEU assessment of what falls within the framework of conduct that is likely to incite violence or hatred against a group or a member of such a group, 'it remains difficult to assess the potential of the severity of criminalizing speech.'[192] Against a backdrop of a lacking judicial extrapolation of key notions and themes, three interesting observations can be made in relation to the list of offences incorporated in the Framework Decision. First, the 'participation in the activities of groups, organizations or associations, which involve discrimination, violence, or racial, ethnic or religious hatred,' as incorporated in the 1996 Joint Action, is not named as an offence. This provision 'was opposed from the outset by nearly all States except Germany and so it was deleted from the draft text.'[193] Second, the public incitement of discrimination, which was incorporated in the Joint Action, has been removed, allowing only for incitement to violence or hatred. Third, the offence of grossly trivialising international crimes, such as genocide, has been added to the list of publicly condoning and denying such crimes. As is the case in the Joint Action, publicly condoning, denying and, now, grossly trivialising an international crime, such as the Holocaust, is only a criminal offence insofar as it is effectuated in a manner likely to incite violence or hatred against such a group, thereby, permitting such expression as long as it does not potentially lead to an undesirable consequence. Article 1(4) provides Member

---

191 Uladzislau Belavusau, 'Historical Revisionism in Comparative Perspective: Law, Politics, and Surrogate Mourning' (2013) *European University Institute* Working Papers, Law 2013/12, 14.
192 Ibid. 15.
193 Mark Bell, *'Racism and Equality in the European Union'* (1st edn. Oxford Scholarship Online 2009) 160.

States with further leniency when faced with the public denial or trivialisation of international crimes, such as genocide, as these can, if a Member State wishes, be restricted to crimes which have been established by a final decision of a national and/or international court. It must be noted that no reference is made to gross trivialisation in this ambit, and one can only assume that this is an oversight by the drafters rather than a purposeful exclusion for which there exists no reasonable explanation. In addition, Article 1(2) grants Member States the liberty to punish all the aforementioned actions and/or expressions only when they are carried out in a way 'likely to disturb public order or which is threatening, abusive or insulting.' The objective of this provision is problematic, given that it can safely be said that the offences listed in this article cannot occur without disturbing public order or without being threatening, abusive or insulting. Thus, not only is it difficult to understand in what types of situation this provision could be enforceable, but also, simultaneously, it indirectly foresees that the type of activities or words described therein can be carried out or expressed without resulting in harm. Further, Article 1(3) interlinks religion with race, colour, descent or national or ethnic origin, adopting the principle of intersectionality as is the case, for example, in the ICERD.

In addition, Article 2 of the Framework Decision provides that instigating, aiding and abetting the aforementioned offences are all punishable activities, marking a positive development in relation to the Joint Action where such activities are not punishable. Article 3 notes that criminal penalties for the offences should be 'effective, proportionate and dissuasive' with the conduct included in Article 1 being punishable by penalties of between one and three years' imprisonment. In addition to the offences incorporated in the document, Article 4 notes that Member States must take the necessary steps to 'ensure that racist and xenophobic motivation is considered an aggravating circumstance' or that it is at least taken into account by courts in the determination of punishment, demonstrating another positive development from the time of the Joint Action. Article 5 is a significant article given that it deals with the liability of legal persons. It holds that Member States must take all the necessary steps to

> ensure that a legal person can be held liable for conduct referred to in Articles 1 and 2, committed for its benefit by any person, acting either individually or as part of an organ of the legal persons, who has a leading position within the legal person…

Importantly, the liability of legal persons 'shall not exclude criminal proceedings against natural persons who are perpetrators or accessories in the conduct…' However, the Framework Decision states that legal persons cannot include 'the State or other public bodies in the exercise of State authority and public international organisations' thereby excluding the State and its institutions from criminal liability in the event that it or they promote racial hatred and/or violence. Thus, this article leaves an 'important discretion for a State to grapple with certain political movements'[194] thereby, equipping it with the tools to combat far-right groups promoting rhetoric and conduct as described in this document. However, and, although no definition of 'State' is provided, one could presumably conclude that a political party that is part of the government would fall within the definition of a State and, thus, outside the scope of this liability. In relation to penalties for legal entities active within the far-right movement, the most relevant include the exclusion from entitlement to public benefits or aid[195] and the placement under judicial supervision.[196]

In relation to the enforceability of the Framework Decision, the 2014 Report prepared by the Commission to the European Parliament and the Council on its implementation noted that

> in accordance with Article 10(1) of Protocol No. 36 to the Treaties, prior to the end of the transitional period expiring on 1 December 2014, the Commission does not have the power to launch infringement proceedings under Article 25 TFEU with regard to Framework Decisions adopted prior to the entry into force of the Treaty of Lisbon.[197]

As a result, the EU and its institutions are left with limited powers to push States in the direction of adequate enforcement. As noted in the recent report, a number of Member States have not fully and/or suitably transposed the Framework Decision's provisions 'namely in relation to the offences of denying, condoning and grossly trivialising certain crimes.'[198]

Thus, the Framework Decision does contribute, at least on a theoretical level, to combatting the far-right, notwithstanding its great leap backwards from the Joint Action *vis-à-vis* the criminalisation of participation in racist groups. Nevertheless, it deals with an array of activities carried out by such groups, embellishes and adds certain notions, such as the consideration of a racist motivation as an aggravating circumstance, and deals separately with the penalties which are to be imposed on legal persons, thereby, encompassing some of the vehicles used to promulgate far-right rhetoric, albeit leaving out the significant vehicle of political parties. The limitations brought by this Decision, as discussed earlier, demonstrate that 'combatting racism can encounter strong political resistance ... [with] the text resembling 'a lowest common denominator.'[199] This, in addition to the

---

194 Uladzislau Belavusau, 'Historical Revisionism in Comparative Perspective: Law, Politics, and Surrogate Mourning' (2013) *European University Institute* Working Papers, Law 2013/12, 15.

195 Council Framework Decision 2009/913/JHA of 28 November 2008 on Combatting Certain Forms and Expressions of Racism and Xenophobia by Means of Criminal Law, Article 6(1)(a).

196 Ibid. Article 6(1)(d).

197 Report from the Commission to the European Parliament and the Council on the implementation of Council Framework Decision 2008/913/JHA on Combating Certain Forms and Expressions of Racism and Xenophobia by Means of Criminal Law COM (2014) 27, 1.

198 Ibid. 9.

199 Mark Bell, *'Racism and Equality in the European Union'* (Oxford Scholarship Online 2009), 161.

limitations of the EU in launching infringement proceedings, as noted earlier, renders the efficacy and actual application of the Framework Decision in a unified and adequate manner in all Member States doubtful, with little progress having been made to date. More particularly, as noted in the 2014 Report on the Framework Decision, 'at present it appears that a number of Member States have not transposed fully and/or correctly all the provisions of the Framework Decision.'[200] In fact, the report urges the 'full and correct legal transposition of the existing Framework Decision.'[201] Indeed, it has been argued that 'the full implementation of the Framework Decision will radically alter the legal landscape in Europe.'[202] This remains to be seen.

European Parliament resolutions

The European Parliament has taken certain initiatives which incorporate regulating the far-right, the most relevant of which are discussed in this section. In 1993, the European Parliament adopted a Resolution on the Resurgence of Racism and Xenophobia in Europe and the danger of far-right violence.[203] It draws attention to the 'proliferation in the Member States of extreme right-wing groups, parties and movements'[204] and holds that 'these practices pose a grave threat to those democratic values which form the basis of the common heritage of the Member States.'[205] It reaffirms the duty of EU institutions to 'combat any group or movement liable to pose a threat to democracy and basic human rights.'[206] However, it does not extrapolate on the term 'combat' and does not provide any further recommendations in relation to how such movements can be combatted. In 1994, it passed a resolution on racism, xenophobia and anti-Semitism[207] which arose following its concern about the electoral success of racist parties in Europe and, particularly, in countries such as Austria, France, the U.K. and Belgium, whilst simultaneously expressing its contentment at the decrease in votes given to the respective party in Germany. The Resolution deplores the fact that 'certain political forces are using the existing crisis in employment and the economy to stir up xenophobic and racist sentiments and exploit them for electoral ends.'[208] It notes

200 Ibid.
201 Report from the Commission to the European Parliament and the Council on the implementation of Council Framework Decision 2008/913/JHA on Combating Certain Forms and Expressions of Racism and Xenophobia by Means of Criminal Law COM (2014) 27, 9.
202 Laurent Pech, 'The Law of Holocaust Denial in Europe: Towards a (Qualified) EU-wide Criminal Prohibition' (2009) *Jean Monnet* Working Paper 10/09, 3.
203 European Parliament Resolution on the Resurgence of Racism and Xenophobia in Europe and the Danger of Right-Wing Extremist Violence, 21 April 1993 (OJ C 150, p. 127, 31.5.1993).
204 Ibid.
205 Ibid.
206 Ibid.
207 European Parliament Resolution on Racism, Xenophobia, and Anti-Semitism, 27 October 1994 (OJ C 323/154, 20.11.1994).
208 Ibid.

'with concern the increasing sympathy with which the positions of extreme right-wing movements and political parties are being received in several Member States of the Union and a candidate country.'[209] Notwithstanding the concern and condemnation of the far-right in this Resolution, the Parliament proceeded to make recommendations for combatting racism through initiatives, such as education and NGO projects, making no reference to the banning and/or regulation of far-right groups, activities and rhetoric. In 1995, it adopted the Resolution of the European Parliament on racism, xenophobia and anti-Semitism,[210] which noted that whenever there is 'a risk that organizations or people with racist, xenophobic or anti-Semitic behaviour make contacts across the borders of a Member State, the criminal aspects should be studied by Europol.'[211] Furthermore, the European Parliament adopted a Resolution in 1997[212] to express 'its regret at racist and xenophobic statements by politicians and parties at national and European Level'[213] and called upon 'democratic parties to use all democratic means to ostracise racist movements and groups.'[214] However, this Resolution makes no reference to the meaning of what can constitute democratic means nor does it make further direct recommendations in relation to the regulation of far-right groups, but instead suggests measures, such as education and national and local projects and youth exchanges, to promote tolerance and understanding. In 2005, the European Parliament called upon States to withdraw public funding from political parties that do not abide by human rights and fundamental freedoms.[215] In 2007, the European Parliament passed a Resolution on combatting the rise of extremism in Europe where it underlined that extremist ideologies are 'incompatible with the principles of liberty, democracy, respect for human rights and fundamental freedoms and the rule of law'[216] and that 'extremist political movements is a European challenge that requires a joint and coordinated approach.'[217] It further went on to stipulate, for the first time so directly, that the combat of extremism must not negatively affect the protection of the freedom of expression and association.[218] It called upon other political forces to avoid supporting and forming alliances with extremist political parties either directly or indirectly.[219]

209 Ibid.
210 Ibid.
211 Ibid.
212 Ibid.
213 European Parliament Resolution on Racism, Xenophobia and Anti-Semitism and the European Year against Racism (1977) (OJ C 55/17, 24.2.97).
214 Ibid.
215 European Parliament Resolution on the Increase in Racist and Homophobic Violence in Europe, P6_TA (2006) 0273.
216 Resolution of the European Parliament on Combatting the Rise of Extremism in Europe, 13 December 2007, P6_TA (2007) 062.
217 Ibid.
218 Ibid.
219 Ibid.

Thus, the far-right has been an issue of concern to the Parliament since 1993. Notwithstanding certain measures to combat this phenomenon, such as non-alliance with such parties and the ostracising of such groups through the implementation of all democratic means, whatever that may mean, no Resolution has been as explicit as the ICERD in mentioning the banning and prohibition of such parties or groups. This could be due to the experience of the limitations imposed on the relevant Article to that Convention, due to concerns over the freedom of expression and freedom of association, and, also, due to the Parliament's concern over this given that it did, in fact, note that any measures must not violate those rights.

Other measures

Following the 1984 European Parliamentary elections and the rise in the success of far-right parties, the Parliament established a Committee of Inquiry into the rise of racism and fascism in Europe which resulted in the Report of the Committee of Inquiry, known as the Evrigenis Report,[220] which provides a comprehensive, definitional and conceptual framework of key terms and phenomena, gives an overview of the situation in Member States and makes recommendations for combatting this phenomenon. Notwithstanding that the Report focusses on the rise of racism and fascism in Europe and extensively discusses the development of the far-right movement in Member States, the recommendations made relating to the direct regulation of the phenomenon are limited, with more emphasis being placed on tackling the causal factors leading to their formation and why they flourish. More particularly, recommendations include the immediate ratification of relevant international conventions,[221] the 'creation of a European legal area in order to prevent the activities of ... extremist organizations ... and the distribution of illegal propaganda material'[222] and that national legislations on combatting political extremism are constantly revised and their application ensured.[223]

In 1990, the European Parliament re-examined the issue through a second Committee of Inquiry which resulted in the Report of the Committee of Inquiry on Racism and Xenophobia, or the Ford Report, which, once again, underlined the need for action, looked at the situation in Member States and produced recommendations to combat racism and xenophobia with some dealing directly with far-right groups. Such recommendations included the establishment of a system for monitoring developments in the field of racism, anti-Semitism and xenophobia, including extreme-right and fascist groups[224] and that a periodic report be prepared every eighteen to twenty four months by the Commission

---

220 European Parliament Committee of Inquiry into the Rise of Fascism and Racism in Europe, Report on the Findings of the Inquiry, 1985, Luxembourg.
221 Ibid. para. 310 (a).
222 Ibid. para. 318 (i).
223 Ibid. para. 313 (d).
224 European Parliament, Report of the Committee of Inquiry on Racism and Xenophobia, 1991, Luxembourg, Recommendation 3.

of the European Communities on the current situation in relation to racism, anti-Semitism and xenophobia, including extreme-right and fascist groups.[225] These reports were valuable initiatives that contributed to the development of knowledge in relation to the far-right.

In sum, these reports are significant in that they reflect the early steps taken by the European Parliament to look into the issue of the far-right and provide concrete recommendations for Member States to combat it. They also allow for an appraisal of developments taken on this level within the framework considered. For example, in 1985, the Evrigenis Report recommended the creation of a European Legal Order to prevent the activities of far-right groups, but this has not yet been realised. However, and notwithstanding that both reports recommend that Member States which have not yet ratified the ICERD do so immediately,[226] and, by extension, request the implementation of Article 4 therein, nowhere in the aforementioned reports are there suggestions pertaining to the prohibition or banning of far-right parties or other less restrictive measures such as non-alliance with such parties.

Chapter conclusion

In conclusion, Article 7 TEU is the strongest tool, with real potential and consequences, which the EU has at its discretion to tackle, *inter alia*, far-right movements. This is not only due to its primacy *vis-à-vis* its positioning on the ladder of EU sources but also due to its innovative, second-chance nature incorporated in the dual preventive–sanctioning mechanism offered therein. Despite some recent actions taken for its use, we have not yet seen it being enforced. According to the letter and spirit of the article, one could come up with a multitude of examples in which this article could and should be implemented, many of those relating to the European far-right. Moreover, the New EU Framework to Strengthen the Rule of Law, which broadens the scope of the second-chance nature approach adopted by the EU to risky situations, the mechanisms proposed by the Tavares report, such as the 'Copenhagen Commission' and, to a much lesser extent the Council's Annual Rule of Law Dialogue, all constitute tools which can be used to protect the rule of law from, *inter alia*, the far-right. However, the efficacy of the tools, apart from Article 7 TEU, is doubtful since they are primarily non-binding, non-consequential recommendations. In addition to this, the EU has come up with other instruments that could be implemented in this sphere. The 1996 Joint Action was the only initiative which sought to criminalise participation in such groups, a measure which was removed by the subsequent Framework Directive. Notwithstanding that the Charter provides for the principle of non-discrimination and limits freedom of expression and association in certain

---

225 Ibid. Recommendation 16.
226 Ibid. Recommendation 51, European Parliament Committee of Inquiry into the Rise of Fascism and Racism in Europe, Report on the Findings of the Inquiry, 1985, Luxembourg, para. 310 (a).

circumstances, regardless of the fact that the Framework Decision criminalises activities and speeches conducted by such movements, and, even though the European Parliament expresses concern in relation to the far-right, the EU has yet to adopt comprehensive and binding legal measures which are particular to the regulation of such movements. Moreover, the Framework Decision focusses solely on racism and xenophobia and related speech and activities, with no penalties on, for example, homophobic or transphobic speech and crimes, demonstrating the hierarchy that exists at a United Nations (UN) level as well. It could be discerned, from the Parliament's Resolutions and the Framework Decision, that the EU wishes to avoid outright bans and prohibitions of such groups, and resorts to other less restrictive measures which have been referred to in more recent years, such as cutting public funding, either due to sincere concern for the freedoms of expression and association or fear of a repeat of the limitations imposed on the ICERD's prohibitive provision. Either way, what can safely be said, and is reflected earlier, is that the far-right is incongruous with European common values but has not yet been challenged by the European family.

Bibliography

Legislation

Charter of Fundamental Rights of the European Union.
Council Framework Decision 2009/913/JHA of 28 November 2008 on Combatting Certain Forms and Expressions of Racism and Xenophobia by Means of Criminal Law, Article 6(1)(a).

Case-law

Case C-288/12, Commission v Hungary, Judgement of the Court of Justice (8 April 2014) ECLI:EU:C:2014:237.
Case C-286/12, Commission v Hungary, Judgement of the Court of Justice (6 November 2012) ECLI:EU:C:2012:687.
Case C-54/07, Centrum voor gelijkheid van kansen en voor racismebestrijding v Firma Feryn NV (10 July 2008) ECLI:EU:C:2008:397.
Joined Cases C-402/05 P and C-415/05, Kadi & Al Barakaat International Foundation v Council of the European Union and Commission of the European Communities (3 September 2008) ECLI:EU:C:2008:461.
Case 294/83, Les Verts v Parliament (23 April 1986) ECLI:EU:C:1986:166.
Case C-216/18 PPU, Minister for Justice and Equality v LM, Judgement of the Court of Justice (25 July 2018) ECLI:EU:C:2018:586.

European Union documents

European Commission

Communication from the Commission to the Council and the European Parliament on Article 7 of the Treaty on the European Union – Respect for and Promotion of the Values on which the European Union is Based, COM (2003) 606 Final, para. 1.4.1.

Communication from the Commission to the European Parliament and the Council: A New EU Framework to Strengthen the Rule of Law, COM (2014) 158 final/2, 3.

Communication from the Commission to the Council and the European Parliament on Article 7 of the Treaty on the European Union – Respect for and Promotion of the Values on which the European Union is based, COM (2003) 606 Final.

European Commission Press Release: 'Relocation: Commission refers the Czech Republic, Hungary and Poland to the Court of Justice' (2017).

European Commission Press Release on Poland: 'College Orientation Debate on Recent Developments in Poland and the Rule of Law Framework: Questions & Answers' (2016).

European Commission Press Release: Hungary – Infringements: European Commission Satisfied with Changes to Central Bank Statute, but Refers Hungary to the Court of Justice on the Independence of the Data Protection Authority and Measures Affecting the Judiciary (2012).

Report from the Commission to the European Parliament and the Council on the Implementation of Council Framework Decision 2008/913/JHA on Combating Certain Forms and Expressions of Racism and Xenophobia by Means of Criminal Law COM (2014) 27.

Council of the European Union

Conclusions of the Council of the European Union and the Member States Meeting within the Council on Ensuring Respect for the Rule of Law, General Affairs Council Meeting Brussels, 16 December 2014.

Council of the European Union, 'Note de Comité K.4 AU Coreper' Ref 7808/1/98/REV 1, 29 April 1998.

Erik Bleick & Mary Clare Feldmann, 'The Rise of Race? Europeanization and Antiracist Policymaking in the EU' Paper Presented at the Conference 'The Impact of Europeanization on Politics and Policy in Europe: Trends and Trajectories' University of Toronto, 7–9 May 2004.

Joint action/96/443/JHA of 15 July 1996 adopted by the Council on the basis of Article K.3 of the Treaty on European Union, Concerning Action to Combat Racism and Xenophobia.

European Parliament

Committee on Civil Liberties, Justice and Home Affairs: 'Report on the Situation of Fundamental Rights: Standards and Practices in Hungary (Pursuant to the European Parliament Resolution of 16 February 2012)' A7–0229/2013 (2013).

Committee on Constitutional Affairs, Rapporteur: Olivier Duhamel, Report on the Constitutionalisation of the Treaties (2000/2160 (INI)), FINAL 15–0289/2000, 12 October 2000.

European Parliament Plenary – Commission Statement on the Situation in Hungary First Vice-President Timmermans Strasbourg (19 May 2015).

European Parliament Resolution of 10 June 2015 on the Situation in Hungary (2015/2700(RSP) (10 June 2015).

European Parliament Resolution of 16 December 2015 on the Situation in Hungary (2015/2935(RSP) (16 December 2015).

European Parliament Resolution on the Increase in Racist and Homophobic Violence in Europe, P6 – TA (2006) 0273.

European Parliament Resolution on Racism, Xenophobia, and Anti-Semitism (27 October 1994) (OJ C 323/154, 20.11.1994).

European Parliament Resolution on the Resurgence of Racism and Xenophobia in Europe and the Danger of Right-Wing Extremist Violence (21 April 1993) (OJ C 150, p. 127, 31.5.1993).

European Parliament, Committee on Constitutional Affairs, Rapporteur: Johannes Voggenhuber, Report on the Commission Communication on Article 7 of the Treaty on European Union, Respect for and Promotion of the Values on which the Union is Based (COM(2003) 606 – C5-0594/2003 – 2003/2249(INI)).

European Parliament Committee of Inquiry into the Rise of Fascism and Racism in Europe, Report on the Findings of the Inquiry, 1985, Luxembourg.

European Parliament, Report of the Committee of Inquiry on Racism and Xenophobia, Recommendation 1991, Luxembourg.

Report on the Situation of Fundamental Rights: Standards and Practices in Hungary (Pursuant to the European Parliament Resolution of 16 February 2012) Committee on Civil Liberties, Justice and Home Affairs, A7-0229/2013.

Fundamental Rights Agency

Fundamental Rights Agency of the European Union, Fundamental Rights: Challenges and Achievements in 2012, Vienna: FRA 2012.

CJEU Press Releases

Court of Justice of the European Union Press Release No 180/14 Luxembourg, 18 December 2014, Opinion 2/13 http://curia.europa.eu/jcms/upload/docs/application/pdf/2014-12/cp140180en.pdf.

Books

Aristotle *'Politics'* (Translated with an Introduction, Notes and Appendixes By Barker E) (1st edn. Oxford University Press, Oxford 1946).

Arnull A, 'The Rule of Law in The European Union' in Anthony Arnull & Daniel Wincott (eds.), *'Accountability and Legitimacy in the European Union'* (1st edn. Oxford University Press, Oxford 2002).

Bell M, *'Racism and Equality in the European Union'* (1st edn. Oxford Scholarship Online 2009).

Cicero M.T, *'The Republic and the Laws'* (A New Translation by Rudd N.) (1st edn. Oxford University Press, Oxford 1998).

Costa P & Zolo D, *'The Rule of Law: History, Theory and Criticism'* (1st edn. Springer, Dordrecht 2007).

Gozzi G, 'Rechtsstaat and Individual Rights in German Constitutional History' in Pietro Costa, Danilo Zolo (eds.), *'The Rule of Law: History, Theory and Criticism'* (1st edn. Springer, Netherlands 2007).

Kochenov D, *'EU Enlargement and The Failure of Conditionality'* (1st edn. Kluwer International, Alphen aan den Rijn 2008) 110.

Krygier M, 'Rule of Law (and Rechtsstaat)' in James D. Wright (ed.) *'International Encyclopedia of the Behavioral Sciences'* (2nd edn. Elsevier, Amsterdam 2015).

Kuijer M, 'Fundamental Rights Protection in the Legal Order of the European Union' in Adam Lazowski & Steven Blockmans (eds.),*'Research Handbook on EU Institutional Law'* 231 (1st edn. Edward Elgar, Cheltenham 2016).

Pech L, 'Rule of Law in France' in Randall Peerenboom (ed.), *'Asian Discourses of Rule of Law'* (1st edn. Routledge, London 2004).

Sajó A, *'Abuse: The Dark Side of Fundamental Rights'* (1st edn. Eleven International Publishing, Utrecht 2006).

Strauss L & Cropsey J, *'Immanuel Kant, in History of Political Philosophy'* (1st edn. University of Chicago Press, Chicago IL 1987).

Tamanaha B.Z, *'On the Rule of Law: History, Politics, Theory'* (1st edn. Cambridge University Press, Cambridge 2004).

Von Hayek F, *'The Road to Serfdom'* (1st edn. The University of Chicago Press, Chicago IL 1994).

Journal articles

Ahtisaari M, Frowein J & Oreja M, Report on the Austrian Government's Commitment to the Common European Values, in particular concerning the rights of minorities, refugees and immigrants and the evolution of the political nature of the FPÖ (The Wise Men Report) 40 *International Legal Materials* 1, 102–103.

Belavusau U, 'Fighting Hate Speech through EU Law' (2012) 4 *Amsterdam Law Forum* 1, 20–35.

Belavusau U, 'On Age Discrimination and Beating Dead Dogs: Commission v Hungary.' (2013) 50 *Common Market Law Review* 1145, 1145–1160.

Craig P, 'Formal and Substantive Conceptions of the Rule of Law: An Analytical Framework' (1997) *Public Law* 467, 467–482.

Editorial Comments: Hungary's New Constitutional Order and "European Unity" (2012) 49 *Common Market Law Review* 3, 871–883.

Fallon R.H Jr. 'The Rule of Law as a Concept in Constitutional Discourse' (1997) 97 *Columbia Law Review* 1, 1–56.

Greer S & Williams A, 'Human Rights in the Council of Europe and the EU: Towards 'Individual', 'Constitutional' or 'Institutional' Justice?' (2009) 15 *European Law Journal* 4, 462–481.

Halmai G, 'An Illiberal Constitutional System in the Middle of Europe' (2014) 5 *European Yearbook on Human Rights*, 497–514.

Jenne E.K & Mudde C, 'Hungary's Illiberal turn – Can Outsiders Help?' (2012) 23 *Journal of Democracy* 3, 147–155.

Kochenov D, 'The EU Rule of Law: Cutting Paths Through Confusion' (2009) 2 *Erasmus Law Review* 1, 1–24.

Kochenov D, 'On Policing Article 2 TEU Compliance – Reverse Solange and Systemic Infringements Analyzed' (2014) 33 *Polish Yearbook of International Law*, 145–170.

Ledford K.F, 'Formalizing the Rule of Law in Prussia: The Supreme Administrative Court 1876–1914' (2004) 37 *Central European History* 2, 203–224.

Merlingen M, Mudde C, Sedelmeier U, 'The Right and the Righteous? European Norms, Domestic Politics and the Sanctions against Austria' (2001) 39 *Journal of Common Market Studies* 1, 61–79.

O'Donnell G.A, 'Why the Rule of Law Matters' (2004) 15 *Journal of Democracy* 4, 32–46.

Pelinka A, 'The Haider Phenomenon in Austria – Examining the FPO in European Context' (2001) 9 *Journal of the International Institute* 1.

Smismans S, 'The European Union's Fundamental Rights Myth' (2010) 48 *Journal of Common Market Studies* 1, 45–66.

Von Bogdandy A & Ioannidis M, 'Systemic Deficiency in the Rule of Law, What it is, What has Been Done, What Can be Done' (2014) 1 *Common Market Law Review* 51, 59–96.

Williams A, 'The Indifferent Gesture: Article 7 TEU, The Fundamental Rights Agency and the UK's invasion of Iraq,' (2006) 31 *European Law Review* 1, 3–27.

Working papers/Research papers

Bárd P & Kochenov D, 'Working Paper: Rule of Law Crisis in the New Member States of the EU' (2018) Reconnect Working Paper.

Belavusau U, 'Historical Revisionism in Comparative Perspective: Law, Politics, and Surrogate Mourning' (2013) European University Institute Working Papers, Law 2013/12.

Bugarič B, 'Protecting Democracy and the Rule of Law in the European Union: The Hungarian Challenge' (2014) LSE 'Europe in Question' Discussion Paper Series (LEQS) Paper no. 79/2014.

Closa C, Kochenov D & Weiler J.H, 'Reinforcing Rule of Law Oversight in the European Union.' European University Institute Working Papers, RSCAS 2014/25.

Kochenov D, 'The Issues of Values' University of Groningen Faculty of Law Research Paper Series no. 19/2013.

Krygier M, 'Rule of Law and Rechtsstaat' (2013) University of New South Wales Research Paper no. 2013–52.

Pech L, 'The Law of Holocaust Denial in Europe: Towards a (Qualified) EU-wide Criminal Prohibition' (2009) Jean Monnet Working Paper 10/09.

Sadurisk W, 'Adding a Bite to a Bark? A Story of Article 7, the EU Enlargement and Jörg Haider.' (2010) *Sydney Law Journal*, Legal Studies Research Paper no. 10/01.

Rosenfeld M, 'The Rule of Law, and the Legitimacy of Constitutional Democracy' (2001) Cardozo Law School, Working Paper Series no. 36.

Müller J-M, 'Safeguarding democracy inside the EU, Brussels and the Future of Liberal Order' (2013) Transatlantic Academy 2012–2013 Paper Series no. 3.

Blog posts

Kochenov D & Pech L, 'From Bad to Worse? On the Commission and the Council's Rule of Law Initiatives' (2015) *VerfBlog*, 2015/1/20 www.verfassungsblog.de/bad-worse-commission-councils-rule-law-initiatives/#.VTo7rdKqqko.

Kochenov D, 'How to Turn Article 2 TEU into a Down-to-Earth Provision?' (2013) *Verf-Blog*, 2013/12/08 www.verfassungsblog.de/how-to-turn-article-2-teu-into-a-down-to-earth-provision/#.VTnrfNKqqko.

Lane Scheppele K, 'Making Infringement Procedures More Effective: A Comment on Commission v Hungary, Case C-288/12 (8 April 2014) (Grand Chamber)' (2014) *Eutopia Law* http://eutopialaw.com/2014/04/29/making-infringement-procedures-more-effective-a-comment-on-commission-v-hungary-case-c-28812-8-april-2014-grand-chamber/.

Lane Scheppele K, 'In Praise of the Tavares Report' Hungarian Spectrum: Reflections on Politics, Economy and Culture' (2013) *Hungarian Spectrum*: https://hungarian spectrum.wordpress.com/2013/07/03/kim-lane-scheppele-in-praise-of-the-tavares-report/.

Lane Scheppele K, 'What Can the European Commission Do When Member States Violate Basic Principles of the European Union? The Case for Systemic Infringement Actions' (2013) *Hungarian Spectrum*: https://hungarianspectrum.wordpress.com/2013/11/27/kim-lane-scheppele-what-can-the-european-commission-do-when-member-states-violate-basic-principles-of-the-european-union-the-case-for-systemic-infringement-actions/.

Other

Ahtisaari M, Frowein J & Oreja M, Report on the Austrian Government's Commitment to the Common European Values, in particular concerning the rights of minorities, refugees and immigrants and the evolution of the political nature of the FPÖ (The Wise Men Report) 40 *International Legal Matters* 1.

Craig P, 'The Rule of Law,' Appendix 5 in House of Lords Select Committee on the Constitution, Relations between the executive, the judiciary and parliament, HL Paper 151 (2006–2007).

6 The United States of America

Introduction

This book focusses on the international and European positions on tackling the far-right and, in particular, its speech, association and assembly. As explored in the previous chapters, hatred, as manifested in speech, association and assembly is restricted by the UN, EU and CoE. Although, for example, the EU, in the form of the Framework Decision on Racism and Xenophobia, includes a much higher threshold of prohibited speech in comparison to, *inter alia*, the UN's ICERD, all three frameworks set out the obligations of States to restrict certain forms of hateful manifestations that meet certain, albeit varying, thresholds. The book includes this short chapter on the key U.S. jurisprudence related to far-right hatred in the form of, amongst others, cross burning and Klu Klux Klan (KKK) speech and assembly. The reason for this is to demonstrate the stark European/International-U.S. variation in the conceptualisation and treatment of freedoms, particularly that of speech, within the framework of a far-right belief system. The central objective of incorporating this comparison is to facilitate further critical understanding of the European and International positions. The analysis will also include an examination of hate crime by the U.S. Supreme Court as a point of relative convergence amongst the frameworks. Notwithstanding the focus of the book on organised or semi-organised groupings, hate speech uttered by individuals not directly affiliated to organised groups will also be looked at in this chapter for purposes of determining the U.S.' position on hatred and the limits to rights which seek to promote hatred in order to demonstrate the stark difference in approaches mentioned earlier. The bulk of this chapter focusses on expression rather than assembly or association, because of the content of the relevant jurisprudence. However, it can safely be said that the country's conceptualisation of speech extends to assembly and association as vehicles of this speech. The Supreme Court underlined that 'the right of peaceful assembly is a right cognate to those of free speech and free press and is equally fundamental.'[1] The freedom of association is not incorporated in the First Amendment or anywhere else in the U.S. Constitution.

---

1 Chief Justice Hughes in *De Jonge v Oregon*, 299 U.S. 353 (1937); *United States v Cruikshank*, 92 U.S. 542 (1876); *Hague v CIO*, 307 U. S. 496 (1939); *N.A.A.C.P. v Alabama ex rel. Patterson* 357 U. S. 449 (1958).

However, in the 1958 case of *N.A.A.C.P. v Alabama*, the Supreme Court held that N.A.A.C.P. did not have to disclose the names and addresses of its members to the attorney general since that would violate their freedom of association. Justice John Marshall Harlan II, in writing for the Court, held that by associating freely with each other for the advancement of ideas is 'an inseparable aspect of the liberty ensured by the Due Process Clause of the Fourteenth Amendment.' The country's position on freedom of association was also emphasised at the time of the ICERD's ratification in which the U.S. held that

> The Constitution of the US contains extensive protections of individual freedom of speech, expression and association. Accordingly, the US does not accept any obligation under the Convention in particular under Article 4 and 7, to restrict those rights, through the adoption of legislation or any other measures to the extent that they are protected by the Constitution and laws of the US.

In brief, the elevated protection of freedom of expression, which will be analysed below, extends to assembly as determined by, *inter alia,* the *De Jonge* case, and to association which, although not a written part of the First Amendment or other part of the U.S. Constitution, has been referred to by the U.S. when seeking to limit its obligations on prohibiting racist groups under the ICERD.

The U.S. and Europe and the treatment of hatred – worlds apart?

This chapter will demonstrate that, in the U.S., there is a 'profound national commitment to the principle that debate on public issues should be uninhibited, robust and wide open.'[2] At the heart of the treatment of hate speech cases and other cases involving potentially problematic speech by the U.S. Supreme Court and its deliberations and discussions revolving around hate crime, lies the First Amendment to the U.S. Constitution, which holds that

> Congress shall make no law respecting an establishment of religion, or prohibiting the free exercise thereof; or abridging the freedom of speech, or of the press; or the right of the people peaceably to assemble, and to petition the government for a redress of grievances.

Free speech is 'the preferred value of the American constitutional order.'[3] As such, in the majority of cases discussed below, one witnesses the scales of the U.S. Supreme Court tilting in the direction of free speech.[4] The Supreme

---

2 New York Times Co. v Sullivan, 376 U.S. 254, 270 (1964).
3 Edward J. Eberle, 'Cross Burning, Hate Speech, and Free Speech in America' (2004) 36 *Arizona State Law Journal* 953, 958.
4 See for example: Whitney v California, 274 U.S. 357 (1927); Tinker v Des Moines Independent Community School District, 393 U.S. 503 (1969); Texas v Johnson, 491 U.S. 397 (1989).

Court has approached speech in such a way as to give it 'breathing space,'[5] which it deems necessary if speech is to function as a vehicle for the democratic and societal participation of each individual. The generalised position is that it is not for the hater to be silent but, rather, for 'the viewer to avoid further bombardment of [his] sensibilities simply by averting [his] eyes.'[6] The First Amendment 'reasonably yields an absolutist orientation'[7] and, in brief, finds that speech and assembly are to be 'free and unfettered, immune from official regulation.'[8] This position can, by reasonable assumption for the reasons discussed earlier, be extended to association. The sanctity of free speech in the American legal order cannot be undermined, with Locke's individualism lying at the heart of the U.S. approach.[9] It could be argued that the individualistic values and their protection override societal interest,[10] whilst the Kantian endorsement of human dignity as the central value upon which a society functions is characteristic of the UN, CoE and EU approaches, to varying levels of course.[11,12] As argued by Hartz, the 'feudal ethos'[13] which has shaped the functioning of Europe's society has not been influential in the U.S. This argument, and the more general Kantian-Lockean variations of the two continents, is manifested in the variation of judicial approaches, extrapolated on further in this chapter, and also by the fact that, when dealing with expression and assembly, which the U.S. Constitution clusters together, there is a reference to the obligation of the State not to intervene in the exercise of these rights, but there is no equivalent to Article 10 ECHR and Article 19 that free speech carries duties and responsibilities. The First Amendment has constituted the justification for reservation grounds imposed on Article 4 ICERD, Article 20 ICCPR and the non-acceptance of a hate speech clause in the Cybercrime Convention, as discussed in preceding chapters. It must be noted that the UN, to which the U.S. is a State Party, is not in agreement with its approach to hate

---

5 Boss v Barry, 485 U.S. 312, 322 (1988).

6 Erznoznik v Jacksonville 422 U.S 205, 210–211 (1975); *Cohen v California* 403 U.S. 15, 21 (1971); *Spence v Washington*, 418 U. S. 405, 412(1974).

7 Edward J. Eberle, 'Cross Burning, Hate Speech, and Free Speech in America' (2004) 36 *Arizona State Law Journal* 1, 958.

8 Ibid.

9 Claudia E. Haupt, 'Regulating Hate Speech - Damned If You Do and Damned If You Don't: Lessons Learned from Comparing the German and U.S. Approaches' (2005) 23 *Boston University International Law Journal* 2, 313.

10 Thomas W. Church & Milton Hueman, 'Hate Speech on Campus' (1st edn. Northeastern University Press, Boston MA 1997) 11.

11 United States v Schwimmer, 279 U.S. 644, 654–655 (1929) (Holmes, J., dissenting) ('[I]f there is any principle of the Constitution that more imperatively calls for attachment than any other it is the principle of free thought-not free thought for those who agree with us but freedom for the thought we hate.').

12 Claudia E. Haupt, 'Regulating Hate Speech - Damned If You Do and Damned If You Don't: Lessons Learned from Comparing the German and U.S. Approaches' (2005) 23 *Boston University International Law Journal* 2, 314.

13 Ibid. 315.

speech regulations and interpretation of free speech in this realm. As noted by institutions such as the CERD, 'the prohibition of dissemination of all ideas based upon racial superiority or hatred is compatible with the right to freedom of opinion and expression.'[14]

When assessing the historical and contextual backdrop of approaches to hate speech, a significant distinction between the two continents and the international framework in the form of the UN should be set out. In the U.S. context, speech regulation was being used in the South for purposes of silencing minorities who were seeking their rights, mainly during the Civil Rights Movement of the 50s and 60s.[15] To this end, 'expanding the rights to free speech in the USA went hand in hand with fighting racism.'[16] On the other hand, the annihilation of human rights in Europe, brought about by the Nazi regime, was a result of Hitler's rise to power and his exploitation of democratic vehicles, such as expression, to do so. The impact of this subsequently led the CoE and the UN, both born from the ashes of the Second World War, to seek to restrict this speech. In fact, Judge Yudkivska, in her concurring opinion joined by Judge Villiger, commented on the variation in historical contexts and the impact of this on current stances to hate speech in the ECtHR case of *Vejdeland v Sweden*. More particularly she said that the U.S. approach

> where hate speech is protected until it threatens to give rise to imminent violence ... is a very high threshold, and for many well-known political and historical reasons today's Europe cannot afford the luxury of such a vision of the paramount value of free speech.

Notwithstanding the general position that the U.S. is a free speech sanctuary and the historical considerations of the issues at stake, it must be noted that, in relation to communist and socialist views and activities that took place in the twentieth century, restrictions and punishments incorporated in relevant statutes were often considered to be in line with the first amendment.[17] The U.S. did not fear taking a militant approach to forces they perceived to be a threat to the functioning of their democracy, nor did they raise any First Amendment issues when allowing such restrictions. Apart from the exception of *Beauharnais*, discussed later, this militancy has not been extended to expression targeting minorities such as black people and Jews.

---

14 See, *inter alia*, General Recommendation XV on Article 4 of the Convention, Forty-second session (1993).

15 Erik Bleich, 'Freedom of Expression versus Racist Hate Speech: Explaining Differences between High Court Regulations in the USA and Europe' (2013) 40 *Journal of Ethnic and Migration Studies* 2, 297.

16 Ibid. 290.

17 Michel Rosenfeld, 'Hate Speech in Constitutional Jurisprudence: A Comparative Analysis' (2003) 24 *Cardozo Law Review* 1 and see, for example, Schenck v United States 249 U.S. 47 (1919) and Whitney v California 274 U.S. 357 (1927).

U.S.: hate speech jurisprudence

The Supreme Court has allowed, *inter alia*, the burning of a cross on the lawn of an African American Family and the hateful speech uttered by a member of the KKK. Drawing a direct parallel with, for example, *Féret's* leaflets considered by the ECtHR, the stark variation in approaches is visibly clear. Although a restrictive approach was embedded in *Beauhernais* and the prohibition of anti-Semitic and anti-Black leaflets, this was quickly overcome. What the Supreme Court has not allowed for is the prohibition of augmented punishments on hate crimes due to First Amendment Concerns. In dealing with speech that could potentially cause harm, the Supreme Court has gone through various stages, developments and tests.

This journey starts with the 1942 decision in *Chaplinsky v New Hampshire*, in which the Supreme Court dealt with an individual who was arrested for disrupting public order. Chaplinsky was a Jehovah's witness who was disseminating leaflets and calling organised religion a 'racket.' His presence was causing public disorder. He was warned and then arrested by a police officer who he called a 'damned racketeer' and a 'damned fascist.' Chaplinsky was convicted under Chapter 378(2) of the Public Laws of New Hampshire which holds that

> No person shall address any offensive, derisive or annoying word to any other person who is lawfully in any street or other public place, nor call him by any offensive or derisive name, nor make any noise or exclamation in his presence and hearing with intent to deride, offend or annoy him, or to prevent him from pursuing his lawful business or occupation.

Here, the Supreme Court found that there are certain categories of 'well-defined and narrowly limited classes of speech'[18] which include 'the lewd and obscene, the profane, the libellous and the insulting or fighting words – those which by their very utterance, inflict injury or tend to incite an immediate breach of the peace.'[19] The Supreme Court, therefore, delineated the limits of unprotected speech, the restriction of which did not bring about any First Amendment concerns since they were considered by the Court to be of

> such slight social value as a step to truth that any benefit that may be derived from them is clearly outweighed by the social interests in order and morality.[20]

So, the first element to be noted is that this case finds all speech to fall within the First Amendment insofar as it does not tick any of these narrowly tailored boxes, none of which are entitled 'hate speech.' This categorisation has been

---

18 Chaplinsky v New Hampshire, 315 U.S. 568 (1942).
19 Ibid.
20 Geoffrey R. Stone, 'Hate Speech and the U.S. Constitution' (1994) 3 *East European Constitutional Review* 1, 78.

described as a 'pragmatic version of absolutism.'[21] It can also be discerned that the Court did not adhere to the individualism that is the foundation of the American legal order but, rather, the protection of societal functioning on the grounds of preserving public order and morals. Therefore, although this case does not involve the targeting of a minority member due to characteristics such as ethnicity or religion, recognised to be in need of protection by, for example, the UN framework, the case is important since it delineates the perimeters of the First Amendment. The case was also relevant to the next case which involved hate speech targeted towards Black people in Chicago. In 1952, the Court was faced with a case of group defamation in *Beauharnais v Illinois*. Beauharnais, the president of the White Circle League[22] co-ordinated and participated in the dissemination of leaflets which called upon the city council of Chicago to 'halt the further encroachment, harassment and invasion of white people, their property, neighbourhoods and persons, by the Negro'[23] and wrote that

> if persuasion and the need to prevent the white race from becoming mongrelized by the Negro will not unite us, then the aggression, robberies, knives, guns and marijuana of the Negro surely will.[24]

Beauharnais was convicted for his participation in the leaflet dissemination. The relevant statute declared unlawful the distribution of any publication which 'portrays depravity, criminality, unchastity or lack of virtue of a class of citizens, of any race, colour, creed or religion' or subjects them 'to contempt, derision or obloquy.'[25] The Supreme Court relied on *Chaplinsky* and upheld Beauharnais's conviction. More specifically, it found that 'libellous utterances are not within the area of constitutionally protected speech'[26] and found it irrelevant that Beauharnais's speech did not create a clear and present danger of serious harm. Interestingly, the Supreme Court held that it was enough that the case did not involve a 'purposeless restriction unrelated to the peace and well being of the State.'[27] The societal factor in the Supreme Court's approach is evident, as opposed to a focus on the individualistic exercise of fundamental rights which marked the construction of the First Amendment and subsequent

---

21 Edward J. Eberle, 'Cross Burning, Hate Speech, and Free Speech in America' (2004) 36 *Arizona State Law Journal* 1, 962.

22 The league was chartered November 9, 1949 with the primary purpose to 'keep white neighborhoods free from negroes.' The League was organised shortly after the Park Manor housing riot of July 25, 1949. Although the League wanted to get a million White Chicagoans into the organization their main focus was keeping negroes out of the Park Manor neighbourhood. The White Circle League's charter was revoked by a Cook county Circuit court on June 29, 1950. The group became inactive as of July 1952.

23 Beauharnais v Illinois, 343 U.S. 250, 252 (1952).

24 Ibid.

25 Ibid.

26 Ibid. 250.

27 Ibid. 258.

case-law. Furthermore, this case is also of interest in that the Court recognised the impact of historical marginalisation against certain groups as an element which constitutes the foundation of Critical Race Theory and an element which is blatantly absent in subsequent case-law. Specifically, the Court referred to the history of Illinois in the ambit of racial conflicts and found that

> we would deny experience to say that the Illinois legislature was without reason in seeking ways to curb false or malicious defamation of racial and religious groups.[28]

Furthermore, in tackling Beauharnais's argument that he should have been permitted to disseminate those leaflets without any issue of libel, on the grounds of truth, the Court found that this ground could be disregarded in the event that the person did not act 'with good motives and for justified ends.'[29] This position moves away from the theoretical marketplace framework which is inextricably linked to the First Amendment. Notwithstanding important elements of this case, such as the recognition of racial tensions and the position of marginalised groups, the limited importance of truth in certain contexts and the importance placed on societal peace, this case has not been relied upon in subsequent cases. Had the line set out in *Beauharnais* been followed later on, there would be no talk of a stark difference in the UN/European-U.S. approach.

The *Skokie* case demonstrated that the steps put forth in *Beauharnais* were not going to be followed. In 1977, the case of the *National Socialist Party of America v Village of Skokie* reached the Supreme Court. Skokie, a suburb in Chicago, had a population of 70,000 persons, 40,000 of whom were Jews and approximately 5,000 survivors of Nazi concentration camps. Collin, the leader of the National Socialist Party of America (NSPA), alerted Skokie officials to a march of approximately thirty to fifty persons in uniforms similar to those worn by the Nazis, including swastika armbands, holding banners with swastikas and messages such as 'free speech for whites.' Skokie officials sought to prohibit the march holding that this would 'incite or promote hatred against persons of Jewish faith or ancestry.'[30] The Circuit Court of Cook County entered an injunction against petitioners. The injunction prohibited them from performing any of the following actions within the village of Skokie:

> [m]arching, walking or parading in the uniform of the National Socialist Party of America; [m]arching, walking or parading or otherwise displaying the swastika on or off their person; [d]istributing pamphlets or displaying any materials which incite or promote hatred against persons of Jewish faith or ancestry or hatred against persons of any faith or ancestry, race or religion.

---

28 Geoffrey R. Stone, 'Hate Speech and the U.S. Constitution' 3 (1994) *East European Constitutional Review* 1, 78.
29 Beauharnais v Illinois, 343 U.S. 250 (1952).
30 National Socialist Party of America v Village of Skokie, 432 U.S. 43 (1977).

The Illinois Appellate Court denied an application for stay pending appeal. Applicants then filed a petition for a stay in the Illinois Supreme Court, together with a request for a direct expedited appeal to that court. The Illinois Supreme Court denied both the stay and leave for an expedited appeal. Applicants then filed an application for a stay with a Circuit Justice, who referred the matter to the U.S. Supreme Court. The NSPA argued that the prohibition deprived it of its First Amendment Rights during the period of review. The Supreme Court reversed the denial for stay and returned the case to the Illinois Supreme Court. More particularly, it found that where a State seeks to impose a prohibition of such severity there must be 'strict procedural safeguards' which could include expedited appeal or temporary suspension of the prohibition which was denied by the Illinois Supreme Court. The Supreme Court declined to review. Therefore, although the Court did not assess the actual content of this case and decipher on whether or not it was protected by the First Amendment, it gave the demonstration a high threshold of protection under the First Amendment and found that the procedural safeguards that should have existed in the event of a curtailment of this kind were great and had not been met.

The 1969 *Brandenburg v Ohio* case involved the speech of Brandenberg, a leader of the KKK and, in particular, the request he submitted to a reporter to cover a KKK meeting in which persons were burning a cross and making speeches whilst wearing the KKK outfits. The speeches referred to, *inter alia*, taking revenge on Jews and alleged that the government was working with non-white groups against whites. Brandenberg made one of the speeches which advocated violence. After this was shown on the television, he was charged under the Ohio Criminal Syndicalism statute for 'advocat[ing] ... the duty, necessity, or propriety of crime, sabotage, violence, or unlawful methods of terrorism as a means of accomplishing industrial or political reform.' The Court found that speech can be restricted if it is likely to incite or produce imminent lawless action and not simply advocate such action. To this end, the Court held that

> accordingly, we are here confronted with a statute which, by its own words and as applied, purports to punish mere advocacy and to forbid, on pain of criminal punishment, assembly with others merely to advocate the described type of action. Such a statute falls within the condemnation of the First and Fourteenth Amendments.

Thus, the Court took a great leap forward from the 'clear and present danger' test articulated in *Schenck v U.S. (1919)*, which involved the dissemination of leaflets against mandatory army conscription by the Socialist Party and developed the imminent lawless action test:

> Freedoms of speech and press do not permit a State to forbid advocacy of the use of force or of law violation except where such advocacy is directed to inciting or producing imminent lawless action and is likely to incite or produce such action.

As such, for purposes of restricting violent speech, the violence in the speech must go beyond mere advocacy to actual incitement or production of action, with an extra safety net incorporated by the Court, namely, that such action must be imminent. However, the Court never actually defines incitement, nor does it set out guidelines on the threshold for such incitement to exist. Moreover, the prohibition of advocacy of violence constituting sufficient grounds to limit speech is in direct contravention with Article 20(2) of the ICCPR. In fact, that Article not only prohibits the advocacy of violence but also of discrimination and hostility, which fall under even lower thresholds. The judgement in *Brandenberg,* therefore, shows the stark difference of the U.S. and UN approach to hate speech regulation. Combining that with the prohibition of content based regulation, set out in *R.A.V* below, the U.S. and international frameworks are complete opposites, with, for example, Article 20(2) prohibiting such advocacy when it is directed to national, racial or religious groups.

In 1992, the Supreme Court was confronted with another case of hate speech, namely *R.A.V. v City of St. Paul,* in which a group of youths had put and burnt a cross on the lawn of an African American family in their predominantly white neighbourhood. The petitioner, one of the teenagers involved, was charged under the St. Paul Bias Motivated Crime Ordinance which provided that

> Whoever places on public or private property a symbol, object, appellation, characterization or graffiti, including, but not limited to, a burning cross or Nazi swastika, which one knows or has reasonable grounds to know arouses anger, alarm or resentment in others on the basis of race, color, creed, religion or gender commits disorderly conduct and shall be guilty of a misdemeanor.[31]

Although the fighting words doctrine had been developed in *Chaplinsky* in a framework beyond hate speech, *per se,* and even though the Supreme Court had not directly struck down the role and relevance of this doctrine, it had not, since then, upheld any conviction on the grounds of the fighting words doctrine.[32] Given the form and context of the expression looked at in *R.A.V.,* the Court could not avoid tackling the question of the doctrine's applicability. Whilst it did not strike it down, it argued that the doctrine could not be applied in this case since the ordinance was content specific, targeting particular groups, thereby, demonstrating State involvement in what and how people should think about particular issues and not abstractly tackling themes of offence and public order as did the ordinance in *Chaplinsky.* Specifically, the Court deemed that the ordinance 'unconstitutionally prohibits speech on the basis of the subjects the speech addresses.'[33]

---

31 R.A.V. v City of St. Paul, 505 U.S. 377, 380 (1992).
32 Geoffrey R. Stone, 'Hate Speech and the U.S. Constitution' (1994) 3 *East European Constitutional Review* 1, 80.
33 R.A.V. v City of St. Paul, 505 U.S. 377 (1992).

At the heart of the Court's decision lies the prohibition of content based regulation. In particular, the Court found that

> Displays containing abusive invective no matter how vicious or severe, are permissible unless they are addressed to one of the specific disfavoured topics. Those who wish to use 'fighting words' in connection with other ideas – to express hostility for example, on the basis of political affiliation, union membership or homosexuality – are not covered. The first amendment does not permit St. Paul to impose special prohibitions on those speakers who express views on disfavoured subjects.[34]

In addition, the Court underlined that 'St Paul's desire to communicate to minority groups that it does not condone the group hatred of bias motivated speech does not justify selectively silencing speech on the basis of its content.'[35]

As such, *R.A.V* underlines that the government is not allowed to determine, regardless of contextual realities in the realm of hatred and discrimination, particular characteristics which are to be protected from phenomena such as hate speech. This is unilaterally different from the approach of, for example, the EU Framework Decision which prohibits, *inter alia*, the incitement to violence or hatred on specific grounds, namely participation in an ethnic or religious group. Of course, as noted in the chapter on the EU, even though the Framework Decision is flawed in that it is contextually ignorant of the target groups of such speech, a European policy maker, judge or academic would find it difficult to imagine such a document without the incorporation of protected characteristics. It appears that the U.S. Supreme Court seeks to prevent the Orwellian concept of some being more equal than others but does so in an absolutist approach, negating all possible value in recognising the vulnerability of certain groups.

Importantly, from the onset the doctrine was eliminated from the Court's discussion. More specifically, it held that

> assuming that all of the expression reached by the ordinance is proscribable under the fighting words doctrine, we nonetheless conclude that the ordinance is facially unconstitutional.[36]

However, it simply assumes this for purposes of making its core argumentation on the prohibition of content based regulation, without ever actually examining whether the cross burning in *R.A.V.* did, in fact, constitute fighting words. As a result, the issue of whether an historically burdened burning cross in America constituted fighting words came about. Furthermore, the Court found that 'there are other ways to punish a defendant for the admittedly reprehensible behaviour

---

34 Ibid. 391.
35 Ibid. 378.
36 Ibid. 381.

of cross burning'[37] but does not provide additional information of what such measures, analogous or not, may be, thereby, limiting the relevance of this reference reminiscent, to an extent, of the proportionality test of the ECtHR. The only indication of what such measures could be were set out in White J's concurring opinion which held that the content based nature of the ordinance did not contribute to the compelling interest of the city to ensure human rights and non-discrimination as these could have been achieved through a generic ordinance (rather than a biased based ordinance). White J found that, in fact,

> the only interest distinctively served by the content limitation is that of displaying the city council's special hostility towards the particular biases singled out. That is precisely what the first amendment forbids.[38]

Therefore, the Court incorporated a safety net on the fighting words exception by holding it to apply insofar as it was content neutral. This demonstrates that it 'highly favoured speech interests over those of equal protection.'[39] The development from *Beauharnais* to *R.A.V.* is dramatic. Essentially, following *R.A.V.*, it could be deduced that no hate speech regulation, even if the speech in question constitutes restrictable speech, such as fighting words, could be legitimate, if the measure to restrict it targeted the speech because of its particular content. The Court's desire to ban content based regulation emanates from its more general premise that, in categories of low value expression, there is an 'equality of status in the field of ideas' and 'above all else, the first amendment means that government has no power to restrict expression because of its message, its ideas, its subject matter or its content.'[40]

The reason for this approach is not because the Court finds no harm in hate speech or that it considers it a fiction in terms of individual and societal impact but, rather, that it prohibits the government from interfering in deciphering the legitimacy of certain ideas and from providing certain groups with enhanced protection over others. As noted the content neutral approach 'delimits official power over estimation of ideas.'[41]

Virginia v Black (2003) involved three individuals, Black, Elliot and O'Mara, who were convicted separately on two separate occasions for violating a Virginia statute on cross burning. Black was charged for violating the statute for his role in a KKK rally on private property, used with the owner's permission. The other two were not KKK members but, instead, burnt the cross in Elliot's black neighbour's yard. All three defendants appealed their convictions, arguing that the Virginia statute is unconstitutional. The statute made it a felony

---

37 Ibid. 377.
38 Ibid. 396.
39 Ibid. 395.
40 Police Department of Chicago v Mosley 408 US 92 (1972).
41 Edward J. Eberle, 'Cross Burning, Hate Speech, and Free Speech in America' (2004) 36 *Arizona State Law Journal* 1, 972.

'for any person ..., with the intent of intimidating any person or group ..., to burn a cross on the property of another, a highway or other public place,' and specifies that '[a]ny such burning ... shall be prima facie evidence of an intent to intimidate a person or group.' The Court placed the statute in an historical context, outlining the 'cross burning's long and pernicious history as a signal of impending violence.'[42] The Court clarified that the First Amendment permits Virginia to ban cross burnings insofar as these are done 'with the intent to intimidate.'[43] In this framework, the Court embraced the 'true threat test' which has been defined as an 'opening' for hate speech regulation.[44] The Court ruled that cross burning can be prohibited if it constitutes a true threat if the purpose of burning is to intimidate, as is the case of cross burning in the yard of the black family.[45] The Court went on to underline that, if there is no true threat of intimidation, then cross burning does constitute free speech. The significance of intimidation for purposes of ensuring constitutionality in the prohibition went further insofar as the existence of a burning cross itself was not sufficient proof of intimidation. On this ground, and despite the previous acknowledgements of the Court, the Court struck down the statute as the evidentiary element was insufficient. More particularly, the Court acknowledged that a burning cross could be a true threat but could also fall in the realm of protected 'messages of shared ideology.'[46] The cross' existence could not constitute *prima facie* evidence of intention. As a result, the Virginia statute was found to be constitutional in terms of its prohibitions of cross burning but unconstitutional in relation to its presumption of intimidation through the existence of the burning cross as the sole justification for the prosecution. This indicates the intricate procedural requirements which come with regulating hate speech, a characteristic which constitutes an extra barrier to hate speech regulation.

In sum, the U.S. judicial approach to hate speech has been summed up well in the case of *Snyder v Phelps (2011)* in which the Westboro church picketed a Marine's funeral with signs that said, *inter alia*, 'thank God for dead soldiers' 'God hates you' 'Fag troops.' In this case, the Supreme Court underlined that

> Speech is powerful. It can stir people to action, move them to tears of both joy and sorrow and as it did here inflict great pain. On the facts before us, we cannot react to that pain by punishing the speaker. As a nation we have chosen a different course – to protect even hurtful speech on public issues to ensure that we do not stifle public debate.

---

42 Virginia v Black, 538 U.S. 343 (2003).
43 Ibid. 347.
44 Edward J. Eberle, 'Cross Burning, Hate Speech, and Free Speech in America' (2004) 36 *Arizona State Law Journal* 1, 993.
45 Virginia v Black, 538 U.S. 343 (2003).
46 Ibid. 354.

This is a polar opposite course to Europe which has embraced a position of militancy and restriction. As a direct parallel to *Snyder*, one could recall *Vejdeland*, in which the ECtHR allowed for the punishment of persons disseminating leaflets, which included, *inter alia*, statements such as:

> Tell them that HIV and AIDS appeared early with the homosexuals and their promiscuous lifestyle' and 'tell them that homosexual lobby organisations are also trying to play down paedophilia, and ask if this sexual deviation should be legalised.

This by no means implies that Europe is on the correct path. It simply reflects the variation in approaches which are not without their problems since hate speech continues to be present on both continents. It is safe to say that the U.S. will only allow for the prohibition of speech which could reasonably result in intimidation or speech which could cause imminent lawless action. The protected characteristic of hate speech, as this has been developed on a European level, is a no go area for the U.S. counterpart since *R.A.V.* prohibits any type of content regulation. Therefore, it could be argued that, for purposes of ensuring First Amendment protection, speech which meets the aforementioned thresholds related to intimidation or incitement to violence is limited insofar as the relevant measure is not protecting only certain groups of persons from such intimidation or incitement. Although this means that no hierarchy issue of who is protected or not arise in the U.S. framework, as it does in relation to the international and European equivalents, an issue discussed in previous chapters, it does appear to defeat the purpose of protecting contextually vulnerable groups from attack.

Hate crime and the U.S. Supreme Court

In 2017, the total number of reported hate crimes in the U.S.' largest cities increased by 12.5%.[47] The Federal Bureau of Investigation defines a hate crime as 'a criminal offence against a person or property motivated in whole or in part by an offender's bias against a race, religion, disability, sexual orientation, ethnicity, gender or gender identity.' Almost all States have some kind of statute criminalising hate crimes which, *inter alia*, find hatred or bias to constitute an aggravating factor.[48] Although the U.S. Supreme Court has found hate speech to fall within the realm of free speech and has found content based regulation unconstitutional, it has argued that hate crimes and their augmented punishment are not a violation of the first amendment. This has not come about without its

---

47 The Center for the Study of Hate and Extremism at California State University found a 12.5% increase reported by police in Chicago, Dallas, Houston, Los Angeles, New York, Philadelphia, Phoenix, San Antonio, San Diego and San Jose.

48 Jeannine Bell, 'Deciding When Hate Is a Crime: The First Amendment, Police Detectives, and the Identification of Hate Crime' (2002) 4 *Rutgers Race & the Law Review* 1, 37.

criticisms from U.S. academics, some of whom have argued that finding a hateful motive and punishing the perceived hate transcends into free speech grounds.[49] In *Wisconsin v Mitchell (1993)*, the Supreme Court was faced with a case on an increase in sentence on the grounds of bias, with Mitchell arguing that this was a violation of his First Amendment rights. After watching Mississippi Burning, Mitchell, who was black, incited a group of black men and boys to attack a white teenage youth. He was convicted under the Wisconsin's bias crime statute, which enhanced penalties if the perpetrator

> intentionally selects the person against whom the crime under par. (a) is committed or selects the property which is damaged or otherwise affected by the crime under par.(a) because of the race, religion, color, disability, sexual orientation, national origin or ancestry of that person.

The jury found that the victim had been targeted because of his race and, therefore, Mitchell received the maximum penalty. Mitchell argued that the aforementioned provision violated his First and Fourteenth Amendment rights. On appeal, the Wisconsin Supreme Court found the statute to violate the First Amendment by 'punishing offensive thought and by chilling speech'[50] and found the statute to be 'constitutionally overbroad.'[51] The Supreme Court 'surprised many'[52] by reversing the decision, finding the statute to be constitutional. The Court found that the First Amendment does 'not prohibit the evidentiary use of speech to establish the elements of a crime or to prove motive or intent.'[53] The Court unanimously agreed that a 'physical assault is not by any stretch of the imagination expressive conduct protected by the first amendment.'[54] On this ground it differentiated its position in *R.A.V.*, which involved an ordinance directed at expression. Therefore, when thoughts, speech and expression transcend into actual physical harm, there are no longer any constitutional concerns and, as such, the use of evidence pertaining to such thoughts are legitimate. Critics to the differential treatment of hate crime cases consider the task of ascertaining motivation 'not only difficult, but one fraught with grave First Amendment difficulties.'[55] More particularly, critics worry that law enforcers will search for

---

49 See, for example Susan Gellman, 'Sticks and Stones Can Put You in Jail, but Can Words Increase Your Sentence? Constitutional and Policy Dilemmas of Ethnic Intimidation Laws' (2991) 39 *UCLA Law Review* 333, 359; Martin H. Redish, 'Freedom of Thought as Freedom of Expression: Hate Crime Sentencing Enhancement and First Amendment Theory' (1992) 11 *Criminal Justice Ethics* 29.

50 Wisconsin v Mitchell 508 U.S. 476, 481–482 (1993).

51 Ibid.

52 Jeannine Bell, 'Deciding When Hate Is a Crime: The First Amendment, Police Detectives, and the Identification of Hate Crime' (2002) 4 *Rutgers Race & the Law Review* 1, 44.

53 Wisconsin v Mitchell 508 U.S. 476, 477 (1993).

54 Ibid. 484.

55 Phyllis B. Gerstenfeld, 'Smile When You Call Me That: The Problems With Punishing Hate Motivated Behavior' (1992) 10 *Behavioural Sciences and the Law* 1, 278.

evidence to demonstrate bias through 'cues from words, thoughts or associations that are protected by the First Amendment.'[56]

As such, notwithstanding the strict protection of the First Amendment by the U.S. Supreme Court, when speech, expression and thought, in relation to a particular group, are subsequently manifested in a physical attack on a person or his/her property, the U.S. Supreme Court has found no first amendment issues, although, in *Mitchell*, the Court had to extrapolate on why, demonstrating the deeply embedded position of free speech and the absolutist precedent set by *R.A.V.*

Chapter conclusion

Speech and its vehicles in the U.S. can be restricted insofar as high thresholds pertaining to threats or incitement to violence are met and so long as the measure seeking restriction is content neutral. On the other hand, in the international and European frameworks, although we witness varying thresholds of what is to be restricted, the common denominator of content specificity, namely, protecting particular characteristics through hate speech regulation, is not only permissible but is a necessity if States Parties are to meet their obligations to the UN, the CoE and the EU. In conclusion, hate speech, as a by-product of the far-right and as conceptualised in the international and European frameworks, is not relevant, in this shape or form, in the U.S. framework. In the U.S., it is speech and its vehicles which are almost absolutely protected, unless they meet the aforementioned thresholds and as long as the restrictions do not seek to protect any particular groups. As well as serving the purpose of demonstrating the stark difference in the approaches, the chapter also seeks to demonstrate that no approach can be considered more effective than the other as long as hate speech continues to be heard in both Europe and the U.S.

Bibliography

International documents

General Recommendation XV on Article 4 of the Convention, Forty-second session (1993).

Case-law

Beauharnais v Illinois, 343 U.S. 250, 252 (1952).
Boss v Barry, 485 U.S. 312, 322 (1988).

---

56 Jeannine Bell, 'Deciding when Hate is a Crime: The First Amendment, Police Detectives, and the Identification of Hate Crime' (2002) 4 *Rutgers Race & the Law Review* 1, 47.
    See, for example: See, e.g., Susan Gellman, 'Sticks and Stones Can Put You in Jail, but Can Words Increase Your Sentence? Constitutional and Policy Dilemmas of Ethnic Intimidation Laws' (1991) 39 *UCLA Law Review* 1, 359; Martin H. Redish, 'Freedom of Thought as Freedom of Expression: Hate Crime Sentencing Enhancement and First Amendment Theory' (1992) 11 *Criminal Justice Ethics* 1, 30.

Chaplinsky v New Hampshire, 315 U.S. 568 (1942).
Cohen v California, 403 U.S. 15, 21 (1971).
De Jonge v Oregon, 299 U.S. 353 (1937).
Erznoznik v Jacksonville, 422 U.S. 205, 210–211 (1975).
Hague v CIO, 307 U.S. 496 (1939).
NAACP v Alabama ex rel. Patterson, 357 U.S. 449 (1958).
National Socialist Party of America v Village of Skokie, 432 U.S. 43 (1977).
New York Times Co. v Sullivan, 376 U.S. 254, 270 (1964).
Police Department of Chicago v Mosley, 408 U.S. 92 (1972).
R.A.V. v City of St. Paul, 505 U.S. 377, 380 (1992).
Schenck v United States, 249 U.S. 47 (1919).
Spence v Washington, 418 U.S. 405, 412(1974).
Texas v Johnson, 491 U.S. 397 (1989).
Tinker v Des Moines Independent Community School District, 393 U.S. 503 (1969).
United States v Cruikshank, 92 U.S. 542 (1876).
United States v Schwimmer, 279 U.S. 644, 654–655 (1929).
Virginia v Black, 538 U.S. 343 (2003).
Whitney v California, 274 U.S. 357 (1927).
Wisconsin v Mitchell, 508 U.S. 476, 481–482 (1993).

Books

Church T.W & Hueman M, *'Hate Speech on Campus'* (1st edn). Northeastern University Press, Boston MA 1997).

Journal articles

Bell J, 'Deciding When Hate Is a Crime: The First Amendment, Police Detectives, and the Identification of Hate Crime' (2002) 4 *Rutgers Race & the Law Review* 33, 33–76.
Bleich E, 'Freedom of Expression versus Racist Hate Speech: Explaining Differences between High Court Regulations in the USA and Europe' (2013) 40 *Journal of Ethnic and Migration Studies* 2, 283–300.
Eberle E.J, Cross Burning, Hate Speech, and Free Speech in America (2004) 36 *Arizona State Law Journal* 1, 953–1001.
Gellman S, 'Sticks and Stones Can Put You in Jail, but Can Words Increase Your Sentence? Constitutional and Policy Dilemmas of Ethnic Intimidation Laws' (1991) 39 *UCLA Law Review* 333, 333–396.
Gerstenfeld P.B, 'Smile When You Call Me That: The Problems with Punishing Hate Motivated Behavior' (1992) 10 *Behavioural Sciences and the Law* 259, 259–285.
Haupt C.E, 'Regulating Hate Speech – Damned If You Do and Damned If You Don't: Lessons Learned from Comparing the German and U.S. Approaches' (2005) 23 *Boston University International Law Journal* 2, 299–336.
Redish M.H, 'Freedom of Thought as Freedom of Expression: Hate Crime Sentencing Enhancement and First Amendment Theory' (1992) 11 *Criminal Justice Ethics* 29.29-42Rosenfeld M, 'Hate Speech in Constitutional Jurisprudence: A Comparative Analysis' (2003) 24 *Cardozo Law Review* 1, 1523–1567.
Stone G.R, 'Hate Speech and the U.S. Constitution' 3 (1994) *East European Constitutional Review* 1, 78–82.

Conclusion

The financial crisis, the arrival of migrants and refugees, combined with the lack of coherent migration and asylum policies on national and regional scales, the global economic and financial crisis as well as the terrorist attacks carried out by, *inter alia*, the Islamic State, as single phenomena or in combination with each other, have created fertile soil upon which far-right political parties, non-party groups and the subculture milieu have mobilised support. In this light, the far-right is a phenomenon tainting the European reality on a national and regional level, the U.S. and beyond, to include countries such as Brazil. The situation in particular countries, such as Greece and Hungary, reveal the significant effects of the rhetoric and activities of the far-right on the rule of law, human rights and, in the case of Greece, on human life. Moreover, the far-right as organised in any form, be it a political party, a non-party group or the subculture milieu, poses a threat to doctrines, such as the rule of law, and is destructive to the rights and freedoms of its victims on a micro (individual), meso (community) and macro (societal) level.

The tragedy of the Second World War prompted the international community to set out mechanisms to prevent the far-right from rising again. To this end, documents, such as the International Convention on the Elimination of All Forms of Racial Discrimination (ICERD) and the International Covenant on Civil and Political Rights (ICCPR) and jurisprudence of their respective committees but also of the European Court of Human Rights (ECtHR), impose obligations on countries to restrict the freedoms of expression and/or assembly and/or association in the ambit of the rhetoric and/or activities of far-right entities, which target, amongst others, ethnic or religious groups. As such, far-right rhetoric and acts are prohibited on international and European levels, albeit with varying thresholds of harm associated with the different levels. What becomes clear is that the Council of Europe (CoE) and the United Nations (UN) are ready to limit fundamental freedoms, such as expression, if such freedoms are utilised in the manifestation of the far-right. Although the intention of the two institutions to prevent the rise of the far-right bodes well with the general spirit of international human rights law, their approach is discredited time and again. An example of this is the ECtHR decision in *Norwood v The United Kingdom*, which was ousted from any Article 10 consideration, despite there being no call for violence against a particular group. Another example includes provisions, such as Article 4 ICERD, which require the prohibition of racist expression with no accompanying threshold test in any correlated documents and no theoretical extrapolation of the intricate line to be drawn between the fundamental freedom of speech, on the one hand, and racial discrimination on the other. Nowhere in the jurisprudence, documents or meeting minutes of the aforementioned institutions has there been a demonstration of a theoretical extrapolation of when, what, how and why fundamental freedoms should be prohibited in the name of regulating the far-right. This book is not propagating a libertarian approach to freedoms, given that the author does not believe in the existence of a free marketplace of ideas, since some humans are simply more equal and therefore have better access to the marketplace. However, , a clumsy prohibition of fundamental rights without an adequate theoretical examination is not a sustainable solution. In fact, silencing the far-right can have the effect of transforming its actors into martyrs who are scapegoated and shut out by the corrupt system. Such actors can subsequently mobilise on this status to attract disheartened voters in a populist manner.

On a UN level, Article 4 of the ICERD lays down a positive obligation on States to prohibit racist expression, racist violence and organisations and propaganda which promote and incite racial discrimination. Article 20 of the ICCPR prohibits any advocacy of national, racial or religious hatred that constitutes incitement to discrimination, hostility or violence. Article 5 of the ICCPR is the non-destruction clause. In its jurisprudence and Concluding Observations, the HRC has embraced the non-permissibility of hateful expression, association and assembly whilst the CERD has underlined, *inter alia*, that prohibiting racist associations is of utmost importance. On a CoE level, although the ECHR does not incorporate a provision similar to, for example, Article 20 of the ICCPR, it nevertheless restricts the tools that can be used by destructive movements, such as the far-right and/or those belonging thereto, namely the freedom of expression, the freedom of assembly and the freedom of association on the grounds of, amongst others, protecting the rights and freedoms of others. This Convention also incorporates a non-destruction clause in the form of Article 17. The analysis of Strasbourg jurisprudence demonstrates that speech and association that fall within the realm of far-right rhetoric are not permissible, without the necessity of such speech or association amounting to and/or inciting, violence. On a CoE level, there also exists the Additional Protocol to the Convention on Cybercrime concerning the Criminalisation of Acts of a Racist and Xenophobic Nature Committed through Computer Systems. This criminalises, *inter alia*, the dissemination of racist and xenophobic material through computer systems as well as racist and xenophobic insults and threats disseminated through such systems. The drafters of this document acknowledged the significant role played by the Internet as a platform for the dissemination of racist and xenophobic expression. The analysis conducted of the European Union (EU) framework found that Article 7 of the Treaty on the European Union (TEU) is the strongest EU tool for tackling the far-right due to its primacy and its capacity to bring direct results to the enjoyment of significant political rights of a defaulting State. However, these positive elements are hampered on a practical level given that this article has not yet been applied by the EU, as demonstrated in its approach to *Fidesz's* Hungary and Poland's *PiS*. Furthermore, there exists the Council Framework Decision on Combatting Certain Forms and Expressions of Racism and Xenophobia by Means of Criminal Law which criminalises activities and speech conducted by racist and xenophobic entities, a tool that can be directly used to combat the rhetoric and activities of the far-right. A conspicuously lacking element of all the aforementioned frameworks is a complete disregard of the actions and speech of the far-right when this is directed to characteristics such as sexual orientation and gender identity. Thus, there are three central conclusions that can be drawn from the analysis of the instruments available at a UN, CoE and EU level. First, overall speech and activities that fall within the realm of the far-right, namely hate speech and hate crime are to be prohibited. However, the thresholds attached to the prohibition of hate speech differ. For example, the ICERD provides that all dissemination of ideas based on racial superiority or hatred, incitement to racial discrimination or incitement to violence against any race or group of persons of another colour or ethnic origin are to be prohibited. On the other hand, the ICCPR prohibits any advocacy of national, racial or religious hatred that constitutes incitement to discrimination, hostility or violence. Thus, the two UN documents are not in conformity with one another when it comes to thresholds, given that the ICCPR necessitates that the particular expression must constitute incitement, whereas the ICERD allows for prohibited expression to include the dissemination of particular ideas without the need for it to amount to incitement. Not only does this limit coherence between instruments of the same institution, but also attaches a lower threshold of protection to religious groups as these are not incorporated into the ICERD. Second, the EU Framework Decision, referred to earlier, prohibits the public incitement to violence or hatred, but not discrimination, directed against a group of persons or a member of such a group defined by reference to race, colour, religion, descent or national or ethnic origin. Member States may choose to criminalise such conduct insofar as it affects public order or if it is threatening, abusive or insulting. Thus, by leaving out the issue of discrimination and incorporating the possibility of criminalisation, if certain grounds are met, such as a threat to public order, the threshold of prohibited speech is raised significantly in comparison to relevant UN provisions and renders punishment more difficult to attain. It must be reiterated that the Framework Decision involves only the criminalisation of hate speech or hateful motive, hence the aforementioned safety nets. Lastly, the result of this is that a country which is a Member State of the EU and a party to the aforementioned international documents has differing obligations in the realm of speech and conduct of the far-right.

Furthermore, during the analysis of the different frameworks, as conducted in this book, one of the most striking issues on a supranational level is the inactivity of the EU to tackle the far-right and its impact. More particularly, Article 7 of the TEU, which is available to EU institutions to tackle the threat of the far-right in Member States, lays dormant, notwithstanding some developments in this realm, as discussed in Chapter Five. This is so, despite the fact that the EU is witnessing a deterioration of the rule of law in certain Member States. Moving mountains and oceans away from the more restrictive approach adopted on an international and European level is the U.S., a libertarian realm where burning crosses in the yard of an African American family is found to be legitimate. The purpose of incorporating the U.S. into this book was briefly to demonstrate an opposite approach to restriction and, by extension, to show that, in fact, no current method is better than another. The reality is that the far-right is present on a multitude of geographical levels, be that Golden Dawn in Greece or Trump and his non-violent yet far-right, nativist and exclusionary policies. As such, any effort to see what should be done with the *by-products* of the far-right in the form of utterances and crime has an expiration date. In fact, limitations to speech which are almost arbitrarily found to constitute hate speech by, *inter alia*, Strasbourg judges, with no theoretical extrapolation thereto, are nothing but patchwork. Unless the international community and national governments look the neo-liberal roots of far-right extremism straight in the eye and make a sincere effort to tackle socio-economic inequalities, nativist constructions of identities and the normalisation of exclusionary approaches to vulnerable groups, this phenomenon is not going to go away. Instead, the far-right, whether suit clad Fidesz' Orbán or militarised Kasidiaris of Golden Dawn, will profit and feed off the resulting buds.

Index

Note: Page numbers followed by "n" denote footnotes.